DATE DUE

AP 09 '98			
MY 07 '99			
MR 06 '00			
JY 07 '00			
APR 14 2005			

DEMCO 38-297

FRANZ SCHUBERT:

THE ARIEL OF MUSIC

FRANZ SCHUBERT

Water color by Wilhelm August Rieder (1825).

FRANZ SCHUBERT:

THE ARIEL OF MUSIC

BY ROBERT HAVEN SCHAUFFLER

G. P. PUTNAM'S SONS   NEW YORK

TO ISABEL AND DEWAR SIMONS

CONTENTS

PART II
THE MUSIC

ILLUSTRATIONS

FOREWORD

THE outer story of Franz Schubert's pathetically short career moves quietly. It cannot boast of Othellian exploits,

> Of moving accidents by flood and field,
> Of hair-breadth scapes i' the imminent deadly breach.

On the other hand, the story of his inner life teems with action. Here we have the heroic struggle of handicapped genius against the hostile trivialities of daily existence, the marshaling of forces to master a pitiable material destiny, the desperate sex conflicts.

Above all there are those thrilling interior adventures for whose sake the memory of Schubert will long be treasured. His music bears evidence of spiritual exploits that far outshine the material ones of the Othellos. What terrific internal commotions must have gone to the making of *The Erl King*, the final symphony, the B Flat Trio, the E Flat Mass, the last quartets, and the String Quintet! The "most disastrous chances" of the Moor of Venice fall short of the action that seethed in the "antres vast" of that amazing imagination!

The following pages have profited by the recent discoveries of the prince of Schubert researchers, Professor Otto Erich Deutsch, which correct numerous misconceptions faithfully handed down from biographer to biographer. To mention a few: the legend that Schubert became a teacher to evade military service has been exploded. We must revise downward the time-honored estimates of the characters of the composer's father and of his favorite brother Ferdinand. And Countess Caroline Esterházy, who has traditionally been made the object of Schubert's hopeless adoration, is now revealed as a pathetic case of arrested development who, at the age of thirty, was still sent by her mother to play with her hoop.

Independently of Professor Deutsch, this book shows that Schubert was a happier man than the biographers have made him out. A psychogram similar to that which I employed in *The Unknown*

Brahms seeks to solve the baffling enigma of his love life. To this day there are still people who resent the suggestion that a man's sexual constitution may vitally affect his character or his creative work. Other conservatives, without going quite so far as this, would set biography back a century by forbidding it either to associate with psychoanalytic psychology or to make any sort of shocking revelation. None the less I believe that a great many well-informed readers today regard that psychology as the biographer's indispensable ally in interpreting the significance of soundly established data, and agree with Stefan Zweig that "the mission of science is to teach men to face the facts."

A new and, I trust, convincing explanation is offered of a problem that has puzzled generations of musicians: why the piano sonatas lag in sustained quality behind the composer's best music. Discoveries have been made about the thematic work that Schubert occasionally employed to lend unity to his compositions. In connection with the songs, some generally unsuspected facts about the relations between poetry and music are given, which may, I fear, anger nine readers out of ten.

If my angle of approach to the music differs somewhat from that of other biographers, it may well be because for years I observed Schubert's compositions from the special viewpoint of the professional violoncellist, and grew intimate with his orchestral works from the successive vantage points of each choir of the orchestra.

Students will do well to read Part II with scores and phonographs at hand. All foreign poems, letters, and documents used here have been freshly translated. Acknowledgment of indebtedness will be found at the end of the volume.

The close of the First World War started a Schubert renaissance which has not ceased to grow and spread. It is as though suffering humanity sought relief from the impact of a hideous, menacing, and brutal world in the serene loveliness and sunlit well-being created by that archmelodist, the Ariel of music.

R. H. S.

New York City,
July, 1949.

PART I

THE MAN

1

THE MILLER'S TRIUMPH

IN THE summer of 1808, the young lads of Vienna were excited about a newspaper advertisement announcing vacancies among the boy choristers of the Court Choir. Two of these youngsters had had a change of voice, and a competition would be held for replacements. Entrants must be at least ten years old. They must sing well, be prepared to enter the first grade of the Latin School, and (vaccination being still unknown) must already have "had smallpox." The winners would enjoy a free education at the Royal and Imperial Convict,[1] a school attached to the university, where strong emphasis was laid on music.

The competition would be judged by awe-inspiring musical dignitaries. Among them was the famous composer and court conductor, Antonio Salieri, who had taught Beethoven and been the archenemy of Mozart. Here was a test fit to appal the bravest youngster.

One of the contestants, a tiny lad of eleven with the diminutive name of Franzl, was a homely fellow, with nearsighted, blinking eyes, a stub of a nose, curly brown hair, and outlandish garments. At sight of him, the other contestants began, boy fashion, to make fun of his clothes.

Even though they once knew that agony, grown-up people are apt to forget how hideously children can suffer from being conspicuously and ridiculously dressed. It is hard to realize how the wretched Franzl felt in that startling light-gray suit, inherited from his brothers and so threadbare as to be almost white.

"Hey, fellows," cried one of the candidates, "here comes a miller. Look, he's all over flour!" And suddenly Franzl was the center of a jeering throng. He was saved from the ignominy of tears only by the start of the examination.

The first five boys did tolerably. Then Franzl came up, accom-

[1] This sinister-sounding word was merely derived from *convictorium*, the Latin for communal house.

panied by a suppressed titter, "Now it's the miller's turn." His heart sank, but when the judges began to ask him questions about music and made him sing at sight, he felt at home. Now he was on his own ground and forgot the tormentors. Promptly and correctly he answered every question. With a lovely, winning quality of voice, and in perfect tune, he sang the hardest pages. The sneering young eyes were abruptly filled with respect. The judges were overcome, first with astonishment, then with kindly sympathy and admiration.

Franzl won with ease. And, by a curious coincidence, another lad whose name sounded a good deal like "Miller" came out second best, though a long way behind the star performer. Salieri sent in this report: *"Fra li soprani li migliori sono: Francesco Schubert e Francesco Müllner."* [1] Dr. Lang, the Convict's director, reported that these two "also excel all the others in preliminary knowledge."

Fifteen years later, when Franz Schubert was clothing his song cycle, *The Miller's Beautiful Daughter,* in imperishable melody, did he recall how, as a youthful miller, he had once turned the tables upon his foes?

[1] "Of the sopranos the best are: Franz Schubert and Franz Müllner."

2

CALIBAN BEGETS ARIEL

IN THE single year of 1797, the Austrian Empire produced, by a curious coincidence, the best of all national hymns and the most Austrian of great composers. Both came from forebears who lived close to the soil. Josef Haydn, who wrote *"Gott erhalte Franz den Kaiser"* ("God preserve Franz the Emperor"), was a farmer's son. And a farmer's grandson wrote *The Miller's Beautiful Daughter* (*Die schöne Müllerin*).

The composer, Franz Peter Schubert, was the twelfth child of a poor schoolmaster.[1] There was nothing glorious or famous about his ancestors. In the Nietzschean sense he was a climax, gradually and obscurely prepared by many generations of humble folk. Quietly, imperceptibly they had accumulated a store of precious combustibles packed with the latent promise of that short and prodigal hour of fireworks which was to begin with *Margaret at the Spinning Wheel* and end with the great Quintet in C.

Franz Schubert's ancestors were peasants. A few generations before his birth, those on the paternal side had removed from the old mountain town of Zuckmantel in their native Austrian Silesia, the land of such poets as Opitz, Eichendorff, and Hauptmann, to the neighboring Neudorf in Moravia, the land of famous singers.

Presently these humble folks began to lift themselves from the soil by their own bootstraps. Without ceasing to be a farmer, the composer's grandfather, Johann Schubert, became a judge of the village of Neudorf. Franz Theodor Florian Schubert, his fifth child, born in 1763, was an amateur 'cellist. He did as Brahms's bass-playing father was to do a generation later, turned his back upon the good earth and set out to seek his fortune in the big city.

[1] Grove and Whitaker-Wilson mistakenly call him the thirteenth, and Landormy, the fourteenth child. (*Grove's Dictionary of Music and Musicians* 3rd ed., New York, The Macmillan Co., 1928; C. Whitaker-Wilson, *Franz Schubert*, London, Wm. Reeves, Ltd., 1928; Paul Landormy, *La vie de Schubert*, Paris, Gallimard, 1928.)

At Vienna, Maria Theresa's recent educational reforms had created a brisk demand for teachers—and few questions asked. So, after a brief normal course, Franz, the composer's father, easily found a job as assistant to his brother Karl, who presided over a school in the Leopoldstadt. Though Father Franz's early chronology is somewhat uncertain, he probably began to teach there in 1784.

Now here he was, securely fixed at the very first try, in laughing, brilliant, careless, charming Vienna, that focal point of the earnest North, the warm, voluptuous South, and the glamorous Orient. At about twenty-one, the provincial clodhopper had actually come and seen and conquered a foothold in the fabulous capital of the Empire. Not, however, that he for a moment approved of the lighter side of his new environment. He was always to remain more grimly serious than most Moravian peasants.

Before long he wisely returned his line to its old Silesian origins by marrying Elisabeth Vietz (or Vitz or Fitz; they were not fussy about spelling). She was a cook, an honorable profession in the annals of music, for Haydn was the son, and Beethoven the grandson of a cook. Elisabeth was the daughter of a Zuckmantel locksmith who had left home in disgrace, under suspicion of having embezzled the funds of his guild, of which he was "head toastmaster." (Perhaps the composer's inability to be realistic about money matters was inherited.) She was six years older than her husband. They set up housekeeping in the suburb Liechtental.

On June 13th, 1786, Franz Theodor was appointed schoolmaster in the region known as the Himmelpfortgrund (The Ground of the Gate of Heaven). The school was probably in the present Säulengasse 3, picturesquely named the Little Black Horse. Tradition says that the same year he went to live near the school in a house called the Red Crayfish. There, on January 31, 1797, in an alcove on the first floor, Franz Peter Schubert, the Ariel of music, was born.

Where but in the old Austria could one find such an alluring verbal *mise en scène?* Today this house, turned into a Schubert museum, is prosaically known as Nussdorferstrasse 54. Anita Silvestrelli[1] draws a vivid picture of what went on around it:

In the background looms a shadowy garden; in the courtyard a fountain plashes. There were then many itinerants moving from house to house: evangelists sang to their harps, peddlers and women selling lavender

---

[1] *Franz Schubert*, Salzburg-Leipzig, Pustet, 1939.

sing-songed their wares; a workman, a fiddler entered the portal, gypsy children danced; sometimes bear leaders and proprietors of flea circuses put in an appearance. It was Schubert's childish realm.

Beyond the garden rose the twin towers of that Liechtental parish church, which was to play such an important role in Franz's creative career. Far from prepossessing, this house of God looks like an enlargement of some appalling insect seen in a nightmare. Its two erect heads are equipped with staring clock dials for eyes and crowned by domes resembling the ugly casques once worn by the Austrian soldiery.

As his portrait suggests, Father Schubert was a bull-necked, hardheaded peasant, thorough, industrious, and frugal. It was natural that his own phenomenal rise from the provincial soil should have filled him with ill-concealed exultation. More than a third of a century after assuming the ferule in his own right, he proudly signed a letter to his son Karl:

> Your faithful father Franz Schubert
> Schoolmaster in the Rossau

The man had suffered a stern upbringing under that magistrate, his dominating father. And, perhaps unconsciously, he sought to compensate himself for early sufferings by dominating his own family with equal sternness. He was a religious bigot with powerful sex instincts which he sadly mistrusted; though mistrust did not keep him from having nineteen children, one of them conceived out of wedlock. And his later opposition to a musical career for his illustrious son sprang even more from what his puritanical soul considered the licentious connotations of the art of music than from economic misgivings. In his convictions he was fiercely dogmatic, and young Franz was to learn all too well how relentlessly he would act upon them.

Father Schubert's portrait is surprising. How could such a Caliban father an Ariel? The bullet head with its wooden features exhibits barely enough intelligence to belong to a stagecoach driver, let alone a good schoolteacher. It suggests the man with the hoe rather than the man who, upon the triumphal return of the Austrian Emperor in 1814, decorated his house with this inscription:

> *Es brennen hier nur Kerzen,*
> *Allein aus meinem Herzen*
> *Spriessen Lorbeerreiser.*

(Here only candles shine;
But from this heart of mine
Shoot twigs of laurel.)

Either the picture or the man's face must have been misleading.
In 1803, after years of official neglect, the powers that were made
him fifth assessor of the Ministerial Bench, on account of his "excellent moral character and absolute integrity." Later his socially
minded efforts on behalf of the community won him the honorary
citizenship of Vienna. From this father the composer inherited his
immense industry, and whatever slight rudiments he could boast
of the solid, the methodical, and the practical.

Mother Elisabeth saw the light in 1757, the year after Mozart's
birth. It is a pity that we have no portrait of her. Quiet, modest,
unassuming, greatly beloved by her children, she was immersed in
continuous maternity, in the cares of an earnestly frugal household,
and in helping to keep in order the inordinate swarms of her husband's pupils. An uncle of hers was for forty years town organist of
Zuckmantel, and a first cousin was a *virtuosus fidicen,* or lute virtuoso. It is probable that the composer's genius came from her side
of the family.

Within little more than a quarter of a century she gave birth to
fourteen children. Ignaz came on March 8th, 1785, two months after
their marriage. He taught school all his life and hated it. The portrait
of this freethinker and democrat shows an attractive, sympathetic,
and highly Viennese countenance marked by pain. The poor fellow
was a hunchback.[1] After him the unfortunate Elisabeth brought
forth in rapid succession eight infants, who perished early. With
Ferdinand, the tenth, born in 1794, they began to live.[2] This Ferdi-

---

[1] Because he was conceived out of wedlock, Ignaz was cruelly excluded from
a share in the family property. Thus Caliban added injury and insult to injury.
Professor Deutsch states that Ferdinand, Ignaz's junior by nine years, "was in
practice regarded as the future head of the family." (Otto Erich Deutsch, *Schubert: A Documentary Biography,* London, J. M. Dent & Son, Ltd., 1946; and as
The Schubert Reader, New York, W. W. Norton & Company, Inc., 1947.) What
a fate: to be hunchbacked and disinherited, with a taint on one's birth, play
second fiddle to a younger brother, and slave for a pittance at a hateful task
under the iron fist of such a father!

[2] A. J. B. Hutchings (*Schubert,* London, J. M. Dent & Son, Ltd., 1945) wrongly
states that the composer "was the youngest of five children; five other children
had died early." The fact is that he was the youngest of four living children;
eight others had died early. His mother was to bear two more and his step-
mother, five.

FATHER SCHUBERT
From an unsigned oil portrait.

Where Franz Schubert was born. Now Nussdorferstrasse 54.

The Esterházy "castle" at Zseliz.

The town of Steyr in Upper Austria.

nand was Franz's favorite brother and was considered by the Schuberts to have special rights in the composer. He was the family's most successful teacher and eventually rose to be director of the Normal School of St. Anna. His youthful portrait also shows typically Viennese traits, but with the years he came to look curiously like a great American—Ralph Waldo Emerson. A Mass of his was almost the last music that Franz was to hear before dying in Ferdinand's house.

Karl, who came along in 1795, became a landscape painter. Another Viennese type. The portraits of all three show young men far better looking than their famous brother and suggest unusual charm. All have the characteristic Schubertian dimple in their strong and well-formed chins. So does that of Maria Theresia, born in 1801.

Father Schubert must have been a natural economist. Though he had no salary, though he taught many poor children free, though the other pupils paid him only one gulden a month, and though he was not sparing of paternity, by dint of Spartan thrift he managed in 1801 to buy, for 3,200 florins, the Little Black Horse schoolhouse. There he went to live. And there, fourteen years later, *The Erl King* was written.

3

RED CRAYFISH AND LITTLE BLACK HORSE

FRANZL spent his first four years in the Red Crayfish. Then, in 1801, the family moved to its newly bought possession the Little Black Horse. There, according to the account written by Father Schubert a few hours before his death, Franzl's formal education began:

In his fifth year I prepared him for elementary instruction, and in his sixth I let him attend school, where he always distinguished himself as first among his fellow-pupils. Even in his earliest childhood he loved company, and was never happier than when he could pass his free hours in a crowd of gay comrades. In his eighth year I taught him the essential first principles of violin playing, and brought him along to the point where he could play easy duets tolerably well. Then I sent him for singing lessons to Herr Michael Holzer, the Liechtental choirmaster, who repeatedly assured me with tears in his eyes that never before had he possessed such a pupil. Said he: "If I wanted to teach him something new—he had already mastered it. Consequently I could not give him any real instruction, but could only talk with the lad and quietly admire him."

It might have been better if Holzer, a little less quiet, had been able to introduce his star pupil to counterpoint. But the lessons were more like play than work. He delighted in hearing Franzl extemporize on a given theme and would exclaim, "Why, the lad simply shakes harmony from the tips of his fingers!"

Without the aid of a teacher, Franzl began learning the piano by himself upon the worn-out "chopping board" (*Hackbrett*) at home. Presently the six-year-old made friends with another small Franzl who had *entrée* into a piano factory and took his pal along to revel in the fine instruments and compare them favorably with the "chopping board."[1]

If an elder brother praises a younger, it usually means something.

[1] A third of a century later the boy Brahms was to enjoy a similar adventure.

10

"When Franz had been studying the piano with me for barely a month," said Ignaz, "he informed me that he needed no more of my teaching and wished to get on by himself. And indeed, before long he had made such progress that I was forced to acknowledge him a master who far surpassed me, and whom I could never hope to overtake."

When Holzer had recovered from his astonishment at Franzl's precocity, he began to be of more use. He had him play violin solos during service in the Liechtental church. He had him accompany the congregation on the organ and improvise preludes and interludes. All this varied contact with what he loved best in the world gave the boy a delightfully happy young childhood and was to be of no small advantage to him as a composer.

In October, 1808, the eleven-year-old changed with a sigh of relief into the uniform of the Convict. The relief was not on account of leaving home, but because the new outfit was literally uniform with the other pupils' clothes. No more grayish white conpicuousness for Franzl! Instead, an open brown coat adorned with a gilt epaulet and brilliantly polished buttons, a white neckerchief, knickerbockers with straps, shoes with buckles, and a smart three-cornered hat.

However, on realizing what kind of place he was now committed to, he heaved a very different sort of sigh. It was a brutally sudden change from liberty, a beloved mother, and the jolly companionship of brothers and friends, to captivity in a strange and gloomy barracks. Within that somber portal Franz, going on twelve, was forced to draw a double bar at the close of his happy childhood.

4

CONVICT LIFE

TO ANGLO-SAXON—though not to Austrian—ears, the word Convict has an ominous sound. And in certain ways the school in the Universitätsplatz was ominous. It had long, dark, clammy corridors and small windows reminiscent of a prison. Except by special dispensation the pupils were not allowed to go out alone, and they were not properly warmed or fed. Luckily for Franzl, the chief emphasis of the curriculum was on music. And this must have been cleverly taught, because instead of regarding it as an imposed chore, the boys all loved it.

For the newcomer the high light of the Convict was the amateur orchestra. It was led by a teacher named Wenzel Ruzicka, from his post as concertmaster. Every pupil who could play at all was allowed to join. A youth named Holzapfel noticed that there was no 'cello section, so he got someone to show him how to play the C major scale—and promptly became solo 'cellist.

The instruments were bad. Zeal so far triumphed over finesse that dynamics were practically nonexistent. Anything less than *mezzo forte* was as rare as in the renditions of the ordinary pianist. But the young enthusiasts loved what they played with fervor enough to atone for many a technical deficiency. Their evening performances drew such an audience in the street outside that the police complained of the obstruction to traffic.

And already they had had a far more distinguished audience. A few weeks before Franzl's arrival, they had been driven in court carriages to the imperial palace to play for the high and mighty. There they found no less a musical personage than Ludwig van Beethoven himself. The great man expressed polite regret that they had not brought along one of his own symphonies. But when someone offered to send for the parts, he jumped up in dismay and brusquely growled that he could not stay long, and besides he was pretty particular when it came to performances of those works.

Franz was assigned to the second violins, and in that modest company he came across his first friend. Josef von Spaun, a law student from Linz, was nine years older. He was the first person to show sympathy and understanding for the lad's compositions. Though he never gained a deep understanding of Schubert's nature, he was destined to be a consistently devoted and helpful comrade. Here is his account of their first meeting:

The tiny fellow did not seem at ease in that institution; for he was always serious and not very friendly. As he was already rather proficient on the violin, he was taken into the small orchestra which, in those days, played an overture and a symphony every evening after supper and, considering their youth, often did very well.

I was the leader of the second violins. Little Schubert stood behind me and fiddled, looking over my shoulder [and probably straining his poor eyes]. Very soon I noticed that the small musician far surpassed me in rhythmical surety. This aroused my interest and made me realize with what animation the lad, who otherwise seemed quiet and indifferent, gave himself up to his impression of the beautiful symphonies which we did.

Once I came upon him alone in the music room, sitting at the piano which his tiny hands could already play very passably. He was just then trying over a Mozart sonata, and said that he liked it very much, but found Mozart difficult to perform well. Under my friendly encouragement he played me a minuet of his own invention. He was shy and red with shame; but my approval made him happy. The lad confided to me that he often secretly wrote his thoughts down; but Father mustn't know about it; for he was dead set against his son's devoting himself to music. After that I sometimes slipped him music-paper.

That was all the more handsome of Spaun because he himself was often hard up. Once, at the start of a vacation, he was so poor from having bought two symphonies and gone once to the theater, that he had to trudge all the way to Linz.

Most of the time, because they reminded the Czech conductor Ruzicka of the folks at home, he made the students play the works of such heaven-inspired Czech and Moravian composers as Pichl, that vigorous bromide Krommer, and Mozart's bitter enemy Koželuh, who exposed the taste of his time by vastly outdoing that genius in popularity. Less often they were allowed Méhul, Cherubini, Haydn, Mozart, and the Second Symphony of Beethoven. Walter Dahms[1]

[1] *Schubert,* Berlin, Deutsche Verlags-Anstalt, 1908.

states that while Schubert was a Convict pupil he also enjoyed Beethoven's Seventh Symphony, but this was not published until 1816,
more than two years after Franzl had left the school.

Certain adagios of Haydn moved the lad deeply. He was enchanted by Mozart's G Minor Symphony and confessed that it broke
him all up without his really knowing why. Its minuet was overpowering, and angels sang along in the Trio.[2] The *Figaro* Overture was
the loveliest in the whole world. "Oh, but I almost forgot the one to
The Magic Flute!"

Beyond the coarse tone of his fellow pupils, the wrong notes, the
out-of-tuneness, the faltering rhythms, and the absence of shading,
Franzl caught the creative intentions of the rare spirits who had conceived this music, and they gave him meat to eat that the others
knew not of. Then too, in the Imperial Choir he had the joy of taking part in great motets and Masses, well performed.

In May, 1809, Vienna was, for the second time, attacked and occupied by Napoleon. Mad with patriotism, the boys begged to be
allowed to join the army, but Principal Lang said no. To a lad they
promptly escaped from school, enlisted, and came back proudly
sporting the red and white ribbons of military men. They were
scolded and sent to their rooms but broke loose next morning and
sallied forth to drill.

Seeing that Lang was powerless, Archduke Rainer took a hand
and sent them back for days of room arrest. Where Lang had failed,
the majesty of an archduke succeeded. The young hotheads gradually cooled down. By good luck a howitzer grenade, which passed
through several floors of the Convict, exploded in a prefect's room,
narrowly missing Schubert.

The Franzl of those days was described by his comrade Anton
Holzapfel as "a short, stocky boy with a friendly round face and well-
marked features. . . . He proved to have one of those deep, still
minds which made shallow instructors misjudge his silence as a
mark of small talent. Even then he was mentally far in advance of
his years."

He was soon made librarian of the orchestra and was kept in that
tedious office until he left the school. He had to distribute the parts,
gather them up, and care for them. He had to restring the fiddles
when the old strings snapped, oil the keys of the wind instruments,

[2] In his E Major Quartet he was unconsciously to plagiarize a passage in the
opening movement of that symphony.

and renew leaky pads and decrepit springs. He even had to light
the tallow candles which furnished the illumination and replace
those that were burned down. It was as though a reincarnation of
John Keats were to be made janitor of the Poetry Society of America.

5

BANISHED

IT WAS September, 1809, and Franzl's pleasure in his best friend was changed to sorrow when Spaun left the Convict and the city, but he found solace in creation. There began to gush the extraordinary spate which Dame Ethel Smythe calls the "music . . . perhaps nearer my heart than any other—that crystal stream welling and welling for ever."

Franzl once told his father that the first piece he had written was a set of piano variations. Brother Ferdinand maintained, however, that the lad's first piano work was a four-hand fantasy dated April 8—May 1, 1810. In June came a Mass in C, dedicated to Holzer, and a setting for voice and piano of Schiller's *Corpse Fantasy*.

With the awakening within him of ceaseless creative activity Franzl, for the time being, changed his nature. The gay, gregarious young person described by his father was metamorphosed into a shy, retiring, somewhat taciturn lad, absorbed in the miracles of his imagination and devoted to a very few friends. Holzapfel and a new crony named Stadler somewhat made up for the absence of Spaun, who, however, in 1811, to Franzl's immense delight, returned to Vienna as a candidate for government officialdom. He reported:

I found my young friend a somewhat bigger boy, and in good spirits. He had long ago been promoted to the first violin section, and had already won a certain prestige in the orchestra, on the management of which he was not without influence. [Notice how Spaun's style already smacks of the government official.] At that time Schubert told me that he had composed a great deal: a sonata, a fantasy, a little opera, and now he was going to write a Mass. His chief difficulty was that he had neither music paper nor money to buy any. He was driven to ruling staves for himself on plain paper; and often he did not know how to get hold of even that. In secret I then provided him prodigiously with music paper, which he consumed in incredible quantities. He wrote extraordinarily fast, and continually used his study hours for composition, so naturally his school work

16

was skimped. Father Schubert, in other respects a very good man, discovered the cause of this backwardness in his studies. Then there was a portentous row. However, the young artist's wings were already too well grown, and nothing more could prevent his upward flight.

Now here is something which Spaun could not have realized, and which none of Schubert's biographers but Stefan[1] has remarked. The fact is that Franzl was, in the main, far from backward in his nonmusical work. Not a single school report had yet marked him as less than "good" in his studies. The boy's backwardness was merely relative, for these same reports showed him "very good" in morals, song, piano, and violin. So that Father Franz's angry reproach that the boy was doing badly in his serious studies was quite unjustified. It can only be explained by the fierce professional pride of a schoolmaster who is determined at all costs to have his offspring excel all comers in his own particular field.[2]

Until that row with Father, Franzl had hugely enjoyed the week ends with the family. Like so many Viennese homes from that day to this, the Schuberts' boasted an amateur string quartet. Ferdinand played first violin, Ignaz, second, Father did what he could on the 'cello, and Franzl, the leading spirit, following Mozart's example and setting one for a future Mendelssohn, operated the viola. When Father mistook the tenor clef for the bass, or forgot the key signature, or started the repeat at the wrong spot, or was just plain sour, the violist suavely passed it off in silence. But if the old man committed the same blunder twice running, the good-humored lad, with superhuman restraint, would mildly murmur, "Herr Father, there seems to be something the matter."

This domestic fiddling was excellent training for a future composer of quartets. Here he learned form, technique, tone color with its infinite possibilities, not from a textbook, but from the voices of the living, vibrating instruments themselves.

Father Franz thought music all very well as a pastime, but he feared and hated to see Franzl get in so deep that he would want to

[1] Paul Stefan, *Franz Schubert*, Berlin, Wegweiser, 1928.

[2] In this connection, one of the more intelligent biographers has been unjust, not to Franzl, but to those in authority over him. Richard Heuberger (*Franz Schubert*, Berlin, Schlesische, 1920) was mistaken in censuring Franzl's teachers for not noticing his musical gift before 1811. In the spring of 1809, his first school report notes that he has "musical talent," and in the fall the notation is "outstanding musical talent."

make it his life work. With a peasant's materialistic conservatism he held that none but a fool would try to extort a living out of what, like Schumann's mother later on, he regarded as "the breadless art." There never had been a genius in the family, and Caliban was as far from a sympathetic appreciation of this one as if Elisabeth had presented him with a leprechaun endowed with the gift of second sight. The more Holzer and the brothers praised the lad's gifts, the more determined the wooden schoolmaster became to nip this dangerous tendency in the bud. Franzl was put upon the carpet, soundly scolded, and given an ultimatum: "Either give up most of your musical activities, or give up your visits home!" Though a flaming sword threatened to bar him from that beloved paradise, the poor lad did not hesitate an instant. With a heavy heart he chose to remain faithful to his gift.

Exile bore hardly on Franzl and on those who loved him. No more gaiety about the family table, no more intimate hours with his adored mother, no more play with the brothers, no more happy wanderings about the picturesque streets or over the hills of the Wienerwald. Now, whenever he went out, it could only be with the other pupils, keeping step in strict formation. Alas! no more string quartets. Nothing but the monotony of the grim, dark, icy Convict, about which he had expressed his true opinion when Spaun had left it: "Lucky chap, now you're escaping from prison!" There was only one thing for the boy to do: find consolation by burrowing still deeper into his art. Father's cruelty was investing music with all the added seductiveness of forbidden fruit.

The year of banishment, 1811, brought a wide range of experimental compositions: a string quartet, a small piano fantasy, a quintet in overture form for Ferdinand, and some of the earliest songs. Considering that Franzl had been thrust out of a dearly loved home and immured in what he called a prison, it is small wonder that these songs continued the grim line started by the *Corpse Fantasy*. They were extremely long, rambling compositions entitled *Hagar's Lament,* and *The Parricide.* The choice of these subjects suggests how fiercely the lad must have resented his father's despotism. Conceived in the manner of the composer Zumsteeg, the object of his boyish admiration, these early songs already show that Schubert's genius was lyric rather than dramatic.

The resentment suggested by these titles must have been deepened by a sudden and terrible disaster. His beloved mother, her health perhaps undermined by the family quarrel, suddenly came down with typhus fever. On Corpus Christi day, May 28, 1812, while the paternal ban still kept Franz from seeing her, she died.

Over her coffin, however, their common sorrow reconciled father and son. The decree of exile was rescinded, and the boy was even allowed to take lessons in composition.[1] On one of his early exercise sheets for Salieri, there is a notation: "18 June, 1812 began counterpoint, 1st species."

This is how it happened. Antonio Salieri, the sixty-two-year-old imperial music director and head of music in the Convict, was a highly distinguished person. He had written dozens of operas, many of which had been successfully staged. As we have seen, he had given some lessons to Beethoven and had been a bitter enemy of Mozart. Indeed, in the delirium of his death bed, he was to accuse himself falsely of having poisoned the creator of *Figaro*.

This authoritative personage had from the first been struck by the qualities of the tiny "Miller." After four years of observation, impressed by such compositions as *Hagar's Lament*, he had allowed him to study musical theory with Ruzicka. It had taken but a lesson or two for that genial Czech to tell Spaun, as Holzer had once told Father Franz, that the little fellow knew everything already. "The *lieber Herrgott* must have had him in hand; for I can teach him nothing." This, however, carried modesty too far. Impregnated as he was with the folk tunes of his native Bohemia, Ruzicka must have filled Franzl with that love for music indigenous to the Austrian Empire's countryside without which his *Ländler* and waltzes and many a more serious movement could never have been written.

Then Salieri graciously accepted the boy as his unique Convict pupil. What a blessing it would have been if Franz could have had as able instruction as Leopold Mozart gave Wolfgang, as Neefe, Schenk, and Albrechtsberger gave young Beethoven, or even as Marxsen gave Brahms.[2]

---

[1] This account of Franz's first banishment is based on Spaun's report of the quarrel (see p. 17), and on Alois Fellner's interpretation of Schubert's autobiographical tale "My Dream" (see p. 108). According to Fellner, Franz's stepbrother Anton, the priest, declared that the composer had twice been banished from home.

[2] In repining over the quality of Schubert's instruction, Whitaker-Wilson— believe it or not—actually wrote: "We should like him to have studied under Mendelssohn for a short period as soon as the C Major Symphony was completed." I feel sure that Clara Schumann would have concurred in this wish.

Salieri did little more than look over hastily and superficially correct certain brief exercises in many-voiced part writing and give practice to Franzl and himself in playing from orchestral scores. They went through a portentous number of Italian operas, one more boring than the other, though they finally studied all the stage works of Gluck. All that the boy got out of the course was Gluck, a little voice leading, and musical contact with the sensuous South, that realm of agreeable sounds whose very language, Robert Schumann was to declare, is like a long-drawn-out A minor chord.

Personally Salieri must have been charming. According to Rochlitz, he was "friendly, obliging, benevolent, full of the joy of life, witty, inexhaustible in anecdote and quotation, a fine, neatly built little man with sparkling fiery eyes, a brown complexion, always tidy and clean, of a lively temperament, easily aroused to anger, but just as easy to pacify."

Unfortunately the man was an anachronistic survival in his profession, representing a point of view long since superseded by the trinity, Haydn, Mozart, Beethoven, with reference to whom he used to growl that music should have ceased with the death of Gluck. What had young Franz, worshiper of that trinity and child of the dawning Romantic era, in common with such a fossil? As we shall see, the worst that Salieri could do against Franz's heroes was temporarily to obscure the boy's admiration for Beethoven.

As sworn enemy of the rising nationalist school of Teutonic music, Salieri commanded Franz to write only in the Italian style and to eschew that pernicious thing, the lied. Especially must he have nothing to do with such unpleasant poetasters as Schiller and Goethe, whose lines were nothing but a farrago of "barbarous words."

Little did the old man realize what a viper he was nourishing in his bosom! If, endowed with prophetic vision, he could have foreseen how, under the aegis of Franz Schubert, the German lied was destined to take the wind out of the sails of Italian song, his peruke would have flown clean across the room.

The course with Salieri did Franzl no harm, except in one important respect. The Italian was never tired of dinning into the lad's ears that opera was the only form of composition worthy of a real composer. And this was the only Salierian dictum that influenced Franz to the bitter end. On other matters their strong differences of opinion finally drove them apart.

In a letter to Luib, Georg Franz Eckel drew a vignette of Franz out of doors:

> When the pupils walked out together, he usually went with head bent down, eyes to the front, hands on his back, fingers in motion as if playing upon the keys. He walked withdrawn into himself as though he were deeply meditating. Never did I see him in a passion. Vivacious he always was; though this was shown more by facial expression than by words, which were usually few, and revealed a profound sense of humor. I seldom saw him laugh; but he smiled frequently, sometimes without apparent reason, as if the smile were the reflex of a thought passing through his mind.

In another letter to Luib, Anton Stadler described young Franz at work.

> To see him compose was interesting. He seldom used the pianoforte, often declaring that this would interrupt the progress of his thoughts. He sat quietly at his small table, scarcely bothered by the conversation and noise of his fellow students—unavoidable at the Convict. He stooped far over a sheet of paper and a textbook; for he was extremely short-sighted. He gnawed at his pen, sometimes playing with his fingers upon the table as if trying a passage over; and wrote fluently and easily with few corrections, as though it had to be just this way and not otherwise.

Schubert was fifteen before he heard a good opera performance. First came Weigl's popular *Swiss Family,* Cherubini's *Medea,* and Spontini's *The Vestal.* More than these he enjoyed *The Magic Flute* and *Don Juan* by Mozart. He also loved Mozart's *Requiem,* Handel's *Messiah,* and Beethoven's Fifth Symphony. In the field of song he cared most for the works of Johann Rudolf Zumsteeg, and these, as we have seen, had a profound influence upon his creative life. This composer laid the foundations for the modern lied and ballad.

Like him, Schubert was a tireless experimenter and a far more stern self-critic than has been generally supposed. He was no lazy denizen of the Land of Cockayne. A happy-go-lucky idler could never have created the modern lied and written some of the loveliest works in all symphonic and chamber music.

6

FRANZL CROWS FOR THE LAST TIME

A SHEET of music once used by the boy choristers of the Imperial Chapel has been preserved. It is a copy of the third alto part of Peter Winter's First Mass. On it a boyish hand once scribbled some flourishes and these words:

> Schubert, Franz,
> Crowed for the last time,
> the 26th July, 1812.

Franzl's voice had broken. Nevertheless he was allowed to stay on for some months at the Convict. Considering that he was surrounded by adoring young friends and that Ruzicka gave him encouragement and discriminating appreciation, his creativeness was probably as well off there as it would have been at home. It is, however, hard to agree with Flower[1] that the Convict was an excellent nurturer of genius, or with Grove that the school had much to answer for. To my mind, it was neither very good nor very bad for his music. He might have fared much worse elsewhere.

True, the following letter of his to Ferdinand describes hardships that seem bitter to us of today but which were then the usual thing in Austrian schools:

November 24, 1812

Let me blurt right out what's on my heart, and so come sooner to the purpose of this letter, and not hold you up by beating about the bush. For a good while now I've been considering my condition, and have concluded that on the whole it is good, but is here and there susceptible of improvement. You know from experience that sometimes one would like to eat a roll and a couple of apples; all the more so when, after a mediocre dinner, one can expect only a wretched supper, and, at that, eight and a half hours later.

This often self-assertive desire now grows more and more insistent, and

[1] Newman Flower, *Franz Schubert, the Man and His Circle*, London, Cassell and Co., Ltd., 1928, and New York, Frederick A. Stokes Co., 1928.

I must willy-nilly (*nolens volens*) effect a change. The couple of *Groschen* which I get from Herr Father always go to the devil in the very first days, and how shall I manage the rest of the time? Those who put their trust in thee shall not be put to shame. Matthew III 4. That's what I think too—So how would it be if every month you let a couple of kreutzer wander my way? You yourself wouldn't feel it, while I, in my monk's cell, would consider myself happy and content. As already mentioned, I prop myself up on the words of the Apostle Matthew, who saith: Whoso hath two coats let him give one to the poor, etc.[1] Meanwhile I trust you will lend ear to the voice that incessantly appeals to you to remember

Your

Loving, poverty-stricken, hoping, and
yet again I say poverty-stricken brother
FRANZ

Despite the precocious humor, parts of this letter sound rather grim. Apparently he had not wholly outgrown the desperation which, years before, had found vent in the remark to Spaun about escaping from prison.

The output of 1812 was a *Kyrie,* a *Salve Regina,* a piano trio movement labeled "Sonate," and an orchestral overture in D.

In the fall of 1813, Franz returned home, having declined the imperial offer of a good scholarship if he would remain in the Convict and improve his mathematics. Professor Deutsch feels that "a disciplinary affair, in which he was not directly involved, may have had something to do with it."

Just before leaving school he had finished his First Symphony, in D. Though almost pure Haydn and Mozart, this work showed that the lad of sixteen had already done no little experimenting with the orchestra. The year 1813 also produced vocal trios, a wind octet, and many dances, including thirty minuets with Trios. In connection with these (now lost) minuets, Kreissle[2] tells that "they were so much

---

[1] These Biblical quotations are diverting instances of the happy-go-lucky Viennese *Schlamperei* that persists to our day. For the first Matthew reference (which Kreissle mistakenly corrects to Matthew II, 4) Franzl was evidently thinking of Psalm XXV, 2: "O my God, I trust in Thee: let me not be ashamed," or of its quotation in Romans X, 11. As for the other citation, it was not Matthew, but Luke (III, 11) who reported the generous proposition: "He that hath two coats, let him impart to him that hath none; and he that hath meat, let him do likewise."

[2] Heinrich Kreissle von Hellborn, *Franz Schubert,* Vienna, Gerold, 1865. English translation, London, Longmans, Green & Co., Ltd., 1869.

admired by Dr. Anton Schmidt, a friend of Mozart, that he exclaimed: 'If these things were really composed by a child, he will
become a master such as few have been.'"

Unsatisfactory though his theoretical studies were, they had already made a profound difference in the lad's creative life. He absorbed them as a damp sponge drinks water. Ambition and ability
had begun to unite, and the first faint signs of originality were timidly appearing.

Eleven months after the death of Mother Elisabeth, Father Franz,
the highly sexed, wrote into the family archives the following quaint
announcement:

1813, the 25th April
I married myself for the second time to the valued virgin (*wertgeschätzten
Jungfrau*) Anna Kleyenböck, b. 1 June, 1783

Her father was a Viennese manufacturer of silk articles, so this second union represented a social step up from Elisabeth, who had only
been the daughter of a country locksmith. Anna was twenty years
younger than her husband. She was to have more luck with her five
children's health than her predecessor, as she brought four of them
through the perils of infancy in that unhygienic age. It is pleasant
to know that she showed young Franz affection, and did her duty by
him.

7

FRANZL IN LOVE

SCHUBERT'S biographers have long agreed that, on escaping from the "prison" of the Convict, he was confronted by a dismaying alternative: he could either be conscripted to serve fourteen years in the army, or enter the one available profession that would exempt a poor boy from military service. And that was why he became a schoolteacher.

This theory has recently been demolished by Professor O. E. Deutsch's discovery[1] that Schubert was then below the military stature of five feet. A conscription form of 1818, which describes him as "weak," shows that, even at the age of twenty-one, he was not much taller than a dwarf, only 4 feet, 11¼ inches. And his profession would not have helped him, for no teachers below the grade of second assistant were exempted from the army, and Franzl was only sixth assistant.

A fine conscript he would have made, with his short sight, weak undersized frame, slow reactions, awkwardness, and utter unfitness for practical workaday existence! Suppose that he had been forced into uniform. During those fourteen years he would not have composed a tithe of what he actually did. And, if he had not been killed in battle, or shot for writing *Du bist die Ruh'* while on guard duty, he would have been discharged in 1828, the year of his actual death. But then, army training might have been so good for his body that he might have lived to a ripe age and produced thrice the masterpieces yielded by his actual thirty-one years on earth.

Franzl must have become a teacher, not from inclination, but because Father decreed it, and because that was the only method he knew for getting three meals a day.

Father of course was delighted. He trusted that, once the lad was well worked into harness as his assistant, he would give up those

---

[1] See *The Music of Schubert*, Gerald Abraham, ed., New York, W. W. Norton & Company, Inc., 1947, p. 11.

silly notions about music and settle down into the sure and respectable paternal profession.

So the young fellow went for a brief normal course in the Normal-Hauptschule. Though weak in five subjects, and very weak in religion, he passed and was licensed to teach. That so-called "weakness" in religion[1] may not have been weakness, after all, but strength —the power to think things out for himself. The year before his death, Ferdinand Walcher was to write him a note lightly alluding to the composer's disbelief in some of the dogmas of the Credo. (See p. 163.) Let those who are shocked by such disbelief reflect that it was far less overt than that of the old Italian composer who rearranged the text the better to suit the turn of his melody: "*Credo! Non credo! Ah, non credo in unum deum!*"

The Mass to Schubert [writes Ralph Bates[2]] was a great musical form of a kind that might secure performance. If his work in that form is often filled with deep feeling, it is for the reason that its imagery, its solemnity and drama awakened the profound mysticism in him, as it does in most of us, a mysticism which probably he mistakenly thought the better part of religion.

Here was Franzl at home again but bereft of his beloved mother, and plunged up to the neck in a profession which he loathed. For teaching little children their ABC's and so on he was paid the munificent sum of 80 florins, A.C.,[3] or $38.56 a year. Of course, money went further then. Today this amount would be worth about $115.68, which comes to a little more than 31 cents a day.

His professional environment was a small, stuffy, low-ceilinged room with tiny windows opening on an airless courtyard. It was packed to suffocation with small children. Their din soon came to be ably reinforced by the wails and screams of his young half-brethren in the adjoining room. The most complicating feature of the situation was that Franzl's genius would not let him alone. Those

---

[1] One recalls the incorrect Biblical allusions in his hungry letter to Ferdinand, p. 23.

[2] *Franz Schubert*, New York, D. Appleton-Century Company, Inc., 1935.

[3] By March 15, 1811, the Napoleonic Wars had so impoverished Austria that the so-called Viennese Currency (hereafter abbreviated V.C.) was introduced. A florin (or gulden) V.C. was worth only two fifths of a florin in the old Assimilated Coinage (A.C. for short), which had a value of 48.2 cents. During Schubert's lifetime these two currencies were used simultaneously. A ducat was worth $2.08. There were 60 kreutzers to a florin.

compelling inspirations simply had to be scribbled on whatever stray scraps of paper he could find and hastily rule. And these impossible conditions for work made him scribble all the faster in the hope of getting them down before they were killed by interruption. On the manuscript of the third B Flat Quartet, written between September 5 and 13, 1814, he noted at the close of the first movement: "Finished in 4½ hours."

Small wonder that he set the children to writing exercises so that he, too, could write. In those days the birch was as necessary a part of a schoolmaster's equipment as blackboard, chalk, and eraser are today. And when the din became too infernal to bear, Franz remembered the old saw about not sparing the rod. According to his sister Maria Theresia, he was often goaded into bad temper and "kept his hands in practice on the children's ears," which seems an odd form of punishment for a musician to choose. "It is true," he once admitted to Franz Lachner, "that, when I was composing, this little crew often angered me so that I always lost the thread. Then, naturally, I beat them well."

Not an engaging picture, but—reader—put yourself in his place. That, however, you will find impossible unless you happen to be an immortal genius of seventeen, living in a cruel age, and brutally torn out of a creative ecstasy. You would have to be a sensitive spirit, dragged from the very gates of heaven to become a pack animal.

"Any one in our shoes," cried his teacher-brother Ignaz, "delivered up like a miserable beast of burden to all the cruelties of a gang of young savages, is the victim of a multitude of abuses; and is besides at the mercy of an ungrateful public and of an imbecile officialdom."

Ignaz meant the doting parents whose offspring could do no wrong and the superiors to whom the brothers owed a strict obedience. How Franzl, too, loathed them all!

This slavery, however, had occasional mitigations. In order to attend the *première* of the final version of *Fidelio* on May 23, 1814, at the Kärntnertor Theater, Franzl sold his schoolbooks.

His old music teacher Papa Holzer was organist and choirmaster of the nearby Liechtental Church that looked like an exaggerated insect. He encouraged Franzl to write him some church music. The boy did not need much urging. It was not that his pious sentiments imperiously demanded musical utterance, for these sentiments, in reaction to the besotted religious bigotry of his peasant father, were of a rather mild nature. Some years later we shall find him writing to freethinking Ignaz about the priests at Zseliz (see p. 71) in such a tone that his apprehensive brother answered, "If you should write to Papa and me together, don't touch on religious matters!"

No doubt Franz composed his early ecclesiastical music mainly because he was sure of the privilege—so alluring to a young composer—of hearing it performed in the local church. In experimental scoring for its modest players, he won invaluable experience and laid the foundation for a later mastery of instrumentation, the freshness, subtlety, and originality of which has not even today been fully appreciated.

Another reason for turning to religious music was that he was more than half enamored of a girl with a beautiful voice, who would sing it. Therese Grob was only sixteen, but her high soprano was precocious. In the social scale she was a step above Franzl, for her father had been a well-to-do manufacturer of silk articles, and her widowed mother carried on the business. Her brother Heinrich was an able performer on 'cello, piano, and organ, and the atmosphere of the house, where the young composer was a welcome guest, was genuinely musical.

Therese was pockmarked, with plain features but a passable figure. In her earliest known portrait she has a long nose, an enormous mouth, and the sort of dress that a homely but egotistical woman would like her paid companion to wear. Franz loved her, not for her *beaux yeux,* but for her *beau voix.* So long after Schubert's death that his memory did not serve him correctly in every detail, Anselm Hüttenbrenner recorded a confession which had been made in 1821:

During a country walk with Schubert, I asked him if he had ever been in love; for, since his attitude in society toward the tender sex was so cold and dry, I was fully convinced that he did not like women at all. "Oh no," he said, "I have loved one of them right tenderly, and it was mutual. She was the daughter of a schoolteacher [sic!], somewhat younger than myself, and sang the soprano solos in a Mass that I wrote, sang them very beautifully and with deep feeling. She was not exactly pretty—had pockmarks in her face; but she was good and kindhearted. For three years she hoped that I would marry her; but I couldn't find a job that would support us both. Then, at her parent's wish, she married another man, which pained me deeply. I love her yet; and since then I've never found another woman that I like as well or better. She just wasn't meant for me.

It is probable that Therese inspired him more than did dogmatic religion in composing his Mass in F. Despite the enormous handicap of youth, this is one of the finest first Masses ever produced. Ebenezer Prout[1] declared it as striking a work of precocious genius as that overture to *A Midsummer Night's Dream* very soon to be composed by another lad of seventeen called Felix Mendelssohn-Bartholdy. Though not quite all of that, it yet remains a miraculous achievement for so young a boy.

And the spirit of this Mass was something new. It registered a remarkable protest against the mode of the time and place. For Viennese church music was then in a bad way. It was dependent on amateurs, who called the tune. And the tune they called was, by preference, far closer to opera, and even operetta, than to the devotional outpourings of a Bach or a Palestrina. The music of the church choir was only a hop, skip, and jump from that of the cabaret.

The Mass in F was given during the centenary celebration of the Liechtental Church, and met with general approval. This, his first public performance, at once made the composer a marked lad in that small suburban community. Josef Mayseder, soon to be famous, was a first violinist. Salieri honored the occasion with his masterful presence and, greatly pleased, went about boasting of Franz as his pupil. Father Schubert actually forgot himself and his prejudices so far as to present his son with a five-octave piano.

On October 26, 1814, the Mass in F was repeated at the Church of St. Augustine in the city, where the Hapsburgs lie buried. This time Franz conducted, while brother Ferdinand presided over the organ.

[1] In *Monthly Musical Record,* Jan. and Feb., 1871.

8

THE MODERN LIED IS BORN

THESE were momentous days for the art of music. On October 19, 1814, the genius of Goethe suddenly inflamed the genius of Schubert to create a perfect song, a new phenomenon, his first masterpiece, *Margaret at the Spinning Wheel.* In the words of Oscar Bie,[1] this date is the birthday of the German lied.

Suddenly, without warning, in the midst of such workaday exercises as the Schiller songs, *An Emma* and *Das Mädchen aus der Fremde,* an inexplicable miracle happened. *Margaret* sprang perfect from the brain of an adolescent. The song was wholly original. It was pure Schubert with no alien admixture. What a feat! As Delacroix told his *Journal:* "To dare *to be one's self* needs great hardihood . . . indeed, the greatest of all hardihoods lies in departing from convention and habits."

Eusebius Mandyczewski, the brilliant editor-in-chief of the Breitkopf and Härtel *Complete Edition* of Schubert,[2] writes that the composer's "genius played him a glorious trick":

Sharply defined, unified atmosphere, logical musical development, freedom in the treatment of key, melodic individuality, in short, nearly everything that afterwards made Schubert a composer of mark, suddenly comes to light here. The fact that this lied emerged so perfect from the turmoil of his inner man must have opened his eyes to new knowledge of himself and brought about in him a tremendous transformation. For immediately he turned, with an almost uncanny industry—an industry as yet new to himself and only explicable in a genius of such power—to the composition of lieder.

[1] *Franz Schubert. Sein Leben und sein Werk,* Berlin, Ullstein, 1925. English translation, *Schubert the Man,* New York, Dodd, Mead & Company, Inc., 1928.
[2] Preface to Series XX, Vol. I. This *Gesammt Ausgabe* will hereafter be referred to as G. A.

To the everlasting dishonor of Professor Salieri, the sole emotion that *Margaret at the Spinning Wheel* caused him was annoyance. "Franz," he grumbled, "it is all very well for you to try your hand at Masses, but do not fritter time away on such insignificant things as lieder. The only thing for a real composer to concentrate on is opera!" How well it would have been if Franz had only disregarded the last bit of bad advice as thoroughly as he did the preceding! [1] Salieri's disservice to Schubert in firing him with ambition to succeed in that hybrid form, opera, for which he was ill suited, can scarcely be overestimated. A few days after producing *Margaret*, he finished *The Devil's Pleasure Castle*, in three acts, words by Kotzebue. It was the first of a series, alas, too long! of operatic love's labors lost.

Near the end of 1814, Josef von Spaun took the first step toward founding Schubert's famous circle of friends by introducing him to the unhappy hypochondriac poet, Johann Mayrhofer. This peculiar creature, a decade older than Franz, hailed from Steyr, had studied theology, entered the tobacco trade, gone in for law, and finally became one of Metternich's censors. As he was, in principle, an ardent champion of freedom of speech and of the press, the job caused him bitter humiliation and self-reproach. Indeed, he once worked himself up into such a fury of enthusiasm on this subject that, like a demagogue of the French Revolution, he sprang upon a table, tearing his hair, raving and shrieking, "Freedom of the press! Freedom of the press!" Whereupon he returned to the office to strangle that same press according to the sternest precepts of Metternich.

Mayrhofer hated women, and loved Young's *Night Thoughts*. This is how he described his first meeting with the composer:

Led by his friend, Schubert entered the room that . . . we were afterward to occupy together. It was in a gloomy street. House and room had felt the might of the years. The ceiling was somewhat sunken, the light badly compromised by a large building opposite. There was a played-out piano and a small bookcase.[2] That was the room which, with the hours passed in it, will not leave my memory. As spring deeply moves

---

[1] He neglected the two poets whom Salieri particularly despised to the extent of setting fifty-seven poems by Schiller and sixty-seven by Goethe.

[2] Another more summary description of this Spartan room says that "it was simply adorned with a guitar, a couple of books, and the obligato tobacco pipes."

the earth, to lavish upon it greenness, blossoms and delicate fragrances, so there overwhelms and enriches a man the perception of his productive power . . .

This fundamental feeling, and our love of poetry and music, made our association the more intimate. I wrote poems and he set them.[1] Many of these owed to his melodies their existence, development, and dissemination.

The essentially Austrian quality of both men helped to make their collaboration more than usually harmonious. It is worth noting that Schubert was the only great Austrian composer to be born in Vienna, for Haydn, Mozart, Bruckner, and Wolf were all provincials. In some ways, however, he was less Viennese than any of the others, for his neat handwriting, his dislike of crowds, his preference for small circles of intimates, and his amazing industry were all inherited from Moravia and Silesia, the land of his parents. As with Beethoven and Brahms, his was a harmony of northern blood [2] and a southern environment.

The mass of music turned out by the eighteen-year-old school assistant in 1815 is almost incredible. Certain composers would have thought it enough for the work of a lifetime. Even the sheer manual labor of putting down so many notes is fantastic. I like Daniel Gregory Mason's remark: "One rubs one's eyes. Compared with Schubert's pen, Aladdin's lamp seems a poor affair." Grove declared that "the spectacle of so insatiable a desire to produce has never before been seen; of a genius thrown naked into the world and compelled to explore for himself all paths and channels in order to discover by exhaustion which was the best . . . and then to die."

This year was the most productive in the life of Schubert or of any other known composer. It yielded the Second and Third Symphonies, four large dramatic works, two Masses, a quantity of minor church music and choral works, a sonata and smaller pieces for piano, and one hundred and forty-five songs, including *Little Heath Rose* (*Heidenröslein*) and *The Erl King,* which runs to more than two and a half songs for every week in the year. And a good many of these were in several different versions. On October fifteenth he finished eight; on the nineteenth, seven. In all this mountain of notes there

[1] Forty-seven of them, more than those of any other poets except Goethe and Schiller.

[2] Comparatively northern in Schubert's case.

is no evidence of carelessness or superficial haste. Bach, Handel, and Haydn were rapid writers, but none of them showed such fecundity as this. So the formidable year of Waterloo, which saw the master of mankind hurled into the depths, countered this carnage by giving evidence that the world's greatest master of song was in the full tide of creation.

Before the winter of 1815, the family quartet had taken on an orchestral character. Haydn symphonies were performed with doubled parts. And so many players clamored for admission that the Schubert home was found too small. The enthusiasts migrated to a house in the Dorotheergasse; wind instruments were recruited, and the quartet became an orchestra. Better and better players were added, some of them professionals. They tackled the music of Weigl, Boïeldieu, Catel, Cherubini, Winter, Spontini, and even those highly modern works, the first two symphonies of Beethoven. There were four moves in all, until the impossibility of finding a suitable goal for a fifth broke up the venture. All through it Franzl played viola, gaining much practical experience. It was probably for this small orchestra that he wrote his Fourth and Fifth Symphonies. One imagines the proud excitement of the little group as they first tried these creations of their young violist.

Late in 1815 Spaun presented to Schubert a Swedish nobleman, Franz, Ritter von Schober, who had heard a Schubert song, had fallen in love with it, and had sworn to know its maker. Before long he was to become one of the composer's dearest, most helpful, and most influential friends.

Schober's mother and his education were both Austrian, and he felt more at home in Vienna than in his native Torup. He was a poet, with occasional flashes of no mean ability, and Schubert was to set a libretto of his and fifteen lyrics. The world can never be too grateful for his lines *To Music* which inspired one of the most memorable Schubertian melodies.

These two youngsters must have been attracted by the law of contrasts. Schober, with his sideburns, goatee, and small mustache, jauntily turned up at the ends, his artificial-looking curls, his sensual, Hapsburglike jaw, and his somewhat cynical, affected expression, looked like a dandified playboy. How different was Schubert's good, honest, ugly peasant countenance! This plain exterior, according to Anselm Hüttenbrenner, was not in the least remarkable or attractive. He was short, with a moon-face, and rather fat. His brow was very beautifully arched. On account of short vision he always wore spectacles, which he did not take off even when he went to bed. The confection of a toilet was simply not in his line, which made him loath to enter fine society where he would have to dress up . . . He hated to bow and scrape; and flattery made him positively sick.

A more detailed word portrait of him was written to Ferdinand Luib in 1858 by the physician Georg Franz Eckel, who had played flute in the Convict orchestra:

Figure short but stocky, bones well developed and solid, muscles firm. Not angular but rather plump. Neck short and powerful, broad, finely curved shoulders, breast and trunk . . . hands and feet small, his walk vivacious and vigorous . . . Hair brown and abundant. Forehead and chin particularly well developed. Face more expressive and forceful than beautiful. Eyes gentle and, if I mistake not, light brown. Under excitement they could flash fire. Well overshadowed by somewhat prominent and bushy eyebrows which made them look smaller than their true size, especially as he often narrowed them in the way of nearsighted folk. The blunt, medium-sized nose somewhat tip-tilted, and a gentle inward sweep joined it to his firm, ample lips, which were usually closed. A deep dimple in the chin. As is usual with genius, the complexion was pallid but vital. In the play of his features one could see the workings of creative genius. When he frowned tremendously and tightened his lips, they were stern. When his eyes beamed and his mouth smiled, they were sweet.

What a foil for Schober, that elegant, loquacious man about town! And the contrast went much further. Schober was an amateur Jack-of-all-artistic-trades: poet, actor, designer, musician, and was easily distracted from one by the other. His instincts were those of Wilhelm Meister, the strolling player, whom he later sought without success to imitate. Schubert, on the contrary, was a man of just one idea, and nothing could turn him aside from a fierce concentration on getting upon paper the beauty that seethed in his soul.

Happily the portraits of Schober, with their impression of conceit, egocentricity, and rather cheap dandyism,[1] do not jibe with what we know of the man's fine unselfish, beauty-loving nature, and real—

---

[1] Robert Pitrou writes of *"son élégance de garçon coiffeur."* (*Franz Schubert,* Paris, Émile-Paul, 1928.)

though semioccasional—creative ability. Schober himself was far better than his portraits suggested. He was always coming to Schubert with the question, "What can I do for you?" And when the answer was, "*Nix*" ("nothing"), as it very often was, he would exclaim, "*Schad!*" ("too bad!") and, like the young man in the Bible, go away sorrowful, though for a more creditable reason.

In time the musician grew so devoted to the dilettante that, with humorous originality, he married their names into the portmanteau word "Schobert." He called the Swede "a fundamentally intelligent chap, a godlike chap." And in 1823 he wrote, "I can never forget you, dear Schober; for what you have been to me, no one else, alas, can replace."

Others of the Circle, however, possibly jealous of the nobleman's grip on their idol's affections, were less enthusiastic. Bauernfeld wrote:

Schober is a sort of man of the world, has great eloquence and convincingness, and is, despite his somewhat crooked legs, beloved by the women . . . Clementine Russ called him "the God Mahadö." [1] She did not, however, demand that he should lift her up in his fiery arms. Moritz [von Schwind] also looks up to him as to a god. I find him rather human, but interesting.

Schober was fully aware that he could never be a creative artist out of the top drawer, and cheerfully, unassumingly, and selflessly he set about doing whatever he could for the greatest genius that he knew.

For the second time Goethe now inspired Franzl to his best efforts. Spaun's memoirs tell how *The Erl King* was born:

One afternoon Mayrhofer and I called on Schubert, who was then living at his father's house in the Himmelpfortgrund. We found him all aglow, reading *The Erl King* out of a book which he carried several times to and fro across the room. Suddenly he sat, and in the shortest possible time the magnificent ballad was hurled down upon paper. As Schubert had no piano, we ran with it to the Convict; and there that evening *The Erl King*

---

[1] She meant Mahadeva, another name for Shiva, whom his Hindu worshipers call "the Supreme Being," and identify with creation, reproduction, and destruction. He is "the lord of the Earth" in Goethe's poem *Der Gott und die Bajadere,* which Schubert set in 1815.

was sung [first by Schubert, then by Randhartinger (?)], and received with enthusiasm.[1] Ruzicka . . . then played it through attentively without the voice. He was very appreciative and the composition moved him deeply. When some of the hearers criticized a recurrent dissonance,[2] Ruzicka sounded it on the piano and explained how necessarily it there mirrored the text; more than that, how beautiful it was and how happily it was resolved.

This appreciation, so intelligent and so far in advance of its day, makes one wonder whether Franzl had not made a mistake in leaving such a forward-looking teacher for the backward-looking Salieri. Little did any of that excited group dream that the honeyed blandishments sung by the *Erl King* foretold one of the most delightful passages of chamber music, to be heard a decade later in the D Minor Quartet.

[1] One wonders what had become of the piano given him the year before by Father Franz after the *première* of the Mass in F. Professor Deutsch doubts Randhartinger's claim to have been the second person to sing this song.

[2] Where G flat, F natural, and E flat sound together at the words: *"Mein Vater, mein Vater, jetzt fasst er mich an!"* To modern ears this seems perfectly natural.

9

FRANZL BREAKS WITH SALIERI

THE Circle that had begun to be so necessary to Schubert's happiness had started auspiciously with Spaun, Mayrhofer, and Schober. Before the end of 1815 it was joined by two lads who had been his fellow pupils under Salieri. Ignaz Assmayer hailed from Mozart's town of Salzburg and became a piano teacher in Vienna. Another provincial, Anselm Hüttenbrenner of Graz, like Handel before, and Schumann after him, escaped from the law to music. Anselm recalled:

At first Schubert was suspicious of me. He thought I wanted only a sort of superficial acquaintance with him, to entertain myself a while with his works and then show him my back. But when, in the course of time, he noticed that I singled out just those portions of his songs which he himself thought most successful, he began to trust me and we became the best of friends. Schubert, Assmayer, Mozatti and I each agreed to compose a new male quartet a week and sing it every Thursday night at Mozatti's house . . . Once Schubert came without his quartet; but when we gently reproached him, he immediately wrote one before our faces and eyes. Schubert set very little store by these occasional compositions, and there are probably no more than a half dozen of them in existence.

When the jovial brothers in music, often as many as ten, sat somewhere snugly together, each had his own gang nickname. Schubert was known as Schwammerl [Little Mushroom]. We were young, gay folk, did ourselves as well as possible in our beloved Imperial city, and each gave the other a lift under the arms.

Now came a chance for Franzl to better his condition and win Therese Grob. In August, 1816, a post as music teacher in Laibach fell vacant. The incumbent must be a fully equipped organist, singer, and fiddler, must know all the wind instruments and be prepared to teach them. Furthermore, he must not engage "in occupations sus-

ceptible of compromising the reputation of a public teacher," a stipu-
lation that stung M. Pitrou to observe, "Here one recognizes again
the puritanism of Franz II, the lover of the danseuse Vigano!" All for
five hundred florins, A.C., a year. Though this was a considerable advance over Franzl's present eighty florins and keep, and he had
rather teach music than the ABC, it was asking much for little.

He applied for the post, modestly omitting all mention of his compositions. But Salieri's testimonial was no more than a dry "I support
the application," and the prince of melodists was rejected. One must
admit, however, that even this support stretched a point; for Franz
was far from being a master of all brazen and wooden tubes. When,
toward the close of his career, we find him with a drop taken, scornfully deriding a hapless clarinetist and his windy comrades (see p.
141), may we possibly trace back this aversion to his Laibach disappointment?

For some time now, the youth had been reacting against the Ital-
ianizing attempts of Master Salieri. The more the old man railed
against his German songs and insisted on his setting Italian *stanze,*
the more Austrian the pupil became. In this he was only following
in the footsteps of that other Salieri pupil, Beethoven, and in those
of Haydn, whose Italian master, Porpora, lived only two streets
away from Salieri.

Franzl was now quite fed up with the old Italian, and burst in
exasperation from the Salieri camp. Even exasperation, however,
could not make the good-natured fellow ungrateful or unjust. Shortly
before the definite break, he wrote a piece for the jubilee on June
16, 1816, celebrating Salieri's fiftieth year in Vienna. These were the
accompanying observations in his diary:

An artist must find it beautiful and life-giving to see all his pupils
gathered about him, each striving to give of his best for the jubilee; in
all these compositions to hear the expression of sheer nature, free from the
eccentric element which dominates the work of most contemporary composers. This element of eccentricity is almost wholly due to one of our
greatest German artists, who unites the tragic with the comic, the agreeable with the repulsive, the heroic with howls, the holiest with harle-
quinades. Who not only unites them but mistakes the one for the other
without distinction, makes men mad instead of dissolving them in love,
moves them to laughter instead of lifting them up to God. To see this eccentric element banned from the circle of his pupils, in exchange for the
sight of pure and holy nature must bring the loftiest joy to this artist who,

guided by a man like Gluck, has learned to know nature and, despite the most unnatural conditions of our times, has clung to it.

It comes as a shock to find that by this "eccentric" composer Schubert actually meant Beethoven, the genius to whom he had in his "*Tragic*" Symphony just paid the sincerest compliment of imitation. The insult was wrung from him in the throes of the painful struggle to break loose from that dominating influence and attain a creative catharsis. As Vetter[1] puts the case, "In its form [this insult] wrongs Beethoven; but essentially it is justified by [Schubert's] most personal artistic urge and will."

Twenty-six of Salieri's present and former pupils came to the jubilee, each armed with a dedicatory composition, and gathered around him in concentric circles. Among them were Assmayr and Anselm Hüttenbrenner. From a distance, Hummel and Moscheles sent vocal pieces, but there is no record of a similar attention by Beethoven. Franzl's offering was a trio for male voices and piano, set to lines of his own which end:

> *Unser aller Grosspapa,*
> *Bleibe noch recht lange da!*

> (Grandpapa of all this throng,
> May you bide with us right long!)

Two different reasons are given for Schubert's break with Salieri. One is the teacher's disparagement of the lied and of the German poets. The other is that in the ms. of the youth's B Flat Mass,[2] he blue-penciled all passages which savored of Haydn or Mozart. This greatly annoyed Franzl. He burst into his friend Doppler's place, hurled the music upon the table, and swore that it was all over between him and the old Italian. This was one of the wisest decisions of his short life.

[1] Walther Vetter, *Franz Schubert*, Potsdam, Acad. Verlagsges., 1934.
[2] Which was not finished until the following month.

10

FREE AT LAST!

FEBRUARY 23, 1816, found Father Schubert in high good humor. In recognition of his public spirit, he had been made an honorary citizen of Vienna. This may have benefited the art of music by presently disposing him to relax his despotic grip upon his genius of a son.

On April seventeenth the devoted Spaun thought to aid Franzl by sending to the literary dictator of Europe some of the settings which that great man's poems had inspired him to write. They included *Shepherd's Complaint, Little Heath Rose, Restless Love, Margaret at the Spinning Wheel,* and *The Erl King* in its third version with the easier accompaniment. With it went a humble complimentary letter in the submissive style of the day. Most contemporary composers were setting Goethe's poems and hopefully offering him their music with similar letters.

Readers of Thomas Mann's *Lotte in Weimar* can well understand how little chance young, proletarian, uninfluential Schubert had of winning the egocentric old Excellency's notice. What feeble inclination for music the snobbish titan possessed, in Dahms's vivid phrase, had "been given a haircut" by his friends, the conventional composers Reichardt and Zelter. Perhaps they weeded out Goethe's musical mail and discarded the more forward-looking scores of their younger rivals. For it seems that the poet never heard *The Erl King* until 1829, when the composer was already in his grave. Then Frau Schröder-Devrient performed it, and Goethe remarked: "So sung, it becomes a veritable picture"—an unmusical approach to the art nicely calculated to give a true musician gooseflesh. The songs were returned without a line of acknowledgment, a stunning blow to the eager expectations of Franzl and his friends.

The young composer was more susceptible to the magic of Milder's voice than was Goethe to that of Schröder-Devrient. Spaun tells of

40

taking his friend, some years earlier, to a performance of Gluck's *Iphigenia in Tauris*. Afterward Franzl was beside himself—"out of the little house," as they say in Austria—with excitement and pleasure at the grand effect of the music. Earth, he declared, held no greater beauty. The voice of Milder, the prima donna, caught him by the heart. And he longed to meet Vogl, the bass-baritone, that he might fall at the man's feet in thanks for the achievement of his Orestes.

Leaving the theater, they ran into the famous poet Theodor Körner, who took them along to the Hunter's Horn in the Dorotheergasse. I translate Spaun's account with a license appropriate to the occasion:

While we were still pleasurably evaporating the evening's musical delight, a University professor at an adjoining table sneered at our exuberance. Milder, he asserted, had crowed like a cock. The less said about her runs and trills the better. In a comprehensive word, she simply could not sing. As for the Orestes, he had feet like an elephant. Our fury at these impudent lies boiled over. Körner [who was no taller than Schubert] jumped menacingly to his feet. So did Schubert; but he was clumsy and had a serious misfortune: he upset his brimming glass of beer. The quarrel grew hotter and hotter and would have come to blows had not peacemakers poured oil upon the inflamed passions.

It was a momentous evening. The beer upset may have averted a duel and spared Franzl to write the C Major Quintet. And that night Körner is believed to have confirmed him in his resolve to go in for a musical career.

Schubert now succumbed again to his besetting temptation, opera. His acceptance of such an incredibly shoddy libretto as *Die Bürgschaft* is to be explained on the sole grounds of his insensate hunger and thirst for dramatic success. Even that, however, could not make him put up for long with the puerilities of the text, and after writing the second number of the third act, he shelved it. One imagines his sigh of mingled disgust and relief. In the music one can hear the horns of Mozartland "faintly blowing," for it has echoes of *Die Entführung, The Magic Flute,* and *Don Juan.*

Of course this experience did not cure him for long of his fatal ambition. The indomitable fellow soon composed another opera, the ms. of which has disappeared and left "not a rack behind." It would be amusing to compare this work with Wagner's masterpiece about musical doings in Nuremberg that followed almost half a lifetime later; for Franzl's was entitled *Der Minnesänger.*

In these days Schubert seems to have been obsessed by Mozart. On June 13, 1816, his diary shows how well he could write words, when adequately inspired:

> So long as I live, this day will always be luminous, radiant and beautiful in my memory. Softly, as if out of the distance, Mozart's magical tones still steal upon my inner ear. With what incredible power, and then again how softly, did Schlesinger's masterly playing print it deep, deep into my heart! Thus do these lovely imprints remain in our souls, imprints that neither time nor circumstance erase, and which bless our beings with their benign influence. Amid the black shadows of this life they reveal to us a clear, bright, beautiful distance upon which we pin our hopes. O Mozart, immortal Mozart, how many, oh how boundlessly many such blessed imprints of a better, more radiant life have you graved upon our souls!— This quintet is, so to speak, one of his greatest smaller works.

One wonders which of those incomparable quintets it was: the dramatic C Minor, the deep, tragic G Minor, the exuberant C Major, the playful D Major, or that in A where clarinet and strings become children of light and sing together with the morning stars.

Schubert's Mozart worship, however, was without prejudice to his feeling for Handel. He loved to play the oratorios four-handed with Anselm Hüttenbrenner, who testified:

> In his admiration of this giant he agreed with Beethoven . . . Sometimes he would exclaim: "Oh, what daring modulations! Even in dreams such things couldn't occur to a fellow like me."

At this time Franzl was so straitly confined indoors by teaching for a pittance, and recording his imperious inspirations for not even that pittance, that he had small time for communion with nature. And this diary entry for June 14, 1816, marks an exceptional occasion:

> After several months I again took an evening walk. There can scarcely be anything more agreeable than, after a hot summer's day, to wander out into the greenery, for which the fields between Währing and Döbling seem made on purpose. Strolling with my brother Karl in the uncertain light of dusk, I had such a good feeling about my heart. How beautiful, I thought, and stood entranced.

Compare this with the utterance, on a similar occasion, of another genius who had far more opportunity to invite his soul in the Wiener Wald. This is how Beethoven felt about it. His words sound more natural in the form of free verse:

> In the country
> Every tree
> Seems to talk to me,
> Saying: "Holy! Holy!"
> In the forest
> Is enchantment
> Which expresses all things—
> Sweet peace of the forest!
>
> Almighty, I am happy
> In the woods,
> Blessed
> In the woods;
> Every tree has a voice
> Through Thee.
>
> How glad am I
> Once again
> To be able to wander
> In forest and thicket
> Among the trees,
> The green things and the rocks.
> No mortal can love
> The country as I do;
> For woods and trees and rocks
> Return the echo
> A man desires.[1]

On June 17, 1816, as one is glad to learn from his diary, for the first time in his ill-paid life, he composed for money. For the birthday celebration of a professor named Watteroth, a cantata on the subject of *Prometheus* was ordered, and paid Schubert 100 florins, or $48.20. The performance, given July twenty-fourth in Watteroth's garden, was well received, and Prometheus remained true to form in shedding some light on the composer's somber and arduous path.

[1] From my *Beethoven: the Man Who Freed Music*, New York, last edition, Tudor Publishing Company, 1946. Reprinted by permission of Henry Holt & Co., Inc.

The manuscript has disappeared. It is said to have contained a slow march of original and extraordinary beauty.

As a diarist Franzl was short winded. He started frequently; but never could keep up the pace. And no wonder. What mortal, assailed by such constant and imperious musical inspiration, could rival the continuity of Delacroix or Pepys? In order to set down all the melodies that crowded in upon him, to say nothing of verbal thoughts, the young man must have longed for the multiple hands of Briareus. Nevertheless he managed to get down a few words that are of signal interest to Schubert lovers.

The diary for 1816 shows him endowed with a wisdom and a capacity for thought unusual in a nineteen-year-old, and most unusual in a musician. Coming from one who made such a sorry mess of his own material affairs, they are all the more remarkable.

Man is like a ball with which accident and passion play.

Natural disposition and upbringing determine man's intellect and heart. The *heart* is master; the intellect *should* be.

Take people as they are, not as they ought to be.

And here is a melancholy entry:

Man bears unhappiness without complaint; but feels it all the more poignantly— Why has God given us the gift of sympathy?

I like Pitrou's comment:

It is in confidences of this kind that we surprise the "second Schubert": beneath the slightly ridiculous shell, the spirit that suffers and weeps. And, let us recognize that here is no *Wertherism,* no romantic *Weltschmerz;* but, powdered over with Viennese lightheartedness, a profound pain . . . the pain of turning the treadmill of an odious occupation; without forgetting the thousand cruel little bruises which, in the life of every day, wounded this timid, this delicate one.

On September 16, 1816, he began the Fifth Symphony for the small amateur orchestra. Although he was occupied at the same time with the first movement of a string trio, it took him less than three weeks to finish. The following October there leaped into his delighted brain that song, *The Wanderer*, which, half a dozen years later, was to inspire and name the piano Fantasy, Op. 15.

It may be wondered how he could write such works in the schoolroom. Fortunately he did not have to try, for one afternoon of the previous spring, Spaun and Schober called on Franzl. That day the children were unusually obstreperous. Two were boisterously playing among the legs of the teacher's desk. Others were quarreling in a corner. Through the open door of the adjoining kitchen came the howls of a baby. Franz, much embarrassed, rose to find chairs for his guests.

"I'm just correcting some papers," he murmured. "It's enough to make a chap run up the walls! But never mind." His genial smile came out. "It's not always as bad as this."

The visitors looked at one another and nodded agreement with their unspoken thought: something must be done!

"Look here," cried Schober. "This sort of thing just can't go on. You've already done quite enough teaching. Come along to live with your friends and get on with your career!"

And so it fell out. By some miracle they got it through Father Franz's thick peasant head that Franzl simply must have a year's respite from teaching.

"*Quelle joie triumphante!*" cries Landormy in describing this happy event. "How he breathed now with full lungs! He couldn't credit it. Free! Free at last to compose at any and every hour of the day! Free now to live for nothing but his beloved music! Free too to enjoy with a few friends the sweet life of Vienna."

From now on, with a few interruptions, his home, usually shared with a friend, was to consist of a cold, bare little room with a chair or two, a hard couch or two, a small bookcase, piles of manuscript on the floor, a small piano, and a candle. But there he could work unassailed by a horde of noisy brats. If he could have read the Bible in English, its least sympathetic verse would have been the one that starts, "Suffer the little children." The first word might have struck him most forcibly. How those little children had made him suffer!

In that spring of 1816 Franzl first went to live with Spaun in what is now Erdbergstrasse 17. In the fall he became the Schober family's guest at Tuchlauben 26. There he found life a fair imitation of the Elysian Fields. He scratched up a few music pupils, but that was no job for him. It reminded him too poignantly of life with Father, and he soon threw up this source of income and lived at Schober's expense, occasionally negotiating small loans from other friends. Happy in the untrammeled exercise of his art, he took, with the touching naïveté of a child, what goods the gods and his fellows provided.

The musical harvest of 1816 was not quite the harvest of the previous year; but for any other composer it would have been a bumper crop, with its hundred and five songs and its wealth of larger compositions. It had been a year of humiliations, one of which was the knowledge that Therese was lost to him forever. But it ended in the stunning triumph of freedom at last.

11

SCHUBERT'S VIENNA

OR many people the word "Vienna," like the "sacred name of Mesopotamia," conjures up sentimental visions of synthetic romance. It makes them imagine a vain thing "that never was on sea or land."

For this, *Blossom Time*[1] is mainly responsible, together with such mendacious films as the French picture which makes Beethoven lose his hearing in a single hour and compose his symphonies in the odd order: VI, V, and III. Misrepresentations like these are as burrs under the collar of any one who truly knows and loves this charming city.

Vienna is two millennia old. The Romans took over from its founders, the Celts, and baptized it Vindobona. Marcus Aurelius, the first of the many famous men associated with the city, died there in 180 A.D. Then came successively: Attila and his Huns, the Mongolian Avars, and Charlemagne who founded the *Ostmark* (Eastmark), which became *Oestreich* (Austria). At Schubert's birth, the city's fortifications were among the strongest in existence, though Napoleon's artillery soon showed that the day of the walled and bastioned town was done. Slavs, Italians, Turks, Greeks, and French arrived as friends or foes, settled in Vienna, and made of the place the animated melting pot it still is.

Though German was its language *par excellence*, many others were spoken. At court one heard French and Italian. The Church talked that clerical Esperanto, Latin. Many a Slavic idiom was used by the servant classes. Peddlers spoke a debased South Slavic Italian. Merchants found advantage in knowing an Oriental tongue or two. North and South met to mingle with East and West. In this bubbling cauldron nothing was static except the Church and the Hapsburg love of absolute power.

[1] George H. Gray remarked that Schubert is now best known as the ghost writer of this preposterous operetta.

Even the nobility hailed from many foreign lands, including Germany, with which Austria was connected by the tie of a common language. Their very names show surprisingly few Teutonic ingredients, while those of the official and officer-gentry classes are largely Slavic.

The reactionary Hapsburgs made up in tyrannical instinct what they lacked in stability, character, intelligence, or wisdom. They swore by the ancient Roman motto *"divide et impera!"* and the later hexameter:

Allii bella gerent, tu felix Austria, nube!

(Leave war-waging to others; you, happy Austria, marry!)

The Hapsburgs were not fond of fighting; they chose their generals badly and were usually beaten. When Schubert was born, Austria within fifteen years had lost 1,150,000 men in battle. The wars into which these impossible rulers ventured were chiefly waged in order to strengthen the power or prestige of the House of Hapsburg. As we have noted, conscription was for fourteen years. The unfortunate conscript's wife or mother was either given a microscopic compensation or a miserably paid job with pick and shovel on the fortifications. Taxes were enormous, but the citizens had no say in the conduct of the war and were forbidden to criticize their superiors.

The powers in the saddle said Austria and meant Hapsburg. They said patriotism and meant unquestioning obedience. But their propaganda always tried to swathe the iron gauntlet in thick folds of velvet as blue as the heavens. For example, in Schubert's time they stressed the fact that the Emperor, that indulgent father of his people, made a point of appearing in person at fires and floods. Unhampered by the least smattering of technical knowledge, he would masterfully direct the technicians. And when he was late in arriving, the firemen would often let the building burn to the ground unwatered, rather than offend His Imperial Majesty by going ahead without him. Then the propagandists would intone paeans about the loving heart of the father of his country.

Once in a great while a more intelligent and merciful type of Hapsburg would appear, only to find hard and brief sledding. When Maria Theresa's gifted eldest son, Joseph II, realized the harm done by various court coteries and began to press for certain reforms, he soon had the court and Church against him and did not live long.

Franz II, crowned Emperor of the Holy Roman Empire in 1792, was delightfully congenial to the reactionaries. The term Holy Roman Empire no longer meant a thing, so, in 1804, he was recrowned Emperor Franz I of Austria. This was an appallingly absolute monarch, a perfect example of the narrow-browed autocrat. He was narrow browed even in the physical sense, inaccessible to human feeling, well nigh incapable of originating a thought. His indifference to the most significant events of the time, his blind stubbornness, his lack of intelligence were devastating.

Under this ruler, who was constantly touted to the skies for those genial human qualities in which he was most deficient, the character of the average Austrian began to change for the worse. He soon saw through the alleged virtues of Franz I and fell to imitating the faults of the real man beneath the camouflage. He developed a blend of specious good nature, spinelessness, cowardice, and that *Schlamperei,* which is best translated sloppiness. With far too great euphemism, the rationalizing Austrian called this combination *Gemütlich- keit,* an expressive word for which no other language has an exact equivalent. When uncorrupted it implies a sort of chronic attitude of peace on earth, good will toward men, tinged with democracy, exuberance, and bubbling humor, with radioactive charm and constructive appreciation of the other's point of view.

To catch the true sense of Viennese *Gemütlichkeit,* however, one must discern, behind the charm, the geniality, and the royal-good-fellow smile—an unhealthy *laissez faire,* an instinct for choosing the easiest way, a defeatism often expressed by the shrugging formula, *nix zu machen* (can't be helped). One must discern a dislike of firmly saying no and a tendency toward making generous promises that lead in the end to nothing. Even today these attractive people remind one somewhat of G. L. Birmingham's west-of-Ireland stories in which the natives, when questioned, ask themselves not, "What are the facts?" but, "What would this person most like to hear?" Remembering that the aborigines of Vienna were Celts, one wonders how much Celtic blood persists in the present population.

Now while all this is true of the average Viennese, one finds, above the average—or found, at Hitler's advent—a truly admirable stratum of humanity: clear-eyed, sturdy, idealistic youngsters; upright, conscientious, and highly intelligent citizenry; sound analytical thought among the scholars; and nearly everywhere a glorious appreciation of the arts. In Schubert's time and before, the Austrian nobility had more taste and a truer feeling for the beautiful than was to be found among the red-nosed, hard-drinking nobles of England, or the dull country squires of North Germany, or the degenerate aristocracy of the French rococo.

Keenly aware of his people's love of freedom, the despot who ruled Austria founded a well-thought-out and highly organized police system. This first of European Gestapos had charge of all matters pertaining to culture, transportation, and domestic economy. It destroyed the privacy of the mails and of family life. A censorship carried through by stupid, bigoted, smallhearted zealots shouldered itself into every phase of mental and spiritual life and turned a magnifying glass upon every fragment of written or printed paper in the search for slights to the imperial house or the Church. It soon had a deadening effect upon all intellectual effort except that of the musician.[1]

Every servant, concierge, waiter, and barber ran to the police with a report of whatever he had overheard that seemed to him in any way suspicious. These semiofficial amateur detectives were called *Naderer*. As spies were set to watch spies and others to watch these, they soon numbered a considerable part of the population. The vicious system bred secretiveness, suspicion, fear, vindictiveness, blackmail, and above all, dishonesty and unreliability. Character is far more readily destroyed than formed.

Shrewd as peasants, the Hapsburgs and their counselors realized, in their lust for power, that so much repression called for safety valves. One of these was the gaily sensuous life of voluptuous Vienna, upon which—so long as it did not grow too scandalous—state and Church bent a complaisant regard.

The very climate of Vienna tempts to a happy, carefree, and passionate life of the senses. A love of intoxicants (though more restrained than in the lands to the north), an amiable playfulness and an exuberant frivolity are in the atmosphere. It is doubtful whether the jolly young Bohemian Circle from which the music of Schubert flowed would have been as successfully productive in a sternly ascetic environment. When puritanism comes in at the door, art, as it did in Cromwell's England, is apt to fly out at the window.

[1] The story goes, however, that a composer who had dedicated a sonata "to the spirit of the departed Hummel" was told by the censor that he must first secure the permission of that spirit.

The other safety valve was music, an art which could fortunately escape from under the ink-smeared thumb of Metternich's censor. So night and day were filled with music, good and bad, joyful and melancholy. And many of these strains aptly harmonized with the sensuous atmosphere which Vienna preserved up to the irruption of the Nazis.

The local mixture of races was an eminently successful blend. This fertile and kindly soil for feminine loveliness has always been justly famous for its beautiful, attractive, and above all, charming girls. There wine, woman, and song have had much in common.

Of the three Schubert chose the first and last as his particular province. But it was not for lack of facilities that he shunned the women. The Vienna of his day enjoyed its stormy love life with zest. The ladies took and gave, thankfully and with delight. No somber cult of austerity stood between the people and the tiny bit of self-determination grudgingly granted them. This mitigation of their hard lot, however, was shadowed by the rampancy of venereal disease and the absence of sex hygiene.

In fact, even general hygiene had as yet reached no more than its first crude stages. A civic sewage system had only begun to develop; the water supply was tainted; the streets were either dust or mud. No wonder that mortality rates, especially among the children, were hideously high. Mother Schubert's loss of eight of her first nine babies was an all too common experience.

One of Vienna's most important characteristics, not always apparent on first acquaintance, is an ethereal quality[1] to which no signpost points an accurate finger. I mean the *genius loci*, the spiritual essence of Vienna and the Viennese, impregnating the town, the buildings, the people, the delightful natural setting, and the very physical atmosphere. This aura has helped to form generations of Vindobona, just as the generations have, reciprocally, helped to form it. It is not to be seen nor touched nor called by a name, but the memory of it, and the longing for it when far away, fills with homesickness those who have once fallen under its spell. No other city except Paris possesses this elusive fragrance. Freedom from care, grace and charm are of its essence. It is as weightless, as indescribable as the euphoria which it tends to induce. It is a hospitable medium for much that could hardly, if at all, survive elsewhere. Could the C Major Quintet have come out of Essen or Birmingham or Pittsburgh?

[1] Sadly impaired since the consulship of Hitler.

No happy accident brought so many great musicians to share that Viennese euphoria which heartened them to give of their best. No encouragement by public, regime, or publishers brought and kept them there. In Schubert's time, two other great composers lived in Vienna: Haydn and Beethoven. Mozart had died six years before Franz's birth, Gluck, ten. Schumann and Brahms came long after his death. Vienna made them all suffer, yet all except Schumann stayed.

Viennese *Schlamperei* soon made bears of those amiable young fellows, Beethoven and Brahms. During his visits there this trait irritated Schumann almost beyond endurance. Yet the *genius loci* was benign to the creative work of all three. As Schubert had, from birth, never known anything different and possessed, moreover, his own share of *Schlamperei* in nonmusical matters, the *genius loci* blessed his works without cursing his disposition.

None of the great composers whose names are identified with this town was ever fully appreciated there until well after his death. Shakespeare might just as truly have been writing of Austrians in *Antony and Cleopatra:*

> our slippery people
> Whose love is never link'd to the deserver
> Till his deserts are past.

Yet if any of these great men had been obliged to choose between instant local recognition and the inspiration of the *genius loci*, I think he would unhesitatingly have chosen the latter.

The physical Vienna of Schubert's day was symbolic of a mental and spiritual Vienna which, denied the breadth of a normal expansion, was compelled to build toward the heavens. The Inner City, clamped between the walls of its fortifications where lateral growth was impossible, grew tall. There was not enough light and air for those who could not live in cloisters or palaces, which had preempted all the best terrain, and even in these, what we of today would call unhealthy slum conditions prevailed. The dust rising from the roadways made it almost impossible to exist below the third floor. In wet weather the deep mud of streets and stairways made walking a problem. Together with the mania for dancing and the scanty clothing of the women, these conditions bred tuberculosis so fast that one person in every six died of it.

Both Inner City and suburbs were rich in cafés, taverns, and hotels which, for little money, offered spendid service, delicious food and drink, and above all, an indescribable atmosphere of well-being. They throve on the discomfort of the homes.

Under the growing centrifugal pressure, the population began to spill over into those suburbs which, in the composer's lifetime, were hamlets and villages. The nobles, too, felt pinched, and began to build grandiose suburban palaces. The late Empress Maria Theresa had started to erect public buildings there, and the intelligent and almost progressive Joseph II put up an excellent hospital and school for surgeons in the Alsergrund.

This suburb's next-door neighbor was Liechtental, the village of Schubert's birth. From there it was but a forty minutes' walk to the woods. Other villages: Döbling, Grinzing, Heiligenstadt, Nussdorf, and Sievering, charmingly embedded in vineyards famous for their products, were sown along the way. It was in this delightful country-side that Beethoven took his solitary and so fruitful rambles.

A special dispensation of long standing gave the vintner the right to sell his new wine on the premises. This was—and is—an excellent though short-lived drink, greenish gold, light and dry. When pure, it is an unmixed blessing, with no unfortunate after effects. Together with the landscape where it is raised, this wine is one of the best tangible symbols of that euphoria-giving *genius loci* already mentioned. Four or five months after it had come from the press and was ready to be enjoyed, the peasant disregarded the old adage, "A good wine needs no bush," and hung above his door a bundle of fir twigs as a sort of green light for the thirsty.

Schubert was a passionate lover of this gracious region. Because the new wine lay in the midst of it, and because the sight of mountain and river, of the vineyards and peasant homes which they adorned, and the sound of folk music were even more inspiring when food and drink and the effervescent spirits of the good companions heightened his appreciation, puritanical criticism of their *élan de vie* should be left to those for whom the *"Unfinished"* is only unpleasant noise. One remembers that Mozart, Beethoven, Schumann, and Brahms were also uplifted by this Arcadian landscape and by the carefree quality of its sometimes Dionysian appreciators. There they could give themselves up wholeheartedly to inspiration.

In the opposite direction, going from Liechtental toward town, one came in twenty minutes to the Glacis, the huge, bare area, once a moat six hundred yards across, which protected the inner fortifications from surprise. Here the dust flew so thick that one had to breathe through a handkerchief.

One entered the Inner City through the Gate of the Scots, named after a huge abbey of the *Scoti*, or Irish Benedictines. It was defended by bastions forming part of the great wall which was Christendom's time-honored bulwark against the heathen hordes of the Orient. Tradition says that the ransom of Richard the Lionhearted had helped to pay for its erection. In a house on one of these bastions, the Mölkerbastei, Beethoven wrote the Fifth Symphony.

From the Gate of the Scots the way led through narrow, winding streets, by the sinister, compact mass of the Imperial Castle, the slim, baroque grace of St. Michael's Church opposite, and the old Burg Theater, where opera was given until Schubert was thirteen. There Goethe, Schiller, and Shakespeare held the boards after having been oddly purged and bowdlerized by Metternich's blue-nosed censors. It is dismal to think of one of them, the poet Mayrhofer, sinning thus, with horrible inner qualms, against his fellow bards.

Then came the center of town and the hoary cathedral of St. Stephen. The view from its lofty tower was praised by the traveler of those days as surpassing even those from Montmartre in Paris and from the Roman Pincio. Beyond the jumble of picturesque roofs and church towers lay the twelve protecting gates with their bastions, then the Glacis, over which the suburbs melted into the vine-clad countryside, the shimmer of the distant Danube, and the mountains enclosing all.

This Vienna [wrote Robert Schumann], with all its memories of the greatest German masters, must be a fertile field for the musician's imagination. Often when I looked down upon it from the mountain tops, it occurred to me how frequently the eyes of Beethoven must have restlessly roved to that distant chain of Alps; how often Mozart may have dreamily followed the course of the Danube, which always seems to swim in forests; and how Papa Haydn may have peered up at St. Stephen's tower, shaking his head at such a giddy height. Put together the pictures of the Danube, St. Stephen's, and the far mountain ranges, cover them with the faint perfume of Catholic incense, and you have a portrait of Vienna. And when the charming landscape comes wholly alive for us, strings may be heard that otherwise might never have sounded within us. At the touch of Schubert's symphony [the great C Major which Schumann himself discovered], and the clear, burgeoning, romantic life in it, the city rises more clearly than ever before me, and most plainly I see again that such works can be born in just such a setting.

The picturesqueness of St. Stephen's was enhanced by the low cloister buildings nearby. They were of chaste and noble architecture, with massive walls sometimes fifty inches thick, wrought as though to resist a siege. In one of them was The Sign of the Green Anchor, a special favorite of Schubert's Circle.

Going north, one came to the Gate of the Red Tower and a small arm of the river, which was later to be disciplined into the Danube Canal. In the opposite direction lay the Kärntner Gate Theater, that predecessor of the present Opera.

A word about the historical situation in Schubert's day. In 1805, after the intrigues and the stupidity of the European princes had made it easy for Napoleon to crush those who would not make common cause with him, the conqueror took Vienna.[1] In 1809 he captured it a second time, razed the fortifications, and sat down well pleased in the great palace at Schönbrunn.

It was hard sledding for the Vienna of the twelve-year-old Franzl. The value of money depreciated alarmingly. The aristocracy, already on the decline through waste and ostentatious display, grew poorer and poorer. The factories lay idle, and nothing flourished but the secret police. A young student named Staps tried to stick a knife into the conqueror and was actually brought to punishment by Austrian *Naderer*.

Napoleon withdrew to prepare his Russian campaign. Presently he married the daughter of the Austrian Emperor. In 1812, that worthy made an alliance against Russia with his son-in-law, only to turn about the next year and join the Prussian-Russian coalition against the Corsican upstart.

These world-shattering events changed Vienna very little, except to destroy the fortifications and impoverish the people. Lovers of freedom began to whisper together, but only out in the open country, for in town the very walls were equipped with the ears of Metternich's spies.

Eighteen thirteen saw the tide turned in the Battle of Leipzig, and

[1] Perhaps one reason why both Schubert and Schumann were so fond of marches is that soldiers marching to music were among their earliest impressions. When Franzl was eight, Napoleon, after Austerlitz, marched into Vienna. On his way to Moscow, he marched into Zwickau when Robert was two. Franzl saw hundreds of wounded French whose ears had been cut off by the Russians. He suffered from the scarcity and the high prices of food, and his father suffered in addition from an assessment of half the amount of his rent, to help pay the conqueror Vienna's fine of ten million gulden.

Napoleon was banished. The following year assembled the diplomats, generals, and princes in the delirious joy of the Congress of Vienna, which was to build a brave new world from the ruins left by the Little Corporal. It was the task of the four allies, Great Britain, Prussia, Austria, and Russia, to settle the fate of those countries which had been freed of French suzerainty by the fall of Napoleon. The work laid down for each delegate was to scramble wildly for more territory and power than any other delegate could secure.

But play was even more important than work. It was essential to enjoy, to the utmost extent of uninhibited natures, the new possibilities of a life of pleasure no longer cramped by a little artillery officer. Gold poured into the town. Ladies and prostitutes, actresses and daughters of the people, duchesses and flower girls had their good season. So did Metternich's spies, who hid under every bed, and who opened every letter, outgoing or incoming. A net of intrigue lay over Vienna and the congress.

Franz Schubert was seventeen. He was short, fat, unkempt, and awkward, but he might have been far more impressive and Chesterfieldian and have still remained unnoticed amid the splendor of the outlanders. Brave in gold, silver, and furs, high officers from all the world strutted and swaggered about. Diplomats perfumed with all the scents of Araby, corseted and romantically clad, gave the Viennese women, long cooped up and starved by war, an idea of the brilliant delights of the world beyond the mountains.[1] There was little attention to spare for a gauche, ugly young composer who was himself unaware of his own greatness.

Though Beethoven was far from an Adonis, he had two enormous worldly advantages over Schubert: an understanding of the value of money and a terrifying roughness that brushed aside any who obstructed his path. Instinctively he hit on the right way of getting on in the world. He scolded barons and princes as though they were schoolboys, *deposuit potentes,* and actually made them almost like it. What an advance over Mozart who, though he humbled his proud spirit to lick exalted boots, yet had to live under conditions that would make every separate hair of a New York swing trombonist of today rise on end

[1] In *Feast of the Jesters,* Manuel Komroff calls the Vienna of Schubert's day, "a sort of little Paris tinged with Oriental barbarism."

Like quills upon the fretful porpentine.

One wishes that the small school assistant might have had enough assurance to use Beethoven's methods with the mighty, and make them work. But the modest drudge never even came within kissing distance of exalted boots. The plane of the lesser nobility was as far up as his social contacts occasionally reached. When he met a higher social order than his own, it was usually in neat Biedermeier parlors amid the nutwood furniture of newly rich tradesmen.

In 1815 the Congress of Vienna closed without having justified the fond hopes of a war-weary world. Then, in a few days, the victory of Waterloo brought French dominance in Europe to an end. This dominance, however, had spread the idea that government could function without princes, and even without the Church. A new revolutionary spirit began to germinate in Austria. The period of ferment, from the Congress of Vienna to the March Revolution of 1848, is known as the *Vormärz*, and Schubert belonged to the movement.

Such then were the place and time that bred and reared the Ariel of music. Though they brought him poverty and an early death, they also brought him fabulous inner riches and immortality. The riches he returned a thousandfold.

12

NOT ENOUGH OF A CHARLATAN

EIGHTEEN seventeen was a brilliant year in the annals of song. January led off with the intimate *Praise of Tears* (*Lob der Tränen*). February brought *Death and the Maiden* (*Der Tod und das Mädchen*). Nine years later Schubert was to choose a part of it as the theme for one of the most enchanting sets of variations in all chamber music—that in the D Minor Quartet. March followed with the setting of Schober's poem *To Music* (*An die Musik*), of which the composer lovingly wrote three versions. July offered more material for future variations: *The Trout* (*Die Forelle*), which, two years after, was to christen the *"Trout"* Quintet. And September contributed *Group from Tartarus* (*Gruppe aus dem Tartarus*). As he felt himself maintaining the perilously high standard of quality which he had set in the song masterpieces of 1815, Schubert must have known a profound satisfaction.

From May to August he wrote seven piano sonatas. His interest in the piano was stimulated by his friends, who proudly took him as a prize exhibit to the houses of wealthy music lovers. All of them owned tempting instruments. Further stimulus came from a friendship with Josef Gahy, a competent pianist and brilliant sight reader, who encouraged him to write four-hand works for them to play together.[1]

In August, Franzl, much against the grain, returned for a while to the crowded family home. His room was needed for Schober's brother Axel.

Toward the end of 1817, Father Schubert was put in charge of a new school whose first principal had been dismissed for a breach of discipline. It was a little nearer to the city, in Green Gate Street, district of the Rossau, or Horse Pasture.

---

[1] Gahy was to suffer a pianistic fate worse than Robert Schumann's, for he lamed two fingers of his left hand. Nothing daunted, he rearranged his friend's music for eight fingers.

The helpful Josef Spaun now tried to get Franzl a publisher and hitched the wagon of his hopes to the triple-starred house of Breitkopf and Härtel in Leipzig. But when the famous publishers received the manuscript of *The Erl King*, they seemed to smell a rat. The only Franz Schubert they knew anything about was a royal church composer and conductor of the Italian Opera in Dresden. And as this song did not sound in the least like that gentleman's product, they sent it to him with an inquiry. When the royal church composer saw his own honorable name attached to this unheard-of piece with its (to him) horrendous discords, his gorge rose with his hair, and on April 18, 1817 he replied:

> To my immense astonishment I answer that this cantata is none of mine. I will keep same in my custody in order to ascertain somehow who has so impolitely sent you such a bungling piece of work, and also to unearth this fellow who has so mistreated my name.

How little did the Dresden Franz Schubert dream that future ages would remember him for only two reasons: (1) because his son Franz would write a little encore piece named *The Bee*, and (2) because he had the same name as the "fellow" who had written that "bungling piece of work," *The Erl King*. We now think of him as "the wrong Schubert," just as people thought of Johannes Brahms's piano-teaching brother as "the wrong Brahms." [1]

Breitkopf never deigned a reply to Spaun. Had Franzl been gifted with prophetic vision, he might have been consoled by foreseeing that this same publisher would also decline *The Erl King* set by Loewe, on the odd ground that "the remarkable songs of Zumsteeg [thirty-six years older than Loewe] no longer find such a sale as their excellence deserves." He would have been even more richly consoled if he could have known that, long after his own death, this same house would bring out a magnificent complete edition of his works, with *The Erl King* as Opus 1.

Were Franzl's friends downhearted over this fiasco? No. At once they turned from Leipzig to Vienna in search, this time, of some famous person as an advance agent for the coming composer. Their choice fell upon the opera star Johann Michael Vogl, who had been the first Pizarro in the final revision of *Fidelio*. He was held in a

[1] Pitrou is confused about this farcical incident. He has our Schubert protesting *"sans efficacité"* against an apocryphal *Erl King* that someone had sent Breitkopf and Härtel, signed with his name.

respect amounting to awe, not only as an artist, but also as the intellectual who, waiting in the wings for his cue, studied the Greek philosophers and the New Testament in the original. This odd singer even translated Thomas à Kempis's *Imitation of Christ* and sent it to his friends. As will be seen from the portrait facing this page, he looked something like Goethe and heightened the resemblance by means of costume, hair do, and pose. He possessed a tenor-baritone voice of immense range and a generous dramatic talent. Schubert afterward punningly called him "a Greek bird [*Vogel*] fluttering about in Austria." In fact, he was a sort of learned Chaliapin at the height of his vogue.

Vogl was a hard person to get at, but Schober finally managed to reach him. In glowing terms he sang Schubert's praises. The singer was not impressed. He had far too often been disappointed by such youthful geniuses. They had invariably come to nothing. The Circle was saddened. Not so the resilient Schober, who had a mulish streak which one would scarcely expect in such a dandified man about town. He pursued Vogl and, one evening, finally captured him, together with the frightened Franzl. The singer had grudgingly consented to see if there could be anything behind all this to-do. I like Landormy's comment: "*Voilà donc Schober qui prépare la redoutable réception.*" Spaun has recorded:

At the appointed time the singer appeared, with immense dignity, at Schober's lodging. As the tiny Schubert, who looked like nobody at all, made him a somewhat awkward gesture of reverence and, in his embarrassment, stammered a few disconnected words about the honor of his acquaintance, Vogl somewhat scornfully wrinkled up his nose and looked down it. To us the acquaintance appeared to have begun disastrously. At length Vogl grunted: "Well then, what have you got there? Accompany me." With that he picked up the first sheet of manuscript, the setting of Mayrhofer's poem *Augenlied,* a pretty song, very singable, but of no significance. Vogl hummed rather than sang, and then said rather coolly: "Not so bad!" Then, as Schubert accompanied *Shepherd's Lament* and *Ganymed* which he [Vogl] sang with only half a voice, he grew progressively more friendly, but left without promising to return. As he went away, he tapped Schubert on the shoulder and said to him: "There's something in you but you're too little of an actor, not enough of a charlatan. You squander your beautiful thoughts without making enough of them."

To others Vogl expressed himself more favorably than he had to us. When he came upon the *Lied eines Schiffers an die Dioskuren,* he told

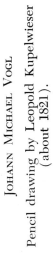

Johann Michael Vogl

Pencil drawing by Leopold Kupelwieser
(about 1821).

Therese Grob Bergmann

From an unsigned oil portrait.

ANTONIO SALIERI

BROTHER FERDINAND SCHUBERT

ANTONIO SALIERI

JOSEF VON SPAUN

Oil portrait by Leopold
Kupelwieser.

FRANZ VON SCHOBER

Pencil drawing by Leopold
Kupelwieser (1821).

them it was a splendid song, and that to find such depth and ripeness coming out of the small young fellow was simply incredible.

The impression which Schubert's songs made on Vogl was quite over-powering. Without invitation he again approached our circle, invited Schubert to his house, worked over songs with him; and when he realized the terrific, overmastering effect which his delivery had upon us, upon Schubert himself and upon all sorts of listeners, he grew so enthusiastic for these songs that he now became Schubert's most eager admirer; and instead of giving up music, as he had thought of doing, he developed new zest for it.

Here are some of Vogl's private reflections about this experience, as revealed in his diary:

Nothing has brought out so clearly the lack of a practical school of sing-ing as Schubert's lieder. If one were in existence, what a prodigious general effect would be made by these truly divine inspirations, these out-pourings of musical clairvoyance, upon every one who knows the German language! [He might better have put it: "for every one who understands the language of tones." Singerwise, he overrated the very modest part which music allows poetry to play in song.] How many would, perhaps for the first time, have grasped the implications of: speech, poetry in tones, words in harmonies, thoughts clad in music.

Vogl used the word "clairvoyance" advisedly, for he himself was enough of a clairvoyant to recognize that Schubert's unconscious mind often ventured out of the depths and came so near the surface that, with small intervention on the part of consciousness, it seemed to take charge of the pen. His friend Josef Hüttenbrenner has testi-fied: "When composing, Schubert seemed to me like a somnambulist. His eyes would protrude and blaze as if they were glasses reflecting light. And all the while he would click with his tongue."

In hearing Schubert's compositions [writes Grove[1]], it is often as if one were brought more immediately and closely into contact with music itself than is the case in the works of others; as if in his pieces the stream from the great heavenly reservoir were dashing over us, or flow-ing through us, more directly, with less admixture of any medium or channel, than it does in those of any other writer—even of Beethoven himself. And this immediate communication with the origin of music

[1] *Dictionary of Music and Musicians.* Copyright, 1904, 1906 and 1927 by The Macmillan Company and used with their permission.

really seems to have happened to him . . . This was the true "inspiration of dictation," as much so as in the utterance of any Hebrew prophet or seer. We have seen one instance in the case of *The Erl King*. The poem of the *Wanderer* attracted him in the same way, and the song was completed in one evening. In a third case, that of Goethe's *Rastlose Liebe*, the paroxysm of inspiration was so fierce that Schubert never forgot it, but, reticent as he often was, talked of it years afterwards.

Clairvoyants are apt to forget what, in the hour of inspiration, they "saw clearly." And the story goes that Schubert once wrote a song that Vogl found too high for him, so he transposed it. A few days after, the composer picked up the transposed manuscript, looked it through, and exclaimed, "The lied is not uneven! Really not bad. Who wrote it?"

Grove, however, was wrong when he went on to say that Schubert took the cash and let the credit go—that he tossed off these products of clairvoyance and let them go as they were. On the contrary, he submitted them to the fierce criticism of his conscious mind and toiled· over them indefatigably, often making numerous versions until completely satisfied.

Vogl and Schubert made a remarkable team, for the older man was still at the height of his powers. "The delectable pleasures now offered us," cried Spaun, "are indescribable." Schubert was satisfied with their perfect ensemble and said that people found it new and unheard of. However, as the aging singer's voice declined, and his ego grew more and more imperious, the team became remarkable in a less satisfactory sense. From the creative standpoint, the composer's intimate association with such a strong character as Vogl was not always ideal. His friend's exceptional compass sometimes led the youngster to write for a range of voice that few other human beings possessed. And Kreissle reported that "to please the singer, Schubert concentrated much more of his energies upon writing songs of a slight character and import than he would otherwise have done." Sometimes Franzl actually revised songs to suit the other. Finally Vogl, who felt that music was hardly music unless written for the voice, while he pressed for more and more songs, discouraged his protégé from creating absolute music. If it had not been for this high and mighty singer and his constricted tastes, we might possibly possess many another masterpiece in the proud class of the last quartets, the String Quintet, and the last symphonies.

In order to have such an amazing influence over a man ordinarily so refractory to criticism and so mulishly obstinate, this Vogl must have wielded a terrific power of suggestion. He told of having taught a lovely young girl a song in which the Queen Mother of heaven appeared. In moving terms the old bachelor explained to her the high significance and noble meaning of the word mother so that her interpretation of the role might have the authentic ring. And he could never forget the lovely innocence of her voice as she begged him, "Make me a mother!"

13

SENT TO EAT WITH THE SERVANTS

SCHUBERT'S keyboard technique was not always impeccable. We know that he altered the triplets in *The Erl King* accompaniment to favor his fingers. And as late as 1822 he stuck fast in the finale of his *"Wanderer"* Fantasy, crying: "The devil may play the stuff; I can't!" He had, however, one precious quality rarely found in pianists, a scrupulous feeling for dynamics. When the occasion called for it, he could actually play *piano* on the piano! "That damned hacking," he insisted, "which even excellent performers make a habit of, is a thing I simply can't put up with. It delights neither the ear nor the spirit;" a sentiment which might well be carved in the rack of every keyboard instrument.

By 1818 his taste had ripened. He had put away the childish notion that Beethoven was "eccentric," to become again the deaf man's wholehearted adorer—and imitator too, as is evidenced by the Sixth Symphony in C, completed that March. He had also developed an enormous appetite for Handel, often playing *The Messiah* and other scores, four-handed, with Anselm Hüttenbrenner at the bass end.

It may have been out of gratitude for all this bass playing that Franzl presented "Hüt's" brother Josef with a manuscript of *The Trout*, accompanied by this characteristic inscription, written after sharing several bottles of Hungarian wine:

21 February, 1818, at midnight.
Dearest Friend!

I'm extraordinarily glad that my songs please you. As a token of my deepest friendship, I send you herewith another one which I have written[1] at Anselm Hüttenbrenner's just now at midnight. I wish that I might pledge closer friendship with you over a glass of punch. *Vale.*

Just as I went in haste to bestrew the thing with sand, somewhat drunk with drowsiness as I was, [instead of the sand box] I took up the inkwell, which I poured over it at my ease. What a calamity!

[1] He means "copied out," for the song was composed in 1817.

We can still see a reproduction of the manuscript with the opening bars almost hidden by a huge blob of ink. (See opposite p. 113.)

This is characteristic of Schubert's happy touch in the matter of inscriptions. Not long before, he had sent one of his brothers a little piece with the heading:

Trio, to be regarded as the lost son of a minuet.

And here is what he scribbled on a copy of the *Trauerwalzer:*

Written down for my little coffee-wine-and-punch-brother, the world-famous composer Anselm Hüttenbrenner. Vienna the 14th of March in the year of our Lord 1818, in his majesty's own lodging 30 florins a month Vienna standard.

Anselm's devotion, however, was not proof against an occasional access of selfishness. Schubert owned the Mozart manuscript of the *Berg-Knappen* music in F, a priceless example of that master's subtle wit. It was a parody full of intentional bloomers in composition. When Hüt raved over the treasure, the greathearted Franzl impulsively said, "Here, take half of it," and got out his knife, like the chief actor in the judgment of Solomon. When Hüt naturally refused to lend himself to such vandalism, Franzl cried, "Well then, take the whole of it!" And to his eternal shame, Hüt actually took it.

His brother Josef was kinder. He kept Franzl's accounts, tried in vain to make him save money, and became the conservator of his friend's songs. For this posterity owes him a huge debt of gratitude, because the composer would always lend the sole manuscript of a lied to the first applicant and seldom thought of getting it back.

In the same month of March Franzl sent an exuberant bilingual effort to Ignaz Assmayer, hitting off the stilted Latin of an academic diploma:

Hier hast Du diesen Deutschen,
Mein allerliebster Asma'r!
Sonst möchst Du mich noch peitschen,
Vermaledeyter Asma'r!
Illustrissimo, doctissimo, sapientissimo,
prudentissimo, maximoque Compositori
in devotissima humillimaque
reverentiae expressione

dedicatum oblatumque
de
Servorum Servo Francisco Seraphico vulgo Schubert nominato.

(Here I send you this German Dance,
Dearest Asma'r!
Lest your club should make me prance,
Cursèd Asma'r!
Dedicated and offered to
the wisest, most distinguished, most learnèd
most prudent, most exalted composer
with the most humble and devoted
expression of reverence
by
his servant of servants Franciscus Seraphicus vulgarly called Schubert.)

This is much the way that young students have always carried on, from Auerbach's Cellar to now. *Gaudeamus igitur!*

Early in 1818, Schubert first appeared in print. His music to Mayrhofer's *Erlafsee* was included in Sartori's almanac, which rejoiced in the elegant name: *Picturesque Pocketbook for Friends of Interesting Localities in the Austrian Empire.* He had already written no less than 350 songs. This was not a very sublime start, but it was at least a start. Here at last was something of his own for folks to read. The beginning of fame! And to crown all, a newspaper called the music "as ingenious as it is lovely."

In June, 1818,[1] Schubert finished the chief religious composition of this year, the Mass in C. But it did not bring in a florin, and now the cupboard was bare. So, with countless mental reservations, he was forced to the bitter expedient of taking a job. It was offered by Count Johann Karl Esterházy von Galánta, one of the lesser nobility, who took the composer to his country place at Zseliz in Hungary and made of him a sort of superior servant.

The cultivation of good music was the joy and pride of the Austro-Hungarian aristocracy. One recalls the elaborate musical establishments kept up by that more exalted Esterházy whose director of music was Haydn, and by Prince Lichnowsky, the friend of Beethoven. Count Johann Esterházy was not in their class, but, in his small way, he sought to imitate them.

The Count sang bass. His twenty-eight-year-old countess, who coyly called herself *Heidenröslein,* or Little Heath Rose, sang con-

---

[1] Dahms was mistaken in giving 1816.

tralto, the sixteen-year-old daughter Marie, soprano, and Caroline, aged thirteen, contralto. Both girls played the piano.

A thrifty bargain was struck with the world's greatest melodist. He was to get his board and lodging free, was to teach the girls piano at seventy-five florins, A. C., a month—and was to know his place and eat with the other servants. One imagines the eruption of rage with which Beethoven would have met such a proposition. But humble, unassuming little Franzl was far from being the man who freed music. In his whole career we shall meet with but few outbursts of anger. We can only regret that the chief one of these was directed at a flabbergasted clarinetist (see p. 140 ff.) instead of at that raw fellow, Count Esterházy.

The family's musical taste did them credit. They liked to stipple away at Mozart's *Requiem* and *The Seasons* and *The Creation* of Haydn. Presently their musical servant began to write vocal and four-hand pieces for local use.

Despite its humiliations, Franz at first rather liked the Hungarian adventure, as appears in a letter to his cronies:

Zseliz, the third of August, 1818.

DEAREST, MOST PRECIOUS FRIENDS!

How could I forget you, who are everything to me! Spaun, Schober, Mayrhofer, Senn, how goes it with you, are you in good fettle? As for me, I'm in excellent shape. I live and compose like a god, just as if it were predestined so.

Mayrhofer's *Einsamkeit* is finished and is, as I think, my best,[1] for when I wrote it I was carefree. I hope that you all are right well and happy, as I am. Now for the first time I'm really living. It was high time, otherwise I'd have turned out to be a spoiled musician . . . Write me jolly soon. Every letter of the alphabet from you fellows is precious to me.

Eternally your true friend

FRANZ SCHUBERT

Three weeks later, however, in an epistle to brother Ferdinand, we find homesickness beginning to set in. Note that it takes a man of some imagination to extract humor from his own foot:

My foot has gone to sleep on me, and that makes me mad. If the chump could write, it would not sleep — — — — — — Good morning, little brother, now I have slept along with my foot . . . Well as it goes with

[1] One need only compare this song with *Margaret at the Spinning Wheel* to know how amazingly he deceived himself.

me, healthy as I am, it makes me no end happy to think of the moment when the word will be: to Vienna, to Vienna! Yes, beloved Vienna, you enclose in your narrow confines the dearest, the best beloved; and nothing but reunion, heavenly reunion, will appease this yearning.

There were, of course, compensations. He found plenty of time for creation. He could actually save some money. And he could broaden his horizons beyond the narrow ways of the home town. There were other people and customs and landscapes, an alien language, a new and delightful folk music.[1] There were young countesses and a pretty chambermaid, Pepi Pöckelhofer, who caught his fancy, and he was learning about women from them.

Then too, there was Baron Karl von Schönstein. This guest of the Esterházys, an official in the Hungarian government, only a year older than Schubert, was musically far more cultivated than his hosts. Vogl had taught him how to use his fine baritone effectively. As soon as he heard the upper servant's songs he was captivated and became a Schubert advance agent and apostle. He sang them everywhere and soon won many of the lesser nobility for his idol. His infectious enthusiasm even did a little something toward lightening the humiliations of Franzl's lot at Zseliz. Later on, the Baron's specialty became *The Miller's Beautiful Daughter*. A decade after the composer's death, Liszt heard him give this cycle and confessed that he had been moved to tears. Schönstein, he declared, sang with such elemental feeling, was so carried away by the music, that he quite forgot his listeners.

Despite the pleasure of this new admirer's company, however, by the eighth of September, Franz was far gone in disillusion and wrote to the friends:

DEAR SCHOBER! DEAR SPAUN! DEAR MAYRHOFER! DEAR STEINSBERG! DEAR WAYSS! DEAR WEIDLICH!

How infinitely the letters from you, one and all, delighted me cannot find expression! When they handed me your pot-bellied epistle, I was at an auction of oxen and cows. I broke the seal and a mighty howl of joy raised itself as I glimpsed the name of Schober. With never ending laughter and childish joy, I read it in the adjoining room. Actually it seemed to me that

[1] Schubert was also influenced by Rumanian and Slovakian folk music, but less than by the Hungarian, which was to leave its mark on the four-hand Fantasy in F Minor, on the *Divertissement à la hongroise*, on the finale of the A Minor Quartet, and much of his other music.

my hands were firmly holding my dear friends'. But I will answer you decently and in order.

DEAR SCHOBERT! [1]

I see already that this transformed name will have to stick. Well, dear Schobert, from start to finish your letter was very dear and precious to me, but especially the last leaf. Yes, yes, the last leaf threw me into full ecstasy; you are a godlike fellow (in the Swedish sense of the term, you understand); and believe me, friend, you'll never go under, for your feeling for art is the purest, truest conceivable. The fact that the Viennese opera folk are so stupid, and that they give the most beautiful operas in my absence, throws me into a small rage. For, in Zseliz I must be all in all to myself. Composer, editor, listener, and I don't know what all. Not a soul here has the least feeling for true art except perhaps now and then (if I mistake not) the Countess. So I am alone with my beloved [his art], and must hide her in my room, in my piano, in my breast. Although on the one hand this makes me sorrowful, on the other, it exalts me all the more. So do not fear that I will remain away any longer than the sternest necessity requires. During this time a good many songs have come into being, and they are, as I hope, jolly good ones. I'm not surprised that the Greek bird [Vogl] flutters about in Upper Austria, as it is his native place, and he is on vacation. Would I were with him! . . .

Now a description for you all:

Our castle is none of the biggest, but very daintily built. The surrounding garden is exceedingly beautiful. I live in the Inspector's quarters. It is tolerably quiet, apart from about forty geese which sometimes squawk together so that one can't hear one's own voice. The people here are good. It is not often that a count's retainers get along so well together as this lot. The Herr Inspector, a Slavonian and a worthy man, is very vain of his former musical talent. At the moment he toots on the lute[2] with virtuosity

[1] As already noticed, this portmanteau word is a combination of their two surnames.

[2] This droll conceit may well have suggested to Gilbert those memorable stanzas in that gem of the *Bab Ballads, The Story of Prince Agib:*

> Strike the concertina's melancholy string!
> Blow the spirit-stirring harp like anything!
> Let the piano's martial blast
> Rouse the echoes of the past,
> For of AGIB, Prince of Tartary, I sing! . . .
>
> Of AGIB; who could readily, at sight,
> Strum a march upon the loud Theodolite.
> He would diligently play
> On the Zoetrope all day,
> And blow the gay Pantechnicon all night.

two German Dances in 3/4 time. [This vignette of the Herr Inspector, proudly seeking to impress a Schubert with his musical ability, is delicious.] The Rent-master is wholly fitted for his office, a man with extraordinary insight into his pockets and sacks . . . The cook is a rather loose fellow . . . the chambermaid, very pretty, often keeps me company . . . the steward is my rival. The two masters of the horse are better fitted for equine than human society. The Count, rather brutal, the Countess, proud but finer feeling, the Countesses, good children. To date I have been spared the roast meat.[1] Now that's all I can think of. I scarcely need assure you who know me that, with my natural candor, I hit it off right well with all these folks . . .

And now, dear friends, the best of good luck to you all. Write me very soon. To read your letters ten times over is my dearest, most valued recreation. With eternal love, your faithful friend

FRZ. SCHUBERT.

And so this noble family consumed the nectar and ambrosia offered by their genius, but grudged him the roast meats in return and shoved him out into the servants' quarters. One imagines the bitter need that made the poor young fellow endure such treatment by the titled snobs and his helpless exasperation. Perhaps if, in Schober's caricature opposite p. 82, the roles had been reversed, and Schubert instead of Vogl had been the tall, majestic one, filled with a tremendous sense of his own importance, he might, in Beethoven's words, have "imposed on" Count Esterházy somewhat as the imperious deaf man "imposed on" Lichnowsky, the Archduke, Lobkowitz, Rasoumowsky, and Co. Which would have been an excellent arrangement for all concerned.

Toward the middle of October, 1818, a letter came from brother Ferdinand:

My piano will be sold and I'd like to take over yours. If you agree, just name the price, and the cash will go to you.

And now be 1000 times kissed, and when you come to Vienna, let me not be the last to see you. In any case you will be welcome here, and doubly welcome if you would like to spend the winter in my house. With true love, your

Sincerely faithful brother
FERDINAND.

---

[1] A ruefully humorous way of indicating his humiliation at not being asked to dine with the family and having to content himself with plain servant's fare. Blom's translation (in Deutsch's *A Documentary Biography*), "So far I have been spared dining with the family," implies the relieved opposite of Schubert's hungry and wistful meaning.

Professor Deutsch[1] recently discovered that the opening of this letter,

which is preserved only in a copy, has been tampered with. The explanation will be found at the beginning of Schubert's reply: it was Ferdinand's confession that he had passed off [Franz's] *German Requiem Mass* as a work of his own, and performed it thus.

To find Ferdinand out as a plagiarist comes as a shock. Our former high estimate of his character must be revised downward, and that of Franz's kindness and generosity still further upward; for this is part of his reply:

Zseliz, 29th October, 1818.

DEAR BROTHER FERDINAND:

You were forgiven the crime of appropriation from the time of your first letter [this refers to its lost beginning], so that there was no reason, except perhaps your sensitive conscience, to delay writing for so long. So my *Requiem Mass* pleased you, and you wept over it . . . Dear brother, this is my most beautiful reward for that gift; don't let me hear of any other.——

If I were not daily getting to know the people about me better, I'd be getting along as well as I did at first. But now I see that, if it were not for a couple of really kind girls, I'd really be alone among these folks. My yearning for Vienna grows daily . . .

Just take my piano; it will please me . . . But it is unpleasant to me that you are forever talking of payment, reward and thanks to a brother. *Pfui*, the devil! . . . [This is really turning the other cheek also.]

You, Ignaz, are still wholly the old man of iron. Your implacable hatred of the entire race of official stuffed shirts does you honor. But you can have no conception of the priestly gang here, bigoted as an old inhabitant of a dungheap, stupid as a brazen donkey, and boorish as a buffalo.

Here we find in Schubert's words the same vivid and passionate power that often erupts into the notes of his dramatic songs.

[1] In *A Documentary Biography*.

14

LA VIE DE BOHÈME

A T LAST, in November, 1818, the exile could return, with his poor savings and his rich manuscripts, to the Vienna of his dreams. Under the most favorable conditions, money never lasted long in Franzl's inflammable pockets. But now the gulden were more transitory than ever, for it was feared that the value of the copper coinage would be raised. Storekeepers returned change only in cardboard tokens. The things were stamped with a seal, marked with the amount, and redeemable nowhere but at the same shop. When the 0 on the 20 kreutzer token was erased by wear, the customer got back merely 2 kreutzers' worth.

Father Schubert was anxious to have the son whom he regarded as the prodigal return, not to the fatted calf, but to the husks of pedagogy. Having once, however, tasted the heady wine of freedom, then renewed bondage at home, and a second—though more varied and interesting—captivity at Zseliz, Franzl balked.

There was another row, another savage exhibition of Caliban's peasantlike rage, and another break between father and son. As in the Convict days, Franzl was forbidden the house.[1]

He accepted the hospitality of the melancholy Mayrhofer's diggings at Wipplingerstrasse 420. The friends' opposite temperaments complemented one another, and Franzl's cheerful nature would sometimes stimulate the morbid bard to indulge in a grim kind of horseplay. With a bayonet fastened to a stick he would make a jocose feint at the man of music, roaring: "What's to prevent me [from spitting you], you little shrimp?" And Franzl would repulse him, bellowing a magic formula in the alliterative style of the *Nibel-*

---

[1] Richard Heuberger discovered a fragment of a paper addressed by Father Schubert to the School Board, asking for Franz's reinstatement as teacher. It looks as though, instead of having been sent in, it had been violently torn and trampled under foot.

ungenlied: "*Waldl, Waldl, wilder Verfasser!*" ("*Waldl, Waldl,* wild author!")[1]

Anselm Hüttenbrenner, calling in wintertime, found Franzl "in a half-dark, damp and unheated little room, wrapped in an old, threadbare dressing gown, freezing and—composing." He recorded the routine in that gloomy hole:

At six o'clock every morning [Schubert] sat himself down to the writing desk and composed without a break until 1 P.M., smoking a few pipes as he wrote. If I visited him in the forenoon, he immediately played me whatever was finished, and wanted to hear what I thought of it. If I specially praised a lied, he would say: "Yes, you see that's a good poem. Reading it makes something sensible occur to me at once. The melodies stream to me so that it's a real pleasure. When you read a bad poem, nothing goes right. You torture yourself with it, and none but dry stuff comes out. I've refused plenty of poems that have been pressed upon me.

Anselm must have enjoyed special favor; for when other friends arrived during work hours,[2] the composer would merely say: "God greet thee,[3] how goes it?" and keep on writing. Whereupon the guest would make an unobtrusive exit.

After the midday dinner, Schubert paid visits or met his cronies for black coffee, tobacco, and conversation obbligati, in the Hungarian Crown, the Black Cat, the Green Anchor, the Snail, or some other of Vienna's characteristic cafés or inns. Good weather lured the friends across the meadows toward the Wienerwald. Or they attended shows or concerts. Or they gathered to hear their music specialist's latest compositions. Until his last days Franzl kept pretty much to this routine.

His sociability, his imperative need of a traveling companion, and his ability to write his best music in the midst of a noisy crowd of friends stamp him as an extrovert, in contrast to introverts like Beethoven, who once said that he loved a tree more than a man, or like Brahms, who could not compose, or even think seriously of creative music, with anyone else in the room. When the son of the Herr Inspector arrived in Zseliz, Franzl wrote, "Right soon I hope to become very fond of him," an indication of how eagerly he sought and

---

[1] The exact significance of *Waldl* is not known. It is a diminutive of *Waldmann,* a South German name for a dog.
[2] As Schwind, who joined the circle the following year, reported.
[3] "*Grüss Di' Gott,*" a characteristic Austrian greeting.

enjoyed companionship. How many of us have ever said such a thing about a perfect stranger?

Now, Franzl had not all his life been consistently keen on sociability. Spaun described him in the first Convict days as "always serious and not very friendly." But before that, as we have found Father Schubert testifying, "in his earliest childhood he loved company and was never happier than when he could pass his free hours in a crowd of gay comrades." So he must have begun as an extrovert, turned introvert in the early school years, and then, as he made friends and tasted their sympathetic appreciation, changed back permanently to extrovert. Spaun bears witness that after boyhood, Schubert did not enjoy eating or any other activity except composing unless it was "seasoned with friendly intercourse." But even the composing was often incredibly accomplished while in a full spate of animated conversation.

The Schubert Circle was still small, but, though including no musician of the first order besides its central figure, it was a choice group. *Parva sed apta.* Here was a phenomenon unique in history. Gathered about a poor, ugly, insignificant-looking little school assistant of proletarian birth, a creature without physical charm or sexual attraction, was a circle of brilliant and absolutely devoted young men, who found their greatest pleasure in supporting and encouraging him, and furthering his genius in every possible way. Schubert was the cement that held this Circle together. "Through him," declared Spaun, "we all became brothers and friends." These friends soon became as necessary to Franzl as food and drink.

When these enthusiastic and exuberant Bohemians met, the occasion was known as a "Canevas." The nickname arose from Schubert's habit of inquiring, in his Viennese dialect, about any newcomer, "*can e vas?*" Which, in High German, is "*kann er etwas?*" or "can he do anything?" [1]

The Canevas evenings brought together a talented crowd. Besides such old friends as Spaun, Schober, Anselm Hüttenbrenner, and Mayrhofer, there was the mighty, vainglorious, and foppish eyeglass-twirler Vogl, the poets Bruchmann, Senn, Von Bauernfeld, and Feuchtersleben, Witteczek, the collector of Schubertiana, Josef Gahy and Josef von Szalay, who were Franzl's leading four-hand partners, the painters Leopold Kupelwieser, Ludwig Schnorr von Carolsfeld,

---

[1] The word "Canevas" is said to have been coined in the Hungarian Crown, where Mozart used to play billiards.

Josef Danhauser, Moritz von Schwind, and Josef Teltscher (who was to sketch Beethoven on his deathbed), and, somewhat later, the composer Franz Lachner and the famous poet Franz Grillparzer.

When this crowd perhaps brought their ladies and met in some friendly home to hear their composer's music, the occasions were called Schubertiads. They sometimes assembled the cultural flower of the middle class and lesser nobility. Poems were read aloud, and there was dancing, while the unterpsichorean Franzl improvised *Deutschen* and *Ländler* and waltzes at the keyboard. But the real *raison d'être* of these gatherings was to hear their great musician's latest songs or piano music.

The musical proceedings were not always strictly serious, as when the composer parodied *The Erl King* by chanting it through that progenitor of the kazoo, a tissue-covered comb. "If sometimes," wrote Kreissle, "he kept quietly to himself, at others he would join in the merriment around him. His laugh was not that of ordinary mirth; it consisted of a hoarse suppressed chuckle."

Concerts given by the violinist Eduard Jaëll on March 1, 1818, and February 28, 1819, were red-letter days in Franzl's life. On the former occasion, one of his "Italian" overtures was played. On the latter, his *Shepherd's Lament* was for the first time heard by the larger public, and the *Allgemeine musikalische Zeitung* of Leipzig referred to "the touching and feeling composition of this talented young man." The Viennese *Allgemeine musikalische Zeitung* reported that "the songs amused the audience." So it appeared that Schubert had performed the impossible. He had written an amusing lament.

15

FRANZL HOAXES THE COUNT

D URING the winter of 1818–1819, a German conductor and composer named Louis Schlösser met Franzl.

I knew [he wrote[1]] that Schubert did not live in luxury, but when I called on him I was astonished at the absence of every comfort. The large ground-floor room where he lived was more like an artisan's workshop than a composer's study. A piano was heaped high with music; stringed instruments, music racks, a table and the needful chairs were in a disorderly jumble. Except for these there was no sign of comfort . . .

From outside the room I heard a piano going; so, very softly, I opened the door, hoping not to disturb him. He saw me, however, and rose. When I begged him to keep on, he played me the variations of the *Impromptu in B Flat Major 2/4.*[2]

It is pleasant to know that Schlösser once took Schubert to one of the finest restaurants in town and ordered the best of everything. His tiny guest was in wonderful form, ate and drank with hearty zest, occasionally scribbled down some musical idea in a small notebook, and told stories about his life at the Convict.

While we were deep in merry talk, a servant in resplendent livery came up and offered my guest a note from Count Esterházy. Schubert opened it, read it deliberately, and told the messenger: "Say to your master that I will come."

He passed the paper over to me. It read: "My cousin Stefan's musical combustibles have again caught fire and flamed up into an art product which nobody but you can decipher. I expect you soon."

---

[1] *Aus Franz Schuberts Leben*, in *Neue Zeitschrift für Musik*, Jahrg. 50, Nos. 33 and 34, 1883.

[2] Schlösser's memory played him false. This *Impromptu*, which is in 4/4 time, was not composed until long after, in 1827.

Schlösser wanted to know what this was all about.

Haven't you ever [replied Schubert] met someone who, very happily endowed with musical gifts, but lacking knowledge, experience, and self-critical ability, has so far succumbed to a mad passion for music that he supposes himself a great composer? This Count Stefan scribbles down any crazy thing that his undisciplined imagination conjures up. Nobody can make head or tail of it. Nor can he himself play it for anyone. It is pure chaos; but he thinks it sublime and quite as good as Beethoven's music. Occasionally he comes on from Hungary to visit his Esterházy relatives here so that I may perform his supposed masterpieces to him.

Schlösser inquired how Schubert could play "chaos."

Let me go on [was the reply]. Some time ago I discovered that this fantastic enthusiast had mistaken the *Variations* by Pixis and Bohn for violin and piano, for the variations in Beethoven's *"Kreutzer"* Sonata. So I plainly saw that I could count on the probability that he was unable to tell one piece of music for another. And that was the way it turned out. I noted the time and key signature on his manuscript, then began with some preluding arpeggios; after which I brought in some rhythmical sentences. My counterfeit composer did not change expression; and when I asked whether I was correctly interpreting his music, he nodded his head. So I bravely kept on improvising variations and turning over the pages of his music to make it seem as if I were performing from them. He had not the slightest notion that I was playing something wholly different from the notes that stared me in the face.

"But how," asked Schlösser, "could you have dared risk being so indiscreet?"

I did it with the knowledge and consent of Count Esterházy and his family. They could not bear to rob their affable cousin of a self-deception that gave him so much happiness. When, at the close of my performance, they called *"bravo! bravissimo!"*, Stefan swam in a sea of felicity. However, this deception weighs on my conscience and I have decided to confess the whole business quite frankly to him. I know Stefan's character, and he will not hold it against me, but will look upon it as a carnival joke. Now, much against my will, the experiment is again to be tried. I have promised, and am too much in the Esterházys' debt to refuse. But after this one repetition, *never again!*

Had the good-natured fellow already forgotten how this family had "spared" him the roast meat? Note the highly singular statement that he performed the hoax "with the knowledge and consent of Count Esterházy." Here we find that remarkably small nobleman in all his caddishness: at one moment intimate enough with the music master to conspire with him to deceive his, the Count's, own cousin, but at the next, treating him like a lackey, and making him eat meager fare in the servants' hall.

Invited by his guest to go along with him to the Count's, Schlösser found that the handsome Stefan alternated intelligent talk with streams of the most arrant nonsense about music. "Two opposing impulses," whispered Schubert, "govern this man's mind: one sane, the other eccentric. At regular intervals they spell each other off." Stefan announced that he had composed a new fantasy which Schubert would now read at sight. The manuscript gave Schlösser a shock.

What did I see? A jungle of queer figures. Like black snakes they squirmed in and out of the staves. And Schubert had to decipher this perfectly undecipherable manuscript!

Yet the dauntless Franzl set the composition on the rack, gave it a cursory glance, and began to improvise as Schlösser had never before heard him.

Melodic pearls in ropes of incomparable beauty rolled from the keys, and little by little grew into a romance of the utmost tenderness, interlarded with episodes and enriched with marvelous modulations. In order not to make the Count suspicious, it was kept in the form of a fantasy. These gentle lyrical melodies introduced a stormy *Allegro con fuoco* full of brilliant coloring.

Schubert had now worked himself up into such a full tide of inspiration that he forgot Stefan, the absurd manuscript, and the reason why he was there. This was so obvious that even the pseudo composer began to suspect that all was not as it should be. He sprang to his feet, and his angry look recalled the sensitive improvisator to the actualities of the absurd situation. With great presence of mind he began again to turn the forgotten sheaves of nonsense. Stefan resumed his seat and once more yielded in ecstasy to the loveliness of what he believed to be his own inspiration. The situation was saved.

A storm of applause greeted the final chord. But in Stefan's praise one could detect a note of irony.

A little later, Schubert went to Count Stefan and, obviously under the stress of emotion, humbly asked his pardon for having deceived him. What he had done was not as bad as it seemed. His eye had been attracted by a certain passage in the manuscript which had charmed him and inflamed his fancy so that he had become guilty of borrowing another man's idea and dressing it up. "But why should a composer who does that be more culpable than a poet whose imagination is warmed by someone else's flame, and who makes an idea that inspires him the subject of his own very different treatment? I did no more than that."

It was a delicate and resourceful turn of Schubert's sensitive feeling. Those who overheard the plea could scarcely refrain from laughing; for Schubert had never before been heard to make such a long and impassioned speech. No one could have been angry with him. The [partially] disillusioned Count soon gave the other his hand in frank and cordial forgiveness. Relieved from the oppressive reproaches of conscience, Schubert returned to the piano and played some of his own German Dances in his own inimitable style.

And so the native hue of Franzl's resolution was sicklied o'er by the pale cast of afterthought. He had assured Schlösser that he intended to make a clean breast of the whole business. But when it came to the pinch, the good-natured fellow could not bring himself to inflict so much pain. So he told a clever quarter truth, giving the impression that he had faithfully read Stefan's music, besides improvising on one of its themes. Whereas the whole performance had been pure Schubert. What a pity that no recording device had yet been invented!

This incident brings up memories of a Viennese restaurant where I was once entertained by an artist no less kindly than Franzl. The service was so execrable that even his enormous patience cracked, and he declared: *"Muss a Bissl schimpfen!"* ("Must scold a bit.") After a geological period the waiter reappeared; but my host merely smiled and murmured, *dolce, "Das muss anders sein."* ("That must be different.") In answer to my quizzical expression, he confided ruefully, *"Kann nicht so recht schimpfen."* ("Can't scold so well.")

16

VAGABONDING WITH VOGL

THROUGH Vogl's influence, Court Opera Director Weigl commissioned Schubert to write incidental music for a deplorable one-acter, *Die Zwillingsbrüder*, which he finished January 19, 1819. Weigl was a specialist in cloud-capt promises which were all too prone to melt into thin air and "leave not a rack behind." Treitschke, the Opera's *régisseur* and official poet, was a similar specialist. The fierce Rossini madness which now swept Vienna induced this precious pair to shelve not only *Die Zwillingsbrüder*, but also far greater works of German genius like *Don Juan, Figaro*, and *Fidelio*.

It shows Franzl's spaciousness of spirit that, despite this harm to his interests, he could praise the Swan of Pesaro. On May 19th he wrote Anselm Hüttenbrenner:

You're a rogue! that's flat!!! It'll be a decade before you see Vienna again. Now this girl, now that, sticks in your head. Ah, if you let the girls bewitch you like this, to the devil with the lot of them! Marry, in God's name, and make an end of the business.— To be sure, like Caesar you can say, better be first in Graz [he spells it Grätz] than second in Vienna. However that may be, I am foxdevilwild [*fuchsteufelwild*] that you are not here . . . In the end I'll go to Graz too and set up as your rival.— In this place there's little new; if one hears anything good, it's always old stuff.— Recently Rossini's *Otello* was given here . . . This opera is far better, I mean more characteristic, than *Tancredi*. One can't deny the man extraordinary genius. The instrumentation is sometimes most original, and so, at times, is the vocal part, if you leave out the customary Italian gallopades, and the numerous reminiscences of *Tancredi.*—

In spite of Vogl, it is hard to maneuver against such rascals as Weigl, Treitschke, etc.— So, instead of my operettas, they produce other abominations, till one's hair stands up like the hills.

For Schubert, as it had been for Mozart, summer usually was the most financially difficult season. The Esterházys had returned to their Hungarian haunts, taking with them all hope of two-gulden music lessons. Duncan[1] points out the shameful fact that Franzl's swiftly moving pen could have earned more by copying the music of nonentities than it did by creating the modern lied.

Now, toward the middle of July, 1819, the situation suddenly improved. A stately *deus ex machina* loomed up in the person of Michael Vogl. "Pack your bag, young Schubert," he rumbled, "I'll take you for a trip. I'll show you the Upper Austria that produced me. And we shall have music wherever we go."

Franzl was wildly delighted. What? Escape the hot, stuffy city; behold at last the mountains, lakes, forests, and picturesque towns that Mayrhofer, Spaun, the Hüts, and Vogl were forever raving about; lead a gay life of adventure, free for a time of the dismal problems of wherewithal? To the town lad who had beheld Upper Austria only in his dreams, the prospect looked like an earthly paradise. And those dreams must have been fantastic, for his one doubt was whether music paper was to be had in "the wilds."

There was, of course, one other drawback, the imperious way in which Vogl often insisted on taking liberties with his songs. But he resolved to pay the price of adventure with as good a grace as possible and hurdle that obstacle in his stride.

A delicious caricature, probably tossed off by Schober in 1825, has come down to us. The caption reads: "Michael Vogl and Franz Schubert launch forth to conflict and conquest." With measured stride, as if advancing upon the buskined stage of tragedy, Vogl stalks solemnly, majestically in the lead. He is swathed in a fabulously long caped overcoat and crowned with a formidable stovepipe hat. His chest is expanded to capacity. His eyes gaze fixedly upon the empyrean with gloomy self-importance as if all witnesses of his progress were expected to shudder with awe.

Behind him trips an abject little rat of a being in spectacles, who seems quite out of countenance. He is not much taller than his mighty companion's waistband. The poor fellow seems to be shivering inside a badly cut overcoat, which outlines his chubby paunch. Each hand is thrust for warmth into the opposite sleeve. A roll of music is gripped under one arm. Another roll protrudes from his pocket, and he is topped by a miserable little hat of mongrel form. His mouth looks pinched as if he were wondering why Vogl could not get along a bit faster.

[1] Edmondstoune Duncan, *Schubert*, London, J. M. Dent & Son, Ltd., 1905.

The design gives the real situation at a glance. The spoiled celebrity, who knew himself infinitely more important than the tiny scribbler that he was pleased to patronize and take under his wing, feels that his word is law. He ordains the tempos, rubatos, ritardandos, and embellishments, while Schubert winces but takes his punishment. Edward Traweger, the son of Schubert's host in Gmunden, wrote, "I remember perfectly well that, in *The Erl King*, Vogl did not sing the words '*das Kind ist tot*,' but spoke them; and in *Der Wanderer*, closed the passage '*dort ist das Glück*' with an improvised scale."

The caricature seems so much like an Edward Lear drawing, especially in the droll little figure of Schubert, that one instinctively feels it should be accompanied by a limerick; perhaps something along the following lines:

> Said Vogl: "My poor little Schuberty,
> Though you look like a lad in his puberty,
> Your music is choice—
> When adorned by *my* voice."
> Said Franz: "Praise indeed from Sir Huberty!"

First stop: the huge monastery of Kremsmünster, where Vogl had had his early schooling. Here the canons and prebendaries came together in the cool summer refectory. They attended politely to Schubert's piano music, but that modern stuff was far over their heads. When Vogl started on his companion's religious compositions, they listened with more understanding. Then, perhaps feeling that offering Kyries and Aves to a monastery was bringing coals to Newcastle, they clamored for secular lieder and applauded them with delight.

Now, on to Vogl's birthplace, Steyr, picturesquely snuggled on both banks of the Enns. Here Franzl fell in love with the charm of Upper Austrian civilization. His heart went out to the venerable half-timbered façades, bowling gardens running down to a swift stream, openwork signs of wrought metal displaying against the light a goose, a flagon, a huntsman, a huge key, a stag with stately antlers, the tutelary Saint Florian with his bucket, pouring wooden water upon a house in wooden flames. And underneath this friendly saint the motto would run:

MORITZ VON SCHWIND
Lithograph by Josef Kriehuber (1827).

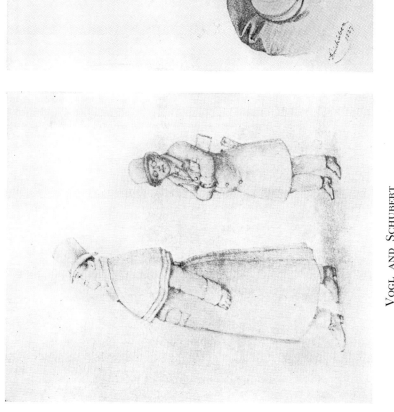

VOGL AND SCHUBERT
Pencil caricature thought to be by Schober.

Grillparzer's friend,
KATHARINA FRÖHLICH
Chalk drawing by Heinrich.

MARIA ANNA FRÖHLICH
Chalk drawing by Heinrich.

JOSEFINE FRÖHLICH
Chalk drawing by Heinrich.

BARBARA FRÖHLICH (Frau Bogner)
Miniature by Peter (1829).

The Four Graces

Heiliger Sankt Florian, du steinbraver Mann,
Schon' unser Haus und steck' Andrer Häuser an!

[Freely translated:]
(Holy Saint Florian, among your blessèd labors,
Spare our dwelling, and burn down the neighbor's.)

In these ancient streets, the upper stories of the houses, successively protruding above those below, almost rubbed foreheads across the way. Their magic casements were glazed with *Butzenscheiben,* discs of iridescent glass with a bubble in the center. And there were glamorous inns, above whose truly entrancing entrances this motto invited:

Willkommen, Wand'rer, hab' kein Angst,
Droben gibt's wass Du verlangst.

(Welcome, wanderer, have no fear;
Everything you want is here.)

The delighted Franzl now first saw and heard that venerable institution, the night watchman. Every hour, on the hour, would come a shuffling of wooden clogs on the cobblestones below, and an ancient man, swathed and hooded in a Loden cape and bearing a halberd and a curious old pierced lantern of tin, would cry in a toothless quaver:

Lost auf ihr Herren und lasst euch sagen:
Der Hammer im Turm hat zehn Uhr geschlagen,
Zehn Uhr!
Lobet Gott und unsere liebe Frau.
Betet für die armen Seelen im Fegfeuer
Dass Gott ihnen allzeit gnädig sei.
Gebt Obacht auf das Feuer
Damit kein Unglück g'schieht.
Zehn Uhr hat's geschlagen.
Gelobt sei Jesus Christus.

[This lyric at once tempts and baffles translation.]
(Hearken, masters, to my rhymes:
The steeple hammer has struck ten times,
Ten o'clock!

Praise ye God and his dear Mother.
From the poor souls in Purgatory's fire
Pray God to turn away His ire.
Pay good heed your fires to smother,
To avoid bad luck.
Ten o'clock has struck.
Praised be Jesus Christus.)

Franzl would doubtless have recognized this as the inspiration for a page of *Die Meistersinger,* had not that work belonged to the distant future.

Besides the art and nature of this smiling land, Franzl loved its cordial hospitality. The good provincials were convinced that, however unprepossessing to look at, any musician whom the immortal Vogl brought along must be a person of note, to be made much of. Though their wine was a bit acrid, their welcome was mellow. Vogl lodged with the Kollers, Schubert with the Schellmanns, of whom, on July 13th, 1819, he wrote brother Ferdinand:

In the house where I live there are eight girls, almost all of them pretty. You see that one has his hands full. The daughter of Herr von K[oller], with whom I and Vogl dine daily, is extremely pretty, plays piano very handily, and will sing various songs of mine . . .

Your

eternally true
brother FRANZ

The country about Steyr is unimaginably beautiful.

Anton Stadler, one of that circle, wrote to Luib:

At Steyr, in Josef von Koller's house, we often had music after an evening walk . . . The very talented daughter, Josefine [Pepi to her intimates], Schubert, Vogl and I enjoyed highly pleasant hours in the alternate performance of Schubert's piano pieces and songs . . .

I recall one interesting episode: the attempt—of course, among ourselves—to sing *The Erl King a tre!* Schubert sang the father, Vogl the Erl King, Josefine the child, while I accompanied.

Alas, poor Pepi! What tasteless, what detestable tricks life can play upon a pretty, slender, and vivacious young creature! From the evidence of the only portrait that has come down to us, this girl, become Frau Krakowitzer, turned into a fat, ridiculous-looking person with a face like a stupid Chinese mandarin and a gross body robed in one acre of black bombazine that billowed pyramidally to earth in all directions.

Note that, in Stadler's account, the composer did not play the piano. That worm, the great opera star's "poor little Schuberty," at long last found the temerity to turn. He asked Vogl not to play ducks and drakes with his songs. And when these timid expostulations were impatiently brushed aside as of no moment, Franzl quietly withdrew from the keyboard. It was agreed that Dr. Schellmann, who did not mind lending himself to Vogl's tricks and manners, should usually accompany him.[1]

This revolt of the little composer was a sort of miniature companion piece to a movement that was just then going on in Austrian society. Anita Silvestrelli has well described it:

> Here in the provinces one could feel more strongly than in Vienna that a new era was dawning, an era in which the nobility gradually ceased to call the tune, while the middle class pushed broadly into the foreground. It no longer imitated the manners and customs of the feudal circles, but, in short order, created a style of its own which made its views, wants and tastes the rule and the fashion. In the Napoleonic wars the nobility had given their all; had bled to death financially; politically speaking had lost their positions to the reigning houses which alone determined alliances and wars. Besides that they had been deprived by Napoleon of so many rights that the attempt fully to make up to them for this deprivation would have met with a certain amount of resistance on the part of the people. The middle class, however, had won because its tremendous sacrifices of life and property had been recompensed by extraordinary concessions. Besides which, after the Corsican's fall, there began a general upswing in business, the professions, administration, and intellectual life.

It follows that his neglect by the high nobility was not so much of a deprivation for Schubert as it would have been for Beethoven, who was taken up by them before their decline. Solid citizens like these Schellmanns and Kollers now meant a good deal more than they would have in Beethoven's youth. They were approaching the crest of the wave. They were beginning to have a dim realization what sort of musical angel they had been entertaining unawares, and to love him, not alone for his genius, but also for his amiable and touchingly simple self. And Franzl was cheered by the feeling that,

[1] On the authority of Professor O. E. Deutsch.

if worst came actually to worst, here were hospitable and congenial
doors with the latch string always out for him. To the end of his days,
both in the provinces and at home, the middle class was to provide
him with friends, enthusiastic admirers, and creative listeners. Spir-
itually—though alas, not materially—they offered Schubert what the
princes offered Beethoven.

In Steyr Franzl made friends with Sylvester Paumgartner, who
commissioned him to write a quintet. This patron played the 'cello
not wisely nor too well but with all the more enthusiasm. Perhaps
these 'cellistic efforts touched Franzl's heart by reminding him of
his own father's Calibanistic scrapings. Anyway he soon delighted
Paumgartner with a more precious gift than any 'cellist had received
since Mozart had written the three delicious "Solo Quartets" for
that amateur 'cellist, the King of Prussia. It was the *"Trout"* Quintet,
Op. 114, for piano, violin, viola, 'cello, and double bass, so-called
from its variations on *Die Forelle*. This was the same song that Franzl
had sleepily baptized with ink instead of sand for Josef Hüttenbrenner.[1]

This charming quintet marks a creative frontier. Beyond it Schubert was to attain full maturity as an instrumental composer. His
contact with the sort of country soil from which his forebears had
sprung had renewed his vitality and filled him with fresh creative
strength. A modern Antaeus, he rose from earth tenfold stronger.
This was natural; for Schubert was second in the great dynasty of
peasant composers: Haydn, Schubert, Brahms, Bruckner, all of
whom did their best work in Vienna, the large city that lay nearest
to beautiful nature.

When the *"Trout"* Quintet was first tried, the 'cello part was rather
too much for Paumgartner's modest technique, but Franzl performed
a notable *tour de force*. There was no time to write out the score.
So he scribbled down the string voices and played the piano part
from memory. This equaled Mozart's feat in 1784 when Madame
Strinasacchi played his new duet Sonata in B Flat (Köchel 454)
from the violin part, while the composer performed his from a piano
manuscript visible to none but his own inner eye. "There were giants
in the earth in those days." When Franzl got around to writing the
score, he presented it to Paumgartner, whose family proceeded to
lose it.

[1] Pitrou refers to this fourth of the five movements as the "finale," while
Stefan calls it the "third."

For Vogl's birthday on August tenth, Franzl dashed off an impromptu cantata to Stadler's words, for soprano, tenor, and bass. Naturally there were references to the singer's stage triumphs and to his dazzling honor and glory, calculated to inflate still further a personality already quite sufficiently puffed up. After three decades the music, with words completely changed by an unknown hand, was published as *The Spring Morning*, Op. 158. Vogl, forgotten in his grave for the last nine years, must have turned in it.

At Linz, of which Franz wrote, "The region is heavenly," he met Spaun's mother and sent a note to Mayrhofer requesting the hospitality of his (Schubert's) bed for a strolling student who would presently stroll through Vienna. The plan to visit the shades of Mozart at Salzburg fell through, and they returned to Steyr, where the composer inscribed a morsel of wisdom in Katharina Stadler's autograph album: "If you always enjoy the present wisely, the past shall be a beautiful memory and the future shall not dismay you." For a young fellow of twenty-two, this shows a precocious insight into the fine art of living. We may be sure that, a month after, he was enjoying the present wisely, if at a price, when he composed the vanished four-hand Overture in F. A notation of his on the manuscript ran, "Written inside of three hours in Josef Hüttenbrenner's room in the Bürgerspital, thus missing the midday dinner."

17

TOO RAGGED TO TAKE A BOW

THE calendar read 1820. Here was Franzl, twenty-three years old, and if the wolf was not at the door, it was only because that sagacious animal knew there was little to eat inside. "I was born for nothing in the world but to write music," he once remarked to Josef Hüttenbrenner. "The state ought to subsidize me." It is humanity's misfortune that Austria did not pension him, as Norway was afterward to pension Grieg, and Finland, Sibelius.

Franzl's inability to market his music, coupled with Rossini's enormous and continuing success, convinced him that a poor devil of a music maker's one hope of worldly success lay in the field of dramatic writing. He decided to take a long chance and give battle to theatrical intrigue, crookedness, venality, and indifference toward any but well-known composers.

And battle he was to give all his short life long, innocently unaware that stage music was not in his line. He was encouraged in this fatal resolve by the fact, fallaciously stimulating to an obscure youth of twenty-three, that this year two of his dramatic pieces were played in the leading theaters of Vienna.

Vogl used his whole powerful influence to secure the presentation of a one-act farce, *Die Zwillingsbrüder*, on June 14, 1820, at the Kärntnertor, himself playing the alternate roles of the two invalids. Franzl, perched with Anselm Hüttenbrenner in the topmost gallery, was overjoyed at the din of applause made by his faithful friends below, all present and working harder than any paid claque. Only when their idolized Vogl appeared did the public join in; otherwise they vainly sought by hisses to modify the partisan transports of the Circle. After the curtain the composer was stormily demanded. Hüt records that Franzl,

however, did not want to go down to the stage because his old coat was a mess. I hastily took off my black dress coat and urged him to put it on

88

and present himself to the audience, which would have done him a lot of good. But he was too undecided and timid. As there was no end to the calls for him, the *régisseur* finally appeared and announced that Schubert was not in the house, which the latter heard with a smile.[1]

After six performances, the piece gave up the ghost. Two months later *Die Zauberharfe* (*The Magic Harp*) was produced in the Theater an der Wien. The text was perpetrated by Georg von Hofmann, the same theater secretary who had been guilty of the book for *Die Zwillingsbrüder*. It was the most arrant twaddle. The fact that Franzl set it shows that he had it in him to be activated by anything from a trade directory up. The introductory number was afterward known and loved as the *Rosamunde* Overture.[2] To the impecunious composer most of the inspiration for this job must have been supplied by a promise of five hundred gulden as remuneration. Alas! he never saw a kreutzer of it, for the theater went bankrupt. Schubert's music kept the play going for a dozen performances before the magic harp broke its last string.

The press notices ranged the entire gamut from jet black to pure white. Franzl's serenity after these two fiascos reminds one of César Franck's after the lamentable first performance of his symphony. "At least," the old man smiled, "they did not hiss it!" "At least," Franzl reflected, "my name is not wholly unknown now to the theatrical public."

Creation presented no problem to Schubert. Producing was as easy as being produced was hard.[3] However, shortly before these two disastrous operatic ventures, a modest publicity had begun to come his way. During the season of 1818–1819, Jäger thrice sang the *Shepherd's Lament* in public. His overtures had several hearings. The Sixth Symphony in C was played in a series of concerts organized by a new and important admirer, Ignaz von Sonnleithner, in his home

[1] Grove was mistaken in writing, "Schubert took so little interest in its production that, like Mendelssohn at 'The Wedding of Camacho,' he did not even stay in the house."

[2] While the prelude which Schubert wrote three years later to *Rosamunde* appeared as the Overture to *Alfonso and Estrella*.

[3] Which reminds one of Wilhelm Busch's choice epigram about another sort of production:

> "Vater werden ist nicht schwer;
> Vater sein, dagegen, sehr."

> ("No trick to become a father;
> But to be one—well just rather!")

at the Gundelhof. There, on January 8, 1819, this influential member of the Friends of Music gave a second performance of the cantata *Prometheus*, with himself in the title role.[1] These concerts, weekly in summer, fortnightly in winter, were among the most important musical events in Vienna. There the best amateurs and the foremost music lovers met and heard the leading professionals.

At the house of Matthäus von Collin, brother of the poet whose *Coriolan* inspired Beethoven's immortal overture, Franzl for the first time sang and played *The Wanderer*. The song roused the enthusiasm of some valuable new acquaintances among the guests: Johann Pyrker, the poetic Patriarch (Archbishop) of Venice, Hammer-Purgstall, the orientalist, Karoline Pichler, the writer, and two personages influential in court circles: the Court Music Count Moritz von Dietrichstein, and the Court Secretary, Ignaz von Mosel, a man mighty in theatrical and concert affairs.

Frühlingsglaube was written in 1820, and the remarkable *Quartett Satz* in C Minor, chamber music's "*Unfinished*." It is the prophetic germ which was to fecundate the superb Quartets in A Minor and D Minor. This revolutionary movement sprang from a mind impatient of the established civil and religious authority of the day. And it is significant that, the same year, Schubert received an official reprimand for consorting with the revolutionary poet Johann Senn.

Another fragment now resulted from an opera idea to which Franzl fell victim. It was the *Sakuntala* story, and though the text was no masterpiece, it was at least preferable to such bilge as he had set in *Zwillingsbrüder* and *Zauberharfe*, and was to honor in *Alfonso and Estrella, Fierrabras*, and *Gleichen*. If Schubert had to write operas, it was a pity that he did not persevere with *Sakuntala* and neglect the others.

For centuries the musical amateurs of Vienna have—as amateurs go—maintained higher standards than the professionals—as professionals go. Among the city's leading dilettantes in Schubert's day were the four charming Fröhlich sisters: Anna, Barbara the painter, Josefine, an opera singer with a drooping eyelid, and—most interesting and attractive of the quartet—Kathi,[2] the "eternal intended" of

---

[1] Flower made an amusing boner when he wrote, "Reissiger, the composer of *Martha*, took part in some of these evenings." In point of fact, Flotow was not to compose *Martha* until nineteen years after Schubert's death.

[2] Pitrou and Silvestrelli place under the portrait of the beautiful Kathi the name of the unattractive girl with the unfortunate eye.

Grillparzer, greatest of Austrian poets. What the poet said of Kathi was true of all the sisters: they intoxicated themselves with music "as drunkards with wine." Their home was a favorite rendezvous for artists of all kinds.

Leopold, the son of Ignaz von Sonnleithner, was a passionate collector of Schubert manuscripts and once took a sheaf of them to the Fröhlichs'. "They are by a young fellow I know, and I think them good." Kathi sat down at the piano and began to read them. Then up spoke Gymnich, an official with a splendid voice, "Look here, what's that you're playing? Not an improvisation?" "No." "Well, its simply glorious, something quite extraordinary! Let's see it." So all that evening Gymnich sang Schubert songs. Enthusiasm flamed high at the Fröhlichs'. In a few days young Sonnleithner proudly brought Franzl to the "Fourmaiden House," and at once the composer found himself delightfully at home.

According to the testimony of Anna Fröhlich, he was a modest, lovable person, with a character unjealously appreciative of the music of others: "Schubert was always overjoyed when something good by another tone-poet was performed. Once, when a large number of his songs were sung, he exclaimed: 'Well, well but now it's enough; now it begins to bore me.'" As Kathi testified: "Schubert had a glorious disposition. He was never envious or jealous like so many others. On the contrary, what pure joy he felt when lovely music was given! Then he would lay his hands together, press them against his mouth, and sit there wholly entranced."

The atmosphere at the "Fourmaiden House" was good for Franzl and his art. Often he would come in, let himself be seated in the place of honor on the sofa, and with a happy smile confess, "Today I've made something that has really come off." In gratitude for what they meant to him, he set the Twenty-third Psalm for piano and four Fröhlichs: two sopranos and two altos. Though curiously uncharacteristic of the composer, the piece is touching in its limpid simplicity. These charming girls soon became the leading spirits among those in musical Vienna who were concerned to give the young master the right atmosphere for work and to secure performances of his compositions.

Leopold von Sonnleithner now made up his energetic mind that something must decidedly be done about getting Franzl's music into print. But he found that the firms of Breitkopf and Härtel in Leipzig, and Steiner and Company in Vienna would have nothing to do with

The Erl King. Those perspicacious local publishers Cappi and
Diabelli declared that they would neither pay a kreutzer for such
trash, nor even take it as a present. Though these merchants did not
quite realize it, their position was: "Why bother with gold when we
can have plenty of tinsel?"

Nothing daunted, Sonnleithner formed a committee with Josef
Hüttenbrenner, Johann Schönpichler, and Johann Schönauer—men
whose memory should be honored by all lovers of music. They put
up enough money to engrave *The Erl King* as Op. 1, and heaped
coals of fire on Cappi's and Diabelli's shameful heads (one hopes
they burned!) by allowing them to do the job and pocket half the
profits.

During a musical evening at the Kiesewetters',[1] a hundred copies
were bought, which provided funds for the printing of *Margaret at
the Spinning Wheel* as Op. 2. And so on for the publication of a
number of the early songs. The choice of them shows the musical
discrimination of the committee. They include such masterpieces
as the *Shepherd's Lament, Little Heath Rose, The Wanderer, Restless Love* (*Rastlose Liebe*), and *Death and the Maiden.*

These publications had some very laudatory press notices, and each
opus brought Schubert an average of a hundred and sixty-five florins.
Count Fries, to whom *Margaret* was dedicated, sent him a present of
twenty ducats. And Johann Pyrker, the Patriarch of Venice, followed
suit with twelve. Franzl's debts were accordingly paid, but he was
such a wretched economist that the balance soon disappeared.

So, after creating hundreds of works: songs, overtures, symphonies, Masses, operas, and chamber music, Franzl at long last
had the satisfaction of seeing his Opus 1 in print. It was a far more
impressive first publication than Haydn, Mozart, or Beethoven could
boast.

[1] Kreissle and Grove were mistaken in thinking that this incident took place at
Sonnleithner's home.

18

SCHWIND, THE SCHUBERT OF PAINTING

BY THE end of 1820, both Schubert and Mayrhofer found themselves fed up with life together. Mayrhofer was too dismally depressing to suit the composer. The poet, on the other hand, did not always find it child's play to live with the genius. Besides, their ideas had become less harmonious, and the bard was hurt because the composer had ceased to find musical inspiration in his poems.

From this time on, Mayrhofer went downhill fast. The antithesis between his lofty principles as a lover of freedom and his vile profession as one of Metternich's censors preyed more and more upon his mind. Eventually, saddened by the fall of Warsaw during the abortive Polish revolution, he tried to drown himself in the Danube, as Schumann later tried to in the Rhine. Failing in that attempt, he threw himself from the third-story window of his office building, suffered forty hours, and died in a hospital. We have him to thank for the texts of many Schubert songs and for having been one of the early founders of the Schubert Circle.

In 1821 much against the grain, Franzl moved to live alone at what is now Wipplingerstrasse 21 until, in 1822, Schober took him in. Schubert felt the loss of Mayrhofer's close companionship all the more because, just then, two dear cronies left Vienna. Anselm Hüttenbrenner went to take over the management of his dead father's estate, and the faithful Spaun moved to Linz for a stay of two years.

These losses, however, were compensated by the acquisition of two young painter friends: Leopold Kupelwieser and Moritz von Schwind. The former had recently abandoned his business as an ironmonger, and scored an immediate success by selling a painting of Faust for 2,500 gulden. He felt greatly drawn to the composer of *The Erl King*.

As a lad of seventeen, Moritz von Schwind, a painter of true genius, was admitted to the Schubert Circle and became fascinated

93

by its central figure. The attraction was mutual, and a David and Jonathan friendship resulted. It was to be disturbed only when the painter moved to Munich in 1827, on the road to glory. For, after Grillparzer and the composer himself, Schwind was the member of the Circle to become most illustrious.

Like Franzl, he was born into poverty. While the musician dashed off little waltzes and German Dances in order to earn a few coppers for dinner, the painter lad cut silhouettes out of black paper, created New Year's cards for the stationer and designs in spun sugar for the festal cakes of the confectioner. Once he ran out of working materials and sent his friends a round-robin begging them for three sheets of drawing paper at thirty kreutzers apiece, adding that when he could not draw he was of all men most miserable.

Seven years younger than Franzl, Moritz was the pet of the Circle, which nicknamed him Cherubim.[1] He occupied very much the same position as the boy Benjamin among the sons of Israel, or as Little Billee among the artists surrounding Trilby, in that British counterpart of *Scènes de la vie de Bohème*. He was a handsome youth, slim, with great blue eyes and finely modeled features. His portraits, painted by himself in 1822 and by Kriehuber five years later, have a strikingly American look.

He was vivacious, impulsive, unbelievably sensitive, lovable, magnetic, zestful, fiery, bubbling with talk. His constant lightning swings from confidence to jealousy, from enchanted delight to lachrymose depression, together with his almost girlish physique, suggest the sort of delayed puberty from which Brahms was later on to suffer. "That," Bauernfeld wrote in his diary, "is a true, genuine artist's temperament, though always in tumultuous ferment; as though he were bent on using himself up."

This passionate lover of Schubert's art declared that he could not paint unless he had his mouth full of music. His motto was, "One should take a spoonful of music every day." He was said to have had no small ability as pianist and fiddler and even tried his hand at composition. *"Der malende Schubert"* was what he came to be called, "the Schubert of painting."

The two friends soon felt themselves to be kindred spirits. The painter wrote to Bauernfeld of the composer: "When one has been living along in the servants' hall of one's own soul—what can be

[1] Probably after the lad in Mozart's *Figaro*.

lovelier than to enter his [Schubert's] best room? There, for the first time, the finest in us comes to our lips, and that in all warmth and most spontaneously."

These lines, and the following ones, written to Schober in 1824, give an idea of Little Billee's ardent temperament: "The greatest things I know on earth are love, beauty and wisdom. You classed me with yourself and Schubert, and the joy of it was more than I could bear. Pain has so purified me that to be third among you means all the world to me."

Schwind lived with his family in Alte Wieden 102, a dwelling as picturesque as its name, the Moonshine House. It was an unforgettable rendezvous for the clan. Built upon a high terrace, it had a splendid view on one side, over a horse market, of the Glacis, the Inner Town, and the Alpine foothills; and on the other, of a charming courtyard garden of lilacs, elders, and acacias, above which the Karlskirche showed its beautiful dome and wafted the music of its organ.

The whole [wrote the painter Führich] made in the midst of Vienna an island of unspoiled rusticity which even great riches could not have conjured up so naturally. Nature and art stood there living and breathing together. The Platzl, as the courtyard was called, was just the continuation of the rooms, the rooms, a refuge from the weather. Drawing and study went on in the arbor. In the evening the rising of a star was observed. Indeed, of a beautiful night, they dragged their mattresses out and slept in the open. There they turned gymnasts and, as in the *Nibelungenlied* (*mit Gehren geschützt*), hurled javelins. In winter they made snow sphinxes and fortifications, and organized complete pitched battles to the accompaniment of Homeric lines . . .

At the old Moonshine House, which also went by the name of *Schwindien*,[1] Franzl and his friends wandered in and out. It was a place of beloved assembly for the Schubertians. Here many a Schubert composition was tried for the first time, criticized, and greeted with jubilation. The poets Schober, Senn, Bauernfeld, and Kenner read aloud from their moist manuscripts. One grew drunk on the works of those forward-looking contemporary poets: Kleist, Brentano, Tieck, Achim von Arnim, Fouqué, and E. T. A. Hoffmann. The German and Nordic sagas, the heroes of the *Nibelungenlied*, whose names the crowd appropriated, awoke to new life. The colorful pages of the minnesingers conjured up before those young eyes

[1] A portmanteau word combining Schwind and *Indien*, or India, thus wedding together in Schwindia the charm of the young painter and the glamour of the gorgeous East.

the splendor of the Middle Ages with their knights and adventures, their palaces and castles.

None who came into contact with the doings at Schwindia could forget the place; and today everybody must admit that the like of it can never be recovered or recreated.

The new friends soon felt the need of sharing all their thoughts, feelings, pleasures, and pains, and of discussing together every creative project. Eventually, early in 1825, Franzl found a room at Alte Wieden 100, in a house next to the Karlskirche, almost wall to wall with Schwindia. He hated living alone; but the curse of it was somewhat mitigated by the painter's nearness. The two inseparables mutually stimulated one another to their best efforts.

One day when Moritz was trying to draw a portrait of the restless Franzl, whom no remonstrances could keep still, somebody put into his hand a copy of *Cymbeline*. Almost at once there leaped at him out of the Second Act: "a wonderful sweet air, with admirable rich words to it." And then the little jewel of a lyric that starts:

Hark, hark! the lark at heaven's gate sings.

Franzl's eyes took on a deep radiance. "I must set this. Where can I find some music paper?" The painter ruled lines on one of his own sheets. And Franzl, immobilized in a creative ecstasy as he dashed down those immortal measures, was now a perfect model. When Little Billee heard the song he caressed the paper: "This is the most valuable design I've ever made!"

Whenever inspiration failed him, Moritz would go to Franzl, lead him to the piano and tell him, "Play—just play whatever comes into your head!" And these improvisations never failed to bring back the lost momentum. It was during these early years of their friendship that the painter first ventured into the Romantic world of fairy story, folklore, fable, and myth that was eventually destined to bring him gold and glory.

Schwind's mercurial jealousy sometimes made his unjealous and patient friend sick at heart. The younger man fell violently in love with Anna (Nettl) Hönig, an attractive girl with whom Franzl liked to play four-hand duets. Moritz hated to have them do it and at these sessions acted more and more like a spoiled child. His friend only turned the other cheek, which excited the painter to ill-bred comments on the contrast between Nettl's beauty and her partner's ugliness, though even as he spoke, his own rudeness hurt him and turned him pale. All that the shocked Schubert answered was, "Well, I can go."

And though Nettl was indignant and tried her best to keep him, Franzl went and took care not to return. Disdainfully she told her lover not to come back before making things good with his friend. The disdain made the boy wild. First he wrote Franzl an offensive letter. Then, lightning-change artist that he was, he swung to the other extreme and, in a second note, deluged himself with reproaches for his "devilish sneering." He begged for a rough and sincere answer. No matter how grievously it put him in the wrong, it would still be better than the fierce self-reproaches that kept torturing him.

But Franzl had already forgiven his friend. His pudgy hand made a brushing motion that swept all unpleasantness aside. "What nonsense a chap will talk when he's in love!" He understood all and forgave all.

Some time later the boy and girl were reconciled and there was talk of marriage. Indeed, shortly before Schubert's death, Little Billee went with great formality to ask her of her family. This is how Bauernfeld described the occasion:

Schwind asked for Nettl's hand and, indeed, in a torn tail coat. The girl's clan was drummed together. A small army of aunts, female cousins, uncles and male cousins, old Privy Councilors and the like, in short a coffee-and-whist party, and incidentally a marriage committee. At first friend Moritz wanted to stay away entirely, or else appear in his painter's costume, as he had no tail coat. This, however, was finally lent him by a friend. [But it was a ruin.] Then, in the first fifteen minutes, he wanted to beat a retreat. The bride had all she could do to keep him there until ten o'clock.

Schubert and I had been in a cafe awaiting the happy bridegroom. He came in all upset and described the philistine gathering to us with a sort of despairing flow of wit. Schubert never ceased his jolly chuckle.

The torn coat impressed the philistines painfully, and Moritz was, in his turn, painfully impressed by the philistines. However, they reluctantly allowed him to become engaged to Nettl.

On October 27, 1828, he finally left Vienna because he could not make a living there, and actually trudged all the way from Linz to Munich. His design, "Stroll Before the Town Gate," was his loving farewell to Austria. In the background is the picturesque old Danubian town of Tulln, celebrated as Tulne in the *Nibelungenlied*. In the right foreground sits the artist, with hat and traveling bag beside him, a sketchbook spread over his knees, and looking almost the spit and image of Du Maurier's Little Billee. On the left the always gallant Schober tips his hat to two girls, while Franzl, at Vogl's side, with his own hat firmly in place, stares stonily past them. Over the high garden wall peers the sad face of the forsaken Nettl.

When Moritz returned from Munich with vastly improved prospects, he found that Nettl had grown tremendously pious and had developed for her dismayed lover ideals of impossible austerity. Nothing about Moritz now satisfied her. Result: scenes of increasing acerbity. In 1829 the last of them ended with the young fellow crying, "Go marry the Pope!" Whereupon the engagement automatically ceased and determined. "As a rule," he told his friends, "I can stand a lot in the way of Catholicism; but too much is too much."

It is good to know that fame, fortune, and even the praise of Goethe came to Schwind before he grew old and gray and fat in that fine house of his on the Bavarian Starnberger See. But one sadly reflects on Schubert's very different fate.

In his later years the painter accomplished a labor of love which has earned him the gratitude of all who care for music. His design, "A Schubertiad" at Josef E. v. Spaun's (see opposite p. 157), shows the Circle gathered intimately about Vogl and the composer, who are fathoms deep in song. There we can meet those pillars of the group: Spaun, Schober, Mayrhofer, Bauernfeld, and Schwind him, self; such celebrities of the day as Lachner, Feuchtersleben, and Grillparzer; such aristocrats as Schnorr von Carolsfeld and Baron von Schönstein. In the conviction that Franzl had been in love with Countess Caroline Esterházy, the painter set her portrait in the center of the background to dominate the scene. Notice in the lower right-hand corner, an old gentleman austere of expression and thin of lip. It is Eduard von Bauernfeld. Though five years younger than Schubert, he was made to look three or four decades more than his true age. Perhaps the painter wished to suggest the maturity of the poet's mind.

19

SCHUBERTIADS

EARLY in 1821 the Imperial Opera was about to become a private enterprise, and Schubert hoped that this change would help his chances of winning a secure position as an opera composer. From old Salieri and Director Weigl he obtained satisfactory testimonials and more enthusiastic ones from Hofrat Mosel and Hofmusikgraf Dietrichstein. However, though the two last-named took over the institution, their good words were never translated into deeds. It was a truly Viennese performance—or rather, lack of performance. As a sop they flung him a small secret job as a ghost writer, and the modest fellow actually composed two numbers to pad out Hérold's opera *Das Zauberglöckchen*. At its *première* on June twentieth, these two were the most applauded.

On April 2, 1821, Eduard von Bauernfeld, writing of a concert at the Kärntnertor Theater, had told his diary, "The best, a quartet by Schubert. A glorious person. I must get to know him." As it turned out, he was not to know him until four years later but was then to play an important role in the composer's life.

For two years now, Franzl had not been heard in public as a song writer, but 1821 brought him encouragement. Several of his pieces were sung at the Gundelhof. At the first concert of the all-powerful Friends of Music, the male quartet *The Little Village* (*Das Dörfchen*) was given. This was repeated and well received in Vogl's "academy" at the Opera House, but the beautiful *Song of the Spirits over the Waters* (*Gesang der Geister über den Wassern*) left the Viennese cold. Vogl, however, scored a sensational hit with *The Erl King*.

Sad to say, this first bit of popularity immediately showed a seamy side. An *Erl King March* appeared; then an *Erl King Galop*, falsely signed with Schubert's name. *Wanderer Waltzes* came out. And Anselm Hüttenbrenner turned musical Judas by perpetrating a set of *Erl King Waltzes*. Whereupon the poet Kanne bitterly inquired:

How does it come that in German lands the terrible shudders induced
by the world of spirits make people dance?
ANSWER: When people began to practice tight lacing, their hearts descended into their legs.

Diabelli, the greedy and dishonest publisher of some of these
atrocities, fancied himself as a creative artist. That spring he invited
Schubert and forty-nine other composers to write variations on a
poor waltz theme hatched by his own conceited self. Franzl meekly
did as he was told. Beethoven, on the contrary, refused with scorn.
Then he chanced to take fire from what he called Diabelli's cobbler's
patch (*Schusterfleck*) and kept on writing variations on it until he
had amassed thirty-three, many of them magnificent. The work grew
into a miniature cosmos reflecting the whole gamut of human emotion. It was published in 1823 as Op. 120.[1]

All this excitement about variations may have moved Franzl to
write the set for four hands on a French song, Op. 10, which he dedicated and presented to Beethoven and which the great deaf man
often played with his nephew Karl. He also dedicated *The Wanderer*
to Johann Pyrker, the Patriarch of Venice, who replied on May 18,
1821, that he was proud to belong to the same fatherland as the composer, and in November followed these words with something more
tangible. "The Patriarch," Franzl reported to Spaun, "has stumped
up (*hat springen lassen*) 12 ducats, which gives me a very fine
feeling."

Since those early days in the Convict, the circle of young enthusiasts about the composer had grown and grown. Nothing short of
the magnetic genius of a Schubert could have drawn and kept together such disparate folk as the self-important and dictatorial Vogl,
Grillparzer the proud and moody, the charmingly Protean but madly
jealous Schwind, the gloomily Byronic Mayrhofer, and that Jack of
all talents, the dandified Schober. Their youthful exuberance and
love of the fine arts would not have been enough to unite them without a deep devotion to the central figure of the group and his music.

Here, one would have supposed, all the necessary ingredients for a
brilliant Schubertian success were assembled: a company of young,
vigorous, enthusiastic disciples, determined to secure the world fame

[1] Whitaker-Wilson incredibly calls this great composition "appalling"!

of a beloved master who united lofty genius with unparalleled industry. Yet their combined efforts were little more efficacious than those of a man trying to hurl a feather through a blanket. In a letter to Holbein, Josef Hüttenbrenner commented on this failure: "In the first place, a *true genius* must have time to obtain the forgiveness of his contemporaries for the tremendous boldness of daring to go his own way; and secondly, those mouthfuls are truly not always the worst which in the beginning do not seem to the world wholly palatable."

These reflections may have occurred to Josef after trying to interest publisher Peters in his friend's music. The man of business replied with some patronizing words about Schubert but excused himself for any lack of interest in the young musician because he had engaged himself to publish all that "the valued composers Spohr, Romberg, Hummel, etc.," sent him, even though he should gain nothing thereby.

First at Schober's, then at the wealthy Von Bruchmann's, later at Witteczek's, and two years before Schubert's death at Spaun's, the inseparable Circle met four evenings a week. On three of these, Schober and young Witteczek read good literature aloud. The *Nibelungenlied* aroused such enthusiasm that the names of its characters were bestowed upon those present. Moritz, for instance, became Giselhêr the Child. The faithful Kupelwieser was dubbed Rüdiger, while Franzl was appropriately named Volkêr after the mailed musician who poured the oil of beauty upon the troubled waters of strife. He rode fiddling in the van of the host. In the intervals of battle his music revived the weary warriors. He also fired them to new exploits with "a strong fiddle-bow, mighty and long, like to a sword, exceeding sharp and broad."

The fourth evening of every week was a so-called Schubertiad, with Volkêr reigning supreme. There his new compositions were first heard and criticized. And he was often beguiled into improvising German Dances, waltzes, and *Ländler* at the piano so that the friends might dance, while he, the nondancer, vicariously enjoyed their fun and stored up in memory the harmonies and melodies that spontaneously sprang to life beneath the stumpy fingers. My friend, the late E. V. Lucas, defined a good man as one who, though a nonsmoker, carries in his pocket excellent, unbroken cigars for his friends. I would describe him as a nondancer who plays that others may dance. But in this case, the recipients of the bounty were less admirable. To exhaust a Schubert by getting him to play dance music all night was little better than using a priceless gold flute as a bat or a Stradivarius violin as a tray for hot sausages.

Not content with entertaining the Schubertians in his home, the generous Schober, on several successive years, arranged outings for them at Schloss Atzenbrugg, twenty-three miles west-northwest of Vienna, where his uncle was steward. These adventures were called "feasts." To cover the incidental expenses, there was a system of forfeits. Anyone whose tongue slipped must pay into the treasury a "slip-of-the-tongue groat." The penalty was not overwhelming; for a a groat, or groschen, was worth three kreutzers, A.C., or about two and a half cents.

Several amusing pictures commemorating such expeditions have come down to us. A water color by Kupelwieser (Kuppel for short) shows a quaint vehicle under way, packed with pretty girls in white, with gentlemen clinging to the running boards and the luggage carrier. The latter are clad in the odd picnic costume of swallowtails and stovepipe hats, one of which has blown off and is being mashed under a wheel. Taking no such chances, Franzl strolls behind, deep in gesticulative talk with Kuppel.

Another water color by the same artist shows the joyous gang inside the *Schloss* doing a charade. Subject: the fall of Adam. Kuppel, who seems to have grown immensely tall since the last picture, makes an excellent Tree of Knowledge. That lady-killer of a Schober is, of course, the serpent. Jenger, an apprehensive Adam, receives the apple from a pert little Eve of unknown identity. Jeanette Cuny de Pierron is the Angel with the Flaming Sword (which looks curiously like a corn stalk). Mounted at the left on what seems anachronistically like a steam radiator, and grasping a long rake as Wotan grasps his spear, looms the tall figure of an unknown who must be representing the Gardener of the Garden of Eden. Seated at the piano, Franzl has the bored look of a fellow who feels that he was not made for this kind of horseplay. And the anachronistic dog behind him, in exactly the same pose, amusingly resembles the composer.

Another design, drawn by Schwind and Schober more in the spirit of caricature, reveals the crowd playing ball with violin and guitar accompaniment and otherwise disporting itself before the ugly *Schloss*, while Schubert, out of it again, languishes inert in the central foreground. Next to him is a high-hatted young guitarist whom

The Schubertians bound for a picnic at Atzenbrugg. Water color by Leopold Kupelwieser (1820).

1 2 3 4 5 6 7 8

The Schubertians do a charade, *The Fall of Adam*, in Schloss Atzenbrugg. Water color by Leopold Kupelwieser (1821). 1 Philipp Karl Hartmann, 2 Schubert, 3 Schober, 4 Leopold Kupelwieser, 5 Jenger, 6 Jeanette Cuny de Pierron, 7 Josef von Spaun 8 Dohlhoff

Professor Deutsch labels "Vogl." But it looks more as if the old singer were the man on the right with the cane, who is trying to make a left-handed catch. Behind the guitar sits Little Billee, for Landormy and Dahms are surely mistaken in supposing him to be the tall ruffian playing the fool with the fiddle.

In the fall Schober took Franzl on a visit to the charming little town of St. Pölten, not far southwest of Atzenbrugg, where a relative of his was bishop. At Schloss Ochsenburg[1] nearby, Franzl reveled in the soft, mellow beauty of the countryside with its gracious woods and meadows and trout streams—as typically Austrian as his own music. There he succumbed anew to his besetting temptation, opera. As fast as Schober scribbled the words of *Alfonso and Estrella*, Schubert scribbled the notes. On November 2, 1821, after their return to Vienna, the librettist wrote to the absent Spaun:

At Ochsenburg the really beautiful country kept us busy and at St. Pölten, balls and concerts. But despite all that, we were industrious, especially Schubert. He's done nearly two acts. I'm on the last. I only wish you could have been there to hear the birth of the glorious melodies.[2] It is wonderful how rich and luxuriant were the thoughts which he kept pouring out. In the evening we always reported to one another what we had done that day, then had beer brought, smoked our pipes and read, or Sofie and Nettl came over and we sang. There were a couple of Schubertiads at the Bishop's, and one at Baron Mink's. . . . All in all, I'm like a man who has gazed into the sun, and now sees everywhere he looks, the fatal black spot—so disturbing is your absence to me, wherever I am.

During the rest of 1821, Franzl did little but pursue the disastrous chimera of dramatic music. By the following February he had finished setting Schober's undramatic lines. Carl Maria von Weber had recently made such a success with *Der Freischütz* in Vienna as to divert popular enthusiasm for the moment from Rossini. He promised to do all he could to have *Alfonso and Estrella* produced in Germany. But Schubert's frank honesty destroyed that hope. When, in 1823, *Euryanthe* met with indifferent success, the younger composer told Weber and others his opinion of its faults. This so enraged the

---

[1] Hutchings confuses Castle Atzenbrugg with Castle Ochsenburg, and the fall visit to the latter with the July visit to the former. Schober had a relative in each place.

[2] A commentary on Schober's taste. The melodies of this pot-boiler are far from glorious.

unsportsmanlike German that he abandoned all idea of helping the Austrian. He is reported to have screamed: "Let the fool first learn something before he undertakes to judge me!" [1] Result: *Alfonso and Estrella* was given its first performance by Liszt at Weimar in 1854. One really solid satisfaction, however, awaited Franzl on his return from St. Pölten. The faithful Spaun, long saddened by the rupture between the Franz Schuberts, senior and junior, at last succeeded in convincing Father that his son was now a made man. Doubtless the naïve old schoolmaster was impressed far more than was warranted by the facts that Franzl's music had actually appeared in print and had received some favorable press notices, as well as by the dim meed of footlight illumination which his operas had enjoyed. Son Ferdinand added his persuasions. So Father Franz forgave the supposedly rising composer and took him to his leathery bosom. "How Austrian," observes Pitrou, "is this peace, concluded under the sign of music!"

The unfounded optimism about Franzl's future was shared by Anton Holzapfel, who had been a fellow student at the Convict. On February 22, 1822, he wrote to his classmate Albert Stadler: "They say that Schubert has made a noise in the world and they also say that he will arrive . . . His rather gruff nature is much to his advantage and will make of him a solid man and a ripe artist. He will be worthy of his art." Holzapfel seems to have been the only friend who found Franzl gruff.

In 1822 Schubert was temporarily estranged from Vogl. The cause is not known. It may have been because Franzl defended Schober, whom the stern old singer charged with sponging on the composer and leading him into a loose way of life. Now Schober was undoubtedly a gay dog. But it is hard to believe that he would have taken financial advantage of the friend whom he had so consistently supported and helped with such open-handed generosity. As this accusation runs counter to what we know of Schober, it may be that the temperamental and probably jealous old singer had either been misinformed, or was lying.

The failure of *Euryanthe* shifted the fickle Viennese fancy again toward Italian music. In 1822 the madness rose to a new height when Rossini arrived in person with a brilliant opera company. Anton

---

[1] There is no authority for the story that Weber went still further and, ignoring the fact that Schubert had already written much for the stage, cried, "First puppies and first operas should always be drowned!"

Schindler described the enthusiasm of the audiences, which grew crazier with each performance, until it seemed as though the screaming, huzzahing mob had been bitten by tarantulas. The Italian mode of the moment was all that appealed to the Viennese. Real music was at a disastrous discount. Very little was bought in the music shops but dances, the platitudes of people like Czerny, and piano scores of the Rossini operas. Beethoven fulminated against this state of affairs:

No one cares any more for the good, the powerful, in a word, for true music! Rossini and Co. are your heroes! Sometimes Schuppanzigh gets out a quartet of mine. You have no time for the symphonies, nor do you want *Fidelio*. Rossini, Rossini means more than everything else to you!

Since the Italians had elbowed the deaf giant out of the way, what chance had poor, unknown, and modestly unaggressive Schubert? One might naturally have expected from him a bitterness surpassing Beethoven's. But no, one of Schubert's most endearing traits was his fair-mindedness and utter lack of jealousy. True, he was fond of inveighing against the bad public taste and the sort of Italian music which he called "*Dudelei*," or "tootling." But no matter what its origin, or how much it countered his own interests, if there was anything good in a piece of music, he was going to enjoy and praise it. Though he could caricature the absurdities of Rossini's orchestral music in his two *Overtures in the Italian Style*, he could, as we have seen on p. 80, grow enthusiastic about the Swan of Pesaro. This is the acme of sportsmanship, to point out the handsome modeling of the foot that treads one into the dust.

And there was sportsmanship too on the Italian side. Delacroix, who knew Rossini well, noted in his *Journal* an admirable remark of the famous composer's: "If I should find a young man of genius, I could set him upon an absolutely new road; and then the poor Rossini would be quite extinguished (*éteint tout à fait*)."

It is interesting to speculate upon the result had Rossini found Schubert, recognized him as the genius whom he sought and, failing to see that the youngster's feet were already set upon a new road, sought to convert him to the advantages of his own thoroughfare. I think that Franz would probably have taken Gioacchino to his heart but would obstinately (and rightly) have refused to change roads.

His own operatic path, however, once more proved to be a *cul de*

20

SCHUBERT'S LOVE LIFE

HERE is an autobiographical document, a prose poem unique among the utterances of the reserved Schubert. He wrote it on July 3, 1822, and called it

MY DREAM

I was a brother among many brothers. Our parents were good folk. I was devoted to them with a deep love.— Father once took us to a banquet. There my brothers grew exceedingly merry. But I was sad. Then Father came and ordered me to enjoy the delicious food. But I could not. So he grew angry and banished me from his sight. I turned away and, with a heart full of boundless love for those who scorned it, I wandered far from there. For years I felt divided between the utmost grief and the greatest love. Then came tidings of my Mother's death. I hastened to see her; and Father, whose heart was softened by sorrow, did not prevent me. Then I beheld her corpse. Tears flowed from my eyes. I saw her lying there like the happy old past, in the spirit of which, according to the desire of the departed one, we were to live, as she herself had lived.

And in sorrow we followed her corpse, and the coffin sank into the earth.— From that day on I lived again at home. Then once more Father led me to his favorite garden. He asked me if I liked it. But I hated the garden and dared not say so. Then, flushing, he asked me for the second time if I liked the garden. Trembling I said no. Then Father struck me and I fled. And for the second time I turned my steps and, with a heart full of boundless love for those who scorned it, again I wandered far away. For long, long years I sang songs. When I would sing of love, it turned to pain. And again, when I would sing of pain, it turned to love.

Thus love and pain divided me.

And once I had word of a saintly maiden who had just died. And a circle was formed about her grave wherein many youths and old men forever paced as though in bliss. Softly they murmured, so as not to arouse the maiden.

From her tombstone heavenly thoughts, like delicate sparks whose sound was scarcely audible, seemed forever to be showered upon the youths. Sorely I longed to walk there too. But they said: nothing short of a miracle can bring you into this circle. However, with slow steps and lowered gaze I approached the tombstone and, before I was aware, I found myself in the circle, which gave forth a sound of wondrous loveliness; and I felt as though eternal bliss were being pressed into a single moment. Father too I beheld, reconciled and loving. He folded me in his arms and wept. But not as much as I.

FRANZ SCHUBERT.

This allegory is revealing. Here we recognize Franz's two periods of exile from home. The feast that Father recommended, of which the brothers partook, is a feast from Father's point of view—his own profession, which Franz loathed. Pitrou is right in feeling that these lines reveal "a secret wound destined to be a source of inspiration for his art."

A psychogram of Schubert by Dr. Edward Hitschmann, the Freudian psychoanalyst,[1] says of *My Dream* that whether it represented an imagined dream, or recorded an actual one, "this serious visionary narrative may rightly be regarded as an allegorical mirroring of his inner development."

According to Dr. Hitschmann, it means that Franz had a special kind of Oedipus complex: he adored his mother, while he simultaneously loved and hated his stern, domineering Caliban of a father. It is significant that among the boy Franzl's earliest songs were *Corpse Fantasy, The Parricide,* and *Hagar's Lament,* in which the son, for whom the angel foretold a great future, is driven out with his mother by a cruel father to famish in the wilderness.

This complex gave rise to a severe conflict in the unconscious, which stimulated Franz's creativeness. "The reactions against the instinctual demands of the Oedipus complex," wrote Freud, "are the source of the most precious and socially important achievements of the human mind." [2]

Dr. Hitschmann holds that, in consequence of this complex, the "eternal, inexplicable yearning" of which Franz complained in a

[1] In *Internationalen Zeitschrift für ärztliche Psychoanalyse,* Vol. III. The whole argument is too long for reproduction here. To this writer, at least, it sounds convincing.

[2] *Encyclopaedia Britannica,* 13th ed., Supplementary Vol. III, p. 254. In describing Stendhal's Oedipus complex, his biographer Matthew Josephson writes: "The ordeal of alienation and conflict in childhood made him refreshingly different from less passionate and more docile beings. It made him Stendhal." (*Stendhal,* New York, Doubleday & Company, Inc., 1946, p. 29.)

letter to Ferdinand of July 18, 1824 (see p. 130), was caused by his inability to feel passion and ideal love for the same woman. Though it fed the springs of his creativeness, this wretched condition may have made him describe himself to Kupelwieser early in the same year as "the most unfortunate, the most miserable person on earth." (See p. 128.) As in the later case of Brahms, it must have forced his sex life down to a distressingly low and sordid level, for more than one friend testified to his great sensuality. Freud wrote of such men: "Where they love they feel no passion, and where they feel passion they cannot love."

Schubert's plight was so terrible that nothing, not even the affection of and for his intimate companions, could make up the loss. Dear as the Circle was to him, Anita Silvestrelli's statement that his friendships repaid him a thousandfold for the lack of happy love, domesticity, and international renown is a tremendous exaggeration.

His realization of this deplorable handicap would explain the apparent contradiction between the love for Therese Grob which he confessed to Anselm Hüttenbrenner (see p. 28), and an entry in his diary for 1816: "For a free man, these days, marriage is a fear-inspiring thought. He identifies it with either sadness or gross lust." [1] That is to say: Marriage on a purely spiritual plane is as sadly incomplete as marriage on a purely physical plane. For Franz to marry either Therese or Countess Caroline (even had such a thing been possible) would have been as fatal a mistake as to marry Pepi Pöckelhofer, the pretty chambermaid of Zseliz, who had an affair with him in 1818, and later married a valet. In the role of husband he would have been an even more complete failure than he had been as a schoolteacher. If it is true that he was fond of the young countess, the realization of his handicap must have helped enormously to alleviate a difficult situation. The fact that she was a case of arrested development may also have acted as a brake upon his feelings. According to Professor Deutsch, "Countess Caroline remained so much of a child that her mother sent her to play with her hoop when she was thirty." At thirty-nine she took a husband, but the marriage was soon annulled.

In his old age, Schober hinted that Schubert had been deeply in love with a third woman, but he never disclosed her name.

The existence of this tragic parallelism, which kept Franz's tender-

---

[1] When asked whether he would not like to marry, Brahms cried in honest terror, "No indeed! Why, I'd run away from her the third day!" See Schauffler, *The Unknown Brahms,* New York, Dodd, Mead & Company, Inc., 1933, p. 280.

ness and his passion—his sacred and profane loves—from ever meeting and coalescing, would seem to be confirmed by what sounds like an intentionally veiled utterance of Bauernfeld's. He wrote that the life of

Schubert, who was rather realistic about some matters, did not pass without a certain amount of enthusiastic sentimentality (*Schwärmerei*). In our friend's case, an ideal love fortunately intervened to reconcile and effect a compromise; and one may look upon Countess Caroline as his visible, beneficent Muse, as the Leonora of this Tasso.

This reference to realistic matters might be taken to mean the sort of purely physical sex adventures to which Brahms was limited.[1] And the "*Schwärmerei*" might mean his sexless tenderness for a type of woman more congenial to him on the mental and spiritual planes. The realization of his peculiar disability would help to explain why, as Hüttenbrenner testified, "he was always a dry customer toward the fair sex, not in the least gallant." He neglected his clothes and his teeth, smelled strongly of tobacco, wore very thick spectacles, was fat, did not bathe too often, and his few inches were against him, for the size of the stronger sex often influences the sighs of the weaker. In a word, physically he was something of a figure of fun and anything but a ladies' man.

I am indebted to my friend Felix O. Derrick for the original manuscript of a prose poem by that typical Viennese man of letters, Peter Altenberg, who set Schubert above all other earthly considerations and sometimes wept over his idol's lack of success with women. It runs as follows:

WIENER BALLADE:
FRANZ SCHUBERT.

Wann man fett-rundlich ist,
und wann man kurzbeinig ist,
wann man kurzhalsig ist,
und wann man kurzathmig ist,
wann man an dicken Krauskopf hat,
und wann man kurze fette Pratzen hat,
dann nutzen Einem bei den süssen süssen süssen Mäderln
nicht "Der Erlkönig," "Die Forelle," "Die Post," "Du bist die Ruh'," "Der
Wanderer"!

[1] See my *Brahms*, p. 252ff.

Und nicht "Am Meer"!
Mit fetten Lerchen geht man nicht gern schlafen!
Armes Armes Franzerl!

PETER ALTENBERG

(VIENNESE BALLAD:
FRANZ SCHUBERT.

When one is chubbily fat,
and when one is short-legged,
when one is short of neck
and is short of breath,
and has a thick, curly head,
and has short, fat paws;
then neither "The Erl King," "The Trout," "The Post," *"Du bist die Ruh',"*
    "The Wanderer"!
Nor "By the Sea"!
help one's cause with the sweet, sweet, sweet little girls.
One doesn't care to *have larks* with *fat larks!*
    Poor, Poor Franzerl!)

None the less, such women as Therese and Caroline may have inspired much of Schubert's work through the same sort of ideal sentiment that Brahms had for so many decent women, without seriously wanting either to marry them or make love to them.

Dr. Hitschmann suggests that the love portion of Schubert's mixture of love and hatred for his father found satisfaction in fondness for such stern father substitutes as Mayrhofer and Vogl, men respectively ten and nineteen years older, and by whom he often willingly let himself be dominated.

Three pictures that suggest Schubert's attitude toward women in general have come down to us. In Schwind's design "Stroll Before the Town Gate" (see opposite page), Franzl, with his stovepipe rammed firmly upon his head, stares stonily past two girls, in contrast to Schober, the lady-killer, who is gallantly uncovering.

The title page of a collection of *Modern Love-Waltzes,* published by a firm of Schubert's leeches, Sauer and Leidesdorf, is decorated with a caricature of the composer ignoring a girl who is languishing upon his chest. This time he has actually removed his hat but merely to hold it out expectantly toward a periwigged father who sits at a table counting out his money. Franzl's gesture looks as though he

The Schubertians play ball at Atzenbrugg. Colored etching by Mohn, Schwind, and Schober.

Stroll before the town gate. Part of a lithograph by Schwind. The tallest man in the central group is Vogl; the shortest is Schubert, with Schober behind him and Schwind holding a sketchbook in the foreground.

The manuscript of *The Trout*, with the famous blot

meant to have the hat filled with thalers.[1] A handkerchief hanging from a trouser pocket suggests his indifference to the arts of sartorial seduction. The caption below this caricature declares:

> *Gar leicht sind Herz und Hand vermählt*
> *Wenn Väterchen die Thaler zählt.*
>
> (How easily heart and hand conjoin
> When little Pa pays out the coin!)

Schwind's title vignette for the same publisher's score of Rossini's *Marriage by Bill of Exchange* recalls the motive of his "Town Gate." Again he shows Franzl gazing fixedly past a girl. Presumably he is looking for a bill of exchange, while she waits solitary on a sofa and Schober peers concernedly in at the door.

All these pictorial suggestions of Schubert's indifference to respectable ladies can scarcely be accidents, but imply that his coldness to them was a standing joke in the Circle, and that this coldness was insincerely and burschikosely attributed to his greedy, calculating desire to make a rich marriage. The nub of the joke, of course, was that everyone knew such a sordid union to be the last thing in the world that Franzl would ever dream of.

It is natural for a man who realizes that he could never make a happy marriage to be somewhat jealous of his friends' greater success with women and to try to conceal his jealousy under a smiling mask. Thus we have found Franzl writing to Anselm Hüttenbrenner on May 19, 1819: "You're a rogue; that's flat!!! . . . Now this girl, now that, sticks in your head. Ah, if you let the girls bewitch you like this, to the devil with the lot of them! Marry, in God's name, and make an end of the business."

Again, on September 18 (or 19), 1825, he reproaches his friends for not joining him in Steyr: "But that is not to be expected of young chaps who, like you, are in love up to the limits of arson and murder. How often will you have been unhappy again, and drowned your sighs and complaints in beer and punch? ha! ha! ha! ha."

Apart from the slight abnormality of not being able to make the

---

[1] Consider in this connection Schubert's amusing, uncharacteristic setting of Metastasio's verses about marrying money: *Il modo di prender moglie* (*The Method of Getting a Wife*), Op. 83, No. 3. And note that the German version, which is so free as to be scarcely a translation, is much less gallant to the girls than the original Italian.

parallel streams of his tenderness and his passion meet, we do not know whether the overt expression of Schubert's sexuality was ever abnormal. About this no more information is available than on the question whether he suffered from a venereal disease. On both points conjecture is unprofitable. His bachelorhood, his love of male companionship, and his comparative indifference to ladies, with none of whom he could enjoy a completely satisfying relationship, can all be accounted for, without reference to more pathological causes, by the presence of an Oedipus complex.

The small activity in Schubert's love life, declares Dr. Hitschmann,

partly directed toward ideal, partly toward lower type women, may be explained by his unconscious fixation [on his mother]. According to his own words, his truly unique love was music. Pain and love—love for parents and brethren—exile and yearning: this complex was the Musagetes of his song. The Viennese girls were not the source of Schubert's creativeness. What drove him upward and apart into a distant land, into dreaming and yearning and invention, were the battles and pains deep within his own breast, strengthened by infantile emotions long sunken into the unconscious. Love and pain "divided" him; and so he became that "double nature which interwove and ennobled Viennese gaiety with a strain of profound melancholy." (Bauernfeld). He remained a dreamer, a man of small practical energy, who timidly recoiled from every activity but artistic creation.

Like all true artists, Schubert had one skin less than ordinary folk. It was the terrible combination of his complex and his sensitivity which made him confess to Kupelwieser in 1824 that the "joys of love" offered him "at the most nothing but torture." The words of the great song *By the Sea* might well be about a man and woman deeply in love but desperately aware that their tenderness could never find physical consummation. It may be that the ghastly poignancy of the music came from Schubert's realization that these lines struck too close home, because the tears of the unhappy woman whom he impotently loved, and who knew he was impotent for her, had "poisoned" him.

21

THE BAD YEAR

EIGHTEEN twenty-three was one of the most ill-starred years in Schubert's brief and luckless life. First of all, he promptly fell ill. Most of those who have written about him, including the accurate Schubert scholar, Professor Deutsch, who says that he probably suffered from syphilis, declare that he had a venereal disease. Many give dark hints about a dissolute way of life, and blame Schober for having led him astray.

In a monograph entitled *The Sick Schubert*,[1] Dr. Waldemar Schweisheimer, a Munich physician, has considered all the reports of Schubert's contemporaries about his health that have come down to us and concluded that the venereal character of his illness can neither be proved nor disproved. What is sure is that an eruption made his hair fall out so that he had to wear a wig until a fresh crop grew. Some time after this, he was troubled by high blood pressure, headaches, and attacks of giddiness.

It was not this illness but typhus that killed him, as it had killed his mother. His resistance, however, had been undermined by the disease of 1823, in conjunction with years of privation, undernourishment, sketchy lodgings, and discouragement, by lack of sleep, by the slow suicide of a too fertile and eager inspiration, and by the fact that the little alcohol he drank was too much for him. Mere bad health, of course, could not dam the creative flow, which in February produced the Piano Sonata in A Minor, Op. 143.

On top of illness came financial troubles and encounters with dishonest publishers. Of these firms, that of Cappi and Diabelli was the most outrageous. Through it, by 1823, the Sonnleithners had published Schubert's first fourteen opuses; and their sale had brought in two thousand gulden, of which the composer received half. Of this half, eight hundred had been made in the first year by *The Erl King* alone. Realizing that Schubert was not only a profitable investment

---

[1] In *Zeitschrift für Musikwissenschaft*, Leipzig, June-July, 1921, pp. 552-561.

but also a mere imbecile in money matters, Diabelli took advantage of a particularly weak moment to buy from him all rights in the fourteen opuses for eight hundred gulden. It was about as honorable as stealing the white cane of a blind beggar. If Franzl had known how to resist such infernally sharp practice, and co-operate in the Sonnleithners' plan, he would have had a steady, growing income, better food, and less worry. He would also have been in a position to dictate terms instead of humbly accepting whatever the thievish publishers offered. And he might have lived years longer to fulfill his tremendous promise.

Financially speaking, however, Schubert existed as much in the immediate moment as a child or a savage, and considerations of their victims' artistic futures were far indeed from the sordid minds of the Viennese publishers. The *"Wanderer"* Fantasy earned Diabelli and his successor 27,000 gulden. Of these Schubert received just 50, which constituted 1/540 of the publisher's winnings. Later on, as Lachner informed Grove, Haslinger bought six of the *Winter Journey* songs for no more than a florin, A.C., apiece! [1]

On Feb. 21, 1823, while convalescing from his illness, Franzl was foolish enough to offer Cappi and Diabelli three works outright for three hundred florins. This time he had a clearer insight into their tricks and their manners. On April tenth he wrote them a letter so denunciatory that, though helpless and hopeless as business correspondence, and utterly unfitted to accomplish its purpose, it fills every Schubert lover with satisfaction:

You Wellborn Ones
have really astonished me with your letter as, according to Mr. Cappi's own words, I supposed the account entirely settled. Since, from the way they acted when publishing my waltzes, I perceived that my publishers' intentions were none too honorable, I could explain this second action of theirs. Consequently, Sirs, you can naturally comprehend why I have entered into lasting relations with another publisher. Moreover, I cannot very well understand your charging me 150 florins, Vienna currency, when, according to your statement, it cost only 100 florins, V.C., to copy my opera. Be that as it may, I believe that the exceedingly low prices you paid me for my former works, as well as that for the Fantasy, which was only 50 florins V.C., have long wiped out the debt which you now unjustly seek to saddle upon me.

[1] Professor Deutsch, on what grounds he does not state, finds this report "quite incredible."

However, as I very much doubt whether you will entertain any such too-human point of view, I politely draw your attention to my just claim for twenty copies of the last, and twelve of the earlier volumes, and to the even stronger claim for the 50 florins which you so craftily knew how to get out of me. Kindly reckon this all up. You will find that my demand is not only greater but more just than yours; though I should never have mentioned it if you had not so disagreeably reminded me of it. Since the debt, as you will kindly recognize, has thus long ago been cleared up, there can be absolutely no question of my letting you publish songs which once again you could not sufficiently undervalue, while at present I receive 200 florins V.C., for a volume, and Herr v. Steiner has repeatedly offered to publish my works. Finally I must ask you kindly to return all manuscripts of my engraved, as well as of my unengraved, works.

With regards
Frz. Schubert
Composer.

N.B. I beg for an exact account of the copies sent me since our first sales settlement, as I find that my statement far exceeds yours.

One groans at the transparency of the bluff about receiving two hundred florins a volume, and at the helpless inefficacy of the whole letter. Its inconsequent logic was doubtless impaired by the fury of a good-natured man who was seldom—but then thoroughly—roused. This fury might never have flared up under the provocation of financial dishonesty alone. But it had, in the first place, been kindled by Diabelli's highhanded procedure in actually tampering with the compositions themselves. The rogue was philistine enough to graft unauthorized interludes into the songs, and to invent fancy names for instrumental pieces, such as *Trauer-Walzer* (*Mourning Waltz*) for Op. 9, No. 2. When Schubert was told of this he burst out, "What kind of donkey ever wrote a mourning waltz?!"[1]

However, this spring Franzl, too miserable for the moment to realize that *Martergang* did not rhyme with *Untergang*, wrote a mourning poem, or rather, doggerel, which he called *Mein Gebet* (*My Prayer*), and which ends with these lugubrious lines:

> *Sieh, vernichtet liegt im Staube,*
> *Unerhörtem Gram zum Raube,*
> *Meines Lebens Martergang*
> *Nahend ew'gem Untergang.*

[1] One wonders if Sibelius, who wrote a real *Valse Triste*, ever heard of this remark.

Tödt' es und mich selber tödte,
Stürz nun Alles in die Lethe,
Und ein reines kräft'ges Sein
Lass' o Grosser, dann gedeih'n.

The translation seeks to echo the faults of the original and the stronger quality of the ending:

(Wrecked in the dust, it lies there low,
The prey of unexampled woe,—
The agony of my existence,
Nearing eternal non-existence.

Lord, hurl it and me to slaughter,
Drown us in Lethe's gloomy water,
And in our stead create ere long
New life, immaculate and strong.)

Despite all his handicaps, annoyances, and griefs, however, Schubert's lot was more enviable than most men's. He carried his own good time around with him. In five minutes he could get more happiness from the music eternally sounding within than most men can find in fishing, hunting, making love, drinking, or playing games all day. Then, too, he had at hand a perfect method for getting rid of negative emotions. One of the best American poets of the last generation, remarking that many of her poems were sad, told me, "That is the reason why I myself am such a cheerful person: I work off all my sadness in my verse." How much more cheerful *The Winter Journey* must have left Franzl! The composer's grandniece, Carola Geisler-Schubert, testified: "Franz Schubert was one of the happiest mortals that ever lived." And she continued:

People should be encouraged to picture his dear, good merry face, instead of the gloomy pining features depicted by plaintive historians. This sentimental, unmanly whining tone, so foreign to Schubert's brave cheerful spirit, must be emphatically contradicted. The fable of the joylessness of his life can be met by . . . the words of . . . Bauernfeld: "The joyousness of heart with which God endowed him at his birth."

The first formal recognition of this young prophet's greatness came, not from his own Vienna, but from the provinces. All honor to the Musical Association of Styria which, in April, 1823, sent this encouraging word from Graz:

The services that you have already rendered the art of music are too widely known to be ignored by the directors of the Styrian Musical Association. As it now wishes to give you a proof of its appreciation, it has elected you a nonresident honorary member of the Styrian Musical Association.

In November, the Friends of Music in Linz followed suit.

One can scarcely blame Schubert for his obstinacy in wooing the theater and never taking no for an answer. In that postwar period of blunted taste, a successful opera was an unknown composer's one chance of making any considerable amount of money. But every time fortune seemed to smile upon Schubert from the footlights, it promptly thumbed its nose at him. Of all Franzl's unlucky loves, the theater was the unluckiest.

Most of 1823 was devoted to a convulsive attempt to capture the stage, for which he wrote three works: *The Conspirators*,[1] a grand opera, *Fierabras*,[2] and incidental numbers for the romantic drama *Rosamunde, Princess of Cyprus*. It is significant that the best of the *Rosamunde* numbers are all absolute music: the Overture (originally written as one of two preludes for *Die Zauberharfe*), the famous second Entr'acte,[3] and the almost equally famous Ballet Music No. 1, in G. These works did nothing for him and were soon buried.

He sent *The Domestic War* to the Court Theater, which kept the package a year and returned it unopened. *Fierabras* was commissioned by Theater Director Barbaja. Schubert actually wrote the thousand-odd pages of manuscript in a little over four months, only to have the work thrown back at him. "Thus," he sadly informed Leopold Kupelwieser, "I've again composed two operas all for nothing."

Rosamunde is a silly play by Wilhelmine von Chezy, whose bad libretto of Weber's *Euryanthe* was largely responsible for that

---

[1] Metternich's censors were shocked at such a subversive title, and hastily changed it to *The Domestic War*.

[2] A Spaniard would wince at the misspelling of this word, just as a Frenchman would at Franzl's spelling of "*Moments musicals*," or at Schumann's of "*Carnaval*."

[3] That favorite melody which he was to use again as the *Andante* of the A Minor Quartet, and for the third *Impromptu*, Op. 142, No. 3.

opera's failure.[1] Schubert's incidental music was dashed upon paper in five days, and survived for only two performances. About the *première* Schwind wrote to Schober:

Vienna, Dec. 22, 1823.

Day before yesterday, in the Theater an der Wien, a play by the disastrous Frau von Chezy was put on: *Rosamunde of Cyprus,* with music by Schubert. You may well imagine how we all attended! As I had a cough which kept me in the whole day, I couldn't arrange to go with the others, so sat alone in the gallery, while they were in the pit . . . [The overture] was unanimously applauded and, to my great joy, was repeated . . . A ballet and the second and third entr'acte passed unnoticed. The fact is, people are used to talking as soon as an act is over, and I don't understand how one can expect them to attend to such serious and praiseworthy things. In the last act there came a chorus of shepherds and huntsmen, so beautiful and natural that I don't recall hearing the like. It was encored, and I believe it will give the chorus in Weber's *Euryanthe* the *coup de grace.* An aria, though horribly sung by Madame Vogel, and a short pastorale were applauded. A subterranean chorus was inaudible and the gesticulations of Herr Rott, who was brewing poison at the same time, did not permit it to come into existence.

Note that, in its noisy frivolity, the Viennese public ignored the best parts of the score.

After this failure, the dust-gathering music lay forgotten for forty-five years awaiting resurrection and life. In 1868 the gifted musicologist George Grove and the composer Arthur Sullivan, neither of whom was to be knighted until fifteen years later, were so stirred by the discovery of the *"Unfinished"* Symphony, that they embarked on what must remain for music lovers one of the most thrilling and delightful of all treasure hunts.

In the hope of unearthing other lost Schubert manuscripts, they rushed from London to Vienna. Spina, the successor of Diabelli, gave them large cigars, a cordial welcome, and turned them over to a Dr. Schneider, who loaded them down with huge parcels of dusty mss., the nature of which he himself did not know. Before long they had in their hands what they had long but vainly sought: the ms. scores of the Schubert Symphonies Numbers 1, 2, 3, 4, and 6. But even these did not satisfy a crusading zeal that was roused to an indignant heat by the coldness of most mid-European musicians toward their great

---

[1] In revenge, Weber referred to her in the neuter gender as *"das Chezy."*

genius. They burned to find, among other treasures, the complete score of *Rosamunde*.

In his *Life of Sir George*, Graves[1] quotes a letter of Grove's to Miss Olga von Glehn, telling how the good companions called on Spina at his house:

Half an hour is spent in mutual compliments, hand shaking, lighting cigars, &c. Then Spina produces a pile of music about as big as a portmanteau and says: "Here is all I have that you wish to see. You shall go into my room with it and do what you like." More compliments, more hand shaking . . .

First we spend an hour in incoherent raptures, then we get more reasonable and part it all into lots and begin to go through it thoroughly. Then we take the things into the other room, and Arthur plays, and we decide to have or not to have. After settling about the instrumental things we open a bundle of about 60 songs, 40 of which at least have never been printed. Some of them turn out *charming*, equal to anything of Schubert's or any one else's, so they have to be played over and over again. Meantime I have got awfully cold . . . and it is some exertion to be cheerful when Spina pops in . . . to talk and purr and press on us endless cigars as big as sausages!

We made a final call on Dr. Schneider,[2] . . . as I now firmly believe, guided by a special instinct. The doctor was civility itself; he again had recourse to the cupboard, and showed us some treasures that had escaped us before. I again turned the conversation to the *Rosamunde* music; he believed that he had at one time possessed a copy or a sketch of it all. Might I go into the cupboard and look for myself? Certainly, if I had no objection to being smothered with dust. In I went; and after some search, during which my companion kept the doctor engaged in conversation, I found, at the bottom of the cupboard, and in its furthest corner, a bundle of music-books two feet high, carefully tied round, and black with the undisturbed dust of nearly half a century. It was like the famous scene at the monastery of Souriani on the Natron lakes, so well described by Mr. Curzon;—" 'Here is a box!' exclaimed the two monks, who were nearly choked with the dust; 'we have found a box, and a heavy one too.' 'A box!' shouted the blind abbot, who was standing in the outer darkness of the oil-cellar—'a box! where is it?' 'Bring it out! bring out the box!' 'Heaven be praised! we have found a treasure! Lift up the box! Pull out the box!' shouted the monks in various tones of voice." We were hardly

[1] C. L. Graves, *Life of Sir George Grove*, London, Macmillan & Co., Ltd., 1903.
[2] Writes Grove, in the Appendix to the English translation of Kreissle..

less vociferous than the monks, when we had dragged out the bundle into the light, and found that it was actually neither more nor less than what we were in search of . . . For these were the part-books of the whole of the music in *Rosamunde*, tied up after the second performance, in December, 1823, and probably never disturbed since. Dr. Schneider must have been amused at our excitement; but let us hope that he recollected his own days of rapture; at any rate he kindly overlooked it, and gave us permission to take away with us and copy what we wanted.

Feverishly the friends copied music and stage directions until two in the morning. Then, to work off their exuberant exultation, while bringing terror to less enthusiastic folk on the floor below, these two middle-aged boys of Englishmen played leapfrog. Never was gusto more zestful than Grove's, especially when Schubert was in question.

So now poor Franzl had composed three dramatic works in a row, all for nothing, and the grueling experience went far toward dampening his stage ardor. For this, music lovers may well be thankful.

Other chagrins multiplied. Kupelwieser went to live in Rome. Schober, Franzl's other self, came into money through the death of an uncle and, deaf to the expostulations of his horrified relatives, planned to leave for Breslau to embrace the romantic vocation of strolling player, à la Wilhelm Meister. So, in the fall of 1823, Franzl had to move from Schober's home. His new environment was not congenial. Until the following spring he roomed at what is now Stubentorbastei 14 with tall Josef Huber, a notorious bore. As if these misfortunes were not enough, his illness returned.

For solace he had made another summer excursion into the laughing Danubian countryside with the magnificent Vogl. The trip was financed from the fatal eight hundred florins for which he had sold his future to the scoundrel Diabelli. From Steyr, on August 14, 1823, he wrote:

DEAR SCHOBER:
. . . I am fairly well, but doubt if I shall ever completely recover. Here I live very simply in every respect, go walking industriously, compose much . . . and read Walter Scott.

With Vogl I get along right well . . . Again I wish you all kinds of luck in your undertaking and assure you of my everlasting love, which will most painfully miss you.

In this bad year, it may have been as medicine for his troubled heart and tortured body that he wrote one of his most serene and reassuring songs, *Du bist die Ruh'*, and the famous *Mill* series. One afternoon, in the midst of his preoccupations with opera, he called on his old friend Randhartinger, the musician who, as a boy in the Convict, claimed to have sung *The Erl King* with the ink still wet on the manuscript.

Randhartinger was called out of the room, and Franzl picked up a book. It was a verse cycle, *The Miller's Beautiful Daughter: Poems from the Papers Left by a French-hornist,* by a man with the appropriate name of Wilhelm Müller. The first lines he read kindled Franzl's musical imagination. Without waiting for his friend's return, he pocketed the volume and rushed home.

The next morning Randhartinger missed his property and went in search of it. Franzl looked up with a shamefaced smile: "Forgive me, you! Yesterday I slipped this little book into my pocket. It pleased me. Look! I'm setting the things to music."

He slapped some notes upon the piano and, in his small composer's voice, began *Das Wandern,* the piece destined to be beloved and bellowed by millions of wanderers under the impression that it is a folk song of unknown origin. "How do you like it? I've already written two more of them."

Of Müller's twenty-five poems Schubert set twenty, little dreaming that, long after his death, this was to become one of the most famous and beloved of song cycles. Some of the numbers were composed in hospital that fall after his return to Vienna, when his illness suddenly grew much worse.

Before starting upon his romantic wanderings, Schober had become engaged to Justina, the sister of Johann von Bruchmann, at whose house many Schubertiads were held. But Justina did not like her lover to be an actor, especially an unsuccessful one, as he turned out to be, so she jilted him. This brought about some friction between the Bruchmanns and the other Schubertians. Franzl himself had another cause for dissatisfaction with that house. He held, and with reason, that to a man of cultivation there is nothing more boring than horse-and-dog talk.

Vienna, Nov. 30, 1823.

Dear Schober!

   . . . As I foresaw, our Circle has lost its central point in you. Since Bruchmann came back from his journey, he has no longer been the same person . . . At his place, if he is absent or ill, one hears for hours at a time . . . nothing but unintermittent chatter about riding and fencing, horses and dogs. If it keeps on like this, I probably will not be able to hold out among them much longer . . .

   How are you? Have you already appeared before the eyes of the world? I beg you to write me very soon how you thrive and strive, . . . and somewhat to still this longing of mine for you . . .

   I hope to get back my health, and this will allow me to forget much suffering. Only you, dear Schober, you I shall never forget, for, alas, nobody else can ever be to me what you have been.

   And now farewell, and do not forget

Your eternally loving
Friend
Franz Schubert

December 9, 1823, Johanna Lutz wrote to her fiancé Leopold Kupelwieser:

Schubert is right well and already shows a renewed inclination to break his strict regime before long. If only he does not destroy himself! Oh, everything would be all right again, if only you were here.

On the day after Christmas, Schwind wrote Schober:

Schubert is better. It will not be long now before he goes about in his own locks . . . He wears a very jolly wig.

22

ANOTHER HUNGARIAN ADVENTURE

JOHANNA LUTZ'S fears were well founded. Schubert broke training and his health went down again. However, toward the close of February, 1824, Schwind reported to Schober that Franzl had laid aside his wig and showed "nice little snail-like spiral harbingers of a fresh crop of hair." As March came in, the composer was persuaded to try a new regimen: the simple life and many baths. And on the sixth, Little Billee sent the same friend more encouraging news.

Schubert is already right well. After a few days of the treatment, he says, he could feel that the sickness had been broken and that everything was different. He still lives on panada one day, and on a cutlet the next, and is superhumanly industrious. A new quartet of his will be performed on Sunday at Zupanzik's.[1] The latter is all enthusiasm; and they say he has rehearsed it with special industry. Schubert is now writing with the utmost zeal at an octet.

The Quartet's debut was postponed from the seventh to the fourteenth of March. After that memorable *première*, Schwind continued to the same correspondent:

The Quartet of Schubert was, in his opinion, played rather slowly, but delicately and with very pure intonation. On the whole it is extremely tender, but of the kind whose melody remains with one like the melody of songs, all feeling and entirely expressed. It received much applause, especially the minuet, which is extraordinarily tender and natural. A fool next to me found it affected and styleless. I'd just like to see Schubert affected!

[1] He means fat Ignaz Schuppanzigh, the leader of Count Rasoumowski's famous chamber organization, who played many of his friend Beethoven's quartets from the fresh manuscript. In this letter it is touching to come so suddenly and simply upon the first mention of two of the most charming and haunting works in all music: Schubert's A Minor Quartet, and Octet.

Although the composer's health had not justified Moritz's optimistic report, he had, on the first of March, finished a work radiant with sunny vitality, humor, and infectious exuberance. The Octet, Op. 166, for string quintet, clarinet, horn, and bassoon, had been commissioned by the ardent amateur clarinetist Count Ferdinand von Troyer and was first performed in private at his home, with the host delightedly playing the succulent part with which Schubert had blessed his instrument. Milord Falstaff (as Beethoven nicknamed Schuppanzigh) was first violinist. Three years later, in one of his subscription concerts, Milord gave the delicious suite its public *première*. Then, for a third of a century, the rare flower blushed unseen until rediscovered by Hellmesberger.

With the same modesty which bade brother Ferdinand ignore his first fifteen string quartets as "experiments," Franzl said of writing the Octet and the Quartets in A Minor, E Flat, and E: "On the whole, in this way I want to lay down a road to the great symphony." Which is a remarkable utterance for a man who had already composed the *"Unfinished,"* but it was justified, for in four years that road led to the great Symphony in C Major.

The year 1824 started dismally enough, with Spaun, Schober, and Kuppel [1] far away. Finances were low, and Franzl could not collect his just dues. Strolling one day with Randhartinger past the office of one of his publishers, he remarked: "If they would only pay me a small part of what is due me! I've often gone to them for my honorarium, but each time they declare that their expenses just then happen to be so enormous, and there's so little sale for my compositions."

His last failures as a musical dramatist weighed heavily on his mind, and to his diary, neglected for the past eight years, he confided:

Nobody understands another's joys and sorrows! One always believes that he is going out to the other; but always goes merely beside him. Oh torture for the one who realizes this!

My creations have been produced by my understanding of music and by my sorrow. Those that sorrow alone has fathered seem to please the world least of all.

This second entry was, of course, inspired by the extravagance of some passing mood. For, if he had stopped to think, he would have

[1] Leopold Kupelwieser's nickname.

recognized that none of his works had been produced without his understanding of music, and that most of them had been fathered, not by sorrow, but by the happiness of a naturally optimistic and exuberant temperament. Richard Wagner came nearer the truth when he wrote, "We should make a serious mistake if we thought the artist could ever conceive except in a state of profound cheerfulness of soul."

Another notation shows Franzl as one of the most modest of all great geniuses: "From the deepest depths of my heart I hate that one-sidedness which makes so many pitiable folk feel that everything they do is the best, and that all else is nothing."

The first thing that happened in 1824 to the Circle was at a New Year's Eve gathering in Mohn's home. Shortly after midnight, Franzl, who had been vainly sought, heralded his approach by hurling a stone through the closed window, which caused no slight uproar. This sort of prank seemed to afford the composer a mysterious thrill. He had an adolescent appetite for breaking glass. When he had had a drink too much, he would amuse himself by smashing all the tumblers on the table. The following autumn he drove back from Zseliz to Vienna with Baron Schönstein, who wrote Count Esterházy: "Schubert broke the rear window of the carriage, which gave the most terrible of cold winds free play about our ears."

On the second of February, Little Billee informed Schober that the Circle had held high festival at the Crown. All hands were very drunk and all were more or less stupid, except the composer, who slept. "Schubert is now fasting and staying at home for a fortnight. He looks much better and is in very high spirits. He is ludicrously hungry, and writes innumerable quartets and German Dances and variations."

Between February 17 and August 12, 1824, the four volumes of *The Miller's Beautiful Daughter* appeared but made little headway with the Rossini-mad public. Schober, boiling with indignation, wrote the disappointed composer:

The dogs have no feelings or thoughts of their own, and succumb blindly to noise and the opinions of others. If only you could equip yourself with a couple of noise-drums of reviewers, who always wrote of you, world without end, in all the papers, your cause would flourish. I know

quite insignificant people who have in this way become famous and beloved. Why shouldn't a man who most richly deserves such rewards use
methods like these?

Apparently the press agent had already been invented.

One should not, however, be too hard on poor, distracted Vienna
for neglecting geniuses like Schubert and Schwind and Beethoven,
to run after cheap Italian opera. War, the exactions of an onerous
officialdom, and the perilous fluctuations of money values had driven
the Viennese to desperation, and desperate people can not be expected to appreciate any art for much more than its escape value.

Toward the end of March, 1824, Franzl's health took another turn
for the worse. This, combined with the last opera fiascos, with money
troubles, and the absence of his dearest friends, brought his volatile
temperament—although for only a happily unique moment, to the
verge of despair. On March thirty-first he wrote to Kuppel and
'poured his soul quite out':

> I feel that I am the most unfortunate, the most miserable person on
> earth. Figure to yourself a man whose health can never come right, and
> who in sheer despair makes it worse instead of better. Figure to yourself,
> I say, a man whose most brilliant hopes have fallen away to nothing, to
> whom the joys of love and friendship offer at the most nothing but torture,
> from whom enthusiasm for beauty (at least the sort that inspires one)
> threatens to flee, and ask yourself if that is not a pitiable, unhappy person.
>
> *Meine Ruh' ist hin, mein Herz ist schwer,*
> *Ich finde sie nimmer und nimmermehr.*
>
> (My peace is gone, my heart is sore,
> Vanished forever and evermore.)

That is now the burden of my daily song; for every night when I go to
sleep I hope never to awake again, and every morning only renews the
woe of yesterday. Thus joylessly and friendlessly would I pass my days
if Schwind did not occasionally look in and bring me a gleam of those
sweet times that are gone.—

As you by now most likely know, our reading club has committed
suicide by reinforcing the coarse crew of ragtag and bobtail specialists
in beer drinking and sausage gobbling . . .

The latest in Vienna is that Beethoven is giving a concert in which he
will bring out his new symphony [the Ninth], 3 pieces from the new Mass

[the *Missa Solemnis*], and a new overture [*The Consecration of the House*].— Next year I am minded, God willing, to give a similar concert . . . I kiss you 1000 times . . .

Your

true friend
FRZ. SCHUBERT

Fare well!
right well!!

The couplet is from *Margaret at the Spinning Wheel.*

A small-beer chronicle of the spring of 1824 shows that in the middle of April Franzl had such pain in his left arm that he could not play the piano. By the middle of May he was "sick again." A fortnight later a friend reported that "he must already have gone away, as the windows of his apartment, which are always shut when he is there, are now quite open." From this one gathers that Franzl shared the general Central European mistrust of fresh air in the home. Late in June, the *Allgemeine musikalische Zeitung* of Leipzig, reviewing the songs Opp. 21-24, which include *Gruppe aus dem Tartarus*, scolded Schubert as if he were a schoolboy for what it called his "modulation mania." This attack was probably written by Fink, the pedant whom Schumann later polished off in his magazine.

Meanwhile the devil of penury had again driven Franzl, despite the galling humiliation, to eat with the servants at Zseliz. This would never have galled the menially minded peasant, Father Schubert. That he felt only pride at his son's association with the Esterházys, even on these dubious terms, is shown in his letter of late June, 1824: "We all rejoice heartily over your beautiful reception in the home of the Count." How Franzl must have snorted when he read that!

However, despite the loneliness and the humiliation of a quasi-menial status, the fresh air of Zseliz was good for him, and by the middle of summer his physical condition took a decided turn for the better.

A most welcome letter from his favorite brother Ferdinand was dated

Vienna, July 3, 1824.

DEAR BROTHER OF MY HEART!

. . . Sometimes your presence is vividly brought to me as I have now begun to play your quartets again, and at least once every week I hear some of your compositions from the [musical] clock at the Hungarian Crown. The first time this clock surprised me not a little when, during a midday meal, I unexpectedly heard it play some of your waltzes. At that moment I felt so strange; I didn't know what was up with me; the music didn't cheer me in the least. On the contrary, such an anxious pain, such a yearning shot through my soul. In the end, melancholy cast her veil over it, and involuntarily there rolled from my eyes—

Reticence forbade the actual mention of what rolled from his eyes. What *was* up with Ferdinand? Perhaps when he heard that forerunner of the juke box, it dawned on him for the first time what a great man his brother really was and how pathetically unfit to steer his way through a tough world. It should be borne in mind that this, the epoch of Jean Paul Richter, was one of the most copiously lachrymose periods in the world's history. Germany and Austria alone annually shed enough tears of sensibility to fill our Great Salt Lake.

A fortnight later Franzl replied:

It would be better if you stuck to other quartets than mine, as they have nothing to recommend them, except that perhaps they please you, who are pleased with anything of mine.[1]

After twitting Ferdy for crying more over the clock waltzes than over the quartets, he went on:

Was it merely the pain caused by my absence that drew from you those tears about which you did not trust yourself to write? Or, in thinking of my person, which is oppressed by eternal, inexplicable yearning, did you feel its sad veil spreading also over yourself? Or did you recall all the tears which you have already seen me weep? Be that as it may, at this moment I feel more clearly that you, or nobody, are my most intimate friend, bound to me by every fiber of my soul!— In case these lines should mislead you into believing that I am not well, or not in good spirits, I hasten to assure you of the contrary. Of course, that happy time is gone when everything seemed to be surrounded by a youthful aureole. Now is the time for the obnoxious recognition of a miserable reality which I seek, as far as possible, to beautify for myself by using my imagination (for which I thank God).[2] People believe that one can find happiness again

---

[1] Grove declared that Schubert was "one of the very few musicians who ever lived who did not behave as if he thought himself the greatest man in the world."

[2] So does every lover of his music.

in a place where he has once been happy; but the truth is that it can be found only within ourselves.[1] Led by the former belief, indeed, I had an unpleasant disillusionment and renewed an experience here which I had already had in Steyr. But now I am more able than I was then to find happiness within myself.

What were these unfortunate experiences? We do not know for certain. But, returning to Steyr in the summer of 1819, he may have been shocked to hear of the engagement of his boyhood's sweetheart, Therese Grob, to a baker. And, returning to Zseliz in 1824, he may have begun to feel a little tenderly toward Countess Caroline, only to have it made cruelly evident that the son of a poor schoolmaster should not make himself ridiculous with impossible aspirations.

All that we surely know is that, judged from their unprepossessing pictures, both girls would have needed superlative spiritual and mental qualities to attract such a sensitive man. Tradition says that when the seventeen-year-old Caroline playfully complained that Schubert had not dedicated any composition to her, he answered: "But why? For, as it is, *all* my works are dedicated to you." Perhaps he meant it. But then again, perhaps this was only a graceful Viennese way of humoring a girl pitiably young for her age and of side-stepping an embarrassing situation.

Be all this as it may, the letter shows clearly that Franzl cared less for life at Zseliz the second time than he had at first.

On August fourteenth, brother Ignaz wrote that he had joined a small musical society.

Only I must tell you that these musical evening parties may not entirely incorrectly be likened to a wagon that often tips over and that is sometimes hard to set in motion again without its capable leader.[2]

The latest is that a mad epidemic of suicide rages here, just as if folks knew positively that in the hereafter they could leap directly into heaven.

Which shows that Schubertian vividness of expression was not confined to the composer.

[1] It is remarkable to find such a profound bit of wisdom in a man who apparently knew so little of how to conduct his own life. In his time, the art of happiness was even less understood than it is today.

[2] A reference to Franzl. Eight years later young Clara Wieck, in writing to Robert Schumann, used much the same vehicular figure about the works of Schneider and Richard Wagner. See my *Florestan: the Life and Work of Robert Schumann*, New York, Henry Holt & Company, Inc., 1945, p. 55.

In August, Franzl wrote Moritz:

Thank God, I still keep well and would be quite contented if only I had you and Schober and Kupelwieser here. As it is, however, despite the attractions of the *star* that you know about, I sometimes feel a cursedly strong homesickness for Vienna. I trust I shall see you again about the end of September. I have written for four hands a long sonata and some variations.[1] The latter are particularly popular here; but as I do not entirely trust the taste of the Hungarians, I shall leave it for you and the Viennese to pass judgment upon them . . .

Good-by now. My greetings to everyone you can think of. And (I warn you) write me soon, *sonst soll Dich— — —*[which is equivalent to: otherwise may the devil fly away with you.]

In fertile spontaneity and ease of composition no other musician except Mozart has ever equaled Schubert. A striking instance of this occurred in September. One morning the senior Countess showed him Fouqué's poem *Gebet* and suggested that he set it for the family to sing. That evening, with her daughter Marie, Baron Schönstein, and the Count, she tried it through from score, with the composer at the piano. In another twenty-four hours the parts were all copied out.

September 21, 1824, Franzl wrote to Schober who was still in Breslau:

I hear that you are not happy . . . Although this saddens me uncommonly, I don't wonder at it in the least for, in our miserable world, this is the lot of almost every intelligent person. And, indeed, what use would we have for happiness, since unhappiness is the one stimulus remaining to us? If only we were together, you, Schwind, Kuppel, and I, I would make light of every mischance. But we are scattered, each in a different corner; and that is really my misfortune. I would like to cry out with Goethe: "Who will bring me back only an hour of that lovely time!" That time when we sat together in intimacy, and each with maternal shyness showed the other his art children, awaiting, not without some anxiety, the judgment that love and truth would deliver. That time when each filled the others with enthusiasm and thus all were inspired by a united striving toward beauty in its highest form. Now I sit here all alone in the depths of Hungary whither, alas!, I have been lured, without having a *single* person with whom I could exchange an intelligent word.

---

[1] The Sonata in C, Op. 140, known as the *"Grand Duo,"* and the Variations in A Flat *On an Original Theme,* Op. 35.

It would seem that the contempt breathing from these last lines is hardly to be reconciled with a Schubert in love with Countess Caroline. As one studies the portraits of the Esterházys, one is shocked by their drearily stupid looks and pities the young genius for having to associate, week after week, with those empty faces and take orders from them. After all, eating with the servants carried with it the signal advantage of escaping the boredom of the family table.

The epistle to Schober continues in a vein of increasing bitterness and disillusion: "Sometimes I endure very miserable days." He generalizes his indictment of the Count's establishment into a condemnation of the world and finally breaks into despairing verse which pillories the dead, uninteresting level of a senile humanity and of a time that, forgetting the glorious days when all the world was young, strives to prevent great accomplishment. The poem closes:

> Nur Dir, o heil'ge Kunst, ist's noch gegönnt
> Im Bild, die Zeit der Kraft u. That zu schildern,
> Um weniges den grossen Schmerz zu mildern,
> Der nimmer mit dem Schicksal sie versöhnt.

[Freely translated:]

> (Thou, holy Art, alone possessest power
> To paint the deeds, the vigor of that age,
> And the sharp agony somewhat to assuage
> That is our tragic fate in this dark hour.)

On October sixth, brother Ferdinand wrote him cheering news. While hunting rabbits near Hainsburg, he had met the leader of the church choir, who had invited him to the choral service the next Sunday.

When I asked him what Mass he would give, he replied: "A very beautiful one by a well-known and famous composer,—I can't just think of his name."— And now, what Mass was it?— I know that if you had been there with me you would have been very happy about it; for it was the B Flat Mass by— —you!

The third week in October, 1824, Franzl reached Vienna and went to live at home in the Rossau until early the following year. Despite the continued absence of dear friends, it was a joyous and satisfying return. On November eighth, Schwind informed Schober: "Schubert is here, well and heavenly light-minded, newly rejuvenated by rapture and pain and a gay life." Which certainly does not look as though he were pining for Countess Caroline.

In his delight at returning, Franzl even bridged the rift between himself and the Fröhlich sisters, whom for two years he had avoided. In a manuscript by Frau von Breuning,[1] Kathi Fröhlich is made to tell how that friendship was revived:

He used to visit us quite often. Then he cultivated somewhat loose companions—I do not mean bad people, but circles that tempted him to let himself go too much . . . For instance, an acquaintance of a family in the Landstrasse told us: "Yesterday we were obliged to carry Schubert from the room. He had had too much to drink . . ."

Schubert fell into debt. After that, for almost two years, he did not visit us. One day I met him on the street. He saluted me and I gave him a stern, reproachful and significant side glance. Very shyly he returned my look. I shall always remember how conscience stricken he seemed. He apologized for not having been to see us in such a great while. As in duty bound, I scolded him earnestly and let him know that his doings and his way of life were no credit to him. He gave me his promise to reform.

Not many days after this, I was sitting at my customary window when there came a knock. Our long-absent Schubert opened the door a bit, inserted his head, and inquired: "May I come in, Fräulein Kathi?"

"But since when," I returned, "has this house become so strange to you? Right well you know that to you it has always been open."

"Ja, ja," he replied, "but I am somewhat timid. That look you gave me in the street—I have not forgotten it."

In November Franzl wrote a charming sonata for piano and arpeggione. This freak instrument, a hybrid of 'cello and guitar,[2] with strings tuned in fourths, had been contrived the year before by Stauffer of Vienna. Since Franzl invested such attractive melodies in this queer contraption, he must have believed in its future, just as, a generation after, Schumann was to believe in that other unsuccessful freak, the pedal piano.

December second finds Schober again encouraging Schubert along operatic lines, a deed as immoral as offering a dipsomaniac a drink. Ten days after that came a letter from a famous woman who had

---

[1] Owned by Professor Deutsch, quoted by Flower.
[2] Kreissle mistakenly calls it "a small harp."

been one of the ideals of his boyhood. Milder-Hauptmann wrote to say how ravishing she found his songs, and wouldn't he like her to get one of his operas produced in Berlin? Transported to the seventh heaven, he sent her *Alfonso and Estrella,* which was promptly refused. The sole tangible result of the incident was that she asked him to write her a coloratura song, and he composed *The Shepherd on the Rock,* a piece utterly unworthy of Schubert's genius.[1] Owing to Viennese *Schlamperei,* she did not receive the song until after the composer's death.

[1] In this she was more successful than Clara Wieck was later to be with Schumann. (Cf. my *Florestan,* p. 160.) Annette Kolb (*Franz Schubert,* Stockholm, Fischer, 1941) calls this somewhat vulgar show piece *"allerliebst"* ("most enchanting"), and Hutchings describes it as "a lovely work."

23

FRANZL EMITS A HEARTY, FREE WORD

ON TWELFTH NIGHT, 1825,[1] Eduard von Bauernfeld's diary told of a masquerade at Schwindia, where the three kings, in full fig, shook dice together. But Schubert was not there, and the diarist, who knew him but slightly, had to wait a month before becoming his intimate.

The following day Schwind wrote Schober about his tribulations with the exasperatingly unreliable and too easily befuddled Franzl.

You just ought to see Schubert and me together . . . That is a real catastrophe. But also as funny as anything in the world. A week ago he went with me to the Hönigs'. That was after he had ten times promised to come, and ten times had failed to come. We met at six and didn't want to arrive till seven, as Frau Hönig was leaving the house then. What to do in the meantime? He wouldn't go to any café but Lenkay's, because he'd always gone there with Senn. A pint of Tokay arrived; and when we had finished the half, it did not seem advisable, without great danger, to proceed further. The remainder was poured into a small bottle . . . As there was nobody at hand who could keep it for me, I took it along to the Hönigs' where, with much laughter, it was produced and drunk up.

The correspondence of the composer's friends is full of dismay over his undependability. On various occasions we find lamentations like this from Little Billee on April 2, 1825: "Schubert had promised to come. I waited for him the whole afternoon, but he left me in the lurch.— I slept, then smoked and incidentally waited, and now I regale myself with the prospect of my ruined Easter." This looks as though Franzl had confused Easter with All Fool's Day.

On another occasion, Franz von Hartmann told his diary: "I go with Fritz [von Hartmann, his brother] to visit Schubert, who had invited us, but who does not put in an appearance."

[1] In German, *Drei-Königsabend*, or Evening of the Three Kings, January sixth, originally the concluding part of medieval Christmas festivities.

Such incidents make less pleasant reading for lovers of music than those in which the composer humiliated the high and mighty Vogl, who so often insulted his little "Schuberty" by his absurd airs and by taking liberties with the lieder. Though the famous singer loathed to be kept waiting a single instant, he would actually hold back the curtain for half an hour because the composer was not yet in his seat. Then, if Franzl did not appear at all, he would only shrug and murmur: "We all must bow before the genius of Schubert, and though he does not come, we must follow after him on our hands and knees." Truly a remarkable change of attitude!

No one expected this genius to practice customary forms of etiquette. Without surprise Sophie von Kleyle wrote: "Schubert once made us happy by coming to our house. He was very amiable and talkative, but suddenly escaped us before anyone realized it."

He was forgiven all the more readily because he could apologize with such charm, as when he wrote to Franz Selliers de Moranville: "I came to excuse myself for recently breaking my word. If you knew how impossible it was made for me to keep same, you would surely forgive me."

When we read passages like these, it grows clearer why Schubert, unlike Beethoven and Brahms, was not soured by the inaccuracy and unreliability of the Viennese. For, an Austrian to his finger tips, he himself was such a prize example of Viennese *Schlamperei* that, when this quality was found in others, he took it for granted with the same good-natured tolerance that others showed him.

In February, 1825, Franzl was forced to look for a new lodging. He could no longer live at home, for the Rossau schoolhouse was already too small for the teeming Schuberts. So the extrovert composer, so pitiably dependent upon constant companionship, was forced for the second time to live alone. In the chapter on Schwind, we found him moving into a room at Alte Wieden 100, which had the signal advantage of proximity to his dear young painter friend's romantic dwelling Schwindia. All the same, this ordeal of solitary living bore hard upon the socially minded Franzl.

One evening Moritz managed to get him to Eduard von Bauernfeld's room to see more of that budding young lawyer, poet, and amateur musician.[1] At once they found one another congenial. The poet declaimed his verse. The composer sang his songs. Four hands raced over the piano. They adjourned to a café until the wee small

[1] He had studied piano with Beethoven's master, Johann Schenk.

hours. So inseparable did the three become that, having antiphonally accompanied each other home, they would eventually compromise on all bunking down in the bleak abode of one of them. None was fussy about comfort. For example, the bare floor with a leathern coverlet over him was good enough for Little Billee.

Once when Eduard yearned to smoke, but had no pipe, the resourceful painter concocted him one out of Franzl's spectacle case. (One wonders whether the resulting flavor did not cure him for good and all of the tobacco habit, and whether the case was ever again safe for spectacles. However, as Franzl slept with his glasses on, so as to be ready for work the instant he awoke, he may have had no other use for the spectacular pipe.)

Whichever of the trio happened to be in pocket quite naturally paid for the others. And it speaks eloquently of the poverty of painter and lawyer that Franzl was most frequently the capitalist. Indeed, at the very end of his life, after taking eight hundred gulden at his own concert, there was no holding him. Though he had already heard Paganini, he insisted on taking Eduard at five gulden a head. When the latter made difficulties, Franzl cried, "Nonsense! I heard him once and was angry because you weren't with me. Such a chap, I tell you, won't come again. And now that I have gold like chaff, let's go!"

They went and, according to Eduard's diary, "were not less enchanted by [Paganini's] wonderful *adagio* playing than highly astonished at his other devilish arts; also not a little amused at the incredibly awkward curtseys of the demonic apparition, which resembled a lean black doll actuated by wires."

Afterward, borne aloft on the crest of enthusiasm, they had one bottle more than usual—and still at Franzl's expense.

But let us return to 1825. In the rhythm of the composer's finances, flood tide always took a long and a weary while in coming, but ebb followed it with stunning promptitude. Late one morning Eduard dropped in at the café near the Kärntnertor Theater to order a coffee with milk and half a dozen crescent rolls. Soon Franzl arrived and did the same. Each expressed admiration of the other's healthy appetite so soon after breakfast. "Look here," murmured Franzl a little shamefacedly, "the real reason for this appetite of mine is that I've had nothing to eat today." Eduard burst out laughing. "The same here," he confessed.

When Teutons reach that stage of intimacy where they feel impelled to dispense with the formal *Sie*, and call each other *Du*, or thou, they link arms, "drink brotherhood" in wine or something stronger, and exchange hearty kisses. Alas, when Franzl and Eduard were moved to enact this ceremony, their purses would run to no beverage more potent than sugar water.

In the cultured middle-class society of Vienna, Schubert now began to enjoy very much the same honored position that, in the younger composer's infancy, the high aristocracy had accorded Beethoven. And, curiously enough, the appreciation of both the nobility and the bourgeoisie was based on pitiably inadequate knowledge of their respective hero's powers. Beethoven won acclaim largely through his trick talent for improvisation at the piano; while most of Schubert's contemporaries knew and loved no more of his immense and varied output than his songs. Even so, however, they showed a truer appreciation of the latter's work than did the Rossini-mad masses or even the professional musicians.

To frequent well-to-do middle-class houses did Franzl good. It rubbed off his sharper corners, allowed his sensitive, receptive spirit to register new impressions, and by degrees taught him to accept the role of cherished favorite among these intelligent and amiable amateurs.

Bauernfeld noted that in April Moritz and he took an outing to Retz on the Bohemian frontier. Schwind painted both their portraits on the signboard of the stagecoach proprietor. This was probably done to defray the expense of the trip and of what they bore home: "Great Schubertiad with friends, musicians and painters. The little cask of Retz wine which we brought along furnished the occasion."

On May 7, 1825, old Salieri died,[1] without in the least suspecting that he had once had as pupil one of the most promising talents in the entire history of music, nor that he himself had tried to enfold that talent in the napkin of formalism and hide it deeply in the operatic earth of his native Italy. But the old master was a curious blend of underhandedness and geniality. And if he had lived a few months longer, he might have been large enough to rejoice in a faint premonition of his recalcitrant pupil's future fame. For, in December, 1825, Cappi and Diabelli put on sale an engraving of Rieder's portrait of Schubert (see frontispiece). His contemporaries, including Schwind, agreed that this was the most faithful likeness of the composer.

[1] Eight years to a day before the birth of Brahms.

It speaks for Franzl's patience and sweetness of disposition that, besides the scenes described on pp. 41 and 169, only two occasions have been recorded when he went off the deep end and passionately blew off the accumulated pressure of his spleen. Be it noted, however, that he was drunk at the time. And small wonder, in view of his depression.[1] Bauernfeld, the chronicler of this astonishing scene, had been drinking with him and may have written with vinous exaggeration.

The incident was astonishing in more ways than one, for instead of making Franzl garrulous, a drop too much usually had the opposite effect. A sincere lover of alcoholic stimulus, he had a poor head for it. The spirit was potent, but the flesh was weak. And when there was much spirit about, his friends had to watch him attentively. A little over his measure would usually send him alone into a secluded corner where, with narrowed eyes, he grew more silent than the double bassoon in the symphony orchestra. His instinct then was for deeds, not words. He would grin genially and smash all the crockery and glassware within reach.[2]

However, despite a love of wine and a weak head, Franzl was no drunkard. In such a short life as his a sot could never have produced so enormous a number of masterpieces, music which he must necessarily have written while in full possession of all his faculties. Here, then, is the story of how Schubert, that mildest of lambs, suddenly turned wolf and emitted what Beethoven, in his place, would have called "a hearty, free word."

With Bauernfeld and Lachner, he had spent the afternoon in Grinzing, diligently sampling the new wine, and the evening in town making a comparative study of the drinks in various taverns. By one o'clock they were in the Café Bogner. In view of what was to follow, it would have been more appropriate had he chosen, not Bogner's, but his favorite beer hall, so delightfully named: Where the Wolf Sermonizes the Geese.

Borne on a tidal wave of eloquence, Franzl was outlining his plans for the future when some members of the Opera orchestra's wind section—in this case it should perhaps be called the ill-wind section —came in, rushed up to Franzl, spoke him fair, and begged him to write them a piece with solos for their respective instruments.

[1] When Anita Silvestrelli asserted that Schubert "was never really drunk," the wish was mother to the thought.
[2] His passion for breaking glass has been noted on p. 127.

"For you I write nothing!" barked Franzl.

Surprised and annoyed, the spokesman grew truculent: "And why not, Herr Schubert? I think we are artists as well as you. None better in Vienna!"

Franzl flared up. "Artists?" The tiny fat man echoed the word ferociously, lurched to his feet, and full of fight as a gamecock, planted himself before the tallest of the players. His eyes narrowed:

Artists? You are musical artisans! Nothing more! One of you bites into the brass mouthpiece of a wooden cudgel; the other blows his cheeks up on his French horn. Is that what you call art? It's a handicraft, skill that brings in the cash—nothing more! Folk like you—artists forsooth!— You pretend to be artists! Don't you know what the great Lessing says?— How can a man spend his whole life doing nothing else than biting into a bit of wood with holes in it? —that's what he said—or something like it . . . And you set up to be artists? You are tooters and fiddlers, the pack of you! It's I who am the artist. *I*. I am Schubert, Franz Schubert, whom the whole world knows and names! Who has created great and beautiful things that you can't in the least understand, and who will create still more beautiful ones—the loveliest in the world! Cantatas and quartets, operas and symphonies. For I am not a mere *Ländler* composer as the stupid newspapers assert and the stupid people echo—I am Schubert! Franz Schubert! Get *that* into your noddles! And when the word "artist" is spoken, it means me, and not you worms and insects who demand solos which I shall never write for you—well do I know why! You creeping and gnawing worms whom my foot ought to crush, the foot of a man who reaches to the stars. *Sublimi feriam sidera vertice!* (Translate that for them.) To the stars, I say, while you wretched tootling worms wriggle in the dust, and with the dust blow away and rot!

This incredible tirade completely knocked the wind out of the startled windsters. It was as if the peaceful and smiling Danube had, under their eyes, changed suddenly into Niagara Falls. Without another word they turned tail and retreated in bad order. His friends had a hard time to pacify the irate master and get him home. Bauernfeld recorded:

The next morning I hastened to visit my friend, whose state had made me uneasy. I found Schubert, bespectacled as usual, sound asleep in bed. In wild confusion, his clothes were scattered all over the room. The table was an ocean of ink from an upset inkpot, and on a single sheet of paper I read: "At two o'clock in the morning." Then came some rather confused aphorisms, violent mental explosions inspired doubtless by the stormy scene of the night before. Among them I found this odd bit: "Enviable Nero, thou who wert so strong as to destroy detestable people to the music of strings and voice."

What was in his addled brain when he wrote this? We may be sure that the composer of the E Flat Mass would not have approved of Nero lyreing while Rome and the Christians burned. Perhaps his befuddled mind anachronistically pictured the Emperor enjoying the luxury of annihilating a whole phalanx of evil clarinetists and French hornists.

Franzl woke up with a laugh. That unique nocturnal orgy of self-expression had evidently proved a mighty relief to his usually so reticent and modest spirit. Adjusting the sleep-drunken spectacles, he sprang from bed.

"Look here," scolded Bauernfeld, "now what will those people think of you?"

"The rogues!" he replied with a merry twinkle. "Don't you know that they are the world's most intriguing rascals? Especially toward me. They deserved what they got. All the same, I must own up to being sorry I went quite so far. I shall probably write them the solos they asked for;[1] and then they'll come and kiss my hand for the gift. Oh, I know that crowd!"

[1] Probably he never did; for no such anthology of wind solos has come down to us.

On what seem insufficient grounds, Professor Deutsch is skeptical of the truth of this story. Writing in 1869, Bauernfeld dated the incident 1824, and Professor Deutsch feels that he did not know Schubert well enough so early. But, in recalling the facts almost half a century later, the chronicler might easily have forgotten the exact date.

24

FRANZL FEELS LIKE AN ENCHANTED PRINCE

IN MARCH, 1825, before Vogl left for a summer in the country, Bauernfeld had met him and noted in his diary: "Remarkable old bachelor, reads Epictetus and is a treasure trove of agreeable mannerism. Moritz was affectedly rude to him.[1] Schubert is always the same, always his natural self."

Toward the end of May, Franzl set forth in the singer's footsteps. He started on one of the most delightful experiences of his career, by way of the great cloisters St. Florian[2] and Kremsmünster. There he was enthusiastically entertained and was cheered to find that his works and his fame had preceded him. The monks were given the first performance of a new piano sonata, probably that in A Minor, Op. 42, which moved them to utter a hoary bromidiom: "Under your fingers the keys are metamorphosed into singing voices." (Strange how many people imagine that the highest of compliments for instrumental music is to call it as good as vocal!)

He joined the singer in that dignitary's native Steyr, which they used as a base for visits to Gmunden, Linz, and Salzburg. At Gmunden they spent six highly enjoyable weeks. The charms of one of the loveliest of Austrian lakes left an indelible impression upon the composer's receptive spirit. And so heartily were they feted that Franzl, freed from the weight of debt and the gnawings of hunger, declared that he felt like "an agreeably enchanted prince." Their host, Herr Traweger, had a fine piano and a burning admiration for Schubert. Almost every day the two visitors took a meal at the palatial home of another melomaniac, Hofrat von Schiller, a salt king and the unofficial monarch of the Salzammergut region.

The chief rival for their guestpitality (if one may venture to coin a

---

[1] Probably in retaliation for the famous singer's condescension to his poor little "Schuberty," and for the gross liberties which he took with the songs.

[2] Where Anton Bruckner, then nine months old, was destined to grow up as a choir boy.

needed word) was Florian Max Clodi, a rich mine owner in nearby
Altmünster, whose trump card was his attractive daughter Therese.
She took Franzl along the choicest lake and mountain trails, which
she knew like her pocket. She kept him charmed with salty tales of
the local peasants and miners. She led him to a part of her garden
that had the name of being bewitched, and there he found it unusually easy to write. It is likely that on this spot most of the songs
from *The Lady of the Lake* were composed. Perhaps, in the back of
his mind, he identified Walter Scott's heroine with Therese, the
lady of the Gmunden Lake.

Franzl wrote Spaun that of these songs the *Ave Maria* was most
liked. Since he was not known to be especially devout, its religious
feeling caused his friends—and perhaps himself—a good deal of
astonishment. As his pious father was inclined to regard his religious
views with suspicion,[1] he may have seen in this song a chance to
mollify the old man and wrote home that the *Ave Maria* apparently
moved all hearts and tuned them to religious feeling.

I believe that is because I never force myself into a devotional spirit
and, except when involuntarily overcome by it, never compose hymns or
prayers of this sort. But when that happens, it is usually the real and
true devotion.

Like Schumann, that younger genius whose name is often coupled
with his, Schubert loved children and had a way with them. During
his stay in Gmunden, four-year-old Eduard Traweger, clad in a
nightshirt, jumped into Vogl's bed on awaking. But the old singer,
fonder of sleep than of youngsters, angrily sent him away with a
flea in his ear. Next morning Eduard tried Franzl's bed and had such
a kind reception that the two became great friends. The little fellow
loved to sit on the man's plump, dressing-gowned knee and rumple
his hair, while Franzl rubbed whiskers against the tiny face, perched
his spectacles on the dot of a nose, and blew smoke rings at him from
a long-stemmed pipe.

When the precocious child proudly exhibited some first attempts
at writing, the generous composer drew from beneath a litter of
music manuscripts a treasure so dear to his own heart that it was always kept in a glass case. This was a leaden writing stand, and it
became Eduard's dearest possession.

---

[1] On p. 28 we found Ignaz warning Franzl to take care how he wrote about
religion to Father.

Franzl taught the lad to sing and began with one of the simplest of the *Mill* cycle: *Guten Morgen, schöne Müllerin.* Eduard often needed coaxing, and even when the composer took him between his knees and began the accompaniment, he could not produce a note. But when his friend urged: "Come on Eduard, if you sing *Guten Morgen* I'll give you a bright new kreutzer," the barriers of shyness melted and, in the words of his later reminiscence, "I squeaked as loud as I could."

When he caught diphtheria Eduard, with a sound instinct to be justified by the later advance of medical knowledge, refused to let the doctor apply leeches. He would not listen to his father's entreaties and turned a deaf ear to Vogl's. But Franzl's coaxing was a different matter. He was so convinced of his new friend's greatness and loved him so much that, without a whimper, he let the composer apply the blood suckers. As a reward, Schubert denuded himself of another prized treasure and gave the little fellow his silver pencil case.

The next stop was Linz. On July 19, 1825, Anton Ottenwalt, Franzl's host there, wrote to his brother-in-law Josef von Spaun:

Schubert looks so healthy and strong, so genial and jolly, so friendly and communicative, as to give one deep joy. Today he has taken possession of the room that was for a while your sleeping quarters. His trunk will be taken there, a table set up for writing, he will be provided with books, and so on. I am ever so proud to have as guest this friend of yours, and all the love and honor that we show him is shown at the same time to you. But it gives me great pleasure that, although you are not here, Schubert still seems to feel so much at home among us. Why, today after dinner he even played parts of his marches with Marie.

And, two days after, Franzl wrote the following on the above-mentioned table:

DEAR SPAUN!

You can imagine how awfully annoyed I am to be in Linz and have to write you to Lemberg!!! Devil take the infamous duties that savagely tear friends asunder, although they have hardly begun to sip from the chalice of friendship. Here I sit in Linz, sweat myself half dead in this shameful heat, have a whole volume of new songs, and you are not here! Aren't you ashamed?

Linz without you is like a body without a soul or like a horseman without a head, or soup without salt. If Jägermeyr didn't have such good beer, and if a passable wine were not to be had on the Schlossberg, I would be obliged to hang myself on the Promenade, with the superscription: *From anguish because the soul of Linz has fled.*

With a characteristic modulation from major to minor, this jocular make-believe abruptly turns into serious pessimism:

All in all, it is really pitiable how everything everywhere ossifies, these days, into flat prose; how most people look on at this process either unmoved or even with approval; and how, quite at their ease, they slither over the slime into the abyss.

Suddenly he lapses into almost as lushly sentimental an imitation of Jean Paul Richter's style as that callow youth, Robert Schumann, was three years later to perpetrate:[1]

Defy foolish fate, and in scorn thereof let your opulent spirit blossom like a garden of flowers that, in the chilly North, you may radiate the warmth of life, and make known your divine origin. Base is the sorrow that steals into a noble heart. Hurl it from you, and trample upon the vulture ere he gnaws his way into your soul.

Now, with another lightning change, he pokes gentle fun at their dear Schober who was about to return to Vienna[2] from his travels à la Wilhelm Meister, with his tail between his legs, having appeared in far less exalted roles than he had anticipated, and with none too brilliant success at that. But the composer ends warmly:

Meanwhile, however, his coming gives me great joy. I hope that he will bring back into our much reduced Circle a somewhat more vital and intelligent way of life.

Anton Ottenwalt was a man of deep musical sensitivity, yet so modest that he did not trust himself to say much about the adored composer's work. After entertaining him a few days, he wrote Spaun a letter which revealed as true and profound an appreciation of Schubert's mind as any contemporary ever put upon paper:

We heard Vogl three times. After breakfast Schubert himself condescended to sing for our intimate circle. He also played on the piano his

---

[1] See my *Florestan*, pp. 19-20. Schubert's may be a conscious parody.
[2] Schubert had not heard that Schober had already returned.

marches, 2- and 4-hand variations, and an overture, compositions of such intrinsic value that it is not for the likes of me to talk about them . . . Schubert was so friendly, so communicative . . . We sat with him until close upon midnight, and never have I seen or heard him thus!—earnest, profound and like a man inspired. How he talked of art, of poetry, of his youth, of friends and other remarkable people, of the relation of the ideal to life, and things like that.

I could not help being more and more astonished at this spirit about whom people kept saying that his artistic accomplishment is so unconscious, that he himself often fails to grasp and comprehend it, and so on. And how simple he made all this appear.— I have no words to describe the extent and totality of his convictions—but those were glimpses of a view of life far from merely appropriated. And the share which noble friends of his may have had in its formation detracts nothing from the personal flavor it manifests.

Therefore it makes me very happy that he seems to like being with me, and likes to show us the side of him that one shows to none but kindred spirits.

It must indeed have been a rare privilege to hear a Schubert, lit by the sacred flame, discourse of art and life in words of a beauty that could stand comparison with his loveliest notes.

Far otherwise was the general quality of his letters home. Most of them have to do with the scenery. In the descriptions of landscape one catches something of the schoolmasterly quality of Father Schubert and Ferdinand, mingled with the factual style of Goethe's letters from Italy. For all that, however, they sometimes show powers of visual observation almost unexampled in a great musician.

Here and there the real Schubert blazes out, as when he turns upon the leeches who had always sucked his blood:

If only one could expect any honest treatment from those——of art dealers; but the wise and benevolent dispositions of the state have seen to it that the artist shall eternally remain the slave of every contemptible little shopkeeper.

One is reminded of the grandfather in Lewis Carroll's delicious poem, *Poeta Fit, Non Nascitur:*

> But, when he thought of *publishing,*
> His face grew stern and sad.

Two days after this outburst, as if to confirm its truth, a Viennese publisher named Hüther wrote asking Franzl about new compositions and enjoining him to make the prices very low because he was only "a beginner." To call Schubert a beginner in 1825, with only three years left to live, is a good deal like calling Shakespeare a beginner when he was at work on *Hamlet*.

Almost at the end of the trip, another characteristic utterance escapes him. Having described Salzburg, curiously enough with no mention of its chief claim to distinction, he writes Ferdinand about the anticlimax of emerging from the beautiful valley of the Salzach into the dirty and pestiferous town of Hallein near the Bavarian frontier. "It seemed like falling from heaven upon a dungheap," or like hearing, "after the music of Mozart, a piece by the immortal A." Though A's identity is charitably veiled, one suspects that the immortal Auber may have been meant.

Of Ferdinand he writes Father:

I'm sure that he has already been sick again 77 times, and 9 times thought he would have to die; as if dying were the worst that could happen to us mortals. If only he could see these divine mountains and lakes, the sight of which threatens to crush or swallow us, he would not love the tiny span of human life too much to look upon restoration to the inconceivable force of the Earth and a new life there as anything but great good fortune.

On reading this somewhat pagan observation, how the pious schoolmaster must have bounded in his armchair!

Early in August came a letter from Ferdinand, wistful about the delights and wonders of the El Dorado his brother was enjoying, but full of warm, generous feeling:

You know how precious every hour in your company is to me . . .
Already I dream how you will be received in England, how through your larger compositions like symphonies, oratorios, or perhaps operas, you will swing yourself aloft from among the German composers, like the Egyptian Joseph from among his brothers.

From the reams that Franzl writes Ferdy in return about Salzburg, some passages stand out:

The way Vogl sings and I accompany, and seem at such a moment to be *one*, strikes these people as quite new and unheard-of.

At the tomb of Michael Haydn he is deeply moved:[1]

I thought: may your calm, clear spirit breathe upon me, you good Haydn; and though I can not be so calm and clear, yet surely no one on earth honors you as profoundly as I do. (A heavy tear fell from my eyes, and we went our way.)

It is touching to find this genius humbling himself before a musician all of whose undeniable calmness and clarity could never avail to carry him artistically within hailing distance of a Schubert.

That summer, for the first and only time, Franzl was offered a nonteaching job. His friend and well-wisher, the Imperial Music Count Dietrichstein, asked him to take the post, shortly to become vacant, of second court organist, at a yearly salary of five hundred gulden. In a jocular epistle of August 14, 1825, Little Billee urged him to accept. If he did, he would have no choice but to live an orderly life so as not to be dismissed.

Otherwise, owing to the absolutely total poverty of your friends, you will be obliged to satisfy your carnal and spiritual need for pheasants and punch in a solitude no less complete than life on a desert island, or Robinsonade.[2]

Franz, however, would have none of it. He declined the offer, partly because he hated to give up his habits as an untrammeled though poverty-stricken Bohemian, but still more because he did not trust his comparatively inexperienced feet to live an orderly life on the organ pedals.

Father Caliban was furious. When he learned that his impossible son had actually tossed away five hundred gulden a year, he came near forbidding his prodigal the house for the third time. But such

[1] One wonders how much more deeply he was moved, in Eisenstadt, a few days before his death, before the resting place of that worthy musician's immortal brother Josef.

[2] The youthful imaginations of that day, even more than of this, were tremendously thrilled by the adventures of Defoe's hero, whose name they pronounced "Róh-been-sohn Cru-so-ä." See my *Florestan*, p. 14.

was Franzl's present fame, as the old man imagined it, that he did not quite dare.

At Bad Gastein, the travelers found an old friend, Johann Pyrker, the poetic Patriarch of Venice, and his poem, *Die Allmacht*, was then and there turned into song. At Gmunden and Gastein, Franz is supposed to have written a symphony of which no trace has been found and which has caused nearly as much speculation as the lost tribes of Israel. Bauernfeld writes of "a symphony composed in 1825 at Gastein, of which its composer was specially fond." And in a chronological list of Schubert's chief works, he lists: "1825, Grand Symphony."

Some writers feel that the four-hand Sonata in C, Op. 140 (the "Grand Duo") is an arrangement of this work, but its weaknesses throw doubt upon the theory. In August, 1825, Schwind wrote Schubert:

> We can allow ourselves good hopes for your symphony. Old Hönig is dean of the legal faculty and in this capacity he will give an academy.[1] This can very well offer an opportunity for—or rather, one counts on—its performance.

The *"Gastein"* Symphony may be the work which Franzl dedicated the following year to the Friends of Music, recommending himself and the score to their protection. This protection was afforded in such overflowing measure, the composition was so carefully put away, that the most diligent search has never been able to discover it.[2] One is glad to learn, however, that the happy-go-lucky organization voted Franzl one hundred silver florins, not in return for the manuscript, but as an encouragement and earnest of its sympathy.

Arguments to prove the identity of the work with the C Major Symphonies of 1818 or 1828 are unconvincing. On the other hand, it is highly significant that such an eminent Schubert authority as Professor Deutsch firmly believes that the *"Gastein"* existed. What fortunate treasure seeker, following in the steps of Schumann, Herbeck, Grove, and Sullivan, will earn The Gramophone Company's reward of two hundred pounds for discovering this fabled sym-

---

[1] An old name for concert.
[2] Note that the ill-disposed sometimes change two letters in *Die Gesellschaft der Musikfreunde,* making it *Die Gesellschaft der Musikfeinde* (The Foes of Music).

phony? That it may yet be found is one of the dearest hopes of the musical world.

On Sept. 13, 1825, Bauernfeld proposed by letter that Franzl live next winter with Moritz and himself, and continued, "How are you, fattest friend? I imagine that your belly will have increased. God keep it and let it flourish."

In reply he was asked to give Franzl's Viennese landlord twenty-five florins. The composer evidently did not dare, particularly in view of the declined organ post, to beg this service of his tight-fisted father. The letter goes on to demonstrate that Franzl had been extracting a little wisdom from hard knocks. The end of the halcyon days in the country was at hand, and he must take a little realistic thought for the winter.

As to our living together, I admit that it would be very pleasant; but as I've had experience of such bachelor and student plans, I would hate in the end to sit on the ground between two stools. Meanwhile, if something really practical can be settled on, I can always find ways of amicably leaving my landlord . . .

Schwind is a true [unprintable epithet, which may have been a slip of the pen] and wool teaser; for, of the two letters which he has written me, one is more confused than the other. Such a nonsensical hodgepodge of good sense and absurdity is new to me. Unless he has made very beautiful things during this time, he can never be excused for such brainless talk.

Vogl went to Italy, and Franzl, the hopeless extrovert, who could never bear to travel alone, persuaded that good pianist, Josef Gahy, to hire a trap with him. From Linz they drove in three days to Vienna.

25

THE CIRCLE DISPORTS ITSELF

A GREAT many of Schubert's best compositions were never printed during the composer's lifetime. Those he saw published were:[1] only 3 chamber works, 56 piano duets (including one sonata), 13 works for piano solo (including 3 sonatas), 193 dances for piano solo, 4 religious works (including 1 Mass), 22 compositions for several voices, and 187 songs. These represent no symphonies or quintets, but 1 of the 19 string quartets, 3 of the 21 piano sonatas, 1 of 7 Masses, and 187 of about 600 songs. Editorial *oui* was an expression that Schubert rarely heard. And for the comparatively few works which they accepted, he had always been underpaid by his publishers.

Now in 1826 he had reached the height of his short career, and his music was growing more serious, more concentrated, far richer in suggestion. But the leeches were actually giving him a fourth less than before.

Hans Nägeli, whose portrait might well be that of Tartuffe, now ordered a sonata from Schubert through Carl Czerny, yet refused to pay his modest fee of one hundred and twenty florins. Anton Diabelli had little eyes more suitable for a pig than for a man, and a crafty, cruel face. He looked the part which he so diligently played: plunderer of genius. Domenico Artaria was another type of bandit, fat, suave, and greasy. Except for its large but shifty eyes, Tobias Haslinger's portrait suggests the moral qualities of Diabelli.

A gentleman who happened to be in Haslinger's office one day reported a scene fit to infuriate every Schubert lover. The door was slightly opened, and a little man with a roll of music peered in through thick spectacles. A wistful question mark was written all over his face. Haslinger made a warding-off gesture and growled brusquely in Viennese dialect, *"Na, na, heut' is' nix!"* ("No, no, nothing today!") The door was sadly closed and the gentleman asked, "Who

[1] According to Professor Deutsch.

152

is that?" Scornfully the publisher replied, *"Das is' a gewisser Schubert. Der kommet alle Tag'."* (That is a certain Schubert. If I let him, he'd come every day.")

In the course of time, these publishing gentry had grown aware that Schubert was often ill and nearly always so desperate for money that they could safely beat him down. Besides, they resented the young upstart's obstinacy in ignoring their requests to make his stuff easier to perform. Probst of Leipzig had refused to pay him the modest fee of eighty gulden a volume for songs. That was too steep. And besides he was very much occupied in publishing Kalkbrenner's complete works! When, at the end of his rope and of his career, the composer offered that opportunist his magnificent E Flat Trio for one hundred florins, A.C., the skinflint beat him down to sixty.

The liberality of publishers has made enormous strides in little more than a century. For the 487 works published during Schubert's lifetime, he received only the equivalent of 2,323 dollars,[1] while today a certain young composer barely worthy to turn pages for a Schubert receives for each new symphony many times that sum.

Franzl was the easier target for the sharpshooting publishers because he now had no fixed source of income, having resigned, or been discharged from, his position of teacher at the Esterházys'. However, as Bauernfeld records,

he still went occasionally to the Count's under the protection of his patron Vogl, who associated with princes and counts as with his equals, everywhere led the conversation, and when he took the composing genius under his wing, comported himself like an elephant driver exhibiting a special rarity from the animal kingdom.

Franzl attended the Sausage Ball [2] at Schober's on January 4, 1826, where, at the piano, he delighted everybody by improvising dances in his best style.

January twenty-ninth should be celebrated as a red-letter day by all devoted quartetists, for then, under the composer's direction, at the home of the fiddling Hacker brothers in the Street of the Beautiful Lantern, the D Minor String Quartet was first tried out before a highly select audience, consisting exclusively of those two creative

[1] Professor Deutsch's estimate.
[2] A modest Viennese festivity where, in lieu of champagne and pheasants, beer and small hot sausages were served.

listeners, Anton Holzapfel and Benedikt Randhartinger. It will be recalled that Randhartinger, as a boy, claimed to have read at sight another wet manuscript on that exciting day, eleven years before, when *The Erl King* was hurled upon paper and tried out at the Convict. Perhaps he was specially invited to the Hackers' to see if he would recognize those wistful echoes of *The Erl King* in the finale of the quartet.

Imagine the thrill of experiencing for the first time in history those Arielesque variations on *Death and the Maiden,* and the mad excitement of the *Presto!* One wonders if that privileged pair realized what an altogether novel kind of music they were hearing, and what an immense influence it was destined to have upon the quartet writing of the future.

Schubert scratched many corrections in the parts and is said to have made a large cut in the finale. Three days after, for a larger audience at the home of the singer Josef Barth, the first public performance was given.

In writing the *"Death and the Maiden"* Quartet, Schubert had made (probably unconscious) use of his art as mental medicine.[1] He had been depressed by poverty, illness, and the world's neglect. Creating the D Minor temporarily cleansed "the stuffed bosom of that perilous stuff" which weighed upon his heart. He was doing with music what Goethe consciously and systematically did with poetry: "I habitually convert whatever rejoices or worries or otherwise concerns me into a poem, and so get rid of it, and at once correct my conception of outward things and set my mind at rest."

Franzl was now cheered by some bits of encouragement. In the Leipzig *Allgemeine musikalische Zeitung* there was a long, favorable review of his Piano Sonata in A Minor, Op. 42, calling it an "uncommonly attractive as well as truly rich work." Another bit was the decision of the Friends of Music to have Jenger write a biography of "Schubert, Franz." [2] Then too, on April 8, 1826, Artaria published his Sonata in D, Op. 53, and the four-hand *Divertissement à la hongroise,* Op. 54.

The friends found the introverted Bauernfeld a good deal of a hermit, so they nicknamed him "Spelunk," from the Greek *spelunx,*

[1] See the preface to my anthology *The Poetry Cure,* New York, Dodd, Mead & Company, Inc., 1925.
[2] Unfortunately this was never written.

meaning a cave or den. This spring Spelunk put down in his diary a
vivid characterization of certain leading members of the Circle.

Schober is mentally superior to us all, and even more so as a talker.
He has, however, something artificial about him, and is in danger of
letting his best powers be choked by idleness.— *Schwind* has a magnificent, pure nature . . . *Schubert* has the right mixture of the ideal and
the real. For him the Earth is something beautiful.— *Mayrhofer* is simple
and natural, although Schober claims him to be a sort of jovial intriguer.
— And I?! Yes, who knows himself? Until I have accomplished something
worth while, I'm not a human being.

A few days after, he added this rider:

Schubert and I hold faithfully together against various Schoberian
follies. Moritz fluctuates back and forth.

Salieri's death and Eybler's succession to his post had left the
second Court Conductor's post vacant. Here was a position that
paid twelve hundred florins a year and that would not oblige
Franzl to run about on the organ pedals. Doubtless impelled by the
pleading of his cronies and by memories of how near Father Franz
had come to apoplexy when his son had scorned the organ job,
Schubert, on April 7, 1826, sent Kaiser Franz II an application:

YOUR MAJESTY!
ALL-GRACIOUS EMPEROR!
In the deepest reverence the undersigned ventures to make the most
submissive petition for the all-most-gracious award of the vacated position
of Vice Court Conductor.

To increase his chances, Franzl submitted a Mass of his own; but
had a freezing reception. He wrote:

Not long ago I took Conductor Eybler a Mass for performance in the
court chapel. On learning my name, Eybler remarked that he had never
heard any of my compositions. Now, I'm certainly not very vain, but for
all that I would have believed that the Court Conductor of Vienna would
by now have heard something of mine. A few weeks later, when I went
back to learn the fate of my offspring, Eybler told me that, though the
Mass was good, it was not written in the style which the Emperor cared

for. On which I said good-by and thought to myself: "So, I'm not fortunate enough to be able to compose in the imperial style."

Bitterness underlay these quiet words, for what the Emperor liked were the pedantic, cut-and-dried Masses of old Johann Reutter, with correct fugues tailored according to the rules in the book.

Among the eight applicants were Anselm Hüttenbrenner, Beethoven's friend Seyfried, and Kreutzer, the well-known opera composer. Not until the following year did they learn their fate.

Eybler was not the only dignitary condescending enough to indicate how Schubert should change himself in order to get along in the world. That spring the famous critic Rochlitz wrote Hofrat Mosel about the composer:

Perhaps this talented artist needs only a scientifically educated friend who would lovingly enlighten him about himself: about what he is, what he possesses, what he wants to do; from all of which, one hopes, he would find out by himself, what he should do.

Fortunately this program was never carried out.

In May, 1826, Franzl moved with Schober and Schwind to the country, in nearby Währing. At first they enjoyed the change very moderately, for the weather was bad, and the composer's companions were both unhappily in love. To Bauernfeld and Mayrhofer, who were touring Carinthia together, he sent this wail:

Don't stay away so long; here it is very sad and miserable— —already boredom has spread too far. From Schober and Schwind one hears nothing but lamentations far more heart-rending than those which we heard in Passion Week . . . I do not work at all [an almost unique state of affairs].—Here the weather is truly fearful; the All-highest appears to have quite deserted us; no sun whatsoever will shine. Here we are in May, yet we can't sit in the garden. Terrible! fearful!! horrible!!! for me the cruelest thing that could happen!

Schubert's fatal hunger for operatic success, indestructible as the Biblical worm that "dieth not," made him spur Bauernfeld on to write him a libretto. This was completed during eight days of the trip and entitled *Der Graf von Gleichen.* Franzl's courageous letter of July tenth to the librettist shows a high quality of sportsmanship:

JENGER, ANSELM HÜTTENBRENNER, AND SCHUBERT
Colored crayon drawing by Josef Teltscher (about 1827).

Schubert's room. Pen drawing by Schwind (1821).

A Schubertiad. Sepia drawing by Schwind.

KEY TO "A SCHUBERTIAD"

1. Karl Pinterics
2. Josef Witteczek
3. Franz Lachner
4. Ignaz Lachner
5. Eleonore Stohl (Frau Schrotzberg)
6. Friedrich Diez
7. Sophie Hartmann (Frau Diez)
8. Karoline Hetzenecker (Frau Mangstl)
9. Marie Pinterics
10. Karl, Baron von Schönstein
11. Benedikt Randhartinger
12. Josef Gahy
13. Johann Steiger von Amstein
14. Johann Michael Vogl
15. Ferdinand Mayerhofer von Grünbühel

16. Anton von Doblhoff-Dier
17. Franz Schubert
18. Josef von Spaun
19. Franz von Hartmann
20. Anton von Spaun
21. ?
22. Kunigunde Vogl (née Rosa)
23. Ludwig Kraissl
24. Josef Kenner
25. Marie Ottenwalt (née von Spaun)
26. Ludwig Ferdinand Schnorr
27. Moritz von Schwind
28. Anna Hönig (Frau Mayerhofer von Grünbühel)
29. August Wilhelm Rieder

30. Leopold Kupelwieser
31. Theresa Hönig (née von Puffer)
32. Anton Dietrich
33. Franz von Schober
34. Romeo Franz Seligmann
35. Ernst von Feuchtersleben
36. Franz Grillparzer
37. Justine von Bruchmann (Frau Smetana)
38. Eduard von Bauernfeld
39. Franz von Bruchmann
40. Johann Senn
41. Johann Mayrhofer
42. Ignaz Franz Castelli

The painting on the wall is of Countess Caroline Esterházy.

I can't possibly get to Gmunden or anywhere else. I have absolutely
no money, and things are altogether going *very* badly with me. But I don't
mind this and am in gay spirits.

However, come to Vienna as soon as possible. As Duport wants an opera
from me, but doesn't like the librettos that I have set, it would be glorious
if yours were favorably received. Then we should have money; if not,
indeed, honor! . . . .

Vogl has married!!!

I beg of you, come as soon as possible.

On account of the opera.

Your
SCHUBERT.

In Linz, just mention my name and you will be well received.

That old bachelor, Vogl, had indeed wedded. To Franzl's discomfort, marriage was in the air and busy tempering down established
friendships, as it has such an uncomfortable way of doing.

When Bauernfeld returned to Vienna late in July, 1826, Franzl
and Moritz spied him through their café window and rushed out
with exuberant greetings.

"Where is the opera?" cried the composer.

"Here!" and Bauernfeld pulled the manuscript with ceremony
from his pocket.

Franzl fell upon it voraciously. Then they joined Schober in Währing, where they spent the night in eager talk.

The history of *Der Graf von Gleichen,* like the annals of the poor,
is short and simple. Schubert immediately began to set it and, in
spite of renewed illness, obstinately persevered. In October the libretto was forbidden by the censor, who was shocked to find that
it dealt with bigamy. But even that could not halt the stubborn composer, who did not drop it until some time in 1827. Even on his
deathbed he spoke of completing the opera. Bauernfeld noted on
his manuscript: "1826. Set by Schubert. The instrumentation is lacking. He died before finishing the work."

After all the rainy weather at Währing, a joyful reaction set in. In
ten crowded days of glorious life, June 20 to 30, 1826, he hurled upon
paper the String Quartet in G, Op. 161. Besides being his last,
longest, and most forward-looking quartet, it is also one of his three
greatest.

This spurt used up all his music paper, so that when he wanted to write songs, he made a book out of the linings of his shelves, ruled staves in pencil, and wrote the immortal pair: *Who is Sylvia?* and the *Cradle Song*. There is a widely believed tradition that, at this time, in the Währing tavern Zum Biersack, amid a noisy crowd of celebrants, Franzl sat with Tietze, turning over the leaves of a volume of Shakespeare. In *Cymbeline* he came upon something that made his eyes gleam. Pointing to the lyric "*Hark, hark! the Lark*," he suddenly cried: "Look, I've found something. A beautiful melody has come into my head; if only I had some music paper." No sooner said than Tietze began ruling lines on the back of the bill of fare, and deaf to the surrounding revelry, Schubert dashed down the great song. There is only one unfortunate thing about this charming story: it is not true.[1] The authentic version was given on p. 96.

On August 12, 1826, the penniless Franzl turned to Germany for help, and appealed to Breitkopf and Härtel. This was the same Leipzig firm which, long before, had jumped to the conclusion that the composer of *The Erl King* had fraudulently used the name of the Dresden Franz Schubert. The first sentence of his letter may be an allusion to that ridiculous incident:

In the hope that my name is not wholly unknown to you, I herewith politely inquire whether you would be not unwilling to accept certain of my compositions for a cheap honorarium, as I greatly wish to become as well known as possible in Germany. You may choose among songs with piano accompaniment,—among string quartets, piano sonatas, etc., etc. I have also written an octet. In any case, it would be a special honor for me to form a connection with such a famous old house of art dealers.

After several weeks' delay the famous old house put a summary end to the correspondence with a reply that redounds to its lasting shame. As they were unacquainted with the mercantile success of his music, they wrote, it would be impossible to pay him anything for the first work or works, but he would have to be content with a number of free copies. Long afterward, when Schubert's fame had encircled the globe, a hideously unjust irony of fate accorded this very firm the signal honor of publishing the complete edition of his

[1] Edward Wilberforce (*Franz Schubert*, London, Wm. Reeves, Ltd., 1866) adds to the misinformation about *Hark, hark!* when he confuses it with that other *Ständchen* by Grillparzer, which Schubert, at the request of Anna Fröhlich, set for female voices.

works, without having to offer the composer even a single free copy. The cheese-paring policy of great houses like this made it all the easier for the small Viennese publishers to flay their local genius alive.

December 17, 1826, was a gala day for the Schubertians. At Spaun's a few of them enjoyed breakfast and four-hand music with Franzl and Gahy at the keyboard. The latter played some of his friend's newly issued dances, Op. 67, and Schubert justly showed anger at Diabelli's effrontery in giving them the fancy title: *"Hommage aux belles Viennoises."* (One is glad that this publisher waited until after the composer's death before baptizing the fine four-hand Allegro in A Minor, Op. 144, *"Lebensstürme"* or *"Life Storms."*)

In two carriages the friends adjourned to luncheon at Nussdorf with the Wanderer family. Presently Frau Kurzrock, one of Vienna's great belles, arrived with her three adorers: Schober, Bauernfeld, and Schwind (whose affections were somewhat fickle). Franz von Hartmann's diary records dancing. Bauernfeld and Schwind played and sang

Schubert songs most lamentably . . . After all these afternoon visitors had left, the old comfortable atmosphere returned; and Schubert sang gloriously, in particular *The Recluse* (*Der Einsame*) . . . and *Withered Flowers* (*Trock'ne Blumen*) from *The Miller's Beautiful Daughter.* Also Betty [Wanderer] sang three *Miller* songs most enchantingly. Then Schubert and Gahy played again with enrapturing beauty. Thereupon everybody went in for gymnastic and sleight-of-hand feats. At last we took our reluctant departure.

They proceeded to the Green Anchor, where Schober joined them, and everyone told funny stories. Spaun said that he had settled for the carriages to Nussdorf and was almost angry when the others wished to pay their share.

In those days the Circle met often, and Franzl was always present. Sometimes they read serious literature aloud. More often they cultivated the fine art of conversation. Their discussions were nothing if not varied. On December 30 they discussed romances of chivalry and convict stories; on March 3, 1827, the Greeks, the Hungarians, and the poet Grillparzer; the following evening, wild animals; on March 27, Byron. On March 29 they talked of Beethoven's funeral from which they had just come. On April 4 they

discussed music and Goethe; on April 29, swimming, and the confusion of the postal service; on April 26, animal magnetism.[1]

These thoughtful young fellows were fully as keen for less serious
amusements. To go back to December 30, 1826, Franz von Hartmann
records:

> As we [doubtless a bit high] emerge from the Anchor, everything is
> deep in snow. The fancy seizes us to snowball, which we promptly do at
> the corner of the Grünanger and Singer Streets. Spaun helps me, and
> Fritz [von Hartmann] and Schober help Schwind. Schober hits me con-
> sistently and well, and I'm equally accurate, especially against him or
> Schwind. Spaun protects himself beautifully against the shots with his
> opened rain-roof [umbrella].

Schubert has no part in the fight, not even on the receiving end.
Perhaps he is spared on account of his spectacles. Reaching home
in a state of high exhilaration, the chronicler rings too exuberantly
and receives a rough tongue-lashing from that curse of Vienna, the
concierge.

A few nights later, in front of the Café Bogner, the friends do
gymnastics and undertake "all sorts of childish operations," while
Little Billee, with fluttering mantle, swoops down the street in a
brilliant imitation of bird flight. The next evening they dance by
Stock im Eisen,[2] ceremoniously saluting that ancient relic in passing.
They dance on about St. Stephen's, making "demonstrations" before
their favorite drinking places and threatening to throw Spaun (who
had a horror of late café life) into Geringer's in the Kohlmarkt. "But,
as we opened the doors, lo! he went in quite willingly, and we all
most calmly tripped in after him."

The next day, Franz von Hartmann notes, after breakfasting at
Spaun's, they hear Gahy play

lovely German Dances by Schubert. Enderes balances sticks, bars, etc.
wonderfully. I try to imitate him, and let a stick with a steel hammer at

---

[1] A subject of natural interest in the town where Mesmer had begun his
career.

[2] This is an old tree trunk, driven full of nails, still preserved opposite the
cathedral. The tree formerly marked the boundary of the Wiener Wald. Legend
has it that a locksmith's apprentice once sold his soul to the devil in return for
the secret of making a lock that could not be opened. The youth naturally went
to hell. In memory of him, every passing locksmith drove a nail into the trunk
until it could hold no more. Hence its name, Stick in Iron.

one end, fall hard upon his forehead, which scares me terribly so that I no no longer hear German Dances, but stay with him as he bathes the place and so fortunately keeps down the swelling.

On the last day of January, 1826, the Spaun brothers entertained the crowd with "glorious Schubert things" performed by Gahy. After supper they dispensed "glorious American cigars" and performed "all manner of surprising tricks."

Metternich's police apparently could close an eye, thankful that the young fellows were working off steam on diversions that had nothing to do with politics. It is good to find the unfortunate Schubert amusing himself so exuberantly with his cronies, almost up to the bitter end.

SCHUBERT CARICATURED
AS A MUSHROOM.

26

SCHUBERT CARRIES ON THE TORCH

FRANZL began 1827 with the wistful hope of bettering his condition by becoming second court conductor. This hope soon turned into the usual disappointment. Like Mozart, who had once vainly applied for the same position, Franzl and his seven competitors were rejected. It was given to old Josef Weigl, a superannuated composer of popular operas, now on pension.

Schubert, as free from envy and jealousy as his successor Schumann (and probably as ill fitted for the exact and exacting duties of such a post), behaved like the magnificent sportsman that he was and remarked to Spaun: "I would have liked to get this job; but as it has been awarded to such a worthy man as Weigl, I must be content with the decision." [1]

Here we have that tolerance and appreciation sometimes shown for the small fry by great souls—if they are great enough. In similar circumstances, Johannes Brahms would probably have said much the same. But one shudders to imagine the thunderbolts of blasphemous rage, fit to batter in the portals of high Valhalla, which that poor, persecuted archegotist Richard Wagner would have launched.

Coming at almost the same time as this bad news, a lighthearted letter acted as a partial counterpoise. The postscript had a smiling allusion to Vogl's theory that Franzl wrote his compositions in a clairvoyant state. The epistle starts with a musical theme set to the words, *"Credo in unum Deum!"* ("I believe in one God!")

Not you, as I well know; but this you *will* believe, that this evening in the Little Music-Society, Tietze will sing your *Night's Brightness* (*Nachthelle*),* [Op. 134], to which performance N. [Nanette, or Anna] Fröhlich invites you by means of the 3 enclosed tickets which, on account of

[1] Schubert's estimate of the gentleman had gone up amazingly since 1819 when, writing to Anselm Hüttenbrenner, he had called Weigl a rascal (*canaille*). See p. 80.

the big snowfall, I have the honor to convey to you by way of the coffee
house of the Jolly Black Pudding.[1]

                              Your highly affectionate
                              WELLWISHER WALCHER.[2]

* In this connection, *Nachthelle* does not mean somnambulism, clairvoyance,
slept-off jag, and so on, but poem by Seidl, music by Schubert, for obbligato
damned-high tenor, with chorus, for which I am engaged for second tenor. And
to that end I have already ordered a superb high F from the baker of Baden
who is said to make the best ones.

                                        Note by the writer.

Early in 1827, Franzl went to live in the Blue Hedgehog, Unter
den Tuchlauben, with his chronic hosts the Schobers. There he was
to stay for nearly all the time remaining to him, reveling in the unaccustomed luxury of two rooms and a "music closet."

None know better than the Viennese how to celebrate the Carnival
season. It was opened by the Schubertians with a grand Sausage
Ball at Schober's. Music: waltzes by Schubert, played alternately by
Gahy and the composer. A wealth of lovely girls. Between dances,
much to eat and drink. Each cavalier would pop one end of a little
sausage into his dancing partner's mouth, and the other into his own.
The most toothsome morsel lay in the middle.

Another affair at Schober's on March fourth was not so successful.
Schubert had invited the friends there to hear his new compositions,
but forgot to come himself. Fritz von Hartmann noted:

> Finally Schwind undertook to sing some of Schubert's older songs,
> which enraptured us. At half past nine we all adjourned to Schloss Eisen-
> stadt [one of their favorite beer halls], where Schubert appeared soon
> after, and won all hearts with his amiable simplicity, even though he had
> betrayed our hopes by the carelessness of genius.

The gaiety of the Carnival may have been good for Franzl's spirit,
but the late hours and all the wine and punch were bad for his body.
This needed a quite different regimen for, since the day when he had
first fallen ill, he had never quite recovered normal health. The first

---

[1] In Viennese, *lustigen Plunzen*, literally, jolly blood sausage, means a jovial
fat man.

[2] Ferdinand Walcher, who later became an Archducal Court Councilor, was
the friend who found the composer drinking beer At the Sign of the Oak, and
haled him to the Friends of Music for the first public performance of his choral
Ständchen, Op. 135 (see p. 170 ff). His remarkably sympathetic portrait by Teltscher shows the long solemn face and quizzical mouth of the born humorist.

fine careless rapture of ebullient youth was gone forever, to be replaced by more and more frequent depressions. These could be
alleviated, but only for the time being, by jolly companionship and
trips to the country. His second song cycle, the somber *Winter Journey*, was begun February, 1827, and completed the following
autumn. Earlier in 1827 he recast his *German Mass* for male chorus;
and in July wrote the *Ständchen*, Op. 135.

March brought Franzl enthusiastic recognition from Johann Hummel, the famous conductor, pianist, and composer. This helped the
younger man by impressing those for whom a prophet in his own
country is profitless. Such were the guests of Princess Kinsky, who
would enjoy his songs without a word or a thought for the insignificant-looking little fellow at the keys. Once when the Princess
apologized for the neglect of her guests, Schubert begged her not to
mind this, as he did not care for compliments, was used to being
passed over, and was more comfortable in the background. He felt
about music as Elizabeth Browning felt about her lover:

> I love thee freely, as men strive for Right;
> I love thee purely, as they turn from Praise.

Yet for all that, the modest young fellow was thrilled when the
visiting star, Hummel, heard Vogl sing Schubert songs at one of
Frau von Laszny's parties, and rushed to the composer, pressing his
hands again and again, and crying, "I thank you! I thank you!" When
urged to play, he improvised long and brilliantly on a Schubert song,
The Blind Boy (*Der blinde Knabe*), which he had just heard. It was
a proud night for the Circle.

The chief European event of 1827 was the death of Beethoven on
March twenty-sixth. It moved Franzl to the depths of his being.
Though, as a lad, he had written foolishly against the great deaf
man (see p. 38 f), that phase had long since been buried under an
overwhelming admiration for the chief musical influence in his life.

Though the two composers lived not far apart and saw one another at Steiner's publishing house and in restaurants, it may well
be that they never exchanged a word. Beethoven's deafness and
defensive unapproachability, coupled with Franzl's modesty and
shyness, make this all the more probable. One must view with extreme conservatism such stories as that the younger man took some
of his music to the older man's rooms, but at the first word of criti-

cism, grew so embarrassed and confused that he rushed abruptly from the house. A more credible version has it that, when he called, the master was out, and he left the score with the servant.

Another doubtful tale has Schubert and Anselm Hüttenbrenner visiting the sick man. Schindler, the factotum, asked Beethoven in what order he would like to see them, and the answer was, "Schubert may come first." When both young men were at the bedside, Beethoven said affectionately, "Anselm, you possess my mind, but Franz has my soul." It is said that three weeks from the end Schubert went a second time with Teltscher, the artist, and Josef Hüttenbrenner. Beethoven, conscious that they were there but unable to speak, gazed at them fixedly and made signs with his hand, whose meaning they could not guess.

Telling against the truth of these stories is Spaun's statement: "Schubert often expressed sorrow, particularly at the time of Beethoven's death, that this man had been so hard to approach and that he had never talked with him."

What we are sure of is that the elder composer liked, and often played with his nephew Karl, the four-hand *Variations on a French Song*, Op. 10, which Schubert dedicated to him in 1821. It is a matter of record that, some time in 1826, Karl Holz wrote in one of the deaf master's Conversation Books: "For song he [Schubert] has a great power of conception. Do you know *The Erl King?*— He always talked in a very mystical vein."

We know that, during the last illness, Schindler handed Beethoven some sixty Schubert songs, including the *Mill* cycle, *Bounds of Mankind* (*Grenzen der Menschheit*), *Viola*, *The Young Nun* (*Die junge Nonne*), and *Omnipotence* (*Die Allmacht*). After reading them raptly and learning that there were five hundred more like them, the great man cried, "Of a truth this Schubert has in him the divine spark!" [1] He demanded to see what the youngster had written in other forms, but increasing illness prevented.

After his death, the two Hartmanns and Ferdinand Sauter viewed the body and bribed the attendant to give them locks of Beethoven's hair. Though Schubert was not present to carry away any part of the great man's body, he was the legatee of the master's spirit and of his position as the focal point of music in Austria.

It is certain that, on March 29, 1827, Franz, wearing a bunch of

---

[1] We are told that Beethoven added, "This one will surpass me." But the remark is probably fictitious.

white lilies, carried a craped waxen torch in the funeral procession and, with the others, symbolically extinguished his against the earth when the coffin was lowered into the grave. In that sad moment, was the modest young genius aware that he was now left in a lamentably tasteless age, as chief torchbearer of the art of music? Probably not, for this was a man who once exclaimed, "Who can do anything after Beethoven?!"

Walking back from the Währing Cemetery with Randhartinger and the composer Lachner, he passed near the poor dwelling where he had been born, never dreaming of the time when it would be transfigured into a Schubert Museum. In the Kärntnerstrasse they entered the Mehlgrube Tavern and called for wine. "To the memory of the great man whom we have just lost," Franz murmured. He drank off his glass, refilled and raised it again. "To him who shall go next." Unconsciously, or perhaps by presentiment, he was drinking to himself, and creating a modern analogue of that upper chamber where, long before, a greater genius had sat at wine and said to His Circle, "This is my blood."

27

BUT WHERE IS SCHUBERT?

ON APRIL 16, 1827, Schuppanzigh gave the first public performance of the delightful Octet, Op. 166. The *Theaterzeitung* found it a "radiant, agreeable, and interesting" work by "a good and happy composer," but complained of its being reminiscent and too long. This last criticism was also made by the *Allgemeine musikalische Zeitung* of Berlin, along with some faint praise. But the Leipzig paper of the same name had only good to report: "Gave much pleasure," "very solidly wrought, thoughtful in design, clear and effective in its working out," "a rarity of our epoch—deserves well-founded praise."

Another chance for a steady income was now thrown in Franzl's way. Lachner, who was employed in the Kärntnertor Theater, persuaded him to apply for a conductorship there, which had just become vacant. All the applicant would have to do was to write a few dramatic scenes to a given text.

Franzl wrote them, and the trial began, but suddenly the prima donna, Nanette Schechner, stopped singing and advanced to the footlights.

"You, Herr Schubert, you don't seriously imagine that anyone can sing such stuff?"

"Why, what's wrong with it?"

"Wrong? Just look here at this impossible passage! And this heavy orchestration. Why, the big bell of St. Stephen's itself couldn't make itself heard through that!"

The composer gave her a friendly smile. "Just try it again, please. This time it will surely go."

The lady gobbled with rage. "When I tell you to change it, you must do as I say. I'm the prima donna here!"

But Franzl was calmly firm. The stage manager and the director, both naturally on the lady's side, labored pontifically to make him revise the score. Their arguments and pleas glanced off the musician like peashooter pellets from an alligator. One is reminded how, for his first Milan opera, Mozart composed a duet twice and an aria seven times before satisfying the vocal tyrants on the stage. One recalls the scene at the Lichnowsky palace when Beethoven's friends pleaded with him to shorten *Fidelio,* and the Princess even got down upon her knees before winning the great man's promise. Nanette did far otherwise. She swooned, and on coming to, she screamed into Franzl's spectacles, "Never will I sing another note of such a mess!"

Schubert was less yielding than his predecessors. Perhaps he did not realize that in opera, as of old, the singer still continued to be more important than the mere composer and was allowed to call the tune. Whether he did or not, his enormous patience was at an end. He banged the score shut, shouted "I change nothing!" and rushed from the theater.

When he had cooled down, his modest common sense asserted itself. Perhaps he knew in his inmost heart that, even if he had been appointed, his tenure of office would have been all too brief, and he told his friends: "It's just as well. I'm not fitted for such a post."

Emotional thunder and lightning like that in the theater was of extreme rarity in the life of the even-tempered Franzl. Once at a picnic in Neustift-am-Walde, part of his conversation with a lady was overheard. As he helped her down from the carriage, he was saying, "Above everything I must not let my temper loose. For God's sake I must not get angry. For, if I do, I knock out of his mouth all the teeth of the miserable wretch who has angered me." The lady was impressed. "Have you often been angry?" An imaginative small boy suddenly stopped being Superman. "Never yet," confessed the self-deflated Franzl.

The Schubertian modesty was not inconsistent with a frequently cavalier way of treating his admirers. When the poet and royal Prussian librarian, Hoffmann von Fallersleben, visited Vienna, he asked his friend Heinrich Panofka to introduce him to Schubert. One suspects that he may have had in his pocket a volume of poems suitable for setting. This is how he tells what happened:

"Very well," said Panofka, "then let us go out to Dornbach, where Schubert is often to be found in the summer. Besides, that would be a far better place to meet him."

One Saturday toward evening, we drive there in a stagecoach. As we enter the "Empress of Austria," our first inquiry is for Schubert. "He hasn't been here for a long time," we are told. "He ought to come on Sunday."

So hope for the morrow brings some consolation. Tomorrow . . . never a Schubert. We have dinner . . . and drive home. Now we try another way of getting to Schubert. We send him a friendly invitation to meet us in "The White Wolf." His place is set. We and the wine await him. He does not come, and we drink his wine. A fortnight later . . . at two o'clock, Panofka and I go . . . to Nussdorf. We pursue the search for Schubert—in vain. We wander on to Heiligenstadt,[1] then on to Grinzing . . . The wine is bad, but the garden makes good sitting. An old fiddler plays. All of a sudden, Panofka cries: "There he is!" and hurries to Schubert who, with his girl [probably a casual acquaintance], is looking around for a place. Panofka brings him to me. In happy surprise I greet him, mention in passing what great pains we have taken to find him, how delighted I am to know him personally, and so on. Schubert stands there before me embarrassed, does not rightly know how to answer and after a few words takes his leave and—does not let us see him again. "No," I tell Panofka, "but that is a bit thick! As matters stand, I'd prefer never to have seen him. Then I would not have had to think of the creator of such soulful melodies as an ordinary, unfeeling or, indeed, ill-mannered person. But as it is, apart from his behavior today, there's no difference at all between him and any other inhabitant of Vienna. He speaks Viennese dialect, like the other Viennese wears fine linen, a well-brushed coat, a shining hat, and has nothing in his face nor in his whole personality that resembles *my* Schubert."

Perhaps Fallersleben should have added to his indictment, "And he never once asked to see the poems in my pocket!"

Franzl's tongue-tied embarrassment may have had to do with the girl he had brought. Whoever she was, it was characteristic of his independent and praise-shy nature to let no mere admirer distract him from his duties as host. In this sad period of his life, one rejoices to find him, for once, smartly dressed, entertaining a girl and having a good day. Hoorah for the fine linen, the presentable coat, and the shining hat! When decked in such unaccustomed style, even his cronies might have had difficulty in recognizing him. It must have been an unusually fortunate windfall that enabled him to lay out a few gold pieces on himself and his own pleasures before lavishing on the Circle the whole contents of his pockets.

In connection with the birth of one of his most engaging choral works, the *Ständchen*, Op. 135, we again find the composer absent-minded and *schlampert*. Here is Anna Fröhlich's sprightly account

[1] Where Beethoven wrote the *"Pastoral"* Symphony.

of what went on. One recalls that Austria's leading poet, Grillparzer, was in love with her sister Kathi and lived with the family.

Every time the name- or birthday of Gosmar[1] came near, I had always gone to Grillparzer and begged him to write something for the occasion; and this time, when her birthday approached, I did it again . . . He answered: "Well, yes, if something occurs to me." But I retorted: "Well, make it your business to see that it does!"

In a couple of days he gave me the *Ständchen* . . . And soon after, when Schubert came to us, I told him: "You, Schubert, you must set that to music." He: "Well, hand it over." Leaning on the piano, he exclaimed again and again: "But how lovely that is—that is beautiful!" For a while he looked at the sheet, and said at last: "So, it is already done. I have it already."

Sure enough, on the third day he brought it finished; but for a mezzo soprano (that is, for Pepi [her sister Josefine's nickname]) and four male voices. Then I told him: "No, Schubert, in this form I can't use it; you see, it is to be an ovation given to Gosmar by her girl friends alone. You must make the chorus for female voices" . . . Soon he brought it back for Pepi's voice with the female chorus it now has.

Schubert promised to play the accompaniment for the occasion, which turned out to be an evening of brilliant moonlight. Anna loaded her pupils into three carriages, drove to Unter Döbling, where Gosmar was visiting friends, stealthily smuggled a piano beneath the young girl's window—and waited for Franzl. But there was no Franzl. Finally a substitute pianist was found, and the charming music filled the night.

Next day Anna took Franzl to task. He was crestfallen and penitent. "I forgot it," he said simply. She then arranged a public performance of the new work in the hall of the Friends of Music, and the composer swore he would be there as accompanist.

The moment came. The hall was filled. But where was Schubert? Probably, like a true genius, he was following the Biblical formula: "Forgetting those things which are behind, and reaching forth unto those things which are before, I press toward the mark for the prize of the high calling." His unborn works always took precedence over the others.

Anna burst into despairing tears. "He has never heard it," she

---

[1] One of Anna's pupils, who later married Leopold Sonnleithner.

sobbed to Hofrat Walcher, "and how I want him to! Who knows where he is hiding!"

The Hofrat did some rapid thinking. "Perhaps he may be at the Sign of the Oak." Walcher ran. Sure enough, there sat Schubert, blissfully unconscious of his second, even more heinous, crime. The horrified and remorseful little man was rushed to the hall and deposited at the piano for a glorious performance. Afterward, as he tried to make his peace with Anna, a transfigured look came into his eyes, and he murmured, "I had no idea that the piece was so beautiful."

28

HIGH TIMES IN GRAZ

IN 1827, toward the end of summer, Franzl made another of those
country visits in which he delighted. His comrade Jenger took
him to visit a family of enthusiastic musical amateurs in Graz.
Frau Marie Pachler was a pianist about whose playing Beethoven
had expressed himself with uncommon approval. She had the gift,
for which young Robert Schumann was even then becoming known,
of characterizing or caricaturing her friends at the keyboard. But
her humor evidently did not begin at home, for she had her portrait
painted in the curious taste of that Biedermeier day. It showed her
in Grecian garb, actually fingering a lyre, and gazing soulfully into
the empyrean, like the muse Erato.

Her husband, Dr. Karl Pachler, was a wealthy lawyer and a bit of
a lion hunter. Through Jenger they had tried, and failed, to entice
Beethoven down as a guest. Now they were to compensate themselves with Schubert, who wrote a characteristically modest acceptance, adding, "Though I do not see how in any way I deserve such a
friendly invitation, . . . nor know if I shall ever be in a position to
offer anything in return."

The express coach took two days for a journey for which today
the Erl Kings of the air need but a few minutes. At the Pachlers' they
were warmly received, and, as in Gmunden two years before, Schubert's first conquest was the heart of a small boy. The eight-year-old
Faust Pachler, vastly impressed by what he had heard of the composer, fully expected to greet some sort of magician or fairy prince.
That evening he refused to go to bed. "I *must* see the Schubert! I
will see the Schubert! Oh, I beg, beg to see the Schubert!" And so obsessed was he with his dream, that when the fat, ugly little man with
the thick spectacles appeared Faust fell in love with him forthwith
and took his beautiful green coat and white breeches as the insignia
of some higher order of humanity. (Who shall maintain that he was
wrong?)

With that small friend, Franzl was instantly at ease. At breakfast he began to joke with the lad and brought a vivid imagination into play for his amusement. Anita Silvestrelli declares that he told Faust, for instance, how naughty boys who wouldn't go to bed were made to play, not only four-handed—but even four-footed—pieces on the piano, and to practice until they could perform the *études* of Czerny with the left foot alone. To the end of his life, Faust never forgot the first overpowering effect of that green coat and those dazzlingly white breeches.

Graz, the picturesque capital of Styria, sown with quaint towers and dominated by the Schlossberg, lies on both banks of the swift and many-bridged Mur. Its terraced gardens mount toward charming country environs, with noble views of the eastern Alps. Something of the magic of Mediterranean lands informs the city, and even enters into the *Gemütlichkeit* of its inhabitants. This attractive place was the nearest that Schubert ever came to enjoying the land of Giorgione. Only eighty-odd miles from the Italian frontier, it offered many a hint of Italy, not only in architecture and landscape, but even in its southern style of speech. If Schubert had enjoyed Brahms's rich opportunities for knowing and loving that alluring peninsula, perhaps Italy would have left on his mind and his music an equally unmistakable mark.

Graz felt agreeably honored by the coming of Vienna's unhonored prophet. Anselm Hüttenbrenner, who presided over the local Music Society, organized a benefit concert for charity. Unfortunately this charity did not begin with Franzl's pocket, though three pieces of his were on the program and he accompanied them. In true Biedermeier style, he was heralded as "an artist and highly extolled tone setter from the capital." And, to extol him further, it was announced that the concert hall would be bright with "a double wax illumination," a splurge of complimentary candles tantamount to a torchlight procession today.

The swiftly flying three weeks in Graz were perhaps the jolliest and most carefree of Franzl's adult life. At the Pachlers' there was much eating, drinking, and laughter. As a matter of course, Franzl improvised abundantly for dancing and later wrote down some of these inspirations as the twelve *Graz Waltzes*, Op. 91, and the *Graz Galop*. Bauernfeld noted that "he had to play his newest waltzes again and again until the endless cotillion was unrolled, and the strong Schubert was dripping with perspiration."

Naturally, Frau Pachler had to display her art. She asked for Schubert sonatas, but Franzl had brought none along. However, far from taking offense that his hostess did not possess either Op. 42 or 53, which had been on the market for a year, he remarked that, as she knew Beethoven's by heart, he did not see why she should bother with his own.

Naïvely intending to give him a treat, the Pachlers took him to hear Meyerbeer's opera *The Crusaders in Egypt*. But, after the first act, he exclaimed in a strangled voice, "I can't bear it; let's get out into the open!" This reminds one of an even more succinct critique on the same composer, written later by Robert Schumann:

"Prophet" by Giac. Meyerbeer.

(Feb. 2, 1850)

Prompted by his wistful longing for dramatic success, he played the score of *Alfonso and Estrella* to Kinsky, the local conductor, who found it very difficult but held out hopes of staging it, if allowed to transpose certain numbers in C sharp and F sharp to the easier keys of C and F. This, mind you, was the same composer who, at the Kärntnertor Theater, had recently refused to "cancel half a line" of his music, or to let the prima donna's tears wash out a note of it. But here in Graz, though much against the grain, he yielded to Kinsky's demands. The pathetic part of it is that, by yielding in Vienna, he might have had a steady income. But in Graz his complaisance profited him nothing. Kinsky never gave *Alfonso and Estrella* after all; and sixteen years later the score,

Unwept, unhonoured and unsung,

turned up at the Pachlers'.

The merry crowd of holiday-makers did much visiting in the charming environs of Graz. The Hallerschlössel was a small, baroque, three-towered castle at the foot of the Ruckerlberg, with engaging views of the city and the mountains, where they spent a few delightful days with the Harings. It was probably here that the ice was so exuberantly broken that the friends were all given nicknames. These were recorded on a jocular playbill dated September, 1827, and headed:

THE FOOTSTEP IN THE HALLER CASTLE

or

DON'T PINCH ME SO!

Hüttenbrenner was called "*Schilcherl,*" from his addiction to Schilcher, the light, pink, pleasant, sparkling Styrian wine. The doctors Haring and Pachler were, in the prevailing fashion, turned into Greeks, as "*Harengos*" and "*Pachleros.*" For this was the Hellenizing age when not only John Keats, but hordes of others as well, were "first looking" not only into Chapman's—but even into Homer's— Homer. The fat Franzl, with his thick short underpinning, went by his old, appropriate nickname, *Schwammerl* (Little Mushroom).[1] On the placard of the Schubert Festival, held at Graz in 1907, there is an amusing caricature entitled "Schwammerl." We see pudgy legs and a roll of music clamped under a thick arm, but the head is obscured by the mottled umbrella of a mushroom.

At the Hallerschlössel, the composer was reminded of that bumptious Dresden musician who had once poured venom upon *The Erl King* and accused its creator of stealing his own name. (See p. 59.) Franz Schubert was introduced to—Franz Schubert. But the Graz namesake, an amateur 'cellist with the long, vacant countenance of a sheep, was as friendly as the Dresden one had been hostile. With others he insisted on performing so much music by the great guest, that the latter finally exclaimed, "Stop playing my stuff! I get enough of that at home. Let me hear something Styrian." Whereupon he was regaled with the folk songs of the region.

For two idyllic days the jolly crowd visited Pachler's elderly aunt, Frau Anna Massegg, in her quaint and tiny sixteenth-century Castle Wildbach near Deutsch-Landsberg. She set a delicious table. The Schilcher flowed in torrents. Best of all, she possessed six charming daughters. Maria, the eldest, had a lovely voice and the soul of a true musician. As dusk fell they would all gather about the piano in the blue room that gave on a picturesque garden. Then Maria would begin with *The Wanderer* and draw tears to Franzl's eyes.

His special favorite was the youngest sister, fourteen-year-old Fanny. Again and again she made him sing her those songs of his which had to do with wandering and high spirits. Even as an old

[1] Not "Fatty," as Flower asserts.

lady, she could forgive no one who seemed skeptical of her claim that, on leaving, Schubert had given her a fatherly kiss. One wonders if it was this tomboy Fanny who set Schubert's portrait above the entrance to the horse shed.

The eager hospitality of Graz proved more than Franzl could cope with, and he followed his frequent plan of accepting invitations, but not appearing. One promise, however, as we shall see, was faithfully kept. It was to compose something for little Faust to perform with Mother on Father's name day. He never disappointed the children.

The three merry weeks had seemed more like three days when Jenger's duties called him inexorably back to Vienna. Heavyheartedly Franzl returned with him to confront care and illness. On September twenty-seventh he sent his hostess a bread-and-butter epistle composed in his best style:

Already I realize that I had too good a time in Graz, and I can't get used to Vienna. It is certainly a bit large, but all the more lacking in heartiness, sincerity, candor, in genuine thought, in intelligent words, and especially in spirited deeds.

Amid all this cross chatter, one doesn't really know whether he is intelligent or stupid; and seldom or never does one attain an inner gladness. It's possible, of course that, with my slow way of warming up, this is my own fault. In Graz I soon perceived the unartificial and open way in which you people live with, and beside, one another, and in which, if I stayed longer, I would surely make more progress. In particular I shall never forget the dear harborage with the dear house mother, the powerful Pachleros, and the little Faust, where I enjoyed the happiest days I have had for a long time. In the hope that I may yet be able to show my gratitude in a worthy fashion, I remain, with all high regard,

Your gracious one's
Devoted
Frz. Schubert.

A fortnight later, the Graz hostess was overjoyed at receiving evidence of the modest composer's gratitude that was indeed "worthy." It was a four-hand *Children's March* in manuscript. On its lower margins was this note:

Herewith I send your Grace the 4-hand piece for the little Faust. I fear I shall not win his approval, as compositions of this sort are not exactly in my line. I hope that Your Graciousness has better health than I have, for my usual headaches have already come back.

29

THE WINTER OF HIS DISCONTENT

EARLY in 1827 these headaches had returned to torture Franzl while he was beginning *The Winter Journey.* In October, under the same handicap, he finished the last twelve songs of that great cycle. In his memoirs, Mayrhofer tells of these dark days:

The choice of *The Winter Journey* is enough to show how much more serious the composer had become. He had been long and severely ill; he had had crushing experiences; for him life had lost its rosy hue; for him winter had set in. The poet's irony, rooted in despair, was congenial to him.

Josef Spaun, a much older friend, is interesting about this period. He tells how gloomy and ill Schubert seemed. He had never fully recovered from his first sickness. Depression, temporarily alleviated by gay companionship, kept returning with increasing frequency and severity. When his friends asked him what was up, all they could get out of him was, "You'll soon hear and understand." One day he told Spaun:

Come to Schober's today; I'll sing you a wreath of ghastly songs. I'm keen to hear what you'll say to them. They've unstrung me worse than my songs ever have before.

Spaun went.

In a voice full of emotion, he sang us the whole *Winter Journey.* We were quite dumfounded by the gloomy atmosphere of these lieder, and Schober said he liked only one, *The Linden Tree.* All that Schubert replied was: "I care more for these songs than for all the rest; and you'll come to like them yet." [1] He was right. Soon the impression of these sorrowful

[1] This recalls something that Beethoven, a few months before his last illness, said to young Von Breuning. "In a Conversation Book some visitors scribbled:

lieder filled us with enthusiasm . . . They were really his swan song.[1] Ever since the completion of *The Winter Journey,* Schubert was in bad health, though not so bad as to cause anxiety. Many believed, perhaps, still believe, that he was a callous fellow whom nothing bothered. Those who knew him better realized how deeply his creations bit into him and in what anguish they came to birth. Whoever has but once seen him composing of a morning, glowing and with radiant eyes, yes, even with a different manner of speech . . . will never forget the impression he received . . . I hold it beyond a doubt that the excitement in which he wrote his most beautiful songs, especially his *Winter Journey,* was a contributory cause of his early decease.

Despite the relief of getting all this morbid emotion off his chest and on paper, the excitement did him more harm than the music cure did him good. The man was literally singing himself to death.

On the whole, the press notices of *The Winter Journey* were favorable, although a Berlin paper monstrously claimed that Schubert's inspiration was as well diluted as the miser's soup where one small lump of fat swims in an ocean of water, and a Munich organ of opinion actually declared the music unworthy of the poems.

The publishers treated Schubert far worse than did the press. As the reader will recall, Lachner assured Grove that Haslinger actually bought six songs of this cycle for one florin, A.C., apiece. And other publishers paid scarcely better for the other twenty works which he sold in 1827. The effect of such shabby treatment may well be imagined. Bauernfeld noted:

The friends and companions with whom Schubert preferred to associate were scarcely in a position to take him helpfully under the arms. He had neither the inclination nor the skill to push his way into higher circles and seek out appreciators who could better his condition. Small wonder, then, that he neither secured a salaried post nor won a success with any of his operas. So, all his life long, he held out in a less than mediocre position. And the music publishers, who quite sufficiently squeezed and exploited him, always remained his sole refuge and source of help. So, from time to time, he found himself quite without courage or hope, staring into the gloomy future.

'Your quartet which Schuppanzigh played yesterday did not please.' When they had gone, the Master tersely remarked to the lad, who had found the entry: 'Some day it will please them.'" (From my *Beethoven,* p. 479.)

[1] His real swan song was the C Major Quintet.

A slight offset to all the misery of 1827 came when Schuppanzigh, with Bocklet and Linke, gave in his own house the first performance of the noble and magnificent E Flat Trio, Op. 100.[1] "It was very well received," Franzl wrote to a friend. The work soon found favor with a steadily widening public. It was his first music to be published outside of Austria.

In November, Friedrich Rochlitz, the Leipzig poet, editor, critic, and Hofrat, tried to get Schubert to set his poem, *Der erste Ton* (*The First Tone*), to music à la Rochlitz. In his long letter, he suppressed the fact that Weber had already set it to the poet's dissatisfaction, and that Beethoven had been vainly urged to attempt it. Rochlitz had the effrontery to write in lavish detail his own ideas of what the music should be. He favored a liberal intermixture of that ghastly form of pseudo art which combines music with the spoken word.[2] As a bribe, he promised to arrange for "the most perfect possible performance in our concerts."

Franzl answered politely, very properly disparaging the spoken word idea but promising to try a legitimate setting. He may, however, have heard later of Beethoven's refusal, for he never set even the first word of *The First Tone*.

Truly, Franzl was one of the most unlucky composers who ever lived. As though it were not enough handicap to be born poor, ugly, low in the social scale, improvident, impotent to care for, or fight for, himself, incapable of refusing anything to a friend—he had to appear on earth during one of the most deplorable periods in the history of human taste. The programs of the time tell the story.

For example, in one Friends of Music concert of 1822, *The Erl King* had been sandwiched between an arrangement by Hummel for voice, guitar, and other instruments, and variations for two guitars by Giuliani, followed shortly by a potpourri for clarinet by Friedlovsky. In another concert at the Court Theater, the same year, Schubert's vocal quartet *Spirit of Love* (*Geist der Liebe*) had been made to associate with an anonymous "Introduction and Variations for French horn . . . wherein same will be made to imitate various instruments."

Among people who liked this sort of thing and were, moreover, infatuated with cheap Italian opera, how could a Schubert flourish?

---

[1] It is shocking to find Annette Kolb calling this glorious work "almost somewhat banal."

[2] The Germans call it *"Melodrama;"* but I prefer to baptize it "melocution."

To make headway against the taste of such a period was a truly desperate undertaking. Franzl could only throw up his hands when one of the world's leading organs of musical opinion offered such crude judgments as this: The *Allgemeine musikalische Zeitung* of Leipzig reported that in a concert of the Romberg Quartet, November, 1827, Bader sang Schubert's *Erl King* to the finished and forceful accompaniment of a young man named Felix Mendelssohn-Bartholdy. The critic felt that this setting did not "come up to those by Reichardt or Zelter, although overrich in modulation and the bizarre."

Even Schubert's own intimate friends did not always understand him any better than that earlier band of disciples understood the Man of Nazareth.[1] Witness their attitude on first hearing *The Winter Journey*.

It does not, of course, necessarily follow that a composer writes gay music because he feels gay nor sad music because he feels sad. But neither is it impossible that Franzl's illness and the deplorable troubles of those days had something to do with the morbid melancholy that breathes from the songs of this period.

[1] Of them all, the musical and poetic Bauernfeld perhaps comprehended and appreciated him most fully.

30

SWAN SONG

NOW that too little time was left for him to enjoy it, the reputation which Schubert had done so very little to cultivate had begun to grow and spread. His name was no longer unknown in Central Europe and was respected—though not by his publishers —at least by his colleagues. It had even crept over the frontier into France and, as early as 1829, was to move the musical circles of Paris to invite him there, only to learn how tragically late they were.

What little celebrity he enjoyed never affected him as it affects many famous men. And even if that celebrity had, during his lifetime, reached the vast proportions of today, one ventures to believe that it would never have spoiled his modest simplicity. Schubert would have remained Schubert.

December, 1827, saw the eight beautiful *Impromptus* finished. At Schober's the good companions drank in 1828, the last year of Schubert's life. Was it through some unconscious premonition of this that, a few days after, in begging Anselm Hüttenbrenner to secure a position for his brother Karl, he signed himself thus?

> Your faithful friend
> until death
> FRANZ SCHUBERT.

On January 2, 1828, an ugly rift threatened the Circle. They were drinking in a beer house when Schober quarreled with Spaun, and a duel was averted only by the latter's perfect behavior. A few days after this came the *première* of the Fantasy for Violin and Piano, Op. 159. Josef Slavik, "The Bohemian Paganini," for whom it had been written, played it in his recital. Alas! the critics did not care for the piece, and the audience acted as though it were the fugue of the witty definition, where "the voices come in one by one, and the listeners go out one by one."

Spaun had returned, after a five years' absence, only to fall acourting. On January twenty-eighth, to celebrate the engagement of this first friend of Schubert's, a final rousing Schubertiad was held, in Spaun's lodgings, where the B Flat Trio had its first performance by Schuppanzigh, Linke, and Bocklet. With the last-named the composer played his four-hand Variations, Op. 35. Bocklet was so moved that he kissed Franzl's hand and declared in a shaking voice that the Viennese had no idea what a treasure they possessed in this genius. A stranger who saw Schubert thus surrounded by adoring friends, playing them his new compositions and happily beaming in the glory of his creativeness, would scarcely have detected how the embarrassments of poverty and illness were insidiously tempering these joys, "like invisible spider webs covering the wings of butterflies." [1] One of the saddest reflections that a devotee of music can make is that this towering genius, who recorded his inspirations with an ease wholly unexampled and possessed a happy, magnetic personality unusual in a composer, should, up to his early death, have been harassed by poverty and the world's neglect.

From that night on, the lusty Schubertiads of the Circle's youth were transformed into the more staid Schubert evenings.

February eighth brought a heartening nibble from Schott, the famous publisher of Mainz, Germany. It seems that Schubert's "well-bornness" had for many years been known to Schott through his "excellently worked-out music pieces," and he would have written before had he not been hindered by publishing "very strong works by the blessed Beethoven." (This at least was a better excuse than Probst's preoccupation with the complete edition of Kalkbrenner.)

Franzl was jubilant. He offered Schott a rare galaxy of masterpieces, including a trio, the String Quartets in G and D Minor, four *Impromptus*, the four-hand Fantasy in F Minor, and the Fantasy for Violin and Piano. He added that he also had ready three operas, a Mass, and a symphony. "I mention these last compositions merely to make known to you my endeavors to attain the highest in art." Franzl apparently felt that the real truth about his larger works would be too much of a shock to the publisher. What on earth would Schott have said if he had known that the composer had ready 15 operas (more or less finished), 5 Masses, and 7 or 8 symphonies?

Schott's answer, reeking again of soft soap, asked for most of the items, but omitted the best of all, the string quartets, and did not fail

[1] As Daudet described, in *Jack,* the money troubles of the Argentan ménage.

to specify "the cheapest possible fee." Schubert offered him the trio at 100 florins, and the *Impromptus* and a vocal quintet together for 60. Schott was shocked at these "high" prices. He ordered only the 60 florin items, which the pained and disillusioned composer dispatched on May twenty-third, but raised his price to 60 florins apiece, and six copies of each work.

Eight months of silence ensued. Answering a dun in October, Schott returned the *Impromptus*. The fee was too stiff! Instead he wanted "something less difficult, yet brilliant, and in easier keys." For the Quintet he eventually sent 30 gulden, but by that time Schubert, on his deathbed, could not enjoy Schott's generosity. As in ancient times, 'the mountains had been in labor and had brought forth a ridiculous mouse.'

All this must have disgusted Schubert with German publishers, for when Brüggeman, of Halberstadt, wrote to ask for short piano pieces, easy to play and to grasp, Franzl apparently did not trouble to answer him. These letters from Schott and the other leeches who fattened upon his blood should serve as hideous warnings to publishers to be a little careful how they place themselves on record as exploiters of genius.

While Schubert's fame grew, his purse dwindled. By March, 1828, thirty-one years old, he was so poverty stricken that Grove aptly applied to the composer's own case the words of his great and tragic song, *The Organgrinder* (*Der Leiermann*):

> *Barfuss auf dem Eise,*
> *Wankt er hin und her,*
> *Und sein kleiner Teller*
> *Bleibt ihm immer leer.*

> (Barefoot on the ice,
> He staggers here and there,
> And his little plate
> Holds but empty air.)

In this crisis he could well have forestalled Foch's valiant words at the Marne: "My left is crushed, my right is in retreat, my center is overwhelmed. I shall attack." And forthwith he proceeded to attack one of the purest inspirations in all music, the great C Major Symphony. Hearing this work long afterward, Von Bülow declared: "One abode in eternal spaces, in a timeless world."

"No more songs for me. I am wholly engrossed in opera and symphony," said Franzl to his companions, as he offered the great C Major to the Friends of Music for performance. Their orchestral players, however, could not become friends of this music. The wrists and fingers of the string choir were not nimble enough. The woods and brasses approached their task

> With stammering lips and insufficient sound.

So, on the composer's advice, they switched to his easier Symphony Number 6, also in C. A decade later, Robert Schumann found the manuscript of the great C Major gathering dust at Ferdinand Schubert's home. He instantly realized what an inestimable treasure trove this was, secured its publication by Breitkopf and Härtel,[1] and its first performance under Mendelssohn at the Leipzig Gewandhaus on March 22, 1839. He also heralded it in his own magazine, with an enthusiastic article.

During March, 1828, in addition to starting his longest and greatest symphony, Schubert composed the cantata, *Miriam's Song of Victory*, a piece with certain traces of Handelian influence. Shortly before writing it, he burst into the Fröhlichs' home, beaming and excited, and told Kathi, "A most delightful thing has happened to me. I have been given Handel's works.[2] For the first time I now see where I am still lacking, and realize how much I have to learn."

The place where he was most lacking was not in his head but in his pocket. Not long before this, he had asked Bauernfeld: "What will become of a poor music chap like me? When I get old, I may well be like Goethe's Harper, and have to slink from door to door, begging my bread."

The poet friend's reply was emphatic:

Do you want my advice? Your name is upon all lips, and every new song of yours is an event. You have composed the most glorious string quartets and trios, not to mention the symphonies. Your friends are enchanted with them, but as yet no art dealer will buy them, and the public

---

[1] Sad to say, he beat Ferdinand down to 180 florins, in order to place the publishers under an obligation to himself and induce them to publish his *Novelletten* and *Fantasy* promptly, which they did. (See my *Florestan*, pp. 134-135.)

[2] Probably the very volumes which, during his last illness, Beethoven had so much enjoyed and admired.

still has no idea of the beauty and grace that slumber in these works. So take a running start, master your inertia, give a concert next winter. Only your own things, of course. Vogl will assist you with pleasure. Bocklet, Böhm, and Linke will feel it an honor to serve a master like you with their artistic skill. The public will compete for tickets. And even if you don't become a Croesus at one blow, a single evening will at least be enough to cover your expenses for a whole year. You can repeat such an evening annually; and if the novelties cause a sensation, as I don't doubt they will, then do you know what you can do to your Diabellis, Artarias, and Haslingers, with their shabby payments? You can raise prices on them, right up to the immeasurable. A concert then, take my advice! A concert!

Though it went mightily against the grain to ask favors of his friends, Franzl took this excellent advice. The only wonder was that he had not tried it long before. Without charge, the Friends of Music lent him their hall in the Tuchlauben for March 26, 1828, which happened to be the first anniversary of Beethoven's death. All of the musicians mentioned by Bauernfeld, and more, were as delighted to assist as Franzl had been reluctant to ask them. Böhm, Holz, Weiss, and Linke started the proceedings with "the first movement of a new string quartet," which must have been either the D Minor or the G Major.[1]

Vogl sang four of the less-known songs, and Josefine Fröhlich brought her Conservatory pupils to do the same Ständchen, Op. 135, which Franzl had twice forgotten to accompany for Anna's performances. There followed the "new trio," the E Flat, Op. 100, played by Bocklet, Böhm, and Linke. Tietze sang On the Stream (Auf dem Strom), with Lewy doing the French horn obbligato.[2] Vogl came back, this time with Omnipotence (Die Allmacht). Then a male choir closed on a note of victory, with the eight-part Battle Song (Schlachtlied).

And victory it was. Standing room only. Every number was wildly applauded. Franzl was kept running to the stage to bow. The net proceeds were eight hundred gulden. There was only one fly in the golden ointment. The Viennese critics were too much engrossed in the coming of Paganini to spare a line for the Liechtental schoolmaster's son. A few correspondents of German papers deigned to grant

---

[1] Duncan says: "The new quartet was probably Op. 163," but this is the opus number of the two-'cello Quintet.

[2] This lovely but little-known composition was possibly written for the concert. It is dated March, 1828.

him a little faint praise. But Berlin hinted that the applause had been due to a claque of Schubert's friends. And Dresden bluntly declared that stars of the second magnitude, like Schubert, pale in the radiance of that comet in the musical sky—Paganini!

Five of those eight hundred gulden, as we have seen on p. 138, took Franzl to hear the infernal fiddler. Ten more to take Bauernfeld to hear him. And then, after paying his debts, Franzl simply had to buy a new piano. Yes, yes, perfectly true that the money was meant to give him a year away from worry. But, after all, the music's the thing. Since he had endured poverty so long, he could endure it a little longer. Next year he would give another evening. Then he would pull himself together and become a hardheaded man of business, and save every kreutzer of the gate receipts.

"But why not repeat this concert at once?" his friends urged. "You would be sure of another packed house."

"All right," Franzl agreed. Then, with true Viennese nonchalance, he did nothing about it. But who shall blame a man from whose mind and heart a horde of masterpieces was struggling to escape? It seems almost incredible that, during the months of life left to him in 1828, he should have found time and strength to write, in addition to his greatest symphony, not only his chief religious work, the Mass in E Flat, but also his supreme effort in chamber music, the C Major String Quintet,[1] to say nothing of those lieder which are called *Swan Song* (*Schwanengesang*), of *Miriam's Song*, the four-hand Fantasy, Op. 103, the Rondo in A, Op. 107, or the last three piano sonatas.[2]

If Schubert had not been too preoccupied by all these undertakings to replenish his purse by giving another concert, he would not have had to decline the Trawegers' invitation to Gmunden that summer, and the Pachlers' to Graz. On July fourth, Jenger wrote Frau Pachler that "the not wholly brilliant financial condition of friend Schubert" was what kept him from accepting her invitation. "He is industriously working on a new Mass, and only awaits the needful money—from whatever quarter it may come—to take wings at once for Upper Austria."

Schubert's friends now conceived the idea—better late than never

[1] There is no record of even a private performance, during Schubert's lifetime, of this consummate inspiration. It was first published in 1853.
[2] The production of which may have been stimulated by joy over his new piano.

—that a little publicity would not do him any harm. Encouraged by the success of his concert, they concocted a laudatory article and sent it to the Viennese *Magazine for Art, Literature, Theater, and Mode* in which several of Franzl's songs had appeared as musical supplements. But its owner, Johann Schickh, reasoning perhaps that the composer was neither painter nor man of letters, had failed in the theater, and was not in the mode, sent the article to his "most valued friend Schubert," referred to his "beautiful, praiseworthy tone works," and explained that the piece was not fitted for his readers, but perhaps Schubert himself would like to peruse it. Dahms's comment on this example of editorial timidity is that the shy and modest Schubert was perhaps all the better pleased to remain unheralded.

We may be sure, however, that Franzl was made happy by sincere appreciation of his music. Witness the last letter he ever sent Probst: "The opus of the Trio is 100. I beg that the edition be without errors, and await it with longing. This work is dedicated to nobody except those who like it. That is the most rewarding dedication." As far as I am aware, Schubert was the first composer to remember his appreciators so graciously. How pleasant that every music lover may have the luxury of knowing that Schubert has dedicated a masterpiece to him! For what music lover in his senses could fail to like the Trio in E Flat?

Schober's finances were now in such a muddle that Franzl, who was living with that old friend, knew it would be a kindness to move away. Besides, the doctor urged that it would reduce the rushes of blood to the head, and the attacks of dizziness and benefit his shaky health in general if he lived in a suburb with quicker and easier access to the open country. Exercise was what he needed. The patient agreed. In those days, a man was a good deal older at thirty-one than he is now. Franzl had had enough of *la vie de Bohème* and felt that it was time to settle down to a more regular existence.

So, on September 1, 1828, he went to live with brother Ferdinand, who had just moved into a new apartment house at what is now known as Kettenbrückengasse 6. Unfortunately the house was too new. The walls were still damp and, together with the rudimentary sanitary conditions of that quarter, gave Schubert's tottering health the last fatal push.

One of the last acts of his kindly existence was to play comforter to Bauernfeld, whose play, *Der Brautwerber*, had its *première* on September fifth at the Burgtheater and scored a resounding failure. The poet was almost paralyzed with grief. "But," cried Franzl, "1 liked the play a lot! All of us did. And we're not exactly asses." Bauernfeld, however, had read the uncomplimentary press notices. "How does that help me if I'm one?"

In September, Schubert's health deteriorated alarmingly, but medi-cine and regimen presently restored his ability to work. Indeed, early in October, with Ferdinand and two friends, he was able to go on a three-day pilgrimage to the grave of Josef Haydn in Eisenstadt, Hungary.

A few days after his return, Anton Schindler, Beethoven's famulus and first biographer, sent Franzl a sprightly invitation to visit him in Budapest, go to the *première* of Lachner's new opera, and give a concert of his own compositions, which would undoubtedly score a huge success.

As one already knows that your timidity and easygoing nature does not lend much of a hand to such an undertaking, I announce and give you to know that you will find people here who will most willingly take you under the arms, heavy as you are . . . To get a few 100 florins into your pocket after this fashion is a thing not to be despised; and alongside this advantage others can peep out. Now go right ahead! Don't worry long. And make no bones of it. You will be assisted most ably and powerfully. [After listing the singers at his disposal—] So all you have to do is to sit yourself down upon your fat behind and accompany whatever is sung . . . And so, God bless you! We all expect that you will act the role of a nice sensible chap, and not kick against the pricks.

So here's to seeing you right soon in the land of mustaches.

How Franzl would have enjoyed such a visit! But he had to refuse; for his pockets were empty of coach fare.

31

"HERE IS MY END"

ON THE last day of October, 1828, the composer dined in a restaurant with an ominous name, the Red Cross. He ordered fish, but after the first mouthful he laid down his fork, murmuring that the food made his gorge rise, and he felt as though he had been poisoned.

That was his final meal. On November third, in a church at Hernals, he heard a Requiem composed by brother Ferdinand. Afterward he took a three-hour walk, a remarkable feat for a sick man who had fasted for almost three days. He arrived home exhausted, but without the faintest suspicion that the end was near, for on the morrow, perhaps under the stimulus of his recent study of Handel, he laid humbly ambitious plans for self-improvement.

With the pianist Lanz, the starving man walked into the city, called on a teacher named Simon Sechter, and arranged for a course in theory, even settling upon Marpurg's *Dissertation on Fugue* as their textbook.[1] He was destined to take only one lesson. But in doing so he left the inspiring example of a great genius at the height of his mastery, so conscious of certain lacks in his equipment that he was willing and anxious to begin anew from the beginning. What a tribute to the science of counterpoint!

Spaun, Lachner, Josef Hüttenbrenner, and Bauernfeld all visited their sick friend. Even with his last strength rapidly ebbing away, Schubert retained the use of his imagination. How vivid is his remark to Spaun: "There is really nothing wrong with me; only I feel so weak that I believe I am going to fall through the bed." He praised the little girl who was attending him, as his "loving thirteen-year-old nurse." It was his stepsister Josepha.

In the list of his visitors there was one striking absentee. Schober, who had been Schubert's most intimate disciple, stayed away, per-

---

[1] Sechter was the leading local professor of counterpoint. Anton Bruckner was to be his pupil.

haps for fear of infection. One cannot help thinking how Simon Peter failed his Master at the end by showing the white feather.

On November 11, 1828, Schubert took to bed, and wrote his absent friend this note:

Dear Schober!
I am sick. For eleven days now I have eaten nothing and drunk nothing, and wander, exhausted and tottering, from chair to bed and back. Rinna is my doctor. Even if I eat anything, I have to give it right up again. So be good enough to help me out of this desperate fix with reading matter. Of Cooper I have read: *The Last of the Mohicans, The Spy, The Pilot,* and *The Pioneers.* If you have perhaps something else of his,[1] I adjure you to leave it for me with Frau von Bogner in the café. My brother, who is conscientiousness itself, will bring it to me most conscientiously. Or something else as well.

Your friend
SCHUBERT.

On November fourteenth, according to Karl Holz, an old friend of Beethoven's, Schubert heard the greatest of that master's quartets, the C Sharp Minor, Op. 131. Holz reported that Schubert "worked himself up into such a state of enthusiasm and excitement that we were all concerned for him." It was Franz's farewell to what was even more necessary to him than food and drink. Holz, Karl Gross, Baron König, and an unknown musician were the players, and the performance must have taken place at Schubert's bedside.

The sick man gamely sat up and tried to correct proofs of *The Winter Journey,* but as his temperature was rising and his strength falling, he soon had to give it up. This was his last piece of work.

After attending him for two days, Dr. Ernst Rinna fell ill. New physicians were called in and, on November sixteenth, they decided that he was going to have typhus (or "nerve fever" as it was then called), but still hoped that he would recover. *Typhus abdominalis*

---

[1] Schober may have sent him *The Prairie,* which had appeared in English only the year before. This writer was just then as popular in Europe as Upton Sinclair is today. The appearance of a new story of his in translation was an important literary event. In his *The World of Washington Irving* (New York, E. P. Dutton & Co., Inc., 1944), Van Wyck Brooks calls this letter "perhaps the most touching tribute to Cooper." How zestfully the composer of *Das Wandern* would have enjoyed the wild glories of the Glimmerglass! The enthusiasm, however, would have been a one-way affair, for the brave pioneers of Cooperstown, New York, would have felt small interest in the ugly little Viennese and his high-brow music.

was what he had, the same disease that had killed his mother. Professor Deutsch writes: "Among the conditions that had helped to bring it about were Schubert's obesity, a certain tendency toward alcoholism, and the bad water of the Neue Wieden district."

En route to Germany in quest of singers for his opera, Lachner called on Schubert, November seventeenth, found him seriously ill, and recorded:

He was fully in his right mind, and I had several hours' conversation with that most unassuming and sympathetic of friends. He told me of various plans for the future; and what made him the happiest was looking forward to recovery, so that he could finish his opera, *Der Graf von Gleichen*.

So we see the exhausted composer still haunted by his fixed idea, the fatal ambition which had always been his curse. Fantastic as it may sound, that same day he actually begged Bauernfeld to write him a new opera libretto. This friend noted:

Schubert was in bad shape and complained of weakness and heat in the head. But that afternoon he was quite himself, without a sign of delirium, although my friend's depressed mood filled me with serious forebodings. His brother came, along with the doctors. By evening, the sick man already began to rave wildly. The most violent form of typhus had broken out.

The whole of November eighteenth, the patient had to be held by force in bed. He begged piteously not to be left "in this corner under ground." When Ferdinand strove to convince him that he was in his own room, he cried, "No, it is not true. Beethoven is not lying here!" His tortured, delirious mind must have told him that already he was dead and in another world—a world where he had confidently expected to make up for the greatest opportunity which he had missed in life. There he would be welcomed by the creator of the C Sharp Minor Quartet, and they would wander away, arm in arm, and be bosom friends forever after. But now he had reached the other side and—Beethoven was not there! Here was the last and bitterest cup, the final disappointment of his tragic life! [1]

[1] That cry of his held a hidden truth. Because both died within a few months of each other, Schubert is often thought of as belonging to Beethoven's time; whereas, being twenty-seven years younger, he was of the following generation, the generation of post-Napoleonic war-weariness. Beethoven was not there.

In a lucid interval that evening, he called Ferdinand to his bedside
and asked, "You, what is happening to me?" The distressed brother
tried to calm him and held out hopes of a speedy recovery. But
Franzl looked him squarely in the eye, laid his feeble hand upon the
wall, and murmured, "Here, here is my end."

The end, just as he was discovering a new world of music, 'before
his pen had gleaned his teeming brain.' No other composer, not even
Mozart, had ever died at such a supreme height and promise of pro-
ductivity. I like Bonavia's words: "The bitterness he felt at the approach of death was no vulgar fear, but the' grief of one who felt
life ebbing away in sight of the Promised land." And what music
lover will not endorse Cobbett's beautiful valedictory?:

> The possibilities of his future as a composer, dating from that moment,
> transcend the bounds of human prevision. He had already composed the
> C Major Quintet, the most romantically conceived work in all chamber
> music, and had shortly before begun seriously to study counterpoint.
> Material was accumulating for the composition of masterpieces to come,
> and one can imagine that vistas of supreme beauty were opening out
> before his inspired gaze while the darkness was closing around him. The
> soul of every true musician aches at the thought that this newly begun
> chapter in his artistic life was fated to come to a premature end.[1]

At three o'clock on the afternoon of November 19, 1828, he gave
up the struggle. The greatest natural musical genius since Mozart
had, like that brother spirit, died poverty stricken in the city which
claimed to be the hub of the musical world. His friends were beside
themselves with sorrow. When Schwind heard the news in Munich,
he cried, "Schubert is dead, and with him has perished our brightest
and most beautiful possession!" He wrote to Schober:

> I have wept for him as for one of my brothers; but now I do not grudge
> it to him to have died in his greatness and to be free of his cares. The
> more I now realize what he was, the more I realize what he suffered.

And these are Bauernfeld's words:

> Yesterday afternoon Schubert died. As late as Monday I talked with
> him. On Tuesday he was delirious; on Wednesday he was dead . . . It

[1] From Cobbett's *Cyclopedic Survey of Chamber Music*, compiled and edited
by W. W. Cobbett, p. 365. Used by permission of Oxford University Press.

is like a dream to me. The most honest soul, the most faithful friend! I
only wish that I lay there in his stead; for he leaves earth in glory!

These poignant evidences of grief contrast strangely with the
letter which tough-minded Father Schubert wrote Ferdinand the
morning of the nineteenth, abounding more in pious commonplaces
than in warm human emotion.

For his coffin, following the fashion of the time, they clad this un-
fashionable extrovert in the least appropriate of garments—the robe
of a hermit.

Father Schubert announced that his son, "tone artist and composer," was to be buried in the Matzleinsdorf Cemetery. But the loyal
Ferdinand had been deeply impressed by Franzl's cry, "Beethoven
is not lying here!" He took it as voicing a wish to lie in death near his
idol. So, at six o'clock on November twenty-first, the morning of the
funeral, he wrote his father urging that the burial should take place
in the cemetery at Währing. This would cost about seventy gulden.
"Much, very much—but for Franz it is surely very little!" And, surprisingly enough, the old man agreed to divide with him the extra
outlay.

There were two funeral services. In the Margarethen Pfarrkirche
they performed the *Pax Vobiscum,* a melody of Schubert's for which
Schober—doubtless remorseful for his white feather—rewrote his
own text of eleven years before. These lines of it are specially
touching:

> *Für viele Rosen hat dies Erdenleben*
> *Dir scharfe Dornen nur zum Lohn gegeben,*
> *Ein langes Leiden und ein frühes Grab,*
> *Dort fallen alle Ketten ab.*

> (Only with piercing thorns were you repaid
> For all the gifts of roses that you made—
> With long pain and a tomb that treats you better
> By loosing every fetter.)

Instead of appropriately giving any of Schubert's larger works,
there was a *Trauermotette* (a *Mourning Motet*) which had been
hastily composed for the occasion by Gänsbacher, the musical director of the cathedral. Gänsbacher's position probably made him so
powerful that none of the dead man's family or Circle dared insist on

having Schubert's music performed instead of the mighty director's poor stuff.[1]

Such paltry considerations also played a part in selecting the program of the memorial service organized for December twenty-third by a committee chosen from members of the Circle. The rehearsal was held in the hall of those Friends of Music who had probably lost the "*Gastein*" Symphony, and had balked at performing the great C Major. On this occasion, instead of giving one of the late composer's noble religious works, they chose a third-rate *Requiem* by committeeman Anselm Hüttenbrenner. Good advertising for Hüttenbrenner![2] It is not pleasant to find the resistance that Schubert had always encountered for his music continued thus after his death even in his own Circle.

There was a second funeral service in the Währing Church of the Saints Lawrence and Gertrude. Then the procession formed anew, the pallbearers in red cloaks, the mourners bearing burning wax candles decked with flowers, and Franz Schubert was buried as close as possible to the bones of Beethoven.

This death aroused Austria to a tardy consciousness of its loss. As soon as Schubert had departed, Vienna, for the first time, stirred from its genial sloth to make much of him. The city might appropriately have adopted as its motto a paraphrase of the inscription often found on sundials:

Musicos non numero nisi mortuos.

[Freely translated:]

(I honor none but dead musicians.)

A short and simple task fell to the official inventorist of Franz's property. It consisted of a few clothes and bedclothes, and "some old music," and was valued at 63 florins, A.C., or $30.37, which would today be worth three times as much. Biographers, assuming that "some old music" included the manuscripts of Schubert's unpublished compositions, have indignantly complained of its value being

[1] This Gänsbacher was a bosom friend of Meyerbeer's. His son became an intimate of Brahms, and received the dedication of the latter's 'Cello Sonata in E Minor.
[2] It will be recalled that this greathearted friend had once allowed Schubert to present him a cherished Mozart manuscript (see p. 65), and that he concealed the score of the "*Unfinished*" Symphony for forty-three years (see p. 106).

estimated at 10 florins, A.C., or $4.82. They have not known that
Franz, regarding his move to Ferdinand's house as a temporary visit,
left his manuscripts behind at Schober's, with the possible exception
of boyhood compositions which his father may have kept for him.
They have also failed to recognize that what Ferdinand and Father
Franz valued at 10 florins was only a pile of old, used music books by
other composers, and that it was to the advantage of the heirs to
keep the valuation as low as possible. The estate included 118 florins,
V.C., in cash. Franz Schubert had given humanity so much for so
little!

Perhaps the friends were conscious how remiss they had been in
the matter of the memorial music, for they decided to erect a worthy
monument at the grave, and sent out a call for contributions. Anna
Fröhlich got up a concert which gave *Miriam* and other works by
Schubert, and the first finale of Mozart's *Don Juan*, the sole concession to popular taste being variations for flute by Gabrielsky. The
successful affair was soon repeated, and the monument was assured.
It cost 360 silver florins, 46 kreutzer. A bust was made by Josef Alois
Dialer, and Grillparzer, whose beautiful eulogy had, the year before,
been spoken at Beethoven's funeral, wrote the following inscription
for the tomb, which was but one grave removed from the older
master's:

DER TONKUNST BEGRUB HIER EINEN REICHEN BESITZ,
ABER NOCH VIEL SCHONERE HOFFNUNGEN.
FRANZ SCHUBERT LIEGT HIER.
GEBOREN AM XXXI JAENNER MDCCXCVII.
GESTORBEN AM XIX NOV. MDCCCXXVIII.
XXXI JAHRE ALT.[1]

(THE ART OF MUSIC HAS HERE ENTOMBED A RICH
POSSESSION,
BUT EVEN FAR FAIRER HOPES.
FRANZ SCHUBERT LIES HERE.
BORN JANUARY 31, 1797.
DIED NOV. 19, 1828.
31 YEARS OLD.)

In those early days, Grillparzer's fine epitaph was unjustly cen-
sured by those who knew the composer chiefly as a composer of

---

[1] The text of this inscription, as given by Kreissle, and followed by Dahms,
Stefan, and others, is grossly incorrect.

songs, and felt that, in this field, art could rise no higher. We know, however, that by the age of thirty-one Beethoven had not progressed beyond his First Symphony, which cannot be compared with Schubert's *"Unfinished"* or great C Major, and that he had yet written no choral works which can be mentioned in the same breath with his successor's Mass in E Flat. We know that Schubert, in his last illness, had begun anew the study of counterpoint. Poignantly we sense the vast promise inherent in the trios, the Octet, the last quartets, and the incomparable C Major Quintet. We know that he was then turning away from song to throw himself with fiery enthusiasm into the larger field. And we are confident that, if he had lived, he would almost certainly have dowered the world with even greater works of absolute music. Richard Heuberger's judgment was sadly at fault when he persuaded the authorities to omit Grillparzer's lines from the present tomb.

In 1863 the bones of the two great composers were exhumed,[1] and given better coffins. In 1888 they were dug up again,[2] and moved to the Central Cemetery, Beethoven on June twenty-second, and Schubert on September twenty-third. By this time the latter as well had become a world figure. Huge throngs accompanied his bones to their new resting place, that greatest of musical pantheons which now also contains the cenotaph of Mozart, and the tombs of Gluck, Wolf, and Brahms.[3]

As for the ceremonial music, it is curious to observe the same odd parsimony in giving the works of Schubert that had, sixty years before, marked his funeral and memorial ceremonies. Wind players from the Court Orchestra merely blew *Death and the Maiden,* but the massed singing societies of Vienna and vicinity poured out a stupendous volume of sound in—the *Libera* of Johann von Herbeck.[4]

---

[1] Measurements showed that Beethoven was 5 ft. 5 in. tall, while Schubert was only 5 ft. ½ in.

[2] When Schubert's skull came to light, it was reverently kissed by Anton Bruckner.

[3] The intrusion of Von Suppé scarcely disturbs the harmony of that august assemblage.

[4] Herbeck, a brilliant and successful conductor, had led the *Männergesangverein* and the chorus of the Friends of Music, and had wielded a very powerful influence. He was a man who, as was said of Theodore Roosevelt, wished to be the bride at a wedding, and the corpse at a funeral. Loyalty to his vivid memory may have led the committee to prefer his music to that of the honored dead. This masterful person had been an opponent of Brahms. His claim to remembrance lies in having discovered and first performed Schubert's *"Unfinished."*

The grouping of genius in the lovely composers' corner may have inspired a tribute in lighter vein. Böhler's charming silhouette shows Schubert in heaven on his hundredth birthday. Though unfortunately none of his own Circle seems to be there, he is greeted by a highly distinguished committee, with Bruckner, Schumann, and Liszt at the far end of the line, and Beethoven and Mozart at the near. Heaven's fare is evidently richer than the birthday celebrant managed to get on earth, for now only Schumann, Handel, and Bach can rival Franzl in the matter of girth. A highly animated orchestra and *corps de ballet* of cherubs provide the airy accompaniment. The 'cellists are brandishing their instruments in a hair-raising manner. The tuba player's heavy horn seems to be bearing him down and out of the picture, while one of the percussionists has come a cropper, and only his chubby legs are visible.

Less happy than this was Vienna's sculptural tribute. Considering the local neglect of Schubert when he was alive, it is astonishing that his own city erected a monument to him before thus honoring Haydn, Mozart, or Beethoven. The cornerstone of Kundmann's atrocity in the Stadtpark was laid on October 12, 1868, with those aged friends, Bauernfeld, Schober, and Sonnleithner in attendance, but with true southern leisureliness, the unveiling tarried until May 15, 1872.

The same old friends were there again, together with Schubert's sister Maria Theresia, Lachner, Baron von Schönstein, and the Fröhlich sisters. The statue itself is heavily idealized. The nose is straightened and lengthened, and the lips refined. The three medallions on the pedestal are supposed to represent instrumental and vocal music, and the musical imagination. They are conceived in the feeblest, most saccharine and sentimental tradition of Thorwaldsen's imitators. That Johannes Brahms regarded this as the beau ideal of a monument for a composer reveals the appalling depth of his taste in plastic art.

Lamentable as it is, this mark of honor cost 8,500 dollars. A small part of this sum might have prolonged the life of the genius whose short thirty-one years knew less fame than famine.[1] Writing of

---

[1] It is perfectly true that Franzl's pockets had a way of turning into sieves; yet even so, less dishonesty from publishers and more generosity from patrons and the public would have meant more vacations in the country and more years of creativeness.

Schubert in Heaven on his hundredth birthday
Silhouette by Otto Böhler (1897).

SCHUBERT

Pencil drawing by Leopold Kupelwieser (1821).

Death mask of Schubert

Vienna's belated monumental generosity, Duncan aptly quotes some
lines of Sam Wesley's, composed in another connection:

> See him, when starved to death and turned to dust,
> Presented with a monumental bust.
> The poet's fate is here in emblem shown,
> He asked for bread and he received a stone.

And the profusion of costly flowers lavished yearly on this absurd
"stone," recalls a more recent poem by Nixon Waterman:

> A rose to the living is more
>   Than sumptuous wreaths to the dead:
> In filling love's infinite store,
> A rose to the living is more,—
> If graciously given before
>   The hungering spirit is fled,—
> A rose to the living is more
>   Than sumptuous wreaths to the dead.[1]

One is glad to remember that the faithful Bauernfeld, who had
brought many a modest rose to his living friend, laid upon his tomb
the beautiful poetic tribute that ends:

> *Er ist nicht tot im ew'gen Reich des Schönen,*
> *Und seine Seele lebt in seinen Tönen.*

> (From beauty's timeless realm he is not gone;
> And in his melodies his soul lives on.)

[1] From *A Book of Verse* by Nixon Waterman. Copyright, 1900, by Nixon
Waterman. Forbes & Co., New York and Chicago.

PART II

THE MUSIC

Their works do follow them.
REVELATION, XIV, 13.

In some ways, the music of this amazing genius is more indispensable to us than that of any other composer.

HAROLD BAUER.

In the following pages, only the more important works of Schubert will be considered.

32

PIANO TRIOS

SCHUBERT'S position among composers of chamber music varies with his vehicle. In their respective spheres, the Octet and the quintets have no serious rivals. The trios rank among the best of their kind. Except for sheer inspiration, Schubert was surpassed in the field of the string quartet by Haydn, Mozart, Beethoven, and Brahms. However, if, like Brahms, he had burned all but his last three quartets,[1] his rank in this department would be higher than it is, though we would have been deprived of much light on his musical development. Samuel L. Laciar[2] is right in saying that those youthful exercises, Schubert's early quartets,

show great deviations from form, some of them fatal to their unqualified acceptance, despite their wealth of musical ideas. These first quartets are very uneven, passages of entrancing beauty frequently standing beside others which are utterly unworthy of the genius of Schubert; moreover, many of the movements are hopelessly verbose.

Particularly as a writer of chamber music, Schubert became the first harmonic impressionist. In his romantic quest for color, the break with tonality becomes progressively evident, to culminate in the G Major Quartet. Willi Kahl[3] writes that Schubert's

link with later times is found, above all, in the development of sensuous sound effect and the breadth of colouring . . . The wider orchestral conception of sound values in chamber music for strings indicated quite new paths in this category, and undoubtedly did something towards making possible a Bruckner string quintet.

[1] There are 15 in the G.A., and Grove mentions 20. Brahms burned his first 20.
[2] In *The Musical Quarterly*, Oct., 1928.
[3] In *Cobbett's Cyclopaedic Survey of Chamber Music*.

One of my most agreeable memories goes back to a year or two
before the Second World War. In Budapest, that chamber-musical
city par excellence, I had the honor of playing in a private gathering
of distinguished musicians. After a few string quartets, a famous
pianist arrived. Someone suggested that we choose by secret ballot the
most purely beautiful of all music for piano and strings and play it
with him. When the ballots were counted, Schubert's B Flat Trio,
Op. 99,[1] like Abou Ben Adhem in Leigh Hunt's poem, "led all the
rest." And the vote was justified; for this rare work contains the composer's most ethereal and Arielesque pages.

The swinging strength of the opening theme[2]

[Ex. 1]

(the Germans would call it a "head theme," but it has heart as well)
is a perfect foil for the transcendent loveliness of the second subject,
that begins

[Ex. 2]

The latter part of this subject is almost as exquisite:

[Ex. 3]

and the spell grows stronger with its delicious variation at diminuendo.

[1] For establishing chronology, the opus numbers of Schubert's works are about
as valuable as the dates on the forged labels of imitation Stradivarius violins.
E.g., *Amalia*, Op. 173, No. 1, was written in 1815, while the A Minor Quartet,
Op. 29, dates from 1824.

[2] Notice one of Schubert's rhythmical mannerisms: a long note followed by
three short ones, as in the opening of the D Minor Quartet, and *passim*. Also its
reverse: three shorts and a long, as in the scherzos of this Trio and of the *"Trout"*
Quintet. One long followed by two shorts (a dactyl) is still more frequent.

The piano part of the whole work is written with almost as discreet a lightness as that of the *"Trout"* Quintet—a lightness refreshingly unusual in piano trios and which makes up for a lack of variety and originality in the keyboard figuration. Unfortunately most composers (like most pianists) have overlooked the disparity in power between the percussion and the bowed instruments; with the result that piano trios usually suggest a howitzer shooting it out against a couple of revolvers. A mere modicum of advantage like this, however, is not enough to suit some keyboard artists. And J. A. Westrup[1] actually deplores the piano part's lack of resonance in the Schubert trios. Fiddlers, however, are of another opinion. They lift up their voices blessing and praising the merciful composer.

In this opening movement of the B Flat, the development, one of Schubert's outstanding attempts to solve a problem that he always found especially difficult, is noteworthy for the success with which the first part of the second subject is handled, and for its well-nigh symphonic quality. This is one of those self-contained and intensely lyrical themes so notoriously refractory to development. The key system of the recapitulation is piquant. Beginning with the surprise of G flat, it only returns to the original B flat when the piano serves out the theme.

The slow movement is one of Ariel's loftiest inspirations. It is "linkèd sweetness long drawn out," but even so, not long enough drawn out for many music lovers. The opening cantabile is in the 'cello's most grateful register:

[Ex. 4]

The violin takes it up; then the piano works it out against a string counterpoint that comes into being as naturally "as the grass grows on the weirs." Relief from the emotional intensities is provided by the second theme with its graceful cascades of thirty-second notes. The strings accompany the piano version of this with a characteristic

[1] In Abraham.

Schubertian richness recalling that of the A Minor Quartet's opening. Here we have the pioneer master of song, who made of the accompaniment a new form of art. When the first theme returns, the hearer is sure that this is one of the greatest melodies that Schubert ever composed.

The succulent counterpoint of the slow movement has prepared one for the airy imitations of the highly successful Scherzo. Ariel begins it

[Ex. 5]

in a blithe, mundane mood, with capricious rhythms and humorous hesitations. But in the Trio he spreads wings and soars:

[Ex. 6]

The finale starts with a merry, highly Viennese, and somewhat frothy tune:

[Ex. 7]

but, as is often the way with last movements and last acts, it does not live up to the standard of the preceding. Besides, it suffers from

Franzl's besetting fault of prolixity, a fault which can be masked only by such a supreme performance as that recorded by Heifetz, Feuermann, and Rubinstein. However, these pages (all but the unfortunate 3/2 passages and the coda) are genuine Schubert in one of his sprightly moods, and are more adequate to end what has gone before than are many finales of other great trios. Think, for example, of the disappointing end of Beethoven's *"Archduke,"* Op. 97!

The fact that this utterly sane and joyful work was probably written in the same October of 1827 that saw the completion of the morbidly sorrowful *Winter Journey,* is a warning not to deduce from a composer's works his emotional state while putting them upon paper.

The diversified richness of tone color in these pages is almost startling.

Daniel Gregory Mason[1] points out that Schubert's

chamber music shows how much he can accomplish with limited means. In his two trios, . . . by making the most of the percussion quality of the piano, as well as of both the pizzicato and the sustained tones of the strings, he evolves a surprising variety from the three instruments.

One of the more mundanely successful ventures of Schubert's unsuccessful life was the E Flat Trio, Op. 100. This was the first work which he sold to a foreign publisher. He heard several readings of it, the last one at the concert of his own music, and each time it was warmly received.

This second Trio has less of the Ariel quality than the first but in other ways compensates so fully as to make a choice between them difficult. It opens, in a three-octave unison, with a more cerebral "head theme" than its mate, one more amenable to development than most of Schubert's sonata-form material. Here is the start, with a significant bit of the continuation:

[Ex. 8]

[1] In *The Romantic Composers,* New York, The Macmillan Company, 1906.

There is a portentous climax, immediately followed, *pianissimo*,
by an addendum to the first subject, a highly Schubertian B minor
theme that recalls the B minor minuet of the *"Fantasy"* Sonata in G,
Op. 78 (see p. 277, ex. 99) which had been composed thirteen
months before, in October, 1826.

[Ex. 9]

Note the characteristic accompaniment of double-stopped strings.[1]
The second subject begins with a soaring melody and leads to

[1] When Westrup (in Abraham) implies a censure of Schubert for this reminiscence, he forgets that allusions like this occur in the work of every composer,
particularly to music most characteristic of himself. These often constitute the
inner essence of his creation and become, as it were, his sign manual. It is significant that the minuet recalled by this theme is the most Schubertian movement in all the piano sonatas.

a rare and mystically beautiful page. It comes from the composer's inner core, and distils his utmost magic:

[Ex. 10]

Consider by what astonishingly simple means such a wonder was created. But, for all their simplicity, who else would have conceived the appoggiaturas in the third and fourth bars, or the little run of eighth notes in the sixth? Surely if any music ever deserved to be called "religious," it is this.

The *Andante con moto* begins with a long 'cello cantabile. Schubert is said to have taken it from a Swedish folk song sung to him by Isaak Berg, who later taught Jenny Lind.

[Ex. 11]

Bars 3 and 4 remind one of the start of the *Adagio* of the C Major
Symphony of Schumann, who was fond of the E Flat Trio and, as
a Leipzig student, gave a party in its honor. This mournful melody,
with its spectral, oddly accented accompaniment, suggests a funeral
march. It gives place to a theme in the relative major ringing with
happy vitality. Now the oil of joy replaces the spirit of heaviness as
blithely as does the major theme in the *Allegretto* of Beethoven's
Seventh Symphony. The joy rises to a resounding climax. The opening minor melody returns to cap this climax with a more powerful
one of its own, whose sorrowful agitation recalls the atmosphere of
those somber outbursts in corresponding portions of the G Major
Quartet and of the String Quintet. Then the major theme, starting
very softly, crescendoes into a page of breath-taking power, marked
by three of the *fff* signs so rarely employed by Schubert. A wraithlike
coda, *Un poco più lento*, puts in the perfect last word.

The Scherzo, like that of the First Trio, one of the composer's
best and most characteristic, offers much jolly canonic imitation
between piano and strings, though the latter are doubled more
than good trio style sanctions. The E major section has a long,
particularly Schubertian free canonic melody in the rhythm of the
opening theme. It starts:

[Ex. 12]

The highly original Trio, which may have served as inspiration for some of Schumann's bolder flights, has some excellent counterpoint, and, like the Scherzo proper, offers a reminder of the ♩ ♩ ♫♫ rhythm with which the first movement (ex. 9) recalled the minuet of the *"Fantasy"* Sonata.

For all its undeniable charm, the immensely long finale, like that of the B Flat, fails to reach the level of the foregoing pages, and shares the other's fault of prolixity. The organic incorporation into it of the first theme of the slow movement (ex. 11) was a more important pioneer innovation than were the inorganic quotations from previous movements in Beethoven's Fifth and *"Choral"* Symphonies.[1]

The economy of material implied by thematic work is, naturally, rare in such a fertile melodist as Schubert; and, when found, is all the more noteworthy. The melodic pattern of the first measure of ex. 1, p. 204, recurs in both trios. This germ motive[2] is in all cases marked by brackets. In the B Flat work it starts the Trio of the Scherzo (p. 206, ex. 6) and recurs twice (the first time with a chromatic change) in the opening subject of the finale (p. 206, ex. 7). Not content with this, Schubert used the same germ motive in both the first and second subjects of the opening movement of the E Flat Trio (see p. 207, ex. 8, and p. 209, ex. 10), strangely enough, with the selfsame notes: B flat, A, B flat, D. And he used it again, slightly modified, in the Scherzo (see p. 211, ex. 12).

Everybody adores Schubert for giving us these priceless trios, but the gratitude of the amateur 'cellist is somewhat chastened by the technical terrors of the B Flat.

[1] The most successful modern use of this procedure is in the Franck String Quartet, where the principal theme of the slow movement functions as an integral part of the finale.

[2] To avoid clumsy foreign expressions, the writer has, in earlier books, been obliged to coin the expression germ motive. It means a germinal melodic phrase, cyclically used to interlock the parts of a sonata, symphony, trio, etc., into a more or less unified whole. In order to escape monotony, its identity is usually disguised by subtle rhythmic and harmonic changes, and even by slight interpolations.

33

OTHER CHAMBER MUSIC WITH PIANO

THE naïve, sparkling exhilaration of the *"Trout"* Quintet, Op. 114, is perfectly harmonious with the atmosphere of the fresh Austrian countryside where it was created. In this it is a younger brother of Mozart's Clarinet Quintet. It opens as purely and sweetly as that immortal work and, with but a single lapse, remains so throughout. One needs but little imaginative help to catch the twenty-two-year-old Franzl enjoying the jolly gurgle of the Danube and the spicy fragrance of crushed fir bark as the logs are jostled together by the current. This work gives the impression of having been composed in that rare state of mind and body when a man is simultaneously stimulated and relaxed. Here we have the true Schwammerl in one of his most radiant and carefree moods.

The instrumental personnel is a unique combination: violin, viola, 'cello, double bass[1] and piano. This probably represents the local talent available in 1819 at Steyr, when and where Op. 114 was written. The *"Trout"* is the first important work ever composed for piano and four strings. From the fiddler's standpoint it is scored for Schubert's own instrument with such merciful lightness and discretion as to be unique in the literature of chamber music with piano.

The first movement is rich in well-contrasted themes. Here is the third, in the violin's condensed version:

[Ex. 13]

This is typical of Franzl's exuberance in holiday mood.

[1] Schubert treated this unusual chamber instrument with an exquisite modera-

At the start of the recapitulation there is subtle humor in his abbreviation of the first subject as if to say, "Well now, the movement has run along an unconscionable time. Let's make short work of it!" And indeed, the recapitulation turns out thirty-six bars briefer than the exposition. This movement is notable for a forecast of one of Schubert's greatest songs. At the twenty-first bar, the piano prophesies the charming phrase to appear seven years later in *Who is Sylvia?*, at the words "That adorèd she might be."

With each encounter I like the *Andante* better. It starts with this happy strain:

[Ex. 14]

The first change of key brings another premonition of a famous song. With tender melancholy, in thirds and sixths, viola and 'cello offer a mellow anticipation of the long interlude in the *Serenade*, to be written nine months later and to become Schubert's most popular lied.

A Viennese friend of mine, whom Hitler had driven to America, was reunited after long years with his beloved wife. Fondly embracing her, he sat down at the piano and, with tears in his eyes, played the soft part of this *Andante*, just before the return of ex. 14:

[Ex. 15]

To both of them it meant the spirit of the old, unspoiled Austria.

There is an infectious humor in the Scherzo. It starts with the same rhythm which, long after, was to do yeoman service in the corresponding movement of the B Flat Trio (see p. 206, ex. 5), and in the

tion that makes many listeners welcome it. But Daniel Gregory Mason wrote this marginal comment on my manuscript, "To some ears it seems to 'queer' the combination almost disastrously—as if a whale had somehow got into the trout's pool and couldn't get out!"

[Ex. 16]

Trio of the *"Fantasy"* Sonata, Op. 78. The jollity culminates in that phenomenon—almost unparalleled in chamber music—a double bass solo. True, it consists only of four loud E's. And, true again, it is not quite a bona fide solo, as it is doubled an octave higher by the 'cello, though the latter is always drowned out by its burly brother. So rare and jolly is the occasion that everyone looks up and smiles at the proud bassist.[1] The Trio is one of Schubert's most ingratiating waltzes.

Those blameless and straightaway variations on Schubert's song, *The Trout*, which christens the Quintet, are so naïve, and follow their theme so literally as to fall a little out of the general picture. It is interesting to compare them with the far more subtle and deeply spiritualized variations on that other song, *Death and the Maiden*, in the D Minor Quartet. Even though he could not do them justice with his bow, one conceives how happy his solos made Paumgartner, the amateur 'cellist who commissioned this work. Let us hope that he was not put to the shame of hearing the contra-bassist excel him in the rapid unison triplets of Variation Four!

The jovial and highly Schubertian finale is an almost worthy companion piece to that of the A Minor Quartet. It starts as a perfect exemplification of Austrian *Gemütlichkeit*, completely relaxed and out to celebrate. After two bars of a unison E, it begins thus:

[1] Perhaps Franzl was inspired by that 'cello solo of Beethoven's on fifteen low B flats, starting the Scherzo of the first Rasoumowsky Quartet. When Romberg, the then famous 'cellist-composer, first played this, he thought he was being "had," grew purple with rage, hurled the music to the floor, and apoplectically danced upon it.

[Ex. 17]

Each phrase is given out by the strings and echoed by the piano. It reminds one of a hymn in a meeting house of the long ago, each line sung out by the precentor and repeated by the congregation, but here with a far more felicitous result. Observe how the first phrase gets the utmost musical value out of a simple turn, and how the second phrase elaborates the first. Schubert was unexcelled in the art of distilling an organic musical effect from turns, trills, grace notes, and other accessories which most composers use unorganically as mere ornaments.[1] Perhaps he caught the idea from Mozart.

The delightful antiphony sweeps us away until we are brought up with a painful jolt against the second subject. Alas! this degenerates into the sort of banality that causes the little rift within many a Schubertian lute. Suddenly, after the powerful climax toward the end of the exposition, come two bars of the thrilling silence which was one of Schubert's specialties. Somewhat wistfully we wonder why this silence could not have occurred at the "little rift," been extended to delete the whole of that unfortunate tune and, temporarily, as Tennyson put it, 'make the music mute.'

The *"Trout"* Quintet has other small defects, such as overmuch repetition, and a too monotonous use of repeated notes and figures, especially for viola and 'cello. However, one should be thankful for the almost pure delight of this highly characteristic, socially minded, carefree, holiday piece, and not look a gift lute in the rift.

The four Sonatas for Violin and Piano, Opp. 131, Nos. 1, 2, and 3,[2] and 162, are pretty and charming, with excellent teamwork for the partners. They are not very important works and boast little of the real Schubert, but make it up in part by offering some presentable Beethoven and generous portions of Mozart. For example, the First Sonata (in D) starts thus:

[Ex. 18]

[1] See *By the Sea* (*Am Meer*), p. 315, *Ave Maria*, p. 322, the *Grand Duo*, p. 295, and the Octet finale, p. 225.

[2] The publisher labeled these three, "Sonatinas."

which sounds curiously like a major version of the first theme of Mozart's E Minor Sonata for Violin and Piano (K. 304):

[Ex. 19]

The scale series in the *Andante* of the A Minor Sonata was evidently inspired by that in the corresponding movement of Mozart's G Minor Piano Quartet (K. 478). Its finale and the second half of the G Minor Sonata contain even more of the Salzburg genius than of their own composer. For example, the second subject of the A Minor's finale is a child of the last movement of the *"Hunt"* Quartet (K. 458).

One finds, however, but few of those cheap, vulgar pages (such as the A flat portion of the A Major Sonata's *Andantino*) that strike a jarring note in so many of Schubert's greater works. There is a delightful crispness and innocent, childlike freshness about the whole D Major, and many pages of the others, which remind one that, when they were written, the composer was a mere youth of nineteen or twenty.

In their own class, these works compare creditably with the first few symphonies. Consider, for example, the strong, surprising and moving harmonies and modulations under the broadly modeled violin melody in the working-out portion of the A Minor's first movement. Note also, in the A Major, Schubert's richer and more original exploitation of keyboard possibilities in chamber music.

The word *brillant,* in a title of Schubert's period, usually prepares one for pure trash. But the *Rondo brillant,* Op. 70, is far from trash. Composed in 1826, the year of the last two quartets, it is stronger, better music than the violin sonatas, and even offers a few gleams of the real Schubert, like the second part of the main theme,

[Ex. 20]

and the last alternative subject, with its dotted grace and charm. Two notes[1] at the beginning and end of the introduction

[Ex. 21]

launch the principal subject, acting as a tiny liaison motive. The rhythmic *élan* of the whole Rondo is infectious. In this piece, and the following, the piano and violin parts are equal in interest and importance.

Though the Fantasy for Violin and Piano, Op. 159, was written as a show piece for the Czech virtuoso Josef Slavik, it has pages of higher quality than any of the foregoing duets. The beautiful *Andante molto*, though demanding too much of the piano in the way of string tremolos, actually looks forward at the fifth bar to the opening of the C Major Quintet. Probably composed in the glorious year of 1827, it cannot help giving us the real Schubert in this movement, in the A minor portions of the exciting and somewhat Hungarian *Allegretto*, and in the theme of the *Andantino*, which is his song *Sei mir gegrüsst*, though altered not wholly for the better.

The first three variations are uninteresting display, but in the fourth Schubert comes back to himself. A bit of the delightful introduction returns, rises to a tremendous climax, and ushers in the exciting and somewhat characteristic *Allegro vivace* variation. After which the *Allegretto* indulges in a welcome memory of the theme, and the *Presto* coda touches off concluding fireworks. The movements run together without a pause, an audacious novelty which, in those days, was hard for both listener and critic to swallow.

The Variations for Flute and Piano, Op. 160, on the song *Withered Flowers* (Trock'ne Blumen) from the *Mill* Cycle, though a welcome addition to the somewhat bare cupboard of flute literature, are musically of no great importance.

In 1823, Johann Georg Stauffer of Vienna invented a six-stringed, fretted instrument that resembled the guitar and was played like the 'cello. He baptized this hybrid the "arpeggione." Schubert liked it and wrote for it a Sonata in A Minor. The arpeggione is now as

---

[1] These are somewhat reminiscent of the start of the *Allegro vivace* in Beethoven's Third Rasoumowsky Quartet, and that of the *"Kreutzer"* Sonata's first *Presto*.

dead as the rebec, but the three good themes which Schubert invested in it are sometimes enjoyed on the 'cello or viola. Gaspar Cassadó even turned the piece into a 'cello concerto.

The *Allegro moderato* starts with this engaging subject:

[Ex. 22]

Then the composer begins to make concessions to the deplorable taste of the time, and sinks by easy stages to approximately the refinement of a Hérold.

The main theme of the lovely *Adagio* is Schubert, pure and undefiled:

[Ex. 23]

Repeating the sorry tale of the first movement, the finale opens with music of quality, a pleasantly carefree, lighthearted lilt full of the composer's Viennese charm, then degenerates to technical ostentation and the salon style of the day.

34

CHAMBER MUSIC FOR STRINGS AND WIND

THE Octet in F, Op. 166, for string quintet, clarinet, bassoon, and horn, was written in February, 1824. Like the *"Trout"* Quintet, it was commissioned by an amateur enthusiast, this time a clarinetist. Count Ferdinand Troyer was chief steward of Beethoven's patron, the Archduke Rudolph. This lucky sponsor was a better performer than 'cellist Paumgartner, and appropriately was gladdened by an even better composition.

It is probable that the Count, having played and liked Beethoven's Septet, asked for a work planned upon the same lines. At any rate, that was what he received. Both compositions have six movements and two introductions (like an old-fashioned suite), of similar general character and for the same instruments, except that the Octet added a second violin. But Schubert did a far more individual job than Beethoven, who in his later years whimsically remarked, "My Septet? It was written by Mozart." [1]

The Octet was first performed in March, 1824, at Count Troyer's home. The host blew the clarinet with pride and joy, and three of the Rasoumowsky Quartet players, Schuppanzigh, Weiss, and Linke, took part. This composition, almost every bit of it, is Schubertian. Heuberger called it "one of the most richly inventive and tonally beautiful works in all chamber music."

After an initial keynote by all hands, the introduction starts engagingly:

---

[1] The fact that Beethoven's work was composed when he was 30, but the Octet when Schubert was only 27, indicates how much earlier the latter ripened than the former. Schubert wrote his mature 9th Symphony at 31; Beethoven, his immature 2nd Symphony at 32.

[Ex. 24]

and proceeds to give veiled hints of the *Allegro's* first subject. This in turn, as easily and naturally as a tree puts forth its leaves, forms the finer second subject:

[Ex. 25]

In the next to the last measure of the above, note Schubert's way of lending richness to a melody at the crucial moment by using a particularly striking harmony, in this case a chord of the dominant thirteenth. When, later on, the horn gives the second subject in the major, it is so satisfyingly hornlike as to suggest that it may have been inspired by the nature of this romantic instrument.

Schubert showed how he loved the second subject by devoting almost the entire development to it. Toward the close of this section he had the felicitous idea of bringing back a variant of the introduction, but in notes twice as long, in order to keep the original tempo. To end the coda, the horn, *ritardando*, breathes a tender

farewell. The lack of contrast between its themes, which, incidentally, is shared by the corresponding movement of Beethoven's A
Minor Quartet, composed the following year, is easily overlooked in
enjoying the purity, freshness, and Schubertian charm of this lovable
music.

Count Troyer must have been overjoyed to find himself beginning
the *Adagio* with one of the composer's longest and most engaging
melodies:

[Ex. 26]

When the first violin took this up, the Count was twice blest with a
counterpoint tune almost as charming. The up and down arpeggio
accompaniment pleased Schubert so much that, a year later, he used
it for the *Ave Maria*. And, indeed, the two melodies themselves have
a trait in common. In great part they depend on his already noted
talent for turning mere ornaments to organic use. (See p. 216.) Com-
paring ex. 26 with ex. 133, p. 322, shows that both tunes are made,
in large measure, from elaborations of the turn.

Despite its fascinating organ points, the second theme of this
Adagio, while still excellent Schubert, does not attain the rich quality of the first. But then, no composer can always stay up in G, and if
he did, there would be no highest, and we should suffer from a
dearth of foils and a monotony of excellence. As it is, the return of
the first subject in the first violin with horn obbligato, and then in the
'cello with clarinet adornment, is doubly effective.

Now comes one of my favorite scherzos. It suggests a whimsical
parody of antiphonal church choral style. One choir starts softly in
unison:

Allegro vivace

[Ex. 27]

Then the other bursts forth mightily with the answer in full harmony:

[Ex. 28]

The humor is made the more piquant by the incongruous suggestion of a scherzo in church. The elastic dotted rhythm scarcely ever ceases its exuberant hopping and skipping. It has very much the infectious momentum of the corresponding movement of the *"Choral"* Symphony.

Lightly scored, and with a toothsome, florid bass, the Trio begins

[Ex. 29]

like a simplification of the start of the finale of Mozart's Wind Divertimento in E Flat (K. 252):

MOZART   (transposed)
Presto assai

[Ex. 30]

This is one of the best among the highly original and characteristic scherzos of Schubert's maturity.

The fourth movement of the Octet consists of variations on a rather commonplace theme from the composer's early musical play, *The Friends of Salamanca*. To all Gilbert and Sullivan addicts this has a strangely familiar sound; for it inspired the sergeant's song in *The Pirates of Penzance*. Despite its pleasantly organ-pointed coda, this movement is the one weak part of the Octet. The variations cling with as old-fashioned literalness to their theme as those in the

"*Trout*" Quintet, and all but the sixth are elegantly embellished with virtuosity's artful aid.

If its Trio were up to the level of the *Menuetto* and coda, the fifth movement would be among the most treasurable pages of Schubert. There is a mysterious but intimate charm in the dusky coloring of the start,

[Ex. 31]

with the feminine appeal of the falling cadence (under the bracket). The first three notes of the first violin recall the introduction (p. 221, ex. 24). This touchingly simple, hearty, and tender movement might well serve as a translation into music of those endearing qualities which have made Vienna the darling of the world.

The somber splendor of that rich tapestry, the introduction to the finale, strikes the one gloomy note in this work. Over a sort of drum

roll, it opens, like the *Menuetto* of the A Minor Quartet, with a quotation from *The Gods of Greece*—the Schubert song that asks,
"Beautiful world, where art thou?"

The answer is immediately forthcoming in the finale, where the
veins of contrapuntal ingenuity are filled, as they all too seldom are,
with the warm, pulsing blood of zestful life. This music catches the
hearer up into a mood like the eager exuberance of a crowd of
youngsters setting forth in high fettle for some such jolly excursion
as that to Atzenbrugg (see cut opposite p. 102):

[*Ex. 32*]

With amusing caprice, the bars are grouped: 3, 5, 2, 2, 4, yet the
rhythm remains sure and convincing. Note the mysteriously organic
effect of the trills. As already remarked, Schubert can make these
ornaments more functional than any other composer, with the possible exception of Mozart. One wonders if the finale of Schumann's
"*Rhenish*" Symphony was not inspired by this infectious movement.
It has the same sparkling gaiety, and the different themes all com-
plement one another with as fertile a resource.

After Schubert's favorite and thrilling device of a two bars' silence,
comes a second subject, smacking of the folk tune and fit to put new
life into jaded feet.

[*Ex. 33*]

What march music could more appropriately accompany the onrush of a crowd of good companions toward a coveted goal?

Abruptly the fun of the recapitulation ends in an echo of the introduction, where seem to shout "ancestral voices prophesying war," then to mutter and groan that "life is real, life is earnest." But all that sort of thing is impatiently brushed aside. And, with the goal in view, the coda becomes a laughing and boisterous foot race, *accelerando*.

There are few *tours de force* so difficult as to write an adequate ending, whether for a play, a symphony, or a work of chamber music. From musicians one hears more criticism of last movements than of anything else. The concluding *Allegro* of this Octet fulfils its function more triumphantly than most finales.

In Schubert's time, people were astonished and repelled by the length of the Octet. Today, despite its wealth of movements and measures, one is sorry to reach the end.

35

CHAMBER MUSIC FOR STRINGS

THE String Quartet in E Flat, Op. 125, No. 1, has been nick-named the *"Haushaltungs Quartett"* (the *Quartetto Domestico,* or *"Household,"* or *"Homebodies'"* Quartet), for it is so easy to play and to understand as to be well suited for family performance. Here is one of Franzl's compositions in which, on Sunday afternoons, Father Schubert probably needed the minimum of admonishment from his sixteen-year-old son.

Musically speaking, the main interest of the E Flat lies in its thematic work. As already noted, Schubert was such a prolific melodist that he rarely resorted to the germ motive. But here he reveled in using it in that unemphatic way which has been noted in connection with the trios. (See p. 212.)

The first movement starts thus:

[Ex. 34]

Here, and in subsequent examples, the germ motive is marked with a bracket. For good measure, he sowed the second theme of the first subject with the germ motive, right side up and upside down:

[Ex. 35]

227

The first four notes of ex. 34 are preluded, interrupted, and varied with scherzoesque appropriateness in order to start the Scherzo:

[Ex. 36]

And then Schubert showed how perfectly these same four notes could be arranged to begin the *Adagio:*

[Ex. 37]

Varied by the interpolation of an E natural, the germ motive starts the finale:

[Ex. 38]

And notice how this subject extends the resemblance to ex. 34 by also ascending the scale to the sixth above.

There is but one serious flaw in the comfortable little Quartet—the second subject of the finale (beginning at bar 80), which is of a vulgarity that would disgrace the cheaper sort of operetta. It is the kind of intrusion that distresses one in too many of Schubert's finer works.

For a lad of seventeen, the B Flat Quartet, Op. 168, is an astonishingly mature composition. Schubert's notation on the ms. records that the first movement was dashed down in four and a half hours of September 5, 1814. There is real value in the clever imitations of the short-winded *fugato* start, and in the dotted portion near the end of the exposition, which pleasantly recalls the corresponding part of Mozart's C Minor Viola Quintet (K. 406).[1]

The *Andante sostenuto,* whose second subject mysteriously recalls *The Erl King,* is deep and tender and, in parts, highly Schubertian. But then the work falls away into a *Menuetto* suited to the boy composer's actual age. It is a not too successful imitation of the more insipid Haydn quartets and suggests a little German band as a more appropriate vehicle.

The cute *Presto* finale is so tricky for first violin that brother Ferdinand must have perspired freely. It has a foretaste of the ♩♩♩♩♩♩ | ♩ ♩ ♩ | rhythm of the scherzos of the G Major Quartet and of the great C Major Symphony. One feels Franzl's desire to emulate Haydn's finale humor, but the joke does not quite come off. In the first half of this surprising Quartet, there are frequent and heart-warming intimations of the composer's future immortality.

The first movement of the G Minor Quartet, with the powerful opening subject and the dramatic second, immediately suggests that the lad of eighteen is writing beyond his years. Note, for example, toward the close of the exposition, this admirable example of contrapuntal quartet style:

[1] A recast of a wind octet, the Serenade, K. 388, christened, in an odd blend of languages, "*Nacht Musique.*"

[Ex. 39]

The principal theme of the *Andantino*, however, though a sweetly charming song, recurs so often as to outlast its welcome. It is reminiscent of a melody in the finale of Mozart's *Haffner* Symphony. Much is made of Schubert's favorite dactylic rhythm | ♩ ♫ |. The *Menuetto* and *Allegro* relapse into Mozart, whose C Minor Viola Quintet finale stands godfather to the last movement.

This succinct little work offers fleeting premonitions of the mature writing for four strings that was to begin five years later. It is by all odds Schubert's best work in this medium before the *Quartett Satz*.

The E Major Quartet, Op. 125, No. 2, was composed in 1816. Despite occasional brief flashes of the real Schubert in the first half, and in the Trio of the Scherzo, it is hard to warm up to the E Major. This may be because it is the composer's one essay at writing a quartet in that virtuoso style which is so foreign to the spirit of chamber music. Though there is less doubling of parts than before, it is awkwardly scored for the instruments. Schubert's inspiration was evidently having an off day, and much of it sounds like "made" music. Moreover, in the *Allegro con fuoco,* toward the close of the development, there is a passage so astonishingly like the corresponding portion of Mozart's G Minor Symphony, as to suggest unconscious plagiarism.

The movement known as the *Quartett Satz,* or *Quartet Movement,* in C Minor, was written in 1820. From this, the unfinished symphony of chamber music, dates Schubert's full maturity as a composer for strings. Here for the first time he used the quartet as an expression of his deepest sorrows, his most desperate inner struggles, and his loftiest joys. It became the confessional of his soul. These pages were the first to distill that potent string magic which was to grow almost steadily to and through the supreme triumph of the C Major Quintet.

Judging from what we have of it, we may regret the fragmentary condition of this work as wistfully as that of the more famous B Minor Symphony. Here we suddenly find the composer writing chamber music quite regardless of Haydn and Mozart, having become every inch himself. Also he has a new and superior way of scoring which makes for an improved quartet style. He has overcome that early weakness, the doubling of parts, and has become a signer of the declaration that the members of the quartet are, and of right ought to be, free and independent instruments.

Laciar cogently remarks:

Beethoven scarcely made a greater advance between the quartets Op. 18 and the Rasoumowsky quartets Op. 59, than did Schubert between the quartets of Op. 125 and the *Quartett-Satz;* besides which, the time which elapsed was three years[1] with Schubert and seven years in the case of Beethoven.

In this great fragment, how satisfying are the dramatic force of the opening,

[Ex. 40]

the blithe, Austrian sweetness of the second theme,

[Ex. 41]

and the lovely modulation of the Arielesque figure toward the end of the exposition, which is derived from ex. 40.

[1] We now know that it was seven years for Op. 125, No. 1, and four years for No. 2.

These pages begin to reveal the composer whom the world loves in that special, intimate way which it reserves for Schubert alone. The *Quartett Satz* is held in reverent affection as the germ which produced the Quartets in A Minor, D Minor, and G, and the great Quintet.

Critics of Grove's time rated the D Minor (*"Death and the Maiden"*) as the best of Schubert's quartets, but our own day has come to feel that the A Minor, Op. 29, of 1824, is the more perfect. Grove indulged in one superlative about the latter when he wrote that it was "not wrongly said to be the most characteristic work of any composer." Perhaps . . . The A Minor is assuredly brimful of the best Schubert. But such a claim seems more doubtful when one considers how characteristic are Schubert's own C Major Quintet, Beethoven's C Sharp Minor Quartet, Mozart's G Minor and Schumann's E Flat quintets, the quartets of Brahms in A Minor, of Dvořák in E Flat, and Smetana's *Aus meinem Leben.*

From the first note to the last, the inspiration of Op. 29 is consistently sustained. The four voices show an even greater independence than in the C Minor fragment of four years earlier. Schubert had always treated bowed instruments idiomatically, with no taint of pianistic mannerism. But here, despite the lyrical quality of the work, he first shows complete mastery of quartet style. It could have been written by none but a great song writer. Filled with the spirit of Romanticism, it sings without ceasing, and is a kaleidoscope of bewitching color.

The opening measure leads off with one of those rich accompaniments, where diverse rhythms are simultaneously opposed, that were until then unknown in chamber music. It bears the hallmark of the father of the modern lied. Over the droning open fifths of the lower strings, the second violin plays a figure reminiscent of Margaret's Spinning Wheel,[1]

pp

[Ex. 42]

[1] Accompaniment figures somewhat suggestive of this occur in the two following movements.

to sustain the first violin's outpouring of enchanted melody,

[Ex. 43]

which then turns from minor to major in a highly Schubertian way.
Laciar calls this theme, "perhaps the most beautiful melodically of
any similar subject in the quartets." The falling triad (marked with
a bracket) constitutes a liaison motive which thematically unifies the
movement. Embellished with a trill, this triad forms the bridge

[Ex. 44]

to the short second subject:

[Ex. 45]

That the notes under the first bracket really form an inverted triad
can be seen by transposing the first G up an octave. It meant unusual
self-restraint for the exuberantly fertile Schubert to pay such tribute
to one of music's cardinal principles, economy of material, as to use
but two themes in this movement, and keep the second down to five
measures.

The more melodically satisfying and self-contained a theme, the
harder it is to develop. Yet the working-out portion, which deals
almost exclusively with the perfection of ex. 43, is one of Schubert's
best. Note the harmonic opulence and the satisfying contrapuntal
exchanges between first violin and 'cello. The part with the figurated
bass is akin in spirit to the stormy section in the first movement of

the *"Unfinished."* The delicious coda ends with a fivefold assertion
of the liaison motive.[1]

Dr. Hugo Leichtentritt[2] and other writers have felt a thematic
unity between this opening movement and the other three, but, to
my mind, the relationships they indicate are too tenuous to be convincing.[3]

The principal theme of the *Andante* was borrowed and altered
from the third Entr'acte of *Rosamunde*, written the year before. This
tune was as much of a favorite with Schubert as the *Prometheus-
Eroica* melody was with Beethoven. One hearing is enough to show
why. Of course he recognized it as the purest essence of himself. It
starts thus:

[*Ex. 46*]

Three years later he was to repeat it again, and altered again, as the
varied theme of the third *Impromptu*, Op. 142. It is remarkable how
these pages can revel in the favorite dactylic rhythm, yet without a
hint of monotony. "The workmanship here," remarks Hutchings, "is
of a far more complicated order than the ingenuous tune would lead
one to expect—a remark which might be applied with equal justice
to minuet and finale." You can stick in your thumb at any point and
pull out a plum. For example, the second violin's unexpected contrapuntal figuration where the *Rosamunde* melody returns after the
second hold.

The poetic *Menuetto* is totally unlike anything that the composer
—or anyone else—had written in this form. Yet nothing could be
more personally Schubertian than this highly original movement,

[1] Of the two closing measures, Daniel Gregory Mason notes on my margin:
"The fine strength of the last statement of the motive (in the bass) *produces
the augmented triad of the harmony, the harmonic interest proceeding, as it
should, from thematic cogency.*"

[2] In *Musical Courier*, Apr. 26, 1928.

[3] Critics seem not to have noticed the important roles played by germ motives
in the E Flat Quartet and the trios.

with its wealth of harmonic surprises, such as the flash of genius at
bar 41, in the ineffable juxtaposition of A flat major and C sharp
minor. The 'cello begins alone, on its deepest string,

[Ex. 47]

with the start of Schubert's song, *The Gods of Greece* (*Die Götter
Griechenlands*), written four years earlier. Curiously enough, in the
fourth measure of that lied, he made the voice intone the liaison
motive of this Quartet's first movement: E, C, A. (See p. 233, ex.
43.) It may be that the composer intended a veiled reference to
Schiller's poem:

> Where art thou, beautiful world?
> Return, O lovely time of nature's blossoming.

Over all the superb movement, except the shy peasant dance of
the Trio where the 'cello is suddenly inspired, there hovers the
silvery shimmer of that "beautiful world," and—despite its simple
lines—a reticent mystery. It is a mystery foreshadowing certain
pages of the Brahms who was to owe so much to Schubert, and to
repay the debt by devoted labors on the Complete Edition of the
elder composer's works.

Writing of these two middle movements, among others, Grove
exclaimed:

> Think of the abundance of the thoughts, the sudden surprises, the
> wonderful transitions, the extraordinary pathos of the turns of melody and
> modulation, the absolute manner in which they bring you into contact
> with the affectionate, tender, suffering personality of the composer—and
> who in the whole realm of music has ever approached them?

Ranging in mood from refined to rough, the gay, mischievous
finale brings a needed contrast by waking one out of the former
movements—"such stuff as dreams are made on," where we "on
honey-dew have fed,"

> And drunk the milk of Paradise.

Bubbling with an infectious humor rarely found in Schubert's pages,
it starts as none but he could have started:

[Ex. 48]

Yet, even in the humor and the mischief, there is a strong admixture
of the Schubertian magic.

The dotted third theme has a slightly dirgelike flavor, but it might
well be a forerunner of Gounod's roguish *Funeral March of a Mari-
onette*. Notice how convincingly, and with what admirable ease,
Schubert blends the capriciously contrasting rhythms of this movement, and how satisfyingly it closes a perfect composition.

Dahms and others attribute the Hungarian flavor of the two last
movements to their having been written at Zseliz. The Quartet, however, was first performed on March 14, 1824, before, Schubert's second visit to the Esterházys' so the Hungarian quality[1] must have
come from memories of his first visit, half a dozen years earlier.

Wilhelm Altmann[2] suggests that, as Op. 29 was originally entitled
"Three Quartets," and as those in D Minor and G were not finished
until 1826, the other two of this opus were written and lost. What
more alluring vision could any musician have than a pipe dream in
which he unearths those two unknown and worthy companions of
the A Minor? I had rather find them than stumble upon an unexpected completion of *Kubla Khan*.

[1] A Magyar violist, a nephew of Karl Goldmark, with whom I used to play
the A Minor in Austria, found nothing Hungarian in this finale, but declared
it, on the contrary, to be the very essence of old Vienna.

[2] *Handbuch für Streichquartettspieler*, Berlin, Hesse, 1928, Vol I.

36

THE LAST STRING QUARTETS

THE D Minor Quartet, the most fiery, and one of the most beautiful of Schubert's chamber works, has called forth a great deal of inept comment. The mere fact that the *Andante con moto* consists of variations on a fragment of Schubert's song, *Death and the Maiden,* and that all four movements are, so unusually, in a minor key, is far from justifying critics in the vandalism of violating this work by gumming a paper program across the marble of its godlike features. Here is music that should be left pure and absolute, to mean a million different things to a million different listeners, and still other things, perhaps, every time they hear it. How puerile to try to cram infinity into a story of death pursuing innocence! Schubert probably chose this melody as the theme of his famous slow movement, not for its literary association, but because he saw that its lack of melodic and rhythmic interest made it excellent material to vary.

The opening *Allegro* is highly original in construction. Five notes twice baldly shout a principal subject of unusual brevity for Schubert:

[Ex. 49]

Its most important feature is rhythmic: three short notes followed by a longer accented one.

There follows a sort of informal introduction, ten soft bars with this rhythm sounding, first fast, then slow. It seems like a genuflection before plunging into the fray. Then come twenty-six measures during most of which the 'cello develops the dominant rhythm, first against strong Bach-like counterpoint in the upper strings, then an-

237

swering the pulse of that rhythm in the first violin. By a long, complicated and alluring harmonic route, the chief statement of the principal subject is finally reached with a sort of fanfare:

[Ex. 50]

After a rapid trip through four major keys, it arrives at a codalike conclusion,

[Ex. 51]

which combines the rhythmic motto with a soft loveliness that prepares charmingly for the mellifluous second subject:

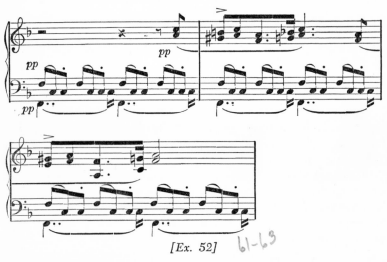

[Ex. 52]

This is almost Mediterranean in its sensuous lilt. It is sung by the violins over remarkable contrasting rhythms in viola and 'cello—a

Schubertian accompaniment as original and stringlike as that which begins the A Minor Quartet. (See p. 232, ex. 42.)

This second subject is at once elaborately worked out in double counterpoint[1] with an exciting phrase in sixteenth notes which is resiliently shuttlecocked about with delightful abandon from voice to voice, and the exposition culminates in a prodigious climax.

The development, unusually ingenious for Schubert, is mainly devoted to ex. 52. Here he exhibits no mean contrapuntal skill. In its twelfth and thirteenth bars he convincingly combines splendidly contrasting material: the second subject (first violin) with a variant of the first subject ('cello) and the Bach-like counterpoint from the quasi-introduction (second violin):

[Ex. 53] 153-154

With great originality the movement ends in two codas, both based on the first subject (ex. 49). The first coda begins softly, mysteriously, and works up, *più mosso*, to an overpowering climax. Then, as if conscious that such brilliance was no fit prelude for the delicate variations to follow, Schubert adds a second coda, quietly secret, tender and sorrowful. Mark the six-measure phrases and, at bars 328 and 334, the harmonic originality of the composer's favorite Neapolitan sixth turned to minor by the G flat. Words cannot hope to convey the magic of this ending.

---

[1] Meaning that the phrase sounds as good below the central theme as above it. One is reminded of champagne, which is recommended for seasickness on the ground that it tastes equally well going down or coming up.

In a letter to Mrs. Bull,[1] Grove described the variations on *Death and the Maiden* which form the second movement, as

> the most poetical, the most mournful, the most *musical* thing in the world
> . . . I am glad to send you the theme, because it is too delightfully
> mournful to play, and the last three notes (mind you make the turn and
> catch the B natural) are like an escape into heaven.

The theme is such an extension and improvement of the original that it may be said to take the song merely as a point of departure. Here are its beginning and end:

[Ex. 54]

How this tune, so homogeneous in its insistently dactylic rhythm, in its melody and in its harmony, can distill such tender, serene magic, is one of the standing, and outstanding, mysteries of the art. The simple, monotonous melody is better adapted for its purpose than any other which Schubert varied, and he made here his supreme essay in this form.

To the nervous restlessness of the first variation, the high, serene 'cello cantilena of the second, sustained by a lower dotted voice in the second violin, and the obstinate ♫ | ♪ rhythm of the viola, and embroidered by the leader with lofty and delicate arabesques, offers a luscious contrast. Midway, as though realizing that, with the best will in the world, brother viola can scarcely provide an adequate

---

[1] Given in Graves's *Grove*, p. 226.

foundation, the 'cellist, to the hearer's joy, leaves the heights of song for half a bar, to deliver himself of one profound and satisfying D. It is all the bass he has time for.

In the third variation Schubert, carried away by a passion for his favorite rhythm, writes a page full of exciting dactyls. Though hard to reconcile with the character of the theme, it provides a valuable foil to the coming major and *pianissimo*. Loud chords, exploded antiphonally by first violin and 'cello,[1] add to the stimulation. If the program makers are right, here in the midst of death, we are indeed in life!

The fourth variation is the work of Ariel and starts with perhaps the loveliest of his characteristic turnings from minor to major. The three lower strings weave a celestial tapestry, while the leader, high above, embroiders even more delicately than in the second variation. Schubert's characteristic use of the 'cello above the viola, while no new procedure, is far more effective than that of former music makers.

The fifth and final variation is one great crescendo to the point where, far below the agitated and diversified rhythms of the others, the 'cello delivers a tremendous pronouncement and, to an interior pedal in the viola, goes wild endeavoring to play both treble and bass, while the second violin vainly tries to emulate the individuality of the 'cello part:

[1] So far as I am aware, such 'cello chords as these were then a startling novelty in chamber music.

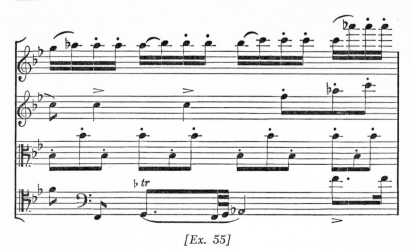

[Ex. 55]

Then the excitement gradually simmers down to the tranquil simplicity of the theme, and the breathless close of one of the most
superb pages in all music.

I recall a quartet evening when the first violin and 'cello parts of
the D Minor could not be found. Our leader, Elsy Stein, suggested
that she and I endeavor to play the slow movement from memory.
Oddly enough, we both succeeded, but the excitement of unexpectedly digging that glorious music out of the inner consciousness
kept me awake all night, and our leader fared no better.

In admirable contrast to the ethereal close of the Variations, the
Scherzo opens with a vigorous tune which, after thirty-one years,
Wagner was to borrow for his Mime in the First Act of *Siegfried:*

[Ex. 56]

Three years before, Schubert had originated this theme in the sixth
of the twelve *Ländler*, Op. 171. The bass of the second part runs:

[Ex. 57]

And similarly the tenor and bass of the D Minor Quartet Scherzo:

[Ex. 58]

Here, however, Schubert capriciously adds two measures more than the ear anticipates.

The whole movement is effervescent with similar rhythmic wit. There are perverse cross accents and periods of such elfinly surprising lengths as 10, 9, and 11 bars. The mischievous Franzl leads us on to expect the usual and conventional thing, then surprises us with the unusual and unconventional. For instance, the first section, where we are made to anticipate 3 times 8, *i.e.* 24 bars, but are brought up short with 22, is as misleading as to say, "Come to my arms and let me—bite your ear off." Moreover, the mischief is heightened by the wide-eyed innocence of the Trio, with its childlike song flowing in blameless thirds. Schubert has reached rhythmical maturity.

The finale is son of the corresponding movement in Beethoven's "*Kreutzer*" Sonata, and father of the Scherzo in Brahms's Piano Quintet, where the headlong end of the dotted first subject contrasts

almost as gloriously with the broad second, as Schubert's wild, reck-
less tarantellalike opening theme,

[Ex. 59]

contrasts, after an impressive silence, with the grandiose detonation
of his second:

[Ex. 60]

After Schubert had written this, the first four notes probably reminded him of the *Erl King's* invitation:

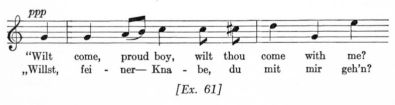

"Wilt   come,   proud boy,   wilt thou   come   with   me?
„Willst,   fei - ner— Kna - be,   du   mit   mir   geh'n?

[Ex. 61]

This the development softly echoes in the second violin, and soon,
more clearly, in the first:

[Ex. 62]

while *secondo's* scurrying eighths might suggest the flight of the
father's steed.

Toward the close of the development there is a sudden respite
from the emotional stress of the movement's wild momentum. Over
a faint, lilting accompaniment derived from the third and fourth bars
of ex. 59, we hear music fit to make

> Every elf and fairy sprite
> Hop as light as bird from brier,

tripping it featly here and there

> On the light fantastic toe,

to a figure taken from ex. 49, or from its inversion in ex. 60:

[Ex. 63]

A mad coda whirls this tremendous movement to a pyrotechnic
close which appals most amateur players. How shall they obey its
direction *"Prestissimo"* when all along they have been fiddling as
fast as they can?

Music offers few things more thrilling to play or to hear than this
tarantella. In fact, as Mason points out, the whole work has "a nervous tenseness which is distinctively modern" for its "closeness of tex-
ture and rapidity of pulse." In independence of part writing and
expressiveness of contrapuntal resource, the quartet style surpasses
even that of the A Minor.

Schubert's contemporaries were unable to appreciate such a forward-looking work. Many of even the most intelligent thought of
the composer as scarcely more than a song writer. The years of relax-
ation after the Napoleonic crisis had led to shallowness and the de-
basement of musical interest. Even the famous Schuppanzigh, the
fat violinist who had been the first to bring out many of Beethoven's

quartets and to whom Schubert had dedicated his A Minor, proved deaf to the signal merits of the D Minor. On hearing it he is actually said to have admonished the composer: *"Brüderl, das ist nichts; das lass gut sein; bleib Du bei Deinen Liedern."* ("Little brother, that's nothing. Let it go. Confine yourself to your songs.")[1] We of today thank whatever gods may be that Franzl ignored such idiocy, and went on to create the G Major, and the great Quintet.

In ten days of June, 1826, Schubert hurled upon paper the remarkable G Major Quartet, Op. 161. Its freshness and vigor followed several weeks of bad weather inaction at Währing, during which the composer's creativeness accumulated and rose to boiling point.

The chief characteristics of the music are a forward-looking modernity surpassing even that of the D Minor, the rhapsodic quality of certain themes, much of Schubert's characteristic wavering between major and minor, the antiphonal play of upper against lower strings, a more marked orchestral quality,[2] a tendency toward horizontal counterpoint rather than vertical harmony, a diffuseness that stretched the work to an inordinate length, and in one tune of the finale a regrettable lapse to the vulgar Italian idiom then popular in Vienna. The outer movements, and parts of the *Andante* are nervous, impatient, vigorous, and somewhat grim, suggesting that *The Winter Journey* is not far distant. Except for a few themes, this music, vibrant with a novel and audacious tone color, strikes with a strange effect upon ears accustomed to the intimate personal communications of the lovable friend who wrote the A Minor, the D Minor, the quintets, the trios, and the two last symphonies.

The G Major shows the influence of Beethoven's final quartets. For example, the opening theme of that master's F Major, Op. 135, nervous, jagged bits of dotted phrase leading to a legato melody, is similar in contour and feeling to Schubert's first subject:

[1] It may be that "Milord Falstaff" (as Beethoven called him) was annoyed at the novel technical difficulties of the D Minor, and knew that he could scold Franzl with more impunity than he himself had enjoyed in the case of the Rasoumowsky series. On first trying those immortal pages, he had roared with laughter, suspecting a practical joke. Then he had complained of certain hard passages. Whereupon Beethoven (who always addressed "Milord" in the third person) angrily retorted, "Does he really suppose that I think of his puling little fiddle when the spirit speaks to me and I compose something?"

[2] Observe the role played by tremolos in the two first movements and, almost throughout, the opulent sonority of the four instruments.

[Ex. 64]

The surprising turn from major to minor in the third measure is especially characteristic of this whole quartet.

Moving within a narrow compass, the second principal theme

[Ex. 65]

is garrulously stated by each of the four instruments in turn and worked out to an extent unusual in an exposition. Counterbalancing this emphasis, the development specializes on the first subject. It is treated with a dramatic power and an imaginative resource not often shown by Schubert in this section of a sonata-form movement.

The recapitulation starts by reversing the opening order of major and minor, but otherwise remains fairly faithful to its exposition. Almost at the end of the coda comes an extreme example of Schubert's favorite mannerism: four bars without benefit of melody, nothing but minor and major chords in sudden alternation. It is a characteristically Romantic color effect.

Mason remarks that the harmonic idiom of this *Allegro molto moderato,*

with its lapses of triads down through intervals of a whole step, is that of César Franck. Schubert is here the prototype of the most advanced modern symphonists, as in his piano pieces he anticipates the methods of Schumann, Chopin and Liszt, and in his songs gives the cue to Franz, Rubinstein, Grieg, and Brahms.

We are in the presence of a novel Schubert who, but for the damp walls and tainted water of Ferdinand's dwelling, might have opened up to us new and even fairer worlds.

The movement suffers from a wearying amount of connective tissue consisting of rapid triplets. Now, when Schubert breaks into triplets, one should prepare for anything from a slight falling off in quality, down to sheer padding. The exceptions where inspiration is perfectly sustained in triplets, as in the opening *allegros* of the Quartets in A Minor and D Minor, are rare. If the composer had lived, he would most likely have trimmed this movement and the finale to more practicable proportions.

The *Andante un poco moto* begins with much the same signal for attention that starts the Minuet of the A Minor and the introduction to the Octet's finale (see pp. 235 and 225). Then comes a succulent theme in the most effective register of the 'cello:

[Ex. 66]

This is a strain of the old familiar Ariel. But after the double bar one descends to second-grade Schubert.

Contrast breaks in with the first of two violent explosions of sorrowful passion:

[Ex. 67]

This recalls the powerful dotted passage near the start of Beethoven's A Minor Quartet:

[Ex. 68]

Whereupon the excitement is immediately intensified in a daring, original, and savage outcry of which this is a representative part:

[Ex. 69]

(But those wild *sforzati* on B flat look more revolutionary than they sound.) And so this unique movement goes on alternating Ariel with Caliban.

At least rhythmically, the Scherzo looks back to the capricious finale of the B Flat Quartet, Op. 168, and forward to the galumphings of the great C Major Symphony's Scherzo. Moreover, it starts by continuing one orchestral feature of the preceding movements, with a (written-out) tremolo:

[Ex. 70]

The Trio, a melting *Ländler* of much contrapuntal ingenuity, is rather too prettily light to fit well into the emotional framework of the Quartet.

Like the closing movement of the D Minor, the finale of the G Major is a tarantella whose headlong rush is stemmed by a broad theme, a confrontation similar to that of ex. 59 with ex. 60 on p. 244. The movement opens impetuously

[Ex. 71]

with a faint resemblance to ex. 59. And, after a second subject almost as dynamic, comes the broad contrast:

[Ex. 72]

Despite the impetus of this finale and its daring harmonic originality, it could not compare in quality with that of the D Minor, even had

Schubert lived to prune its endless length and to remove its chief blemish, the cheaply Italianate transition tune which binds the first subject to the second:

[Ex. 73]

This is the one serious blot on a great quartet.

37

THE STRING QUINTET

SCHUBERT'S swan song, the Quintet in C Major, Op. 163, for 2 violins, viola, and 2 'cellos, came into existence in September, 1828, only a few weeks before his death. It has been wittily characterized by Josephine Braider as "the quinte*t*ssence of beauty." Cobbett, calling it "the most romantically conceived work in all chamber music," declared that "from the lyrical and dramatic point of view, nothing so ideally perfect has ever been written for strings as this inexpressibly lovely work."

According to Laciar, it has

all the poetry, romance and inspiration of the G Major Quartet . . . all the intensity of the D Minor and the subdued melancholy of the A Minor; a workmanship never before approached by Schubert and equalled in chamber music only by Mozart, Beethoven and Brahms; in short, it crowns Schubert's entire creative life in this field, if not in all forms.

It is a sad thought that he never heard Op. 163 performed. In 1838, Schumann unfortunately missed it in the pile of dusty manuscripts where he discovered that companion work, the great C Major Symphony. It was first exhumed and played by Hellmesberger twenty-two years after the composer's death, and published four years later.

In choosing his instruments, Schubert was influenced by the 'cellist-composer Boccherini, who wrote 112 quintets for this combination. The advantages of two 'cellos are obvious. One of them can provide for the cantilenas of the other a far more satisfying bass than any viola could manage; the pair can sing in thirds and sixths of a delicious tone color; and how firm a foundation their unison lays down! Also the five instruments can split up into antiphonal coteries of three, with the viola adhering to both parties.

The reverent regard in which musicians hold this Quintet is shown by an incident of my callow youth at Princeton. My 'cello teacher, Alwin Schroeder, a member of the Kneisel Quartet and solo 'cellist of the Boston Symphony Orchestra, was at that time considered the world's foremost chamber musician. During one of our lessons he found on the stand the second 'cello part of the C Major Quintet.

"Vat iss dis doing here?" he cried in astonishment.

"Oh, a piece I'd like to play with the Quartet at one of your Princeton concerts."

"My poor young friend," growled the master, "let me tell you something: dere iss not another 'cellist in de Boston Symphony worthy to blay with us dis subreme masterpiece!"

In *Fiddler's Folly*[1] I remarked that when good fellow-'cellos get together to do the C Major Quintet, they usually stage the same old comedy.

At first each hypocritically insists on the other's playing first 'cello. When this Alphonse-Gaston business has gone on long enough to satisfy the demands of a hollow etiquette, one of them finally proposes that the question be settled by the laws of chance. The other amends this by moving that whoever wins the toss may have the first choice of two movements.

The winner then elects to play the lead in the outer movements, thus falling heir, with agreeable qualms of misgiving, to the notorious second-'cello ordeal of the *Adagio*.

Most of the time, from the opening chord of this Quintet to the closing, Ariel holds the pen. The first violin starts:

[Ex. 74]

[1] New York, Henry Holt & Co., Inc., 1942.

Then the first 'cello, rising above the dusky golden coloring of the three other lower strings, magically completes the incomparable thought:

[Ex. 75]

Deep down below a militant counterpoint, the combined 'cellos develop this theme. Then, after a quiet legato bridge passage, Ariel soars to rarer heights for his second subject.

In England, four quite unsentimental chamber musicians, among them Alfredo Piatti, the famous 'cellist, and the quartet leader John Saunders, happened to discuss what music they would choose to hear on their deathbeds, and all of them declared for this Quintet. Saunders, indeed, had the 'cello duet of the second subject inscribed upon his tomb:

[Ex. 76]

Beneath it stand these lines from Shakespeare's Eighteenth Sonnet:

> So long as men can breathe, or eyes can see,
> So long lives this, and this gives life to thee.

Note, in the first three bars of this example, the sudden, delightful pivot modulation from G to E flat.

After first violin and viola have developed this theme in ethereal counterpoint to a place where almost any other composer, with nothing new to say, would be ready to rule a double bar, Schubert still cannot halt the creative flood. There comes a soaring legato theme more blithely Arielesque than its fellows, and a soft, staccato march:

[Ex. 77]

With this march the development is almost exclusively concerned. One is tempted to imagine that, as he neared the end of the exposition, the composer, like God in the first evening of creation, looked upon his material and found that it was good—but not so good for the working-out portion. So he appended the eminently workable ex. 77. Alas! he found it so apt for development that he could not bear to stop. So that the middle section of the movement, with its endless reiterations, is the one weak page of the Quintet. As already observed, when Schubert breaks into triplets, it usually means a letdown of interest, and this section is well diluted with them.

At last, however, comes the superb approach to the recapitulation and re-entry into the celestial regions. Here the tone color of the first subject is even more alluring than at the start. So is that of the second subject's elaboration, because this time the first 'cello takes the viola's former place in counterpointing the first violin. Schubert made the recapitulation ten bars longer than the exposition, as if loath to have done, and that is exactly the feeling of most players and hearers, for they are in the seventh heaven. The brief and highly Schubertian coda lifts them to the eighth.

For the Schubert centenary celebration in 1928, the *Adagio* of this Quintet was chosen as his most representative movement, to be played on the gramophone in all schools and wherever people came together to honor the Master's memory. Westrup[1] remarks that it begins "with a divine tranquillity, the tranquillity that only mature artists can achieve because only they have sufficient confidence in their powers . . . The simplicity of this movement must be the admiration—and the despair—of every budding composer." It starts with the three middle voices whispering a long, calm melody, while the first violin makes recitativelike comments under its breath, and the second 'cello's deep pizzicatos sound as though they came from a softly tapped kettledrum. As Hutchings aptly comments, "Schubert

[Ex. 78]

[1] Reprinted from *The Music of Schubert,* edited by Gerald Abraham, by permission of W. W. Norton & Company, Inc. Copyright 1947 by the publishers.

was probably unconscious that he was using a Dorian idiom when he changed the harmony of his opening theme at its first repetition and gave it a flavor found in Brahms or Dvořák."

Suddenly the calm of this Elysian mood is disrupted by an F minor section whose wild and anguished turbulence is akin to the passionate outbursts of sorrow in the slow movement of the G Major Quartet. The first violin and first 'cello carry the despairing melody while, far below, the second 'cello utters rapid and savage outcries.

Even in the return to the major and the first subject, an undertone of somber mystery is lent the serene melody by the deep, rapid, sinister runs, spiced with chromatics, of the second 'cello.[1] This low part is the rock on which most amateur attempts upon the work are shattered; for it is hard to find a player fully equal to its formidable demands.[2] At last the excitement simmers down to perfect peace in a close as ideal as any *adagio* was ever blessed with.

The lusty Scherzo has been nicknamed "*La Chasse*," from the hunting horns that, in the main portion, seem to spur the chase on. This fiery movement starts:

[Ex. 79]

Beginning at bar 115, notice the tricky cross accents characteristic of Schubert's rhythmical maturity.

That high point of the work, the *Andante sostenuto* Trio, is unlike any scherzo Trio that ever was "on sea or land." It is veritably

The consecration and the poet's dream.

[1] In the *Largo sostenuto* of his E Minor Quartet, at the letter G, Smetana made the first violin echo Schubert's second 'cello runs.

[2] At the opening of the chamber-music hall which that musical Maecenas, Mrs. Frederick Shurtleff Coolidge, presented to the Library of Congress in Washington, Op. 163 was performed. All but one of the players had discovered how to adapt their instruments to the then too resonant stage, but the uninhibited fifth turned the Quintet into a concerto for second 'cello and string quartet.

Its mood of elegiac mystery makes it the most significant part of this, the Master's swan song. Poignant cadences enshrine what is to my ear the most sensuously beautiful single note in all music: the first 'cello's G flat in the following:

[Ex. 80]

This note, more precious than rubies, comes four times in the first 'cello, and twice in the viola. One wishes that it would return for ever. The twenty-three G's of the transition back to the Scherzo proper emphasize Schubert's mannerism of repeated tones, especially while marking time before a change of mood.

With its fire, its grace notes, and its syncopated accompaniment, the finale gives an immediate hint of Hungarian folk music.

[Ex. 81]

Under a C major signature it starts, with mischievous perversity, in C minor, and the sentences which one expects to be eight bars long are curtailed to six. The mischievousness even extends to the structure of the movement, for Schubert has made it hard to decide whether we have here a highly irregular sonata-form or a new and revolutionary sort of rondo with most unconventional bursts of sonata-form development.

The roguishly graceful second subject sounds like a folksy Schubert song that never managed to join the six hundred-odd lieder:

[Ex. 82]

Notice in the first two bars, the composer's favorite dactylic rhythm.

There follows something quite new in chamber music, a fascinating introductory passage with the 'cellos echoing the violins, while the viola alternately runs with the hares and rides with the hounds:

[Ex. 83]

This must have been at the back of young Brahms's mind when he wrote the delectable antiphonal bits in the first movement of the G Minor Piano Quartet, and in the finale of the B Flat Sextet.

Then comes what at first seems like a wholly new theme:

[Ex. 84]

On closer examination, it turns out to be adapted from the first subject (ex. 81). It is a moving 'cello duet, accompanied by the introductory echoing figure, ex. 83, now no longer antiphonal. This theme also had a profound influence upon Brahms, as is evident from the duet for 'cello and viola which is the last subject in the finale of his A Major Piano Quartet. And Brahms was but one composer of the many who have found Opus 163 a perpetually yielding mine of inspiration.

The recapitulation ends with the 'cello duet, this time in the most effective register, preceded, accompanied, and followed by an even more Arielesque version of the exquisite antiphonal passages.

The fireworks of the *Più allegro* coda flare up into a jubilant *Più presto*, and the mighty C Major work puckishly closes with a tremendous trill on D flat, and a D flat *acciaccatura* before the final C.

How superbly right is Schubert's chamber-music style from start to finish! Though the *Adagio* and the Trio are two of the most sublime pages in the entire literature of music, when I recall this Quintet, I always think first of those enchanted spots in the outer movements where the 'cellos sing together like the children of light.

38

THE EARLIER PIANO SONATAS

SCHUBERT'S solo sonatas for piano are a mine where one can pick up, here and there, gems of entrancing beauty and purity, quantities of semiprecious stones, and many not so precious. With the exception of dramatic and choral music, the solo sonata is, on the whole, his weakest branch of composition. Considering that the piano was far more his chosen instrument than the viola and that his keyboard facility was respectable, it is astonishing that Schubert should have produced in this field nothing comparable to the wealth of works of pure genius, informed with his unique personality, which he so lavishly created for some other vehicles.

What is the reason for this extraordinary state of things? Some critics say that he was cowed by his great deaf contemporary and recall that he once exclaimed to Spaun, "Who can still do anything after Beethoven?!" But why, then, did not that giant have an equally paralyzing effect upon his other fields of endeavor?

Others, like the late Olga Samaroff,[1] declare that Schubert's insufficient piano technique was at fault because it hindered effective writing for the keyboard. But if so, why did it not equally handicap him, and veil his true personality, in writing the best of the *Impromptus* and *Moments musicaux*,[2] the four-hand Fantasy in F Minor, and the piano parts of the trios and *"Trout"* Quintet?

Laciar[3] feels that the sonatas were too intimate to mirror Schubert's development and that he wrote into them "many things which were intensely personal rather than impersonally artistic." But if so, why do we hear the note of the authentic Schubert all through the greatest symphonies, chamber music, and songs, but too rarely in the sonatas?

Hans Költzsch[4] thinks that Schubert's lyrical nature was cramped

[1] In *Musical Quarterly*, Oct., 1928, p. 599 f.
[2] There is no point in repeating Schubert's faulty French, "*Moments musicals.*"
[3] In *Musical Quarterly*, Oct., 1928, p. 516.
[4] *Franz Schubert in seinen Klaviersonaten*, Leipzig, Breitkopf, 1927, p. 74.

by trying to square it with the demands of classical form, and that the outer movements of all the sonatas except the A Minor, Op. 164, were thus robbed of spontaneity. But why should not this same classical form have had a like effect upon his best music? Költzsch argues that he was more at home with the orchestra and the string quartet. True, he was not a great piano virtuoso, but it is hard to imagine him more at home with strings, brass, and woodwind than with his chosen ivory keys.

Költzsch further brings up the nature of Schubert's themes, which were inclined to be self-sufficient, and which he tended to regard as serving their own purposes rather than as means to an end. This further aggravated his weakness in the art of development and encouraged that tendency toward prolixity which, instead, needed discouragement. But why did not this lyrical instinct equally handicap him in other fields?

I have an idea that the cause of the mystery may have been Schubert's remarkable gift for improvisation, an art too quick on the trigger to allow much opportunity for thought or sufficient time for ripening ideas. We have no certain information about how he composed these sonatas, but many of them sound as though he had dashed to the keyboard and improvised them, using the first tunes, good, bad, or indifferent, that poured from his exhaustless imagination. Why should he bother to invent rhythms when he had only to appropriate Beethoven's? Sometimes he went further and used Beethoven's brand of melody and harmony as well. The deaf giant so pervades these sonatas as often to shoulder Schubert himself out of the picture.

This, then, may be the reason why there are no such supreme masterpieces among the sonatas as we find liberally strewn about other fields of his activity. One does not improvise for string quartet or orchestra, or even for four hands.

However, these sonatas hold so many pages of entrancing music that we are drawn back to them again and again. It is tantalizing to see by what a narrow margin some of them miss greatness and interesting to discover why. Let us consider, in chronological order, the most significant dozen of the twenty-one.

The A Minor Sonata, Op. 164, is the first of six written in 1817 and the best of them. The swinging, infectious start takes us back to the spirit, and not far from the letter, of Beethoven's E Minor Sonata, Op. 90. But Schubert cannot keep it up. In the fourth bar he lapses into conventional sixteenth notes that seem to have no legitimate place there and give almost the effect of padding. With the downward driving force of the opening,

[Ex. 85]

the second subject is beautifully contrasted.

This movement offers some novel features. Surprisingly enough, the development avoids all but subtle rhythmical suggestions of the material of the exposition, and its new material thumbs its nose at sacrosanct tradition by covertly hinting at a waltz. Then too, the reprise starts in the subdominant, one of the less admirable Schubertian habits.

Not until the *Allegretto quasi Andantino* do we find the real Schubertian note. It begins:

[Ex. 86]

That the composer himself was aware of the improvement is shown
by his use of the first theme once more to start the finale of the
posthumous A Major Sonata, where it is still more beautiful.

The *Allegro vivace* opens promisingly enough but, at the change
of key, is disadvantageously influenced by Weber. And the *dolce*
tune that follows sails perilously close to the sweetly banal. On the
whole, however, this is a worth-while piece and boasts a little more
Schubert than most of his sonata movements.

The E Flat Sonata, Op. 122 (whose first version was in D flat)
starts with some good Beethoven that reminds one of the opening of
that master's own Sonata in E Flat, Op. 31, No. 3. But, with the
appearance of the second subject, Schubert switches to bad Rossini:

[Ex. 87]

This is the sort of concession to the atrocious taste of that period,
which we have noticed all too frequently in the chamber music. We
hear these things and weep.

The same thing happens in the other movements. They start agreeably, then let one down. In the *Menuetto*, the best of the four, with
its interesting five-bar periods, its jagged melodic line, harmonic
piquancies, and novel technical effects, there is a foretaste of the
new piano style which Schubert and Weber were to create.

The third sonata of 1817 is the B Major, Op. 147. It is one of the
composer's weakest but has several amusing anticipations of famous music, for the discovery of which this book is indebted to
Augusta Scheiber. At the eighth bar of the first movement, we look
down the years to the opening of Brahms's *Vergebliches Ständchen*.
Five bars after the second change of key we surprisingly encounter
Lord Jeffrey Amherst:

And he looked around for more when he was through.

Toward the end of the exposition, we hear Schumann, in the spring of his life start the *Dichterliebe* with *Im wunderschönen Monat Mai*. The *Andante* is another sweet, though unspecific, anticipation. This time it is of Mendelssohn, upon whom the movement must have made a profound impression. The Scherzo is palely pretty, its Trio still weaker. The finale, full of terribly banal tunes, makes the Schubert lover hang his head.

The little A Major Sonata, Op. 120, of 1819, instead of anticipations, is filled with what seem like reminiscences of more youthful ideas. Considering who wrote it, the work is astonishingly short. It take only three sides of old-style twelve-inch phonograph disks. At the outset we are reminded of its lyricist composer's often observed tendency toward making his sonata-form themes so self-sufficient as to resist development, toward regarding them as ends rather than as means to ends. Here the first subject is actually a complete song of nineteen measures. At the risk of offending certain readers, I am frank to say that for me this tune, so fragilely sweet as to cloy, does not wear well. It starts:

[Ex. 88]

Then comes a bridge passage in scale triplets, and one is braced for the sort of padding that Schubert's sudden triplets often announce. It is a relief that they last only one measure. The develop-

ment, however, makes up for this self-restraint by expanding the
single bar into eight of dreary bathos. Költzsch speaks of their
"*leere Verlegenheitspathetik*" ("empty pathos of embarrassment").

With its characteristic dactylic rhythm, the second subject shares
the fault of the first in being more of a song than a sonata subject
should be, but it is a little more Schubertian.

For all the rhythmic interest of its seven-bar periods, the *Andante*
is on the dull side. The finale, despite the cute first subject's
suggestion of a music box, is the most successful movement of the
three.

This too saccharine sonata is tantalizing. One often feels it hover-
ing on a knife edge between the great Schubert on the left and
triviality on the right. Unfortunately it never once loses its balance
to the left.

The A Minor Sonata, Op. 143, written in 1823, modulates from
the earlier sonatas to the finer group of 1825. This is the promising
start:

[Ex. 89]

In the charmingly simple second subject the composer exploits the
wistful sweetness of the suspension, that seems to ask the former
chord,

How can I bear to leave thee?

This suspension magic is one of the many wise men's gifts that Schubert passed down the years to Brahms. Another is the trick, enlivening the first theme of the finale, of beginning the same figure successively in different parts of the measure.

The opening movement has fine themes that bring us nearer than do the preceding sonatas to the composer's true individuality. The other day, turning on the radio in the midst of this *Allegro giusto*, before identifying it, I knew that it was by Schubert. And I might have made as good a guess if it had been the really moving *Andante*, or the Viennese felicity of the luscious waltz tune in the finale. One feels that Schubert, if only for the time being, has stopped imitating Beethoven and is trying to be himself. Never once does he relapse into the cheap mode of the moment. The one weak spot in the work is the first movement's development which at first is thrillingly impressive, but then surprisingly sinks to a page of feeble dots. Bates[1] suggests that the debacle happens "because the might of the orchestra was needed to support this nobility."

In Op. 143, both harmonically, melodically, and rhythmically, we come nearer to its maker's personal touch, yet the work stops below grade A Schubert.

The three sonatas of 1825 are more interesting. The unfinished C Major Sonata, known as the "*Relic*," is laid out on the heroic scale of those other large works in the same key, the last Symphony, the String Quintet, the "*Grand Duo*," and the "*Wanderer*" Fantasy. The two movements which were finished are built on broad and noble lines—too broad, indeed, for such a vehicle as the piano. Like

> The high that proved too high, the heroic for earth too hard,
> The passion that left the ground to lose itself in the sky,

like the poet's

> Fancies that broke through language and escaped,

Schubert's thoughts, which had begun pianistically, soon turned purely musical. And the music broke through mere pianism to escape into the proper realm of the grand orchestra. If we did not

---

[1] Ralph Bates, *Franz Schubert*, New York, D. Appleton-Century, 1935.

know that the fabled *"Gastein"* Symphony had four completed movements, we might imagine that this was it.

The simple beginning,

[Ex. 90]

is pianistic enough; but soon there follow passages fit only for strings and wind. We wonder at the daring modulations, as in the transition to the second subject, which is in Schubert's beloved key of B minor, and begins:

[Ex. 91]

This harbors an anticipation of Chopin. Note another of those accompaniments that hint of the pioneer song writer's technique.

Except near the end, where monotony and suspense are slightly overdone, the development is one of Schubert's most convincing. It is concerned only with ex. 90, whose interesting rhythmical transformations should be thoughtfully appreciated. And the reprise is brought in with such harmonic magic that the hearer does not know where he stands. As pure music, this seems to me one of the

finest movements in all the piano sonatas, even though it has little
that is characteristic of the Schubert we love.

The beautiful *Andante* has a strong tang of Beethoven. For a
musician supposed to be shaky in counterpoint, how cleverly he
combines the treble first theme (a page before the change of key)
with the tenor second!

[Ex. 92]

The unfinished *Menuetto* leans more heavily than the preceding
on Beethoven. Here inspiration begins to flag, though the first part
has the dusky coloring which Schumann learned to use. In the Trio it
slips lower. But by the start of the unfinished finale, Schubert has
reached a strain as unworthy of him as is that miserable tune in the
last movement of the G Major Quartet. Its superficial banality is
scarcely mitigated by the more respectable second theme.

When Ernst Křenek completed the movement, he performed a
work of supererogation. Schubert must have felt about his abortive
attempt as he had felt, three years earlier, about the scherzo sketch
for the B Minor Symphony: it was not worth finishing. Such a
minuet and such a rondo would only belittle the immensity of the
"*Relic's*" first two movements.

The Sonata in A Minor, Op. 42, has a Hungarian tang, which
relates it to the finales of the "*Trout*" Quintet and A Minor Quartet,
and to the *Divertissement à la hongroise*. This musical paprika

seasons the first movement and, still more, the last. The opening
theme is self-contained like a song:

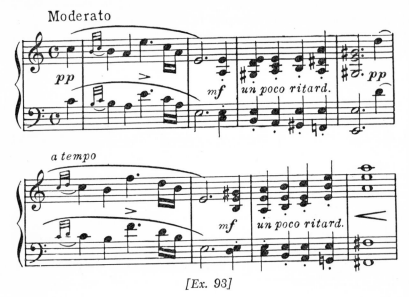

[Ex. 93]

With Schubert the development is often a weak portion, but in this
movement it is the glory of the sonata. The cumulative suspense
which gradually works up to the reprise is both beautiful and terrible. It is all managed by the left hand under high tremolos, with
deep questionings and higher answers, until the first theme returns
in canon form, delightfully modulating back to the A minor start.
Another high point is the powerful coda.

The theme of the *Andante, poco mosso,* is a song. Unless inter-
preted by one of those rare artists who can make music sound
better than it was composed, the variations that follow are apt to
be wearisome.

The richly exciting Scherzo, full of inventiveness and driving
force, is marred by a Trio on a lower level. The finale, too, is exciting, especially the Hungarian second theme and the page where
this fights with the first subject for a hearing, and the hint at bar
181 of a mighty tune in the future finale of the great C Major
Symphony. Though full of splendid, original music, with a minimum of vain repetition, this Sonata is not very characteristic of its
composer.

Despite its uneven quality, the D Major, Op. 53, the last of the
1825 sonatas, is justly popular. It starts by rapping out a virile,
rousing, and somewhat Beethovenian theme,[1]

Allegro vivace

[Ex. 94]

and then hastily resorts to the padding of almost meaningless
triplets.

A second subject unworthy of the first is followed, at *Un poco più
lento*,[2] by a remarkable passage foreshadowing the piano technique
of the future:

Un poco più lento

[1] Note the resemblance to the student song, *Wer kommt dort von der Höh?*
which Brahms was to use with such effect in the *Academic Festival* Overture.
[2] In the ms. *"e con capriccita"* was added to this direction.

[Ex. 95]

The development is organically weak, but to atone for this characteristic failing, the first three movements are notably brilliant exemplars of tone color.

In spots the *Con moto,* one of the loveliest pages in the series, comes near to the great Schubert. Költzsch calls it "the most important and stylistically characteristic slow movement" among the sonatas. He points out that here, as so often, Schubert builds his melody out of repetitions of a short phrase, in a sort of musical pointillist style.

[Ex. 96]

In the 198 measures of this movement, the rhythm $\frac{3}{4}$ ♩♩♩|♩. actually occurs no less than 160 times, either in its original form or in more elaborate variants. One might think of it as a rare sort of chaconne, not in the melodic, but in the rhythmic sense. That so surprisingly little monotony results is a tribute to the sheer magic that could successfully counteract Schubert's besetting Viennese sin of repetition. Sometimes the tender happiness of this music rises to sheer ecstasy. And sometimes, as in the preceding movement, it anticipates future piano style:

[Ex. 97]

With its wild exuberance, the Scherzo is an effective musical pick-me-up. The insistent dotted rhythm, however, does not avoid monotony quite so successfully as does the pointillist figure of the slow movement.

The rondo finale begins with a theme that is charmingly childish, though it accords ill with the maturity of the preceding. The movement is actually more effective when divorced from its setting, and goes very well as arranged for violin and piano by Friedberg, and recorded for the phonograph by Szigeti and Földes.

"*Fantaisie, Andante, Menuetto et Allegretto*" was a name gratuitously coined for the G Major Sonata of 1826, Op. 78, by its publisher, Tobias Haslinger. It is now called the "*Fantasy*" Sonata, and is the most widely known and liked of these works. This is perhaps due to its lovely beginning, and to the *Menuetto*, the most Schubertian movement in all the sonatas. Unfortunately, the G Major has serious drawbacks. While it can soar to lofty heights, it can also slump to moderately low depths.

The dreamy start, that vaguely recalls the opening of Beethoven's
G Major Piano Concerto, is for a page and a half one of the treasures of keyboard music:

[Ex. 98]

But when the somewhat barren octave scale passages of the second
subject intrude, one is reminded of how the deaf master, when he
improvised and felt the emotion of his hearers growing tense, would
abruptly break the spell with something quite incongruous.

The development repeats the same disappointment. While the
first subject (ex. 98), now in G minor, works up its canon to an
overwhelming *fortissimo* climax, we are carried along breathless.
Then the improvising Schwammerl rudely drags in the second subject to shatter the tension of our delight. On the last page he makes
amends with one of the most comely of codas. Tobias Haslinger
was wrong, as usual. This movement, far from being a "fantasy,"
sticks closer than its maker usually does to accepted classical form.

The *Andante* offers a little Schubert and much Beethoven, though
the latter would not have tolerated such platitudes as bars 4–6, and
17–18. In Schubert's cherished B minor, the delicious *Menuetto*
starts thus:

[Ex. 99]

See how the composer indulges his habit of repeated notes. This, as we have noted, is close to a theme of a year later in the first movement of the E Flat Trio:[1]

[Ex. 99A]

How characteristic of Schubert's best dance music is the finely etched Viennese waltz of the Trio![2] This minuet has a flavor of Hungary, and might almost have been cut from the same cloth as the *Marcia* of the *Divertissement à la hongroise* of the same year.

In its *espressivo* melody, which returns with enhanced beauty in the major, the *Allegretto* reminds one again of Hungary. But, except for these passages, the effect is anticlimax. It is pretty, sprightly restaurant music, unworthy to end such a sonata.

[1] Compare it also with No. 16 of the *Valses sentimentales,* Op. 50 and with Nos. 5, 7, and 11 of the *Valses nobles,* Op. 77.

[2] Mason notes on the margin, "The distinction of this Trio is due to Schubert's doing here what he does not do in most of the sonatas, that is, using development of a rhythm to secure the fascinating modulation from G sharp major to B major at the end. Indeed, this whole Minuet and Trio are truly *composed,* —not juxtaposed."

39

THE LAST PIANO SONATAS

THERE remain to consider the three last, and posthumous, sonatas, written in 1828, shortly before the composer's death. He intended to inscribe these to Hummel, but Diabelli, in publishing them a decade after, changed the dedication to Robert Schumann.

The C Minor is the least interesting. It begins with some impressive Beethoven, the rhythm carrying one back to the *Egmont* Overture; but, at the twenty-first bar, the effect is spoiled by a theme that Beethoven might have written on an off day under Italianate influence. The choric, legato theme in E flat is a vast improvement. Then, as in the A Minor Sonata, Op. 143, the development goes to pieces.

The hand of a less inspired Beethoven is heavy on the *Adagio*, and on the enormous lengths of the rather commonplace tarantella-like finale. With its Hungarian rhythmic tang, the *Menuetto* is interesting music.

There is little Schubert in the C Minor. It casts a melancholy side light on the taste of his day when that studious old biographer, August Reissmann, whose life of the composer appeared in 1873, actually pronounces this to be the best of all the sonatas.

The opening movement of the posthumous A Major is laid out upon a grand scale, with longer, simpler lines and broader planes, but instead of sounding grand, it sounds slightly labored—all but that beauty spot, the beginning of the second subject:

[Ex. 100]

Note also the fascinating harmony in development[1] and coda and the subtle, forward-pointing allusiveness with which the reprise is prepared.

Beginning with some rather dry Beethoven, the *Andante* rises, at the second change of key, to a superb climax. The Scherzo, with its sprightly leaps, comes at times perilously near the salon music of that day. At other times, Schubert is close to being himself. Then, in the rondo finale, this *rapprochement* is completed. There, with renewed pleasure, we greet again that truly characteristic subject which we learned to love in the *Allegretto quasi Andantino* of the A Minor Sonata, Op. 164, this time a little more lively and charming:

[Ex. 101]

Perhaps because it is unusually grateful to the fingers, pianists are more prone than others to favor this Sonata.

With the possible exception of the little A Major, Op. 120, which is far below it in musical value, the posthumous Sonata in B Flat is the most consistently sustained of them all. In the opening movement we find not only the form but also the spirit of the grand manner—grand also in simplicity, long lines, large planes. The broad first subject, with its luscious dusky coloring, has as much of Schu-

---

[1] Where the passages in thirds have a suggestion of Slavic folk music.

bert himself as of Beethoven,[1] and comes back as the most moving
and satisfying return to a reprise that the composer ever conceived
for the piano:

[Ex. 102]

The development, one of Schubert's more characteristic, is an
effective preparation for that return. Though it has little to do with
the classical rules of sonata-form, this development's sudden, breath-
catching start in C sharp minor out of F major, the lovely Episode
it creates and, before the return, the dramatic expectation and suspense, shimmering back and forth between major and minor, dis-
tinguish this as one of the Master's most poetic pages.

The other material of the *Molto moderato* is almost worthy of
the fine opening theme. So is the *Andante sostenuto,* with its
religious atmosphere where, amid all the Beethoven, one finds a
gratifying modicum of its own composer. The third movement
has a strong affinity with the scherzos of the trios. This is praise,
indeed, and implies a generous Schubertian content. Here is the
start:

---

[1] It has much in common with the beginnings of Beethoven's *"Archduke"* Trio,
Op. 97, the first Rasoumowsky Quartet, Op. 59, No. 1, the F Sharp Major
Sonata, Op. 78, and the finale of the A Major 'Cello Sonata, Op. 69.

Allegro vivace con delicatezza

[Ex. 103]

In the finale the Beethoven feeling markedly increases. Nevertheless, with a hint of Hungary here, and a premonition of Schumann there, it is delightful and, but for a hint of cheap contemporary style in the coda, brings the last sonata to an almost satisfying conclusion.

Here then, in this series of sonatas we have one long tantalization. Frequently they offer us pages of deep interest, precious emotional value, entrancing beauty, and occasional flashes of the real Schubert. But even those which, like Opp. 164, 42, 53, 143, and the B Flat, have the fewest weak spots, share with their brethren the defect of remaining considerably below the level of the last symphonies and quartets, the String Quintet, and the best songs. Even Robert Schumann, who praised the G Major far above its deserts, admitted that the piano sonatas "are not first class."

The view expressed above, that Schubert's habit of improvisation was responsible for this discrepancy would seem to be buttressed by Költzsch, who is the chief authority on these sonatas:

The fact that almost always in sonata form Schubert sketched merely the subject matter is highly significant for him. In the last analysis, what interested him was only the nascent present, the tone color, the theme. He was less interested in the purposeful working out and its contemplation. So the developments . . . often come into existence as if through the inspiration of the moment. On that account they are in part less organic, in part strangely fluctuating and iridescent with rich colors, but also fundamentally without energy and purposeless. [His way of approaching his theme-complex from the outside rather than from the inside] makes all the parts to be "worked out" unfree and lifeless.

40

OTHER TWO-HAND MUSIC FOR PIANO

NOW comes a lusty composition of 1822, written soon after the *"Unfinished."* Unlike the piano sonatas, the Fantasy in C, Op. 15, which is called *"The Wanderer,"* bears the composer's hallmark on every page. One gladly condones its faults of overmuch repetition and occasional bombast. Technically it is Schubert's most difficult work for the keyboard. As the reader will recall, he once broke down in the finale and cried in exasperation: "The devil may play the stuff! I can't!"

The plunging start has an infectious verve,

Allegro con fuoco, ma non troppo

[Ex. 104]

an exciting exploitation of the favorite dactylic rhythm, which turns out to be the germ cell of the entire piece.

This theme is neatly scherzified in the *Presto:*

[Ex. 105]

And the *dolce* tune of the first movement

[Ex. 106]

is condensed and transformed by this Scherzo into a fast Viennese waltz:

[Ex. 107]

Hutchings writes as if this unifying device of thematic work were an invention of Schubert's: "The 'transformation of themes,' a technique supposedly adumbrated and developed by [Liszt], is here a *fait accompli.*" The fact is that thematic transformation began some time before Mozart became adept at it and that Beethoven did far more with the germ motive than Schubert, whose extraordinary melodic fecundity discouraged this kind of economy. And the difference went far beyond the quantitative. Schubert's thematic work was usually more forthright, naïve, and obvious; Beethoven's was done with more of that subtlety of disguise which forestalls the danger of monotony.

Though the first movement of the *"Wanderer"* Fantasy is here and there a bit prolix, and is none the worse for a little discreet barbering, its rich and vital quality lasts to the end. It suffers from none of those barren displays of mere finger twiddling which mar so many virtuoso pieces. This latter virtue, shared by the other movements, may have influenced Schumann's reform of the concerto.

The *Adagio* variations, based on a part of the composer's song, *The Wanderer,*

[Ex. 108]

are rich in dreamy loveliness. The movement, and indeed the whole
work, belies the gloom of that song in which the sun has turned cold
and joy is always where the wretched Wanderer is not. Joy and exuberance pervade Op. 15 from start to finish.

The Scherzo returns to, and even outdoes, the sparkle and verve
of the opening pages.

Thus far the quality has held up consistently, but the finale brings
a slight letdown. Its *fugato* subject

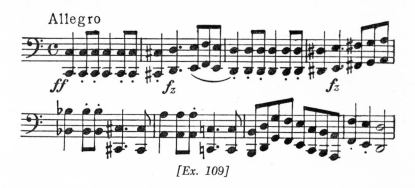

[Ex. 109]

is obviously derived from the development of ex. 104. When they
venture into this learned polyphonic domain, most composers inevitably smack of Bach. Here Schubert triumphantly remains himself, and one cannot help wondering if he might not have made of
this excellent theme a really great fugue, had he been spared to continue the fresh study of counterpoint which he began just before his
death. As it is, this finale lags only a little behind the others in interest and inspiration.

Franz Liszt found a congenial task in revamping Op. 15 into the
more conventional form of a concerto (alas! a bit too Lisztian) for
piano and orchestra.

In three sets of late piano pieces there is far more of the real Schubert to the page than in all of the sonatas. They are: the 6 *Moments
musicaux*, Op. 94, the 4 *Impromptus*, Op. 90, and the 4 *Impromptus*,
Op. 142. Four numbers of Op. 94 were written in 1825–1827, and the
Impromptus in 1827.

Schubert did not invent this kind of small, detached piano piece, though he was probably unacquainted with those by Couperin, Rameau, and Scarlatti. But he probably knew Beethoven's *Bagatelles*, Field's nocturnes and romances, the *Eclogues* of Tomašek, published in 1810, and the 1822 *Impromptus* of that worthy's pupil Vořišek, another Czech composer. However, though Schubert did not originate such pieces, he wrote them so much better than his forerunners that they were the first music of the sort to win a lasting place in the world's pianistic repertory. And, far more than the earlier ones, they influenced Chopin, Schumann, Mendelssohn, Grieg, Brahms, and a host of other composers down the line.

In the *Moments musicaux*, Schubert's Ariel side is dominant. We find it in the exquisite first theme of Number 1, in the tender, intimate loveliness of Number 2, which begins,

[Ex. 110]

in the D flat delicacies that make a sort of Trio in Number 4, and in the consecrated harmonies of Number 6:

[Ex. 111]

Contrasting moods also abound, as where Number 1, in changing to G major, modulates from Schubert to the future Schumann. There is the Hungarian playfulness of Number 3 in F Minor, which is so immensely popular that it has invaded the brass band, the music box and, yes, even the accursed jukebox. Number 4 begins with an adumbration of the Chopin of the Études, and Number 5 looks down long years to the Brahms of the E Flat Rhapsody.

In the *Impromptus*, Ariel appears less often; but when he does, he soars even higher than in Op. 94, particularly in the celestial melodies and harmonies of the G Major of the first set,[1]

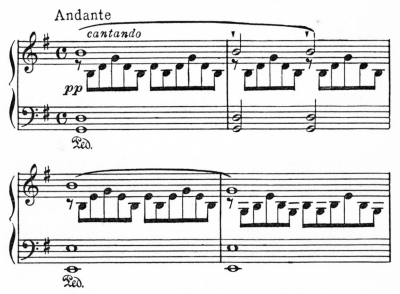

[1] Which Schubert, who preferred the fresher, less-used, black keys, wrote in G flat.

[Ex. 112]

in the A Flat of the second set,

[Ex. 113]

and parts of the Variations, Number 3, which follow it. Their theme
is a slight variant of the Third Entr'acte of the incidental music to

Rosamunde, and of the *Andante* of the A Minor Quartet. (See p. 234, ex. 46). In connection with the latter it was noted that Schubert seemed as fond of the tune as Beethoven was of his *Prometheus-Eroica* melody. Curiously enough, this variant of the *Rosamunde* theme begins with much the same intervals as those of Beethoven's favorite.

[Ex. 114]

The high point of this *Impromptu* is the sublimely passionate outburst of the third variation. The Arielesque quality of the theme and what immediately follows is rudely contradicted by the salon music of variations 2 and 5; but is restored by the coda that suddenly turns from modish frivolity to end the piece with a reminder of the inimitable theme.

Nobody realized more clearly than Schubert how soon unrelieved Ariel will cloy the listener, and these *Impromptus* range broad fields of contrasting emotions. The C Minor, which starts the first series, is in a novel form: a double set of variations on alternate themes, both of which represent the composer at a high level of poetic inspiration. The five-bar phrases of the second theme have a mysterious, elusive charm, while the sinuous delicacy of the first

[Ex. 115]

soon develops unexpected dramatic force. At its climax, one is reminded of *The Erl King*, and indeed, the excitement is followed by a cadence in triplets borrowed whole from that song, just before

"*Sei ruhig, bleibe ruhig, mein Kind.*" The whole *Impromptu* is as fully characteristic as any of the more ethereal pages of the others.

Number 2 is a foretaste of the Chopin Études. The contrast between the somewhat frivolous first theme and the four-square might of the second is completely satisfying. There is another contrast no less satisfying—and no less Chopinesque—in Number 4, between the flying sixteenth-note figures and the solid chord sequences. And the lovely "Trio" in C sharp minor lifts to a climax which almost outvies the future Polish master.

Most exceptionally for these pieces, Op. 142 starts quite uncharacteristically and, in bars 9–10, surprises us with a whiff of Beethoven. Then, after a couple of pages, the composer comes delightfully to himself in the *pp sempre legato* melody. It took the unworldly Schwammerl, whose eye was so often directed accurately away from the main chance, to end these *Impromptus* with the least interesting number of the lot. The most arresting features of Number 4 are the imitations of 4/8 rhythm in its 3/8 framework. The piece sounds rather like a premonition of a gypsy dance by Bizet, with here and there a little Slavic coloring.

Unlike many of his successors, Schubert nobly resisted the temptation to make program music of these shorter pieces, by attaching literary titles to them. Apropos, Heuberger neatly observed, "This music can almost speak; but its greatest charm is that it does not."

The legion of dances which the good-natured Franzl improvised at the piano so that his friends might amuse themselves is a well-nigh inexhaustible mine of melody. The most famous of them is Op. 9, No. 2, which, to the composer's indignation, the publisher absurdly baptized "*Trauer Walzer,*" or "*Mourning Waltz.*" This is the tune which Servais, in turn, called "*Le Désir,*" and varied for the 'cello; and which runs through that travesty of Schubert's life, *Blossom Time.* Somehow the idea got around that this waltz was Beethoven's, and the misconception died hard.

At times we find, hidden away among these dances, music which the composer used afterward in more famous works. We have already seen (on p. 243, ex. 57) in the twelve *Ländler*, Op. 171, which is one of the best examples of terpsichorean Schubert, a bass passage almost identical with that in the second part of the D Minor Quartet's Scherzo.

Many other composers have lit their miner's lamps and delved with delight in these rich subterranean deposits. The excellent parodist, Robert Schumann, knew them well, for he fooled Töpken into believing that the original D minor form of Number 8 in the *Papillons* was a Schubert dance. Numbers 3, 4, and 8 of those same *Ländler*, Op. 171, and Numbers 6, 7, and 9 of the *Deutsche Tänze*, Op. 33, sound also as if they were *Papillons;* while Numbers 2 and 10 of Op. 33 could have had more than a little to do with the origins of *Carnaval*. To my ear, the last of the *Valses nobles*, Op. 77, might well have inspired the *March of the Davidsbündler against the Philistines*, which is the finale of Schumann's amusing suite. And Number 5 of the *Last Waltzes*, Op. 127, has a Trio that opens with a transparent paraphrase of the *Granddaddy Dance* which is used in both *Papillons* and *Carnaval*.

In his dances Schubert lavished a treasure of first-rate melody that would have set up almost any other composer for life.

41

FOUR-HAND MUSIC

EVEN more than Mozart, Schubert is the four-hand composer par excellence. This branch of composition, scorned by vain performers who wish to shine, is essentially home music; and, from Schubert's time on, it has suffered through the inroads made on home music by the growing popularity of the concert stage.

Schubert did not wish to shine. He was one of the most modest and socially minded of creative artists. His friends were his home. Surrounded by them, he liked to share the keyboard with Gahy, Gros, Szalay, Anselm Hüttenbrenner, and others. It was for them that he so lavishly enriched the social literature for twenty fingers.

In 1871, Mme. Audley wrote that Kreissle, in his enthusiasm for Schubert's music, made certain reserves, "notably with regard to some of the compositions for four hands, in which he regretted to find too much abandon (*trop de laisser aller*) and too much familiar phraseology." Now these are two of the very qualities which today endear the best of those splendid works to the few that know them.

The F Minor Fantasy was written in 1828 and dedicated to Countess Caroline Esterházy. It is more consistently Schubertian than any of the solo sonatas, taken as a whole. Moreover, it lies gratifyingly for the fingers. The tender, yearning melancholy of the opening theme is immediately captivating;

[Ex. 116]

and the movement maintains its depth of feeling and high level of quality.

The glory of the piece is its characteristic and inimitable Scherzo. In a somber mood, we have heard Schubert declare that he knew of no merry (*lustig*) music. But here is one instance of how light, gay, and really *lustig* music can be, even in the minor:

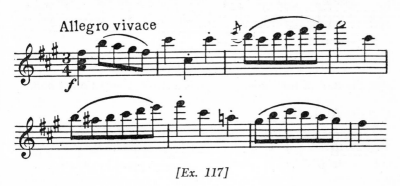

[Ex. 117]

This most impressive composition is a treasure and should be heard far more often.

The four-hand Sonata in C, Op. 140, known as the "*Grand Duo,*" is less consistently sustained. Grove must have had a moment of aberration when he called it "that splendid work in which, with Beethoven in his eye, Schubert was never more himself." During most of the *Andante*, Beethoven was certainly in his eye; but the real Schubert gratifies us all too rarely. I find him neither in the excellent opening of the first movement,

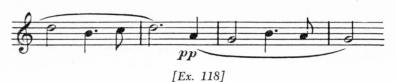

[Ex. 118]

nor in the still finer second subject:

[Ex. 119]

At the start of the *Andante* there is a strong suggestion of him;

[Ex. 120]

but the music grows progressively derivative, and comes to lean
heavily but brilliantly upon the *Larghetto* of Beethoven's Second
Symphony.

The Scherzo is a poor imitation of the deaf master, and is unworthy of its composer. The finale brings good cheer. It starts with
a long, unpianistic E that recalls the corresponding moment of the
"Trout" Quintet. Then it launches into a perfectly delightful Schubertian gypsy tune, a little like that which starts the last movement
of the B Flat Trio, but even more infectious:

[Ex. 121]

This may have encouraged Brahms to begin the finale of his Piano
Quintet. More than once we have noticed Schubert's mysterious talent for making ornaments significant and organic. Here the trills are
very much so. Alas! the movement presently loses touch, not only
with its composer, but even with the standards of first-class music.

The whole work sounds startlingly orchestral. If, as Professor
Deutsch and others suggest, this uneven composition is really a four-
hand arrangement of the vanished *"Gastein"* Symphony, the disap-
pearance of the orchestral score is no tragic loss.

Flower was wrong in stating that the composer dedicated the
"Grand Duo" to Schumann's sweetheart, Clara Wieck. At the time
of Schubert's death she was only nine years of age. Not until a decade later was the piece inscribed to her by publisher Diabelli.

The B Flat Sonata, Op. 30, was composed in 1818. The first movement starts with a pleasant reminder of Mozart and has interesting
harmony in the development. The *Andante con moto*, a delightful
movement, leads off with a charming and rather Schubertian theme:

[Ex. 122]

After its initial taste of Mozart, the *Allegretto* finale loses in interest, and ends the work in anticlimax.

One of the best four-hand pieces is the *Allegro* in A Minor, Op. 144, composed in the spring of 1828, half a year before Schubert's death. The publisher gave it the fancy title, *Lebensstürme* (*Life's Storms*). Bad taste on Diabelli's part, but at least it was not so bad as that other superscription, "*Hommage aux belles Viennoises.*" The work is well sustained. One is equally delighted by the headlong, fiery start, by the soft, lyrical melody that follows,

[Ex. 123]

and by the *ppp* chorale-like theme two pages further on, which presently returns with exquisite figurations.

There are differing stories about the origin of the *Divertissement à la hongroise*, Op. 54, which was probably put upon paper in 1824. Some say that, walking across the fields at Zseliz with Baron von

Schönstein, Schubert was impelled to write it by hearing a cow-girl sing a folk song. Others are sure that this song came from the kitchen. Perhaps it was sung by the pretty chambermaid who had taken Franzl's eye during his former Hungarian adventure.

Whatever the inspiration, a piece resulted that is full of rhapsodic color, capricious contrasts, national syncopations and cadences, and langorous lyrical outpourings jostled by rousing marches. Unfortunately the outer movements have all too many pages that sound as cheap as the cheaper Liszt Rhapsodies. The best part is the *Marcia.* It has a strong affinity with a more Teutonic piece, probably written a year earlier, the Ballet which is Number 9 of the *Rosamunde* music.

Of the many four-hand works in march form, the *Marche militaire,* Op. 51, No. 1, beloved of brass bands, is the most famous. There are others equally suited to that brazen vehicle, which I prefer, such as the *Deux Marches caractéristiques,* Op. 121. They have abundant 6/8 swing, snap, and excitement, and their Trios might have lurked at the back of Brahms's mind when he composed some of the *Liebeslieder Walzer.*

Then there are the *Six marches héroïques,* Op. 40, especially Nos. 2 to 5. Their Trios are even better and grow more and more characteristic, until that of Number 5 offers us

> a beaker full of the warm South,
> Full of the true, the blushful Hippocrene,
> With beaded bubbles winking at the brim,
> And purple-stainèd mouth.

(Two-hand arrangement)

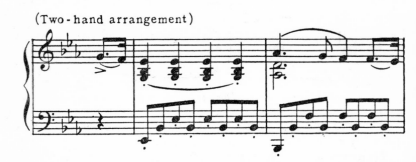

[Ex. 124]

It is odd that in the *fugato* finale of the "*Wanderer*" Fantasy, dating from 1822, Schubert should have emancipated himself from the style of Bach, yet in the four-hand E Minor Fugue, Op. 152,[1] a few months before his death, he should be writing under the aegis of Johann Sebastian. A realization of this retrogression may have influenced him in making those humble arrangements to study with Sechter, which reflect so much credit upon the composer of this highly respectable fugue.

His four-hand music, however, looks forward far more often than backward. The F Major Polonaise, Op. 61, No. 2, is the prototype of Schumann's *Papillon* No. 11. And there is a hint of the latter's *Widmung* in an avoided cadence of the *Grand Rondo*, Op. 107. Its sweetly pretty and ingratiating first pages were perhaps intended to captivate the not too musical ears of folk like the Esterházys. Then despite this purpose, Schubert grew deeper, more serious, more himself as the pen raced along. The fourth variation of the agreeable *Andantino varié über französische Motive*, Op. 84, No. 1 smacks less of Schubert than of Brahms. In another adventure among French motives, the *Divertissement en forme d'un marche brillante et raisonnée*, Op. 63, the second subject gives a foretaste of the best Mendelssohn.[2]

The three early fantasies have little more than a curiosity value. They show what can be done by a lad at the ages of thirteen, fourteen, and sixteen, provided he bears deep within him the germ of genius. The first of these also shows an iron endurance that can run to thirty-four mortal pages.

[1] Also for organ.
[2] It will be recalled that Mendelssohn was the first to interpret Schubert's great C Major Symphony.

Though there is some interesting stuff in the *Variations on a French Song*, Op. 10, one regrets that there was not more of its composer in this, perhaps the first piece of Schubert's that Beethoven encountered. The final variation is especially unworthy. There is far less dance music for four hands than for two. I care less for the polonaises than for the brief simplicity of the *Vier Ländler*, of which Number 4 is unusually delicate and charming.

L. Dunton Green[1] writes of Schubert's four-hand music:

Both in bulk and in quality, his works in this medium excel those that came before or after him. Mozart wrote some lovely sonatas for four hands, and a fugue which is far better than the one Schubert left us; but it is difficult to sustain that any of these achieve the grandeur of the Fantasy in F Minor.

[1] In *Chesterian*, Vol. X, No. 74, p. 64.

42

THE FATHER OF MODERN SONG

SCHUBERT did not, as some suppose, invent the lied. Far from it. His artistic forebears, the first of whom began composing in the mists of antiquity, came to include Englishmen like Purcell and Dowland, and Teutons like Schütz, Schulz, Haydn, Mozart, and Beethoven. Indeed, it is extraordinary that Mozart, in *The Violet*, and Beethoven, in *Die Ehre Gottes in der Natur*, and the cycle *An die ferne Geliebte*, should have hit so close to Schubert's epoch-making discovery of the modern lied, and yet have missed it.

Two North German composers, Reichardt and Zelter, and the Swabian Zumsteeg, all born about the middle of the eighteenth century, directly inspired Schubert in creating the new form. This he accomplished by an emotional treatment of the words until then unheard of, and by giving the accompaniment the expressive richness which absolute music had but recently attained. He made it suggest not only the exterior, but also the interior setting of the poem: both its outer world and the character of the dramatis personae. But this original achievement would have been far less significant without his two greatest gifts: a melodic opulence and fecundity unequaled before or since, and a harmonic endowment almost as phenomenal. Even if Schubert had confined himself to song writing, his accomplishment would have made him a composer of the first rank.

The striking characteristics of Schubert's best songs [wrote Philip Hale[1]] are spontaneous, haunting melody, a natural birthright-mastery over modulation, a singular good fortune in finding the one inevitable phrase for the prevailing sentiment of the poem, and in finding the fitting descriptive figure for salient detail. His best songs have an atmosphere which cannot be passed unnoticed, which cannot be misunderstood.

[1] In *The Looker-On,* Jan., 1897.

I shall not, like some writers, classify the songs according to the poets who wrote their texts, because these texts have a less important part in the final product than is generally supposed. Their chief function was fulfilled as soon as they had inspired Schubert to write music for them. That done, they were destined to play an insignificant, not to say ignominious, role. For, when harnessed to notes, the pace of all verse except patter doggerel is so disastrously slowed down as to destroy that most precious and essential part of poetry, its word music.[1] Those things that go to make the melody of verse: alliteration, vowel- and consonant-arpeggios, and rhyme, are obliterated. The magic is gone, and of the poetry little remains but a residue of argument which turns the notes into a sort of program music.

A friend of mine feels that, in some mysterious way, the music stimulates the memory and enables the ear to retain, *e.g.*, the sound of a rhyme longer than would be possible without the excitation of the notes. But I think he deceives himself, and that the notes, with their vastly more powerful sensuous appeal, distract attention from their own unfortunate effect on the far more delicate and vulnerable music of the verse.

Of course, while subtracting so much of value from its text, music undeniably adds to the combination glorious riches of its own; but does it at so great an expense to its partner as to sadden every true lover of poetry who becomes aware of what happens when these two arts join forces.

The foregoing will doubtless make many a reader boil with rage; but the truth seeker may easily verify my statements by looking up pp. 384–388 of my life of Schumann,[2] and trying the simple experiments there described. Those pages will also demonstrate how impossible it would have been for Schubert to do what even so accomplished a critic as Alfred Einstein supposes that he did; enhance "the value of the text with his music without ever doing it violence or obscuring it." [3]

The fact is that, in addition to the violence which all song composers are forced, by the inevitably slower tempo of music, to wreak upon their texts, Schubert further mistreated his poets by unauthorized repetitions of words, phrases, and whole lines, by altering me-

[1] Joseph Addison must have realized this sad fact when he wrote: "Nothing is capable of being well set to music that is not nonsense." (*Spectator*, March 21, 1711.)

[2] *Florestan: The Life and Work of Robert Schumann.*

[3] *Mozart*, New York, Oxford University Press, 1945, p. 375.

ters, and by faulty declamation. A singsong schoolboy does not injure fine poems more grossly than Schubert often did by accenting the wrong syllables, by arbitrarily changing words, and even omitting or rewriting whole sentences or stanzas, transforming their aspect like a facial surgeon, and going so far as to hack out hunks of the living flesh.

This was returning evil for good with a vengeance, for great poetry often inspired the composer to surpass himself. The importance of the poems as Schubert set them does not lie in the effect of the word-music upon the listener (for the word-music has largely disappeared), but rather in their initially stimulating effect upon the composer. Bearing this in mind, one can better understand how Heine came to denounce what he called "song-rubbish," when he found what Schubert had done to the word-music of his lyrics.

Even in this field, where he was and is supreme, Schubert's quality is extremely uneven. It would, indeed, be against nature for any man, within the brief span of two decades, to write more than six hundred songs and not let the dross of the commonplace and the tinsel of the melodramatic greatly exceed the pure gold of supreme inspiration. I would rate but one tenth of them as his best. Compared with those of the two other greatest song writers, this ratio is modest. In my opinion, one seventh of Schumann's 260 solo songs were his best, and as many as one fourth of Brahms's 198.

The subjects of Schubert's best songs,[1] however, range over a considerably wider field than those of either Schumann or Brahms. Three celebrate the joys of wandering, four sing the praises of nature, fourteen treat of happy love, seventeen of unhappy love, a single one of melancholy, nine of wretchedness, seven of death, three of religion, and there is one each about the sleep of a child, courage, and the art of music.

Two bright, crisp songs of wanderlust, *Wandering* (*Das Wandern*), and *Whither?* (*Wohin?*) open *The Miller's Beautiful Daughter* (*Die schöne Müllerin*) cycle. With carefree gaiety the former celebrates the joys of the open road. It has an elemental quality that reminds one of Alfred Einstein's words: "The Schubert songs grew up in mysterious ways out of the folksong." This is the most primitive of his lieder.

---

[1] Compiling a list of this sort is a matter so highly personal that I do not expect any reader wholly to agree with my choice. But then again, I do not expect any reader wholly to denounce it.

The accompaniment of *Whither?* suggests the murmur of a brook. The eternal boy in Schubert's nature took a youthful delight in such imitations. Brooks and rivers abound in his songs. We hear the whirr of a spinning wheel as in the *Gretchen* song, the gallop of hoofs (*The Erl King*), rustling leaves (*The Linden Tree*), a post horn (*The Post*), a hurdy-gurdy (*The Organ-grinder*), leaping fish (*The Trout*), and barking dogs (*In the Village*).

Such effects, especially the last named, are all managed with more delicate sophistication than earlier composers had shown. They are more subtle than even those in the *"Pastoral"* Symphony and pay more regard than Beethoven himself paid to his own guiding motto: "More expression of feeling than tone painting." Schumann was to use such imitations less, and Brahms, very little.

The second, and far greater, cycle, *The Winter Journey* (*Die Winterreise*) begins like the first with a song of wanderlust. *Good Night* (*Gute Nacht*) is a sad, cynical companion piece to *Wandering*. It celebrates, not the innocent open road to which youth takes "afoot and lighthearted," but a wearier wandering from one love adventure to another. At the start of the last verse, the beauty of the transition from minor to major is enough to bring a lump into the throat. There are enchanted, iridescent depths in this music. *Wandering* wears splendidly, but *Good Night,* far better.

One feels that the gay adventurer who starts his vagabondage in *Wandering* should choose such a morning as one naturally associates with that delicious song of nature, *Frühlingsglaube.* (Certain song titles do not bear translation well.) The music is as fresh and pure as the opening buds, the young leaves, the shining heavens, the bird notes, and the loamy, aromatic fragrances of the banner day of spring. How close to nature the city-dwelling composer came is shown by this well-loved song. Note how the rhythmic figure | ♪♪.♪♩ | is almost obstinately sustained, yet without the least sense of monotony, and consider the exquisite musical tact of interrupting this figure at the words, *"Nun, armes Herze."*

Little Heath Rose (*Heidenröslein*) had been written by Goethe to a fine folk tune, but Schubert's own music actually outdid the other. That the composer was as much at home on water as on land is evidenced by a *jeu d'esprit, The Trout* (*Die Forelle*),[1] with its witty

---

[1] Used as the theme of the variations in the Quintet for Piano and Strings, Op. 114.

leaping-fish accompaniment, and by the gliding liquid motion and sunset peace of *To Be Sung on the Water* (*Auf dem Wasser zu singen*), with that meandering between major and minor so characteristic of Schubert.

It is a commentary on his extraordinary imaginative powers that this young composer, whose own love life left so pitifully much to be desired, should have written fourteen of his best songs about happy love. They have a variety that ranges from the pianissimo whisperings of *Sei mir gegrüsst*, whisperings broken by a few vivid outbursts, and the shy, limpid *Early Greeting* (*Morgengruss*), to the tender playfulness of his last song,[1] *The Pigeon Post* (*Die Taubenpost*), and the restlessness of *Impatience* (*Ungeduld*), the first truly great lied of the *Mill* cycle,

[Ex. 125]

which culminates in the fervid "*Dein ist mein Herz.*" The yearning impetuosity of this song carries one completely away. Professor Deutsch points out that the words, "I'd carve it on the bark of every tree," are reminiscent of a poem by Edmund Spenser, "Colin Clout's come home again" ("Her name on every tree I will endosse"), and notes that the poet, Wilhelm Müller, was also a translator from the English.

There are the strongly masculine strains of *To the Lyre* (*An die Leyer*), matching Anacreon's lines. Here is "a song that is fit for men," into which a baritone can throw his whole soul. Though with

[1] Also last in a group of fourteen which was baptized *Swan Song* (*Schwanengesang*) by the publisher. This is no cycle, but a miscellaneous collection of his final lieder.

small thematic resemblance, it has much the same enthusiastic atmosphere as *To Music* (*An die Musik*).

The Fishermaiden (*Das Fischermädchen*) is bright with something of the dewy sparkle of that sheer inspiration, *Hark, hark! the Lark* (*Ständchen aus Cymbeline*):

[Ex. 126]

Ranking this among Schubert's fifteen or twenty greatest songs, Mason[1] says of them that the composer

strikes at once, and in each case . . . the exact tone and style needed to transfigure the particular feeling with all the magic of music, and throughout the song maintains the mood perfectly, with no mixture or

[1] In *The Romantic Composers*.

clouding. And this, too, with the greatest actual diversity in the different songs, to which his art flexibly responds.

There is the *Serenade* (*Ständchen*), its measures so famous that, like the heavens of the psalm, "their [melodic] line is gone out through all the earth, and their words to the end of the world." The interlude between verses, with the characteristic alternation of major and minor, recalls a treasurable page of the *"Trout"* Quintet (see p. 214).

Numbers 9, 11, 12, and 13 of *The Miller's Beautiful Daughter* range from the placid tenderness and contemplative delight of *The Miller's Flowers* (*Des Müllers Blumen*), through the mad exaltation of *Mine* (*Mein*),[1] to *Pause*, where the lover's joy begins to be overshadowed by a dim premonition of disaster. The poignance of this is heightened by the accompaniment, much of which sounds like the innocent, artless tune of a children's game. At the twenty-first measure there is another reminder of the *"Trout"* Quintet.[2] *With the Green Lute Ribbon* (*Mit dem grünen Lautenbande*) conveys with delicate sweetness a touching sense of the lover striving to keep up his courage.

Musically speaking, *Who is Sylvia?*, the greatest of these superb songs of happy love,

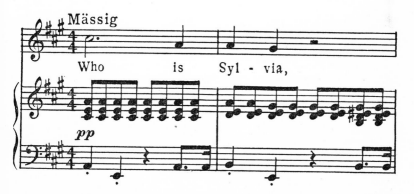

---

[1] So difficult to perform up to tempo that I have never yet heard it done cleanly. As the saying goes, "he who touches pitch is defiled," but the singers defile this song because they do not touch pitch. The magic of *Mine* is chiefly in the accompaniment, as is evident when one sings the voice part alone.

[2] Finale, bar 137.

What is she,— That all our swains com-

mend her?

Ho - ly, fair—— and

[Ex. 127]

is an inspiration fully as consummate as Shakespeare's lyric. Hutchings calls attention to the artistry that produced the octave leaps near the end of the last example, "which might otherwise have been these dull ascending notes":

[Ex. 128]

Here, in the words and in the music, we have two matchless works of art, yet the notes, while gloriously echoing the spirit and atmosphere of the lines, proceed to wreck those lines. This can be heard by anybody who will take the trouble to time the vocal part of the score and then read the poem aloud—in English or German—without the notes, at exactly the same tempo. Taken thus slowly, the word-music simply vanishes.

Having called *Who is Sylvia?* the greatest lied in this division, I would take it back in favor of *Du bist die Ruh'*, were it not that this, perhaps the supreme example of Schubert's genius in song,

[*Ex. 129*]

is less of happy love than of yearningly hopeful love. One wonders if the subtle suggestions of suffering in the accompaniment, and in the poignant bar of silence near the end, point to Schubert's own agonizing consciousness that, in such an ideal love, there could be no "peace" for himself. Here are simplicity, power, serenity, sincerity, and an infallible instinct for beauty all fused into one of the loveliest and purest little works of art that this world has known. A woman who was tenderly but somewhat calmly in love, wrote to her lover, "There is an indescribable something in Schubert's music that speaks to the heart in the way that my darling speaks to mine." The song, however, is a pitfall for the unwary performer. The music looks deceptively easy, yet, to any but a supreme singer with perfect breath control, it brings not peace but a sword.

Close to the border line between these songs and more somber regions, is the quivering expectation of *The Post,* with that most eloquent bar's rest, during which the lover finds that the postman has no letter for him today. This flare-up of adoring love against the somber background of reality is like nothing else in music.

One thing strikes us in all these love songs and those to follow. Not one of them has in it the ecstasy of full sexual consummation; not one is erotically quite adult. But this is only to be expected from an unfortunate man for whom the two streams of ideal tenderness and physical passion could never meet and coalesce. Schubert was physically stirred only by the sort of woman to whom he would never pour out his melodic soul. Those for whom he felt tenderness could not move him to the depths. Hence the ethereal, Arielesque quality of his love music.

43

SONGS OF UNHAPPY LOVE, WRETCHEDNESS, DEATH, AND RELIGION

A̲S WAS natural for such a luckless young man, Schubert wrote more great songs of unhappy, than of happy, love. He was only seventeen when, in a frenzy of inspiration, he dashed upon paper *Margaret at the Spinning Wheel* (*Gretchen am Spinnrade*)—and the modern lied was born.

Herz_____   ist   schwer;

[Ex. 130]

Poetry of this sort had never before won from a musician any such response. It was almost as unheard-of as a visitant from an outer star. The fact that this perfect thing was preceded and followed by many an inferior piece of work would seem to lend color to Vogl's theory that his protégé sometimes composed in a clairvoyant state. It needed something like clairvoyance for such a youngster to realize so vividly and truthfully Margaret's love and torture. The hearer, too, is carried away by that realization, especially at the moment when she remembers Faust's kiss, and the wheel stops whirring, and the girl's voice falters. Robertson[1] traces this memorable effect in "a perfect work of art" back to Gluck's Orpheus, who "breaks off his sorrowful plaint to cry out the name of his beloved." The second violin figure which opens the A Minor Quartet is one of the yarns spun by Margaret's magic wheel. Robert Franz was right in declaring that Schubert took Goethe's poetic bone and "sucked out its musical marrow to the last particle."

These songs of unhappy love have almost as broad a variety as the happy ones. How differently Schubert could treat such a theme as that of *Margaret*, is shown in *The Maiden's Lament* (*Des Mädchens Klage*). We shudder at the miserable whisperings of *The Town* (*Die Stadt*), with the elaborate and original accompaniment, its obstinate soft arpeggios suggesting the "damp breeze." Nobody can forget the tremendous and terrible climax when the lover beholds the spot where he lost his beloved.

In *The Doubleganger*[2] (*Der Doppelgänger*) one hears the melo-

---

[1] In Abraham.
[2] A legitimate English word.

dist *par excellence* invent a new sort of melody, wonderfully free and recitativelike. Here Schubert created the speech song which was to be further developed by Wagner and Wolf. Observe how perfectly it is knit with the somberly inflexible accompaniment, as the hero expostulates with the Scrooge-like figure of his own former self for apeing his woe. Note the magic of the modulations, the characteristic use of the echo phrase in the piano part, and turns as organic as those in *Ave Maria* and *By the Sea* (*Am Meer*). A grim, powerful song. It is a passacaglia, founded on the same spectral and inexorable bass which starts the *Agnus Dei* of the Mass in E Flat, also composed in 1828. How appropriate is the implied connotation of "*miserere nobis!*" ("have compassion on us!") How faithful to the spirit of the poem is this incomparable setting!

With simple means Schubert suggested the innermost essence of Heine's *By the Sea* (*Am Meer*). I like what Mason wrote about it.[1]

Four chords at the beginning, and again at the end, bring the sombre, majestic ocean visibly before us, while the sudden dissonance introduced with the line "*Fielen die Thränen nieder*," bring home to us with terrible poignancy the human tragedy which the poet has so vividly outlined against this stern natural background.

Here is the beginning and part of the end:

[1] In *The Romantic Composers*.

weit hin-aus im letz-ten A-bend-schei - ne,

Thrä - nen.

[Ex. 131]

Musically, that last turn is fecund, for not only the opening strain, but also a good deal of the song varies it more or less freely. (In the *Ave Maria*, p. 322, we shall find much the same procedure.) Note the infinite tenderness of the echo phrases in the accompaniment after "*alleine*" and "*fortgetrunken.*" On p. 114 it was suggested that this music was lent added poignancy because the poem depicted Schubert's own sexual plight.

The *Mill* cycle has three songs of unhappy love which are more charmingly pathetic than devastatingly tragic. In *The Favorite Color* (*Die liebe Farbe*) the characteristic major-minor wavering is effective. And in *The Detested Color* (*Die böse Farbe*) this device grows even more masterly. Here the carefree spirit of *Wandering* has

turned dismal. The accompaniment is the most original feature of
this song.

Withered Flowers (*Trock'ne Blumen*) ranks high among the
lieder. The composer evidently thought so too for, the year after it
was born, he made it the theme of the Variations for Flute and
Piano, Op. 160. The change to E major, where the lover thinks of the
miller's daughter walking by his tomb in May, is particularly touching and romantic.

The unhappiness of the nine *Winter Journey* songs in this category is more grim and virile, also more beautiful, for they were
written in 1827 at the height of Schubert's powers. Dahms has well
described the perilous state of their composer:

> *The Winter Journey* shows a step further on the road which Schubert
> took in *The Miller's Beautiful Daughter*. One finds here full mastery of
> artistic methods, an almost unheard-of expressiveness in depicting shades
> of mood, and indeed—this must be emphasized—by the simplest means.
> His piano parts are clear as crystal. They have been raised above the
> sphere of scenic depiction, of mere illustration and intensive character-
> ization, and become the very fluid of soul-life. Harmonies vibrate like
> sensitive membranes. Melodies have become antennae of the soul. Such
> tones as sound here had never yet been heard with lyric poetry . . . It
> was a strange world in which no one had before set foot. Some of the
> songs nearly touch the boundaries of the pathological. The intensity of
> their expression of pain has risen to madness. No further rise would be
> possible. Here is an inner event such as took place in Hugo Wolf. Sen-
> sitivity and irritability of soul have reached their highest imaginable limit.
> Any attempt to go further must have turned crisis to catastrophe. A kindly
> fate protected Schubert from the night of the soul and a living death. His
> victorious nature, life-loving and sensuous as it was, overcame the inhibi-
> tions and found the way back.

Splendidly somber, *The Weathervane* (*Die Wetterfahne*) points
the way to *Frozen Tears* (*Gefror'ne Thränen*). One shudders to
think of the hideous cacophony which many a living composer
would feel bound to unleash if he should set these words. But no
depth of sorrow could divorce Schubert from the worship of beauty
or turn these mournful notes to ugliness. Note the prevalence of the
favorite dactylic rhythm.

With its impetuous, unhappy *élan*, *Benumbed* (*Erstarrung*) belies
the cold torpor of the title. *The Linden Tree* (*Der Lindenbaum*)

is a sweet, simple song of unhappy love, and the introductory murmur of the wind through the leaves, one of the composer's most
subtle and charming imitative devices. At the second change of key,
the return to the major is particularly effective. More in Schubert's
earlier manner, this song is easier to grasp immediately than the rest
of *The Winter Journey,* and, at the first hearing, Schober must be
pardoned for preferring it to its deeper companions.[1]

There is far more magic in the stream songs of this unhappy love
series: *Watercourse* (*Wasserfluth*) and *On the River* (*Auf dem
Flusse*), than in the brook music of the *Mill* cycle. *Looking Backward* (*Rückblick*), with the inimitable turn to major after the hold,
is one of the loveliest of the *Winterreise. Dream of Spring* (*Frühlingstraum*), with its appallingly vivid contrasts of imagined delight
and actual woe,

[Ex. 132]

---

[1] The venerable linden tree of Müller's poem stood for six hundred years in
Allendorf an der Werra, and finally fell in 1912, leaving its old fountain un-
shadowed.

is worthy to stand beside Dante's vision of the bliss of Paolo and Francesca, which ends with the realization that the lovers are enduring the tortures of the inferno. And *Loneliness* (*Einsamkeit*), where the lover recognizes his plight, is a postlude to unhappy love, all the more poignant for its brief simplicity.

When these mournful memories die away, *The Winter Journey* depicts the wanderer's utter wretchedness in seven lieder that remind one of Rembrandt's genius for bringing out the beauty hidden deep under ugliness and misery. Despite their redeeming loveliness, however, singers and listeners who are nervously unstable would be wise to avoid the haunting morbidity of songs like these.

In *The Hoary Head* (*Der greise Kopf*) the frost had made the wanderer's hair look white. Disappointed to find this an illusion, he utters the memorable cry, "How far still to the coffin!" Equally heart-rending is his apostrophe, in *The Crow* (*Die Krähe*), to the bird who follows him in the hope of picking his bones: "Oh let me at last see faithfulness, even unto the grave!" Here Schubert actually distilled loveliness out of cynicism. How inevitable seem the crazy cross-rhythms where the traveler's state of mind is depicted in *Last Hope* (*Letzte Hoffnung*), and how perfect the piano's imitation of the poor man's shivering. Highly original and sublimely sad music.

In the Village (*Im Dorfe*) offers a touching contrast between the gracious, serene notes of the voice, the hopeless resignation of the words, and the insistent barking of the watchdog accompaniment. Then, in *The Stormy Morning* (*Der stürmische Morgen*), there is a magical little vignette of storm—at once exterior and interior. *Illusion* (*Täuschung*) brings the moving realization that this bright, simple, happy music represents merely a phantom delight and a wretched soul for whom "only illusion is gain."

The Organ-grinder (*Der Leiermann*) is the last, and perhaps the most original and terrible of the songs of wretchedness in this cycle. It was a signal inspiration to have all the words sung to the simplest of drone basses and to let the interludes consist of just the three snatches of melody in the repertoire of the old beggar's wheezy and ruinous grind organ. With heavy hearts we hear the words, "And his little plate holds but empty air," which remind us once more how the world treated the man who put these notes upon paper. "What porridge had"—Franz Schubert?

After the still depths and the reticent economy of means which move us in these pages of *The Winter Journey*, two other outstanding and more vigorous songs of wretchedness prove not quite so stirring. *The Wanderer* and *Resting Place* (*Aufenthalt*) are earlier and less reticent. It is noteworthy that one of the most quiet and direct strains in the former (after the first hold) is the best part of that famous song. Schubert must have thought so too, for he varied it in the "*Wanderer*" Fantasy (see p. 284). The two middle sections have an astonishing lack of distinction, which is redeemed by the pathos of the final page. The poignant music of those last whispered words of anguish, "There where thou art not, all joy is there," came from the heart of a man who realized that for him a perfect love would always remain a will o' the wisp. Except for *The Erl King*, *The Wanderer* was the most popular of the songs during its maker's lifetime.

When, after the undemonstrative pain of *The Hoary Head* or of *Last Hope*, one hears the excited music of *Resting Place* loudly complain of the discomforts of woods life and of the streams of tears that flow eternally, one feels that, by comparison, for all its heroic dramatic power, it "doth protest too much" and comes perilously near ranting. With its fast pace and its just stresses, this song does the music of verse less injury than notes usually do to poetry; though its unauthorized repetitions remind one of Tennyson's growl, "Why do these damned musicians make me say a thing twice when I say it only once?"

Schubert evidently did not care much for half measures. Among his best there lies midway between joy and sorrow only one outstanding song of melancholy—that musical *Il Penseroso, Praise of Tears* (*Lob der Thränen*)—to balance all those of unhappy love and wretchedness, and the seven superb ones dealing with death.

Three of these last come near the end of *The Winter Journey*. No more lovely and touching music has ever been written about the ultimate bourne than *The Guidepost* (*Der Wegweiser*). It begins a good deal like a minor version of that exuberantly happy song in the *Mill* cycle, with the cognate title *Whither?* The modulations that end the first verse and start the second are peculiarly Schubertian. When the wanderer sees the ultimate guidepost and murmurs, "I must travel a road from which none has ever returned," his voice almost abandons melody for a trancelike repetition of the same note, sung over unearthly harmonies. How human his fluctuating attitude toward that road! In *The Hoary Head* he had complained that the coffin was too distant. Here he is overwhelmed because it seems too close. (One recalls with compassion that Schubert corrected the proof of this lied on his deathbed.)

In the next song, *The Wayside Inn* (*Das Wirtshaus*), his mood
veers back, and he reproaches that green tavern, the cemetery, for
turning him away. The music is as serenely exalted as Whitman's
lines:

> Come lovely and soothing death,
> Undulate round the world, serenely arriving, arriving,
> In the day, in the night, to all, to each,
> Sooner or later, delicate death . . .
> I float this carol with joy, with joy to thee, O death.

In *The Mock Suns* (*Die Nebensonnen*) Schubert made a song
worthy of these two others. Except for eight measures which are
almost as simple, the melody confines itself to the first four tones of
the scale, yet how eloquent it is! There is nothing in all the arts more
tragically moving than *The Winter Journey*.

In sharp contrast is the tumultuous drive of *To Postilion Chronos*
(*An Schwager Kronos*), a song of the joy of youth, aware of the
inevitable end, and gallantly asking only to descend to Orkus "drunk
with the last ray of sunset" and "be welcomed at the portal by a
friendly host." Even taken alone, much of the piano part is interesting in its own right. Throughout one hears the "rattling trot" of
hoofs, combined at the end with the postilion's horn.

There are few lovelier pages in the whole literature of song than
Litany (*Litanei*). With its magical bass progression, the single measure of prelude is enough to establish the quiet atmosphere of "Rest
in peace, all souls departed." And there is yet more magic in the
chromatic bass of the fifth measure, and in the ineffable harmonies
of the closing three, after the voice has finally whispered "rest in
peace." Such richness in such simplicity suggests, as only music can,
the splendor of the eternal, blossoming out of the simplicity of death.

Death and the Maiden (*Der Tod und das Mädchen*) is a worthy
companion piece to these great songs. Directness and chaste reticence, brought to a high tension by strong underlying emotion, make
its pathos unforgettable. What the composer thought of this inspired
page was shown by his taking a slight variant of the piano introduction as the theme of his finest set of variations—that in the D Minor
Quartet. Arranged for wind instruments, this theme was played
when his bones were transferred to rest beside Beethoven's in the
Zentralfriedhof.

The D Minor Quartet also quotes from another death song, but one as unlike these others as may well be. In the Quartet's finale we hear fragments of that thrilling ballad, *The Erl King*. There the eighteen-year-old youth captured the innermost spirit of Goethe's lines. Note his lavish fecundity in giving the spectral king a different melody whenever he is heard. The galloping triplets of the piano part turned out to be so difficult that neither Schubert, nor many a pianist since his day, could manage them, and he curbed their fury into an easier eighth-note version. But the original triplets are so effective that when Moussorgsky accompanied Mme. Leonova at Elizavetgrad in 1879, he wrote, "After *The Erl King* they loudly applauded even poor me." Which was a tribute to a wonderful piano part as well as to a superb pianist.

Two things influenced Goethe in writing this poem. One was literary, the other a bit of real life. He knew the Danish ballad in which Sir Olaf, riding through a forest to his marriage, meets the daughter of the Erl King[1] and perishes. And his imagination fused this with a memory of an actual occurrence. One evening he saw a horseman riding furiously past the garden gate. Later he learned that a farmer had been rushing his sick baby to the doctor.

Schubert made four versions of *The Erl King*. Then he stowed them all away in a drawer until, five years later, Gymnich sang one of them for a select circle at the Sonnleithners'. Later the voice of Vogl started the song on its illustrious career. This ballad of death has, incongruously enough, furnished no little amusement. In burlesque mood, Schwammerl was capable of performing it upon a comb covered with tissue paper. And an American baritone once contributed to the gaiety of nations by mispronouncing the adjective in "*das ächzende Kind*" ("the moaning child"), so that the audience was electrified to learn:

> *Dem Vater grauset's; er reitet geschwind,*
> *Er hält in den Armen das achtzehnte Kind.*

> (The father shudders; his gallop is wild,
> He holds in his arms the eighteenth child.)

Schubert wrote three outstanding religious songs. Two of them, *The Young Nun* (*Die junge Nonne*) and *Omnipotence* (*Die Allmacht*), are powerful, turbulent, highly dramatic, shuddering with

---

[1] The name of the ballad is a mistake which can be traced back to Herder's mistranslation of the Danish *ellerkonge* as *Erlkönig*, instead of *Elbkönig* which means Elfking.

tremolos, scourged by stage thunder and lightning. They were conceived in what Sir Charles G. D. Roberts used to call "the big
bow-wow style." In their way, these songs are moving and effective,
especially where, at the close of *The Young Nun,* underneath the
calm voice of the chapel bell, one is conscious of the storm still
raging.

With the third religious song we find ourselves on that other
plane of purity, tenderness, and almost folk-songlike simplicity
where Schubert worked out his happier inspirations. There is an
ineffable magic in the direct, intimate strains of the *Ave Maria* from
the Walter Scott songs. Here is elemental wearing quality. And the
wonder of its appeal grows when one realizes that the melody, like
that of *By the Sea,* is spun out of what, for most other composers,
would remain a mere unorganic ornament. For it consists largely of
the commonplace turn, or its variants.

[Ex. 133]

Schubert's versatility as a song writer was as wide as his melodic and harmonic fecundity. There is no cradle song sweeter and more reassuring than his. There is no more remarkable song of courage than *Muth*, in which the hero of *The Winter Journey* whistles to keep up his spirits, though we feel the depression beneath this outburst. And finally, we have in *To Music* (*An die Musik*), the most treasurable tribute ever paid by a composer to his art:

[Ex. 134]

Whatever the faults of friend Schober, we pardon him everything
for having written the poem that inspired this glorious outburst. As
Alec Robertson[1] has well said, "It is a song a musician would wish
to be sung at his own passing; every bar and phrase of it is immortal."

[1] In Abraham.

44

PART SONGS

IT IS odd that Bach, Handel, Haydn, Mozart, and Beethoven should have remained characteristic in their choral works, but that Schubert and Schumann, as soon as they wrote for more than one voice should, as a rule, have stepped out of their skins and abandoned their own personalities. To anyone who expects to find in them the master's endearing idiom, Schubert's part songs will prove disappointing; but, as they offer some excellent pages, the best plan is to forget their creator, consider these works "*sans père et sans proche*" and enjoy the music for itself alone.

God in Nature (*Gott in der Natur*), for female voices and piano, is impressive if one likes "the big bow-wow" style. Though the *Serenade* (*Ständchen*), Op. 135, for alto solo and female choir, which was written and rewritten at Anna Fröhlich's request, has been a good deal overpraised, still it is dainty, charming, and original. There is some interesting canonic imitation at "*Sucht' ein Weiser nah' und ferne.*"

In the more notable music for men's voices, Schubert took special pains to declare and preserve the independent individuality of the different parts, which often disport themselves in clever counterpoint. Though unidiomatic, these works won for him the distinction of being the most important composer of male part songs.

La Pastorella, with piano, is suave and sweet. *Night Song in the Forest* (*Nachtgesang im Walde*), Op. 139b, accompanied by four horns with agreeable echo effects, comes at first tantalizingly near the Schubertian, then lets the disappointed hearer down. *The Spirit of Love* (*Geist der Liebe*), Op. 11, No. 3, with piano or guitar accompaniment, is saved from the commonplace by its rustic and primitive charm.

A descriptive piece, *The Little Village* (*Das Dörfchen*), Op. 11, No. 1, also accompanied by piano or guitar, is so naïvely folksy that at times it draws perilously near the "close harmony" of the street corner. It shows the taste of the period that, when this was sung in the same concert with the composer's greatest part song for male voices, a setting of Goethe's *Song of the Spirits over the Waters* (*Gesang der Geister über den Wassern*), the audience vastly preferred the former. It was something which they could grasp at a first hearing. Schubert made several versions of Goethe's poem. The final one, Op. 167, for four tenors, four basses, two violas, two 'cellos, and double bass, has the deliciously rich, dusky coloring which Schumann and Brahms inherited and used to such advantage. The notes manage to suggest the motions of water and wind without sinking to the usual level of imitative music. But Schubert overdid his favorite dactyls, just as Schumann was to overdo his beloved dotted rhythm.

Close in quality to this fine piece is the *a cappella Chorus of Angels* from Goethe's *Faust,* for mixed voices, powerful, impressive, and serenely beautiful. It sounds as if Schubert were experimenting with a new style.

For mixed voices with piano, there are the solemnly moving *Burial Song* (*Begräbnislied*), and two pieces from Op. 112: *God, the Creator of the World* (*Gott, der Weltschöpfer*), somewhat on the order of Haydn's powerful chorus, *The Heavens Are Telling;* and the finer *Hymn to the Unending* (*Hymne an den Unendlichen*). *To the Sun* (*An die Sonne*), ranks high among the part songs.

We have heard Schwammerl, in contrary mood, deny that there was any such thing as jolly (*lustig*) music. Of course he had penned —and was to pen—many a truly *lustig* piece. Among them two terzettos deserve honorable mention. One is a side-splitting parody of Mozart, *Die Advokaten,* Op. 74, in which a pair of lawyers, tenor and bass, endeavor to collect their fees from a tenor cheat.[1] The other, *The Wedding Roast* (*Der Hochzeitsbraten*), Op. 104, for soprano, tenor, bass, and piano, has an Italian flavor. After an unpromising start, it grows more and more "unbuttoned" and uproarious. Here is music perfectly adapted for the most alcoholic moment of a Schubertiad.

---

[1] This was, however, merely a recasting of Anton Fischer's terzetto of the same name, published in 1805.

45

DRAMATIC MUSIC

IN READING A. Hyatt King's enthusiastic chapter on Schubert's *Music for the Stage,*[1] I feared that I must have grossly underestimated this part of his work and inexcusably overlooked many a page of beauty, charm, and dramatic power. But, on turning back with high hopes to the numbers specially praised, I was disappointed to find that most of them would have done small credit to a Boieldieu, to say nothing of a Schubert. For instance, the unaccompanied male chorus, *O theures Vaterland,* Act II, No. 14, of *Fierrabras,* which Mr. King calls "grand," sounds to me like an early harmony exercise by a not too talented student. The finale of *Alfonso and Estrella,* which he calls "tremendous," seems almost incredibly poor and barren, and so on.

The same disappointment persisted in other works. In none of Schubert's seventeen dramatic attempts except *Rosamunde,* could I find first-rate music, or anything truly Schubertian. King implies censure of critics like Grove and Hadow for dismissing the operas in a few lines. But I think that the eating of this inferior pudding proves those gentlemen justified in their neglect.

The reason usually given for Schubert's artistic, as well as financial, failure in opera is that he lacked a practical eye for the technical tricks and manners of the stage. Vogl's remark at their first meeting, "You are not enough of a charlatan," has frequently been used to explain his ill success on the boards. In a sense, Vogl was right. It is true that Schubert, like his successor Schumann, had but little dramatic instinct and almost invariably chose impossible librettos. In working for the stage, he was handicapped by his very virtues as a lyrical creator of songs and absolute music. His instinct for unity in accompaniments hindered conformity to the necessary suppleness

[1] In Abraham.

of movement. He could not make the bad librettos a part of himself and live in them. (Who could?) The vocal melodic line lost in magic. Everything leaned toward a perfunctory standardization.

The stage [writes Alfred Orel] [1] demands far and away coarser means of expression than the song, and these were unknown to Schubert. The dramatic accents in his works for the stage grow very much too much out of the lyrical; they do not breathe out the essential hot life of the dramatist . . . Seen at the far greater distance of the theatre audience, the delicate colours in which Schubert here works grow pale.

The chief reason, however, why we cannot today enjoy sixteen of his seventeen stage works, is that he was, in another sense, not too little, but too much, of a charlatan. He wrote these things in order to make money, and he must have felt that his best chance of doing so was to prostitute his art and compose in a style that would appeal to the cheap taste of the time. Dashed off at top speed, much of his stage music sounds as though influenced for the worse by Rossini, the operatic giant who obstructed his path. He was following Salieri's pernicious advice to keep the preferences of the great public in mind and not go deep. Here the Italian was only echoing Goethe's unworthy counsel when, in 1790, he wrote Reichardt: "In order to make [a musical play], one must ape the noble Italian example, lay aside all poetic conscience, all poetic shame."

This humiliating concession to the groundlings was made, alas! in vain. It only managed to get Schubert a mere handful of stage performances. Finally the composer perhaps realized that his pocket might have been little worse off if he had given opera of his best, instead of pandering to the popular taste. At all events, in the incidental music to a nonsensical play called *Rosamunde,* he came to himself, and left us some of his most charming and characteristic pages.

The *Allegro vivace* of the sprightly piece known as the *Rosamunde* Overture[2] leans upon Mozart, who was so frequent a source of Schubert's inspiration. It begins

---

[1] Quoted by Vetter.

[2] This was originally written for *The Magic Harp* (*Der Zauberharfe*); and the overture which Schubert originally wrote for *Rosamunde* was shifted by him to *Alfonso and Estrella.*

[Ex. 135]

with a reminiscence of the second theme of the opening movement
of the "*Jeunehomme*" Piano Concerto in E Flat (K. 271).

Ten numbers follow. After working through the unworthy pages
of sixteen attempts at stage pieces, one finds with joyful relief that
most of *Rosamunde* is not only good music but—what is saying more
—real Schubert.

The First Entr'acte starts propitiously with a truly tragic atmosphere and a symphonic breadth and depth. Then comes the First
Ballet, with a heart-warming march that goes into an *Andante un
poco assai* of the most exquisite childlike purity and charm:

[Ex. 136]

The Second Entr'acte has been undeservedly neglected, perhaps
because difficult to recall. It is, for the most part, merely delicious
harmony without much definite tune. The *Romance* for soprano,
"*Der Vollmond strahlt*," soars so high in quality above the songs
in the other dramatic works as almost to fall within my selection of
Schubert's best lieder.

The Third Entr'acte opens with a delicate scoring of the B flat
melody which is what most people first think of when they hear the
name *Rosamunde*. This unforgettable tune was, as we have seen,
used later in the A Minor Quartet and in the B Flat *Impromptu*.[1]
It was very dear to Schubert's heart. Here he secured a happy con-

[1] See pp. 234 and 288 f.

trast by alternating the dactylic first part with minor mode triplets
in the two Trios.

After *Shepherds' Melodies,* very simply scored for clarinets, bassoons, and horns, and of a calculated monotony which might be good
medicine against insomnia, come two choruses, a highly dactylic one
of shepherds, and a swinging one of huntsmen, culminating in an
uproar calculated to scare all the game for leagues around. These
two sink down close to the composer's ordinary opera level. But the
Second Ballet redeems the occasion with a bit of the choicest Schubert,

[Ex. 137]

which is akin to the toothsome last example.

Taken by and large, *Rosamunde* is one of the composer's most
creditable achievements. To find this jewel in his dramatic dustbin is
a memorable experience. One can well understand why, on digging
part of its score out of Viennese oblivion, Grove and Sullivan were
moved to play leapfrog in the small hours.

46

RELIGIOUS MUSIC

JOHANNES BRAHMS told Robert Kahn that when he copied the original manuscript of Schubert's uncompleted religious drama *Lazarus,* he was touched to find in its unread pages some of the sand with which the composer had dried the wet notes. This he piously collected and preserved.

After studying *Lazarus,* I imagine that Brahms's act was dictated more by love of the man who wrote the String Quintet, *Hark, hark! the Lark,* and the Last Symphony than by reverence for the Easter oratorio itself. True, the third part, which would have offered more stuff of dramatic vitality and interest, was never completed, and the second breaks off in mid-career; but what has come down to us, though on a somewhat higher level than most of the shorter religious pieces, is disappointingly dull. A few pages here and there, like the orchestral introduction of Part II, are solemnly impressive, but the interest is not long sustained. One feels nowhere the exuberant warmth that radiates from the composer's best works. Strange that a genius of his infinite resource should have gone in for these long, dry recitatives, and allowed the orchestra, for page after page, to settle into the rut of block chords. Here the religious Schubert was no more successful than the operatic in endowing his characters with flesh and blood. True, the work's novel form foreshadowed the oratorio of the future, and its substance was strikingly independent of the influence of earlier composers. But today, for all that, one cannot recommend the raising of *Lazarus* from the dead.

Miriam's Song of Victory, Op. 136, is in no better case. One hears much about its Handelian quality, but, in fact, it offers little more real Handel than real Schubert—which is nil—and in the end, the clatter of the busy piano accompaniment grows wearisome.

The smaller religious pieces do not offer much of interest. The *Salve Regina,* Op. 149, of 1824, for male quartet unaccompanied, is sweet, but full of trite phrases and commonplace cadences. The

blameless little *Twenty-third Psalm,* Op. 132, for female voices and
piano has, I suspect, made its way more through ease of execution
than through more positive qualities. Another Psalm, the Ninety-
second, for mixed choir *a cappella,* with Hebrew words, shows a trifle
more distinction, and the occasional Hebraic quality of the music
speaks of Schubert's imaginative mobility. Of these short church
compositions, the choicest, written shortly before Schubert's death, is
Intende voci, for solo tenor, mixed chorus, and orchestra. Here is
moving and truly devotional music, but like the others, it offers little
clue to the identity of the composer.

The best of the religious works are some of the Masses. These
would be still better, if, like Bach and Beethoven, Schubert had set
the sacred text without regard to the hampering and formalizing
exigencies of performance as part of a church service. But he should
be given immense credit for writing truly devotional compositions
at a period when church music had very generally sunk close to
operetta and tavern levels, when the *Kyrie* often sounded like a
triumphal march, and the prayer for peace at the close of the *Agnus
Dei,* like a *marche militaire* in *presto* time.

The naïve *German Mass (Deutsche Messe),* with its straightfor-
ward homophony and its atmosphere of simple trust in the divine, is
dearer to the hearts of the Austrian country folk than the more
sophisticated works with Latin texts.

The First Mass in F [1] is a most remarkable achievement for a boy
of seventeen. He composed the delightful soprano solos of the *Kyrie*
for Therese Grob, with whom he was in love, and the worshipful
spirit of the whole composition is full of the youthful freshness of
Franzl's worship of her. Perhaps that was why the *Dona nobis pacem*
which ends the Mass returns to the music of Therese's *Kyrie.*

The *Gloria,* with the dew still on it, is actually more successful
than that of the mature Mass in A Flat of a decade later, for the
Andante con moto is one of Schubert's most fortunate essays in religious music. Which shows what love can do for a musician's creativeness. It could even make the dryest reaches of the *Credo* sparkle
like Therese's eyes, and make the lovely *Benedictus* truly a blessing
to music lovers. Parts of this Mass bear the composer's sign manual
after the manner of some of the lesser songs, but it is strange that a
work written the same year as the intensely Schubertian *Margaret
at the Spinning Wheel,* when his faculties were all heightened by

[1] Disregarding the childish Mass in C of 1810.

the intoxication of love, should not have been more characteristic of
its composer.

In one respect the F Major was a pioneer. As Schering noted in
Messe und Requiem seit Haydn und Mozart, it was the first to bring
back the principal theme of the *Credo* at the words "*Credo in spiri-
tum sanctum,*" thus establishing a new form which, a few years later,
Beethoven was independently to follow in the *Missa Solemnis,* and
which has become classical.

This work, so astonishingly ripe for an adolescent, was dashed
down in little more than two months. Due perhaps to Therese's influence, it surpasses his next four Masses in various respects. One
can understand why, after hearing it performed, Salieri embraced
the boy composer and cried, "Franz, you are my pupil and are going
to do me proud!"

The cheerful, almost gay, Second Mass in G, modestly scored for
string orchestra, and finished in five days, is less than a third as long
as the First and, curiously enough, though written a year later,
sounds less mature. The sweet, innocent *Kyrie* is no more extensive
than one of the longer songs. The forthright *Gloria,* though equally
naïve, hints at the future power of its composer. Dahms well described the *Credo* as "childishly trusting." It is an effective chorale-
like movement of long chords over a brisk bass of staccato quarters.
This goes on a considerable time, but any suggestion of monotony is
dispelled by the enthusiastic *Osanna* fugato of the tiny *Sanctus,*

O - san - na in   ex - cel - sis, O - san - na   in   ex - cel   -   sis

[Ex. 138]

and by the interest and color of the *Benedictus,* which also ventures
upon a bit of contrapuntal imitation. This, with the even more expressive and dramatic *Agnus Dei,* closes the work with its best and
most characteristic movements. And the last pages carry us within
measurable distance of the quality which we think of as Schubertian.
Ariel has had a finger in this pie.

Let those critics who habitually complain of Schubert's diffuseness
consider the admirable brevity of a work which gave him complete
expression in a *Kyrie* of five and a half pages, a *Sanctus* of three, and

an *Agnus Dei* of four. Even more remarkable was the achievement of compressing such inelastic things as the *Gloria* and the *Credo* to seven and nine and a half pages. Throughout the quality holds up consistently.

Two decades after the composer's death, a rogue named Robert Führer paid the G Major Mass the compliment of printing it in Prague as his own composition.

The less distinguished and scarcely longer Masses in B Flat and C will not detain us. For almost three years, from 1819 to 1822, and again just before his death, Schubert toiled over the lengthy Fifth Mass in A Flat, known as the *Missa Solemnis*.[1] He lavished on it what was for him an unusual amount of revision, but what would have been unusually small for Beethoven. He replaced the poor *cum sancto Spiritu* fugue in the *Gloria*, and the *Osanna* ending the *Sanctus*, with pages but slightly better. However, at the close of his labors, he had a work in the grand style that improved consistently from start to finish, in one long crescendo of quality.

The *Kyrie* of the A Flat is good sound choral music but is far from bearing its composer's signature. The same may be said for the exciting *Gloria*, except for the remarkable modulation at *miserere*, and the breath-taking climax so thrillingly worked up to from the quiet *Quoniam*. The most treasurable portions of the *Credo* are the eight-part *et incarnatus est*, and the rousing *Amen*, which almost begins to sound characteristic.

And then the movements grow more and more beautiful, through the *Sanctus* with its flowing violin accompaniment, and the *Benedictus* with its delightful pizzicato bass, to the *Agnus Dei*, whose haunting melody and deliciously changing harmony bring us close at last to the real Schubert.

The Sixth and best of the Masses is in E Flat. Johannes Brahms loved this music so dearly that he actually took time from his own creative work to arrange the orchestra part for piano. Written in 1828, it was one of the composer's final achievements, and is worthy of a place beside the world's chief choral masterpieces. In the six years which separated it from the bulk of work on the A Flat, Schubert had reached the height of mastery. The harmony is richer, more subtle, more passionate; the polyphony is on a higher plane. The

---

[1] This tautological designation might seem absurdly to imply a distinction between solemn Masses and jocular ones; but in this instance it may have meant that the A Flat was to be taken more seriously than the cheerful little G Major.

orchestra, which had begun to be more prominent in the A Flat, now has things of far greater import to communicate.

In the *Kyrie,* Schubert might have been experimenting with a new style. It strikes a note novel for him or for his predecessors. I recall no other such dazzling effect in liturgical music as that of the brilliant *Gloria,* suddenly bursting from behind the clouds of the *Kyrie.* And, after all the exuberance, how effective is the soft ending of the *glorificamus, laudamus te!*

The *Miserere* works up to one of the most thrilling of choral climaxes. Immediately there follows the sheer inspiration of couching the *Quoniam* in the opening strain of the *Gloria.* Then comes the powerful and elaborately developed fugue, *cum sancto Spiritu,*

[Ex. 139]

and a resounding *Amen.*

The *Credo* brings contrapuntal imitations so satisfying that one marvels at the composer's humility in resolving, soon after writing them, to study counterpoint with Sechter. In the last pages before the somewhat Schubertian trio, *et incarnatus est,* Ariel gives forth such ethereal strains as to remind one how few of his last days separated this Mass from the String Quintet. Schubert must have written the profoundly moving choral portions of the *Crucifixus* with his heart's blood.

Did he conceive the ineffable harmonies which open the *Sanctus* with some dim—perhaps unconscious—premonition of how soon he was to know "the life of the world to come"? One feels an unearthly exhilaration in the free *Osanna* fugato,

sis   De ————— o,

[Ex. 140]

with its unexpected harmonies. Heuberger calls this *Sanctus* "one of the strongest movements in modern music," and feels that its composer stands on an even footing with Michelangelo and Beethoven.

The *Benedictus*, too, is the music of heaven, though of a new heaven for which Schubert had never before written incidental music. Here, in ever increasing beauty, solo quartet alternates with choir, hymnlike passages with fugued passages. But in the *Agnus Dei*, the greatest movement in any of the Masses, we are suddenly brought back to a realization of the poor sick composer's wretched plight; for it starts with the bass theme which opens that song of unutterable woe, *Der Doppelgänger:*

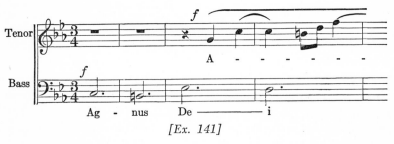

Ag - nus   De ——————— i

[Ex. 141]

Touching in its tender simplicity and in the moving antiphonal accents of solo quartet and choir, the *dona nobis pacem* has the quality of those lieder in which Schubert caught the inner essence of folk song. And it is still more touching when one remembers how soon the composer himself was to be caught up into the eternal peace.

47

THE SYMPHONIST

IN WRITING of Mozart's universality, Alfred Einstein[1] dismisses
the claims of other music makers, then adds:

And this would bring us to Schubert, the composer of the *"Unfinished"*
and the D Minor Quartet, and of hundreds of perfect songs, the only one
who could be compared to Mozart, if it were not that, although he wrote
operas too, the dramatic, the scenic, the feeling for the stage, were denied
him.

But why not set those hundreds of perfect songs against Mozart's
handful, and place the two composers upon the same lofty level of
universality?

The myriad-minded Schubert was a great symphonist. It is customary to condemn him for departing from the more classical models of
Beethoven, and creating the lyrical symphony of Romanticism. He
bequeathed this invention to Schumann, and much that I have written about the latter as symphonist[2] applies (with a change of names)
to the former:

What ineluctable lawgiver has laid down the rule that, until the crack
of doom, all symphonies worthy the name must be of one kind only?
What final ukase has decreed: "Thou shalt have no other symphonic gods
before me"?

I, for one, think that genius must be allowed the last word in this
matter. And I zestfully enjoy the Romantic variety that [Schubert] im-
ported into sonata-form. "In my Father's house are many mansions."
Within the spacious city of art, side by side with all the tremendous epic
monuments, there is abundant room for lyric symphonies like these. In
them we find the same exultant joy in life, . . . the same intimacy, dreamy

---

[1] *Mozart.*
[2] In *Florestan,* p. 390 ff.

tenderness, opulence of fancy and continuing excitement which we enjoy in the piano works, the songs, and the chamber music.

It is true that, while some of Schubert's development sections were everything that could be desired in a working-out portion, many were not as imaginatively resourceful as one would expect from a mind such as his. Often he merely contented himself with running large blocks of his subjects through various keys.

But I think that the strident outcry which the critics have raised about this is unjustified. If we refused to enjoy any composer who does not always develop his material like Beethoven, we miserable perfectionists would have to subsist upon a diet of pure L. v. B. and Brahms. And in these radio-saturated days, when the prudent listener is forced to ration his enjoyment of any composer for fear of surfeit, how long would that last us?

Hugo Leichtentritt declared:[1]

The principal charge brought against Schubert for a century is that his working-out sections are excessively long, loosely constructed, too little organic in the sense of Bach and Beethoven. Now . . . the musical world ought to be advanced enough to recognize that these apparent faults are faults only if Schubert's works are considered from the point of view appropriate to Bach and Beethoven. But it is evidently unjust to impose such demands and conditions upon a master who can be fully appreciated only if we find the point of view appropriate to him alone. Schubert's exposition and working-out section in the sonata-form follow their own law, which is not identical with Beethoven's law . . .

The reason for this departure from the classical model lies in the nature of the Romantic imagination, less inclined toward the plastic and architectural tendencies of classical music, but rather desirous of breaking away from the predominance of the tonic and dominant keys, and of bringing in quickly the brighter and richer colors of harmony.

It is true that Schubert's lyrical instinct was a handicap when it inclined him, as it often did, toward choosing self-contained, song-like themes whose very completeness made development difficult. Indeed, some claim that we can understand this composer only through his song writing. This, however, is as foolish as to claim that we can understand Edison only through his invention of the electric

[1] In *Musical Courier*, Apr. 26, 1928.

bulb, or George Washington only through his feat in making a silver dollar go so far. And let us not forget how many self-contained, song-like themes were used by Haydn, Mozart, and even Beethoven. An important part of friendship consists in forgiving the other for what we consider his failings. So, if we would be friends with this incomparable genius of a Schubert, we must comprehend the reason for—or at least excuse—his un-Beethovenian developments and over-look his diffuseness, love of repetition, and occasional descents from inspiration to banality. There is a higher alchemy that overrules the laws of the musicologists. It allowed Schubert to indulge in these practices and even to be less contrapuntal than the professors ap-prove—yet to charm more potently and wear with a more steel-like perdurability than the ninety-and-nine just composers who observe all the rules, and need no repentance. Shakespeare went far on "small Latin and less Greek." One striking evidence of Schubert's transcend-ent ability is that he could make his greatest compositions, like the last symphonies and chamber works, wear so well with so little counterpoint. I doubt if even Mozart or Beethoven could have per-formed such a miracle. It was making bricks with too little straw. It was lifting himself to the empyrean by his bootstraps. In short, it was sheer magic performing the impossible. The feat is as hard to explain in words as is the power of that high explosive called charm. In the matter of counterpoint, no one else has ever accomplished so much with so little.

What positive qualities he had wherewith to offset the negative! Tovey[1] thought Schubert a no "less great master of large forms than Shakespeare up to the time of, let us say, *Richard II*." In his supreme works, this greatest maker of melodies, this convincing combiner of them, this pioneer in spontaneous harmonic alchemy, this intoxicat-ing master of driving, compelling rhythms, which, toward the close of his life, grew constantly more original and more compelling, this magical orchestrator, this communicator par excellence of intimate personal charm, this wielder of the ample brush with the wide sweep, had an equipment which makes us gladly discount his obvious faults. Lay them in the balance opposite his virtues, and they kick the beam. Grove was right: "He did nothing to extend the formal limits of symphony or sonata, but he endowed them with a magic, a romance, a sweet naturalness which no one has yet approached."

[1] Donald Francis Tovey, *Essays in Musical Analysis*, Vol. I, London, Oxford University Press, 1935.

48

THE EARLIER SYMPHONIES

THE First Symphony, in D, is the most remarkable work in this form ever written by a boy of sixteen. It sounds as though, in 1813, Franzl had summoned all his courage, enthusiasm, and energy for the purpose of mastering the genre in one impetuous frontal attack.

The Second Symphony, in B Flat, marks an astonishing advance. Begun a year later, it was finished in March, 1815. If we compare this with Beethoven's First, written at the age of thirty, and consider that Franzl was still a boy while Beethoven was a mature man, and that both were still strongly influenced by Haydn and Mozart, the lad's feat is the more remarkable. In the senior's composition one finds a little more of the future Beethoven than in the other's of the real Schubert, but not nearly enough to make up for the age disparity.

In the lad's Second Symphony there is also some Beethoven influence. The first subject of the opening *Allegro vivace* is a son of the corresponding theme in the deaf man's First Symphony. The second subject, as well, is Beethovenian, and ends in the phrase, a descending F, D, B flat, A flat, G, that introduces the second subject of the *Coriolanus* Overture with these very notes. Unfortunately the last two pages of the movement lapse into a vulgarity such as might be expected from the weaker moments of popular operatic composers like Boieldieu, Hérold, and Nicolai.

The gem of the Second is the theme of the *Andante* variations.

[Ex. 142]

They are of the unsophisticated, straightaway kind, clinging close to their theme for protection, that Schubert was to write as late as the *"Trout"* Quintet. Gamboling vigorously, the Minuet and its playful Trio seem at first to offer much Haydn and little Schubert, but, as with the *Andante,* the more it is heard, the more characteristic it sounds.

With the snap and go of eager youth, the finale overworks the composer's favorite dactylic rhythm in some rather commonplace Haydn. But suddenly, sixteen bars before the first hold, there comes a bit of brass-band music that would have made the Papa of the symphony and of the quartet bound in his chair. Other tributes to the mode of the moment are the second subject and the noisy passages that follow it. Despite such blemishes, however, the Second marked a phenomenal advance and is still heard with pleasure.

With the Third, in D, comes a falling off in quality that is not recovered until the Fourth, the *"Tragic,"* Symphony in C Minor. Here Schubert's evident intention is to be weightily serious. Much is made throughout of the ♩♩♩|♩ rhythm which we associate with Beethoven's Fifth in the same key. But, after a somewhat imposing *Adagio molto* introduction, the *Allegro vivace* sounds all too much like a task done to order. The uninspired scherzolike Minuet is odd without being reminiscent of anybody—even of its own composer. The dull finale suffers from repetition and diffuseness, and the *"Tragic"* would be a tragic failure but for the admirable *Andante,* which goes far toward redeeming the work. Its first subject

pp dolce

[Ex. 143]

distantly reminds one of that German toast-song, *"Hoch soll er leben!"* The spontaneous freshness and joy in creation breathed out by this lovely movement is an earnest of symphonic pleasures to come.

The Fifth Symphony, in B Flat, is a little treasure and, even though more redolent of Mozart, Beethoven, and Haydn than of Schubert,

is a perennial delight. This musical pearl has none of those unfortunate blemishes that disfigure so much of its creator's best work. Perhaps because the amateur orchestra for which it was intended had
been reduced in numbers, Franzl scored it modestly, without benefit
of clarinets, trumpets and drums, for a single flute, oboes, bassoons,
horns and strings, which lent it some of the intimate quality of
chamber music.

This Symphony does not, like the preceding, go on stilts, nor has
it anything to do with the "sceptred pomp" of "gorgeous tragedy."
The themes, simple and, as Baedeker would put it, "unpretending,"
are exquisitely adapted to the handful of moderately skilled amateur
players for which they were conceived.

At times [declares Eugene Goossens[1]], particularly in No. 5, Schubert
gets away from tradition and boldly strikes out into new effects, a foretaste of the superb orchestration of his last two symphonies. His woodwind writing in particular has a conversational quality, a tenderness, and
a delicacy which atone for any paucity of contrapuntal effect . . . These
scores display a degree of self-confidence unequalled by any composer
since Mozart.

After a charming four-bar wisp of introduction, the principal subject of the *Allegro*,

Vlc.
[Ex. 144]

opens with a rising triad figure (marked by a bracket) which suggests the beginning of Mozart's G Minor Quintet with two violas,
K. 516, but sounds none the less like Schubert. The subject is largely
made up of repetitions of that triad, joined by connective tissue. Such
economy was rare with the prodigal melodist.[2]

[1] In *Chesterian*, Vol. X, No. 74.
[2] It becomes all the more remarkable when one notices that this triad arpeggio
is a germ motive which recurs, with simplified rhythm, in the sixth bar of the
second subject; comes (diminished) in the second subject of the *Andante con
moto*, begins each section of the *Menuetto*, is inverted at the start of the Trio,
recurs in the finale at bars 49–50, and both inverted and rising at bars 88–89.

Here is the delightfully pert and mischievous second subject of the opening movement:

[Ex. 145]

To counteract the insistent | ♩. ♪ ♩ ♩ | beat of ex. 144, ex. 145 offers unusual diversity of movement, by varying the rhythm of each successive two-bar phrase. It may be left to the curious reader who has a score to discover how the fourth bar of ex. 145 recurs, shorn of its first or last note,[1] in the other three movements of the Symphony.

The development is one of the composer's most successful. It starts by concerning itself so busily with the introduction that one wonders whether this had not been prefixed to the movement as an afterthought, for use as working-out material.[2] Perhaps Schubert realized how unfitted the self-contained second subject (ex. 145) was for development, and how brief was the scrap of phrase on which he had built the first subject (ex. 144). Here he attains a more interesting symphonic style. Instead of literally quoting his subjects in various keys, he offers mere imaginative suggestions of them and, with clever imitative work, dramatically plays one against another. The whole development is one great Schubertian crescendo and diminuendo.

Mosco Carner points out[3] "the clear structural plan of the section as a whole. The latter feature is seen at its best in the gradual shortening of the phrases from four bars to one bar."

The *Andante con moto* is none the less beautiful and moving because its principal subject suggests the main theme in the rondo of Mozart's F Major Violin Sonata, K. 377,[4]

[1] Schubert's characteristic way of modifying his germ motives.
[2] For a similar hypothesis about the *"Unfinished,"* see p. 30.
[3] In Abraham.
[4] As Tovey shows.

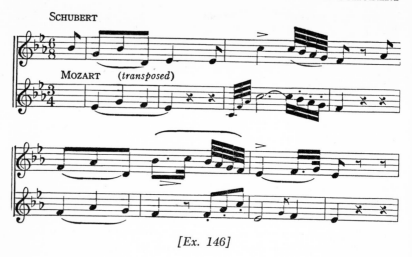

[Ex. 146]

and its second subject floats us to the tranquil atmosphere of the Heiligenstadt brookside in Beethoven's *"Pastoral"* Symphony. Then, with incomparable grace, we are wafted back to the Mozartian commencement.

The *Menuetto* is excellent Mozart, with an opening fit to hold up its head beside the more elaborate corresponding movement of the older master's G Minor Symphony, while the falling chromatics at the end recall a similar passage in the Minuet of the *"Jupiter."*

The Trio

[Ex. 147]

reinforces the most limpid Mozartian honey with a spoonful from Schubert's own personal hive. Its second part dishes up a mellifluous canon in D minor between first violin plus bassoon, and flute plus oboe.

Here is the main theme of the merry finale,

[Ex. 148]

which mingles the sweetness of Mozart and the jollity of Haydn.

What with its firmer handling of form, its spontaneity, heightened creativeness, and more frequent foretastes of the Schubert to come, the Fifth is far and away the best of the early symphonies. There are none of the "lengths," "heavenly" or otherwise, that Schumann found in the Ninth. Devoid of prolixity and vain repetitions, it has an almost epigrammatic conciseness foreign to most of Schubert's larger compositions. Perhaps the amateur group he had in mind was as limited in playing hours as in personnel.

The Fifth was begun June 16, 1816, only two days after Schubert had gone into raptures on hearing a Mozart quintet.[1] This sixteenth was the very day of Salieri's anniversary celebration when Franzl had gone so far as to inveigh against what he called the "eccentricity" of Beethoven. (See p. 38). The Beethovenian second subject of the slow movement shows how promptly he was to recant that absurd heresy.

Two years later, the Sixth Symphony, the so-called "Little C Major," showed more of Beethoven's influence than of any other composer. But the pages thus sponsored are not to be compared in quality with the Mozartian strains of the Fifth. In reminiscent vein, Schubert was, as a rule, more happily inspired by Salzburg than by Bonn. He felt more akin to his great fellow Austrian than to the great German.

This shift to the deaf master, however, cannot wholly account for the mysterious and lamentable falling off in quality of the Sixth. The fact that the first movement, pertly theatrical as it is, shows the influence of such small fry as Hérold and Boieldieu, would suggest that here, for once in his symphonic work, Schubert succumbed to the temptation that helped to vitiate most of his operatic writing, and

[1] See p. 42. The first subject of Schubert's Fifth (ex. 144) might suggest that the Mozart quintet in question was the G Minor, K. 516.

tried to win a popular success by pandering to the ears of the ground-lings in the style of the day.[1] Later, when the Friends of Music boggled at playing the Ninth Symphony, this hope may have led him to substitute the Sixth, as being more to their taste. Which it doubt-less was.

The lack of rhythmical subtlety in Schubert's early works is spe-cially marked in this one, and the plethora of simple cadences adds to the monotony.

The approach to the recapitulation is Beethoven to the life. With the middle movements, the not wholly happy influence of Bonn in-creases until, in the Scherzo,[2] imitation of the deaf man's First Sym-phony grows almost pedestrian.

The finale, full of exuberant drive, offers some lusty Haydn, a little Mozarting that would justify the term "cute," and a suggestion of Schubert's own popular *Marche militaire* of the future, but it soon slips back into Beethoven and lets fall a curious hint of the, as yet unwritten, *Ode to Joy*.

Hutchings is justified in remarking that this work "on the whole would make a pleasant accompaniment to tea in Shallow's orchard." Fit indeed for nothing much better than a foil for conversation. Its somewhat shoddy quality is leagues from the fresh, sparkling, spon-taneous loveliness of the Fifth.

Except for the introduction and a part of the first *Allegro*, which were fully scored, the Seventh Symphony in E Minor remained a mere sketch, of which the most interesting portion is the very be-ginning:

---

[1] Note also the bits of Rossinian tinsel in the introduction, *Andante*, and finale.
[2] Schubert's first use of the designation in a symphony.

[Ex. 149]

When he had finished his outline, Schubert, the quartet player, perhaps realized that the first four notes of the above melody were simply those of the *Adagio* of Beethoven's E Minor Quartet, Op. 59, No. 2:

[Ex. 150]

and the next four moved in the rhythm of that immortal inspiration. Then, looking over the rest of the material, Schubert perhaps saw that, despite the appeal of the lyrical *Andante*, his themes were not up to the mark, so he impatiently shelved the whole work. However, it would be unjust for us to judge in advance the quality of an unborn composition from a mere outline sketch. In 1883, an Englishman named J. F. Barnett, and in 1934, Felix Weingartner, completed the E Minor; but these attempts did not find favor.[1]

The earlier way of numbering the symphonies after the Sixth was to call the Great C Major the Seventh, and to assign no numbers to the unfinished ones in E Minor and B Minor. Today the E Minor sketch of 1821 is known as the Seventh, the B Minor, *"Unfinished,"* of 1822, as the Eighth, and the Great C Major of 1828, as the Ninth.

On my first acquaintance with the early symphonies, I found those parts the best which sounded like Haydn or Mozart; but the better I knew them, the more they began, and continued, to sound like the real Schubert.

[1] For a discussion of the legendary *"Gastein"* Symphony, see p. 150.

49

THE LAST SYMPHONIES

DESPITE their occasional corruscations of genius, their charm, and scattered hints of the ripe Schubert to come, the first six symphonies and the sketched Seventh stop far below the wholly Schubertian quality of the best songs of this period. It is startling to realize that the Second and Third Symphonies were contemporaneous with such characteristic and epoch-making inspirations as *Margaret at the Spinning Wheel* and *The Erl King*.

From the first seven to the *"Unfinished"* Symphony, the Eighth, in B Minor, Schubert took an enormous stride. Carner[1] calls that composition

the only successful case of a symphony being suffused by lyrical feeling while preserving the essential features of a large-scale symphonic work. [But this is true of the Ninth as well.] It is the consummation of Schubert's instrumental lyricism expressed in a medium—and that applies particularly to the first movement—that the classical tradition had nearly always excluded from the expression of personal and strongly emotional accents. It is in the breaking down of these stylistic barriers that Schubert's revolutionary departure lies. It was something that only a lyrical genius of his calibre was able to achieve.

This work is as warm, personally intimate, and emotionally fresh as one of the composer's best songs, yet it miraculously combines these lovable qualities with what Mason calls "the nobility and seriousness suitable to symphonic style." Here we have one of the high lights of Romantic music.

Antonin Dvořák[2] called this symphony and its successor

unique contributions to musical literature, absolutely new and original, Schubert in every bar. What is perhaps most characteristic about them

[1] In Abraham.
[2] In *Century Magazine*, 1894.

is the song-like melody pervading them. He introduced the song into the symphony . . . In originality of harmony and modulations, and in his gift of orchestral coloring, Schubert has had no superior.

The Eighth justifies the name "*Unfinished*" only in the sense that the Scherzo was never completed, and there is no evidence of any work on a finale, but the pair of movements that we have are among the most highly finished that Schubert ever wrote. It seems probable that, having started the Scherzo, he looked upon his work and saw that it was not good as a continuation of the first lyrical symphony of the Romantic movement. And the disappointment cooled him off to such an extent that he could not immediately try something else in its place. So he put the manuscript aside and, in the press of other inspirations—perhaps for the "*Wanderer*" Fantasy, the A Minor Sonata, Op. 143, and *The Miller's Beautiful Daughter*—forgot all about it, just as he once forgot having written the song which he admired when calling on Vogl. (See p. 62.) It is an eloquent commentary on the wealth of ideas that were forever competing in his mind for utterance, that he should have lost sight of the work which is now one of the most famous and best loved in all symphonic literature.

The 'cellos and basses start with a mysterious low unison, *pianissimo*, which proves to be the theme-of-all-work, for the development is almost exclusively concerned with it.

Allegro moderato

[Ex. 151]

There follows one of Schubert's unique song-accompaniment figures,

[Ex. 152]

sustained by the contrasting rhythmic throb of ♩♩♩|♩ in the lower strings. This ushers in and enriches a song of the clarinet, doubled by the oboe:

[Ex. 153]

Brent-Smith[1] has the ingenious thought that ex. 153 is "undoubtedly the first real subject of the movement," and was the composer's initial idea for beginning the work. Then he realized that this wistful, romantic tune was no fit material for starting a symphony and wrote four bars (see ex. 152) by way of preparation.

But again, feeling that these bars might not catch the full attention of the listeners, he prefaced them with [ex. 151], which has just the requisite feeling of mystery and suspense to make the arrival of the principal theme [ex. 153] absolutely satisfying.

Perhaps he also realized that ex. 153, with its lyrical character, would resist development as heartily as ex. 151 would co-operate in the venture.

After a long hold on D and a characteristic modulation which sets one to guessing the outcome, and guessing wrong, the syncopated clarinets and violas introduce the well-known second subject, a tune that has become an almost universal human possession, with a popularity rivaling that of the *Ave Maria* and the *Serenade*. It has even been desecrated into a popular song. Bie calls it "the most famous melody in the world."

[Ex. 154]

---

[1] Alexander Brent-Smith, *Schubert*, Vol. I, London, Oxford Univ. Press, 1926.

Note the symmetrical grouping of its phrases. The second and third measures match. So do the first and fourth. This causes the snake of music to bite its own tail. It is the excellent arrangement known to a sister art as the rhyme scheme ABBA.

In writing this 'cello solo, Franzl may have meant to please his 'cellist father, for in order to make his every note fully tell, the accompaniment keeps well above and below the soloist's range. The melody is repeated by the violins, but just as it seems about to end on the expected tonic G, there comes one of those sudden, dramatic Schubertian silences, followed by the G, which has surprisingly deserted the tonic to become the fifth of a tremendous C minor chord, the first of an agitated series[1] in stunning contrast to the delicate textures of the second subject. After some imitative sport with phrases from that subject, comes one of Schubert's ablest and most dramatic developments. It plays with the first four notes of ex. 151. Then, following some brilliant passages which bear no relation to the thematic material, it plays with the next four notes of that opening subject. Grove pointed out a subtle touch in the suggestive use of the syncopated accompaniment of the second subject (ex. 154) without the melody. It is as if we were shown Prospero's wand, to remind us of the absent Prospero.

Glimpses of the syncopated wand are interspersed with wild chord sequences. These naïve transitions, though alien to the subject matter, are in themselves elementally moving. A massive statement of ex. 151 as a whole builds up to a tremendous climax, shot through with exciting rhythms.

This development has none of the passive, stale air of textbook music. It is as fresh and spontaneous as an exhilarating scramble in the high mountains. The thematic material is not merely worked— it works. Here is none of the haphazard flinging down of themes side by side, nor of the spur-of-the-moment repetition and the planless modulation so often encountered in Schubert's earlier music. The logic of this development is convincing; its emotional quality, sincere and infectious. The section ends with a masterly *morendo* subsidence to the recapitulation, which starts with ex. 153 and, after insisting on that subject at somewhat too great length, brings back the famous ex. 154, this time in the 'cello's most brilliant register.

---

[1] It begins with a falling fifth in the high woodwind, recalling the start of ex. 153. One of Schubert's rare miscalculations let this be smothered by the outcries of the other instruments.

The coda plays delightfully with ex. 151, which is, at last, crowned
with a perfect cadence, to end an almost perfect movement.

The "Unfinished" is lent thematic unity by the simple device of
repeating the first notes of ex. 151, three notes of an ascending scale,
in all the other themes of the movement, and even in the accompaniment figure (ex. 152). These also occur in two themes of the slow
movement (ex. 155 and 157). This germinal phrase is marked
throughout by brackets.

Such melodic, harmonic, and contrapuntal enchantment as the
Andante con moto offers is hard to find elsewhere. It opens

[*Ex. 155*]

with two anticipatory bars so full of beauty and meaning that they
pervade much of what follows. Those descending pizzicati of the
double basses must have been in Tschaikowsky's mind when he
closed the first movement of the Symphony *Pathétique.*

In the third bar of the above example, at the start of the principal
theme,[1] the 'cello has the same delicious kind of counterpoint as at
bar 37 of the A Minor Quartet's *Andante.* After adventures in various keys, the melody returns to the original E major, "breaking," as
Brent-Smith well says, "into one of the loveliest and most tender
passages in orchestral music. It is a passage of simple tonic and
dominant harmony, childlike in its simplicity but touched with a
magic which seems to have been a secret known only to Beethoven
and Schubert."

[1] Carner (in Abraham) points out the resemblance between the start of this
theme and *The Linden Tree,* at the words, *"so manches liebe Wort."*

[Ex. 156]

Then, over an admirable staccato bass, derived from the two opening measures and played by strings and bass trombone, the woodwinds and the other trombones give out this tune:

[Ex. 157]

But the bass is so important that it steals the spotlight.

After a six-bar prelude in the composer's rarest vein, the second subject, accompanied by syncopated strings,

[Ex. 158]

is breathed by "the melting clarionet." Schubert's consummate use
of this instrument, here and elsewhere, makes one wish that he had
written a clarinet quintet, for such a work might well have stood in
the supreme class of those by Mozart, Brahms, and Reger. This second subject is characteristic of Schubert's melodic inspiration, the
rising and falling halves complementing each other, and finally producing a sense of unity as satisfying as the more famous second subject of the first movement.

Oboe and flute elaborate on this theme. Then it reaches the lower
regions in a cataclysm of double counterpoint, accompanied by a
hurricane of thirty-second notes, finally joined by those dignitaries,
the double basses, who end by tearing loose and gamboling like
young roes upon the mountains.

The coda is a miracle of amazing harmony and vivid instrumental
color. When it brings back and transforms the introduction to the
second subject, the modulations are iridescent with

> The light that never was on sea or land.

Tovey calls this "as subtle a stroke of genius as can be found anywhere in music." The movement expires in an inimitable *morendo.*

Here is a work that comes from the heart and goes to the heart. It
is almost as original as if no other symphony had ever existed.
Schubert may not have fully mastered the art of making fugues
according to Sechter; but in the B Minor and its successor, we find
him wreathing beautiful melodies in counterpoint as freshly, spontaneously, and convincingly as Nature herself when she mingles the
honeysuckle with the wild rose. And the orchestration is as fresh,
spontaneous, and convincing as the counterpoint.

The great Ninth Symphony in C Major gives the illusion that
writing a long piece for orchestra is more play than work. Apparently all a composer has to do is to set down some tune that is
running in his head, which in turn gives rise to another tune, and so
on. The fun is heightened by apportioning these among a lot of
varied instruments.

Unlike the *"Unfinished,"* whose sweet melancholy is interspersed
with occasional outbursts of pain, the Ninth is predominantly the
music of gay exuberance and high fettle. Its inventive opulence and

uproarious spirits remind one again that, even at the close of his career, its creator was a young man, and that all of his compositions are early works. In felicity of instrumentation, transparency of coloring, and grandeur of scale it is well-nigh unique. Hutchings remarks that "the one and only complete symphony of Schubert's last years makes it impossible for the mind to conceive the glories that were silenced by his death." Its faults, too little concentration and textual detail and too much prolixity and repetition, are the faults of youth. One gladly accepts them in return for the richness of imagination and the fresh spontaneity. Despite these faults, the profound and overwhelming effect of the Ninth, particularly in the finale, is due less to any details, however happy, than to its magnificent structure.

In a program note, the late Lawrence Gilman left a notable tribute to this work:

The discourse, almost throughout, is like that of a speaker who knows and loves and cunningly employs "the shape and hue and odour and sweet sound of words." It is full of surprising and inexhaustible subtleties of design and procedure, of delicate felicities accomplished with so perfect an art that they wear the innocence . . . of natural processes . . .

If the finale, especially, is not the pure, brave ecstasy of tone, then that ecstasy was never captured and released. Here indeed, as Francis Thompson said of *Prometheus Unbound*, "poetry is spilt like wine, music runs to drunken waste. The jubilant voices sweep down the wind, flight after flight, till we cry for respite from the unrolling splendors."

The long introduction is concerned with a hymnlike theme, given out at first by two horns in unison:

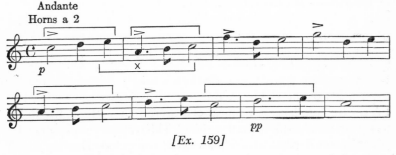

[Ex. 159]

More than half of this melody consists of repetitions of the germ motive of the "*Unfinished*," three rising diatonic notes, which is also, remarkably enough, the germ motive of the Ninth. It will be marked throughout by brackets. Notes 3–6, designated by (x), are to play an important role in the following movement.

The unusual time structure of ex. 159, in phrases of 3, 3, and 2 bars, is one more evidence of that rhythmic vigor and richness which the composer's maturity had developed. This theme is stated by different instrumental combinations and punctuated by a little development of the opening measures. The excitement of string triplets and a crescendo pedal point seem to herald some portentous event—and the *Allegro ma non troppo* is launched.

After all the grandiose preparation and suspense, however, the start of the movement unfortunately impresses one *non troppo*. It opens with this baldly unattractive unison "head-theme":

Allegro ma non troppo

[Ex. 160]

In the original version it was still more bleak:

[Ex. 161]

Schubert realized this and corrected it throughout the score. That he himself did not much like ex. 160, he showed by referring to it as little as he well could. Repetitions of it, with its | ♩. ♪♩. ♪| beat, are interspersed with harmonized woodwind chords in the strongly contrasting rhythm of | ♩ ♩ ♩ ♩ ♩ ♩ |. This play of triplets against more direct rhythms strongly flavors the outside movements of the C Major. Brent-Smith is justified in saying that the device "produces a richness of texture somewhat similar to the result of good contrapuntal writing. This rhythmic substitute for counterpoint is characteristic of another composer—Dvořák."

The antithesis of these two rhythms is found, vertically, in the more interesting continuation of the first subject,

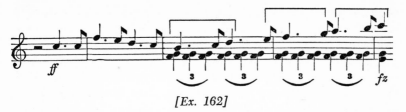

[Ex. 162]

and again, horizontally in the E minor second subject, where the movement begins to develop the real Schubertian flavor:

[Ex. 163]

Coming back in the major, this tune grows positively hilarious:

[Ex. 164]

Those "potent, grave, and reverend signiors," the trombones, seem to register disapproving protests in the phrase (x) borrowed from the introduction (ex. 159). But, deaf to the accents of authority, the other instruments continue the high jinks, hopping and skipping from key to key with an infectious levity that finally wins over the *signiors* to hurl dignity to the skies and join the revels. One is reminded of the constable in Wodehouse's tale, *Buck-u-up-o*, who, as I recall it, undertakes to arrest the bishop and his uproarious crew, but, having also indiscreetly sampled that superstimulant, *Buck-u-up-o*, plunges wholeheartedly into the spirit of the occasion, and proposes to turn the garden hose upon the slumbering curate, a proceeding which, he declares, will afford "much fun and merriment."

In the development, where the barren first subject is rightly accorded no more than a mere passing glance, the trombones, having presumably slept it off, resume the awful voice of authority, with the unexpected result of persuading the woodwinds to abandon levity and turn dreamily poetic.

Despite its brilliant coloring, infectious rhythms, and exciting modulations, the coda seems at first to lack the authentic ring. But just when one fears that Schubert has abandoned true eloquence for rhetoric, inspiration comes from on high, and one is carried away by the beauty of ex. 159, delivered with the power and splendor of the full orchestra. It is a perfect integration of an introduction with what it introduces.

Schumann spoke of the C Major's "heavenly lengths." This phrase applies best to the *Andante con moto*. The movement gives one the impression that, by a sort of clairvoyance, it wrote itself. Crammed as full of melody as a coconut is of meat and milk, it starts with one of Schubert's unique song accompaniments. Whereupon the oboe, in a strain that sounds as if suggested by that instrument's own sweetly acid quality, conjures the listener to the plains of Hungary:

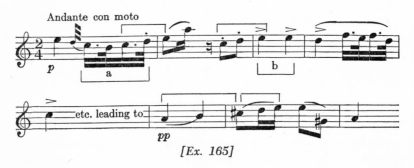

[Ex. 165]

This tune is vigorously supplemented by a brave theme which makes much of phrases (a) and (b) from the preceding example:

[Ex. 166]

Then, with different instrumentation, we hear it all again before the entrance of the serenely consoling second subject,

[Ex. 167]

which opens with the same hymnlike quality as the introduction.
A good deal is made of the last two chords of the above, in a passage
leading to the final part of the second subject, a charming antiphonal
duet for clarinet and oboe:

[Ex. 168]

Tovey writes that the mysterious return from this to the first
subject "is famous as one of the simplest and most romantic
passages ever written for horns. They toll like a bell haunted by a
human soul."

The recapitulation of the first part makes one noteworthy departure from the original. It works up to a terrific climax and
a characteristic measure of silence (bar 250). Then, accompanied
by soft pizzicati, the 'cellos insinuate a new melody in the rhythm
of the first subject (ex. 165), joined by a charming oboe counterpoint.

[Ex. 169]

The coda rolls under its tongue the most toothsome morsels of the first subject.

Though lengthened by much repetition, this movement is so magically saved from monotony by Schubert's delicate, varied, and resourceful modulation, phrasing, and orchestration that one would not wish "to cancel half a line."

As in Beethoven's "*Choral*" Symphony and First Rasoumowsky Quartet, the main body of the Scherzo is in compressed sonata-form. It opens with a burschikosely stamping and galumphing unison,

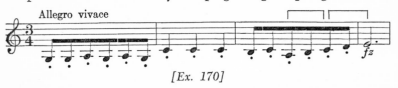

[Ex. 170]

whose origins go back to the finale of the B Flat Quartet, Op. 168, and the Scherzo of the G Major Quartet, Op. 161 (see ex. 70, p. 250).

The resilient second subject

[Ex. 171]

is accompanied by winds in the rhythm of ex. 170, and imitated, behind its back, by the 'cellos.

At bar 113, the development brings, in the woodwind, a premonition of the notable four-note motive in the second subject of the

finale. It also contributes new material in the shape of an ingratiating
Viennese waltz, while the mischievous 'cellos chime in with a travesty of ex. 171.

[Ex. 172]

And, a moment later, the fountain of melodic inspiration still gushes
so exuberantly that Schubert cannot refrain from adding one more
new and graceful theme to a section which, according to the Hoyle
of form, is supposed to contribute no fresh material, but merely to
work out that of the exposition:

[Ex. 173]

Notice the playful false accents on the weak third beat of each
measure.

This highly original development is followed by an original recapitulation, for its treatment differs as much as it dares from that
of the exposition. The coda touches on one of the new melodies
(ex. 172) that had been smuggled into the development, and lets
off a rocket or two for a brilliant finish.

Tovey calls "the huge single melody" of the Trio one of the
"greatest and most exhilarating melodies in the world."

[Ex. 174]

While such praise is perhaps extreme for the naïve thirds and sixths
which reduce its wearing quality, it offers rich enjoyment when
heard in moderation—always provided that conductors take care to
chasten the overexuberant accompaniment of the strings. Note the
distinction lent by the chord marked (x), an implied thirteenth.
From this tune, one of the principal themes of Liszt's tone poem
Les Préludes drew its inspiration. At bar 367 of the Trio, mark the
sudden, succulent modulation from A to B flat.

As a rule, the weak point of most dramatists and most composers
has always been the last act and the finale. Schubert, as we have
seen, was no exception to this rule. His few great finales, those of
the Quartets in A Minor and D Minor, the Octet, and the String
Quintet, are far more felicitous endings than he achieved for most
of his compositions; but that of the last Symphony ranges like an
Everest above even such masterpieces.

The most evident characteristic of this outstanding finale is a
rhythmic impetuosity and *élan* more powerfully compelling than in
any other movement I know. Its irrepressible triplets develop a
momentum like that of a jet-propelled plane which, with the last
note, vanishes into the stratosphere.

The gist of the lengthy, fanfarelike first subject[1] is as follows:

[Ex. 175]

[1] In 1844, when Mendelssohn brought the great C Major to London, the first
rehearsal was broken up at this point by the scornful laughter of the orchestral
players, who openly asked one another if they had yet discovered any signs of
a tune. The answer was always in the negative. Justly enraged, Mendelssohn
withdrew the work, and England never heard it until twelve years later.

In a dominant organ point, the subject continues with a play of
quarters against triplets, recalling the contrast of rhythms in the
Allegro ma non troppo:

[Ex. 176]

From the G. A. *Revision Report* (*Revisions Bericht*) of this work
made by no less a person than Johannes Brahms, we learn that when
Schubert arrived at the second subject, which is the presiding genius
of the movement, he shaved disaster by a narrow margin. After one
of his characteristic silences, he had scarcely set down the first pre-
monitory horn notes when his fancy decoyed him aside into a dull
little fugal theme:

[Ex. 177]

But, by good luck, this was no sooner scribbled down than the great
inspiration descended upon him; and hastily striking out the fugal
whimsy, he wrote,

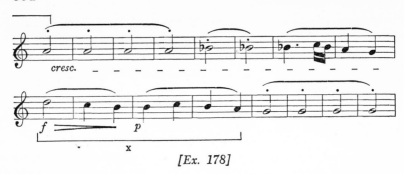

[Ex. 178]

against the relentless rhythm of  taken from the fanfarelike first subject. This is typical of Schubert's tendency to combine a
marked rhythmic heartbeat with a flowing cantabile. Tovey comments: "The danger was past, and instead of a weak facility, we
have the momentum of a planet in its orbit . . . Throughout the
movement, the four repeated notes are as powerful and terrible as
anything in Beethoven or Michelangelo." From now on, this great
theme is to dominate the finale. After a vivid harmonic kaleidoscope,
the exposition culminates in a *fff* climax on phrase (x) of ex. 178.

   The development is one of Schubert's most remarkable and satisfying. Phrase (x) is lengthened,

[Ex. 179]

so that it bears a startling resemblance to a part of the *Ode to Joy*
theme in Beethoven's *"Choral"* Symphony. This must have been a
deliberate salutation to Schubert's demigod, for the *"Choral"* had
been produced five years earlier and was undoubtedly familiar to
the younger composer.

   After ex. 179 has indulged in piquant contrapuntal repartee and
some engaging fairy music, the opening measures of ex. 178 are
thundered forth *fff* by low strings and brass battery. The 'cellos take
them over, *piano;* the movement dies down to a lull between two
storms; then the recapitulation crashes in with the full power of the
first subject.

In its mystery and suspense, the transition to the coda is nothing short of sublime.

[Ex. 180]

This coda is the greatest that Schubert ever conceived, a gloriously appropriate end to his symphonic career. No one has paid it a more fitting tribute than Brent-Smith:

> The closing bars cannot be described or analyzed. They are a vision of heavenly glory and happiness revealed to Schubert . . . by the world and circumstance, and this vision—"Behold, I see the heavens opened"— he has translated into sound for us. And we, to whom the revelation has been made, can never adequately show our admiration either by our words or by applause; we must listen spellbound to its mighty workings, lost in admiration, and be dumb.

When Grove had nearly finished the Schubert article for his *Dictionary,* he wrote to a friend some valedictory words which the present writer heartily endorses:

> Alas, I shall soon have to say good-bye to my beloved friend, Franz Schubert, and I do not know how to. We have been such inseparable companions for months and months, and close friends for years, and how lovable he is! I have got to know him so intimately—and yet—how *dare* I say so? In his great Symphony in C he towers so high, so far above [all] but a very few of the "Chosen and Elect," that it is presumptuous in me to say I understand him. I can only gaze and worship him, and humbly thank God for having given us such a genius.

ACKNOWLEDGMENTS

FOR criticizing the ms. and proofs of this book, hearty thanks are due to Mr. Earle Balch, Miss Marion Bauer, Mrs. Josephine Braider, Mr. Felix O. Derrick, Mr. Daniel Gregory Mason (Part II), Mr. Howard Nichols, Mr. Kennett L. Rawson, Mrs. Augusta Scheiber, Mr. William Sloane, Mr. Bedřich Váška, and Miss Eunice Wheeler.

For other help I wish to thank Mr. Monroe Bare, Mr. and Mrs. Sydney Beck, Miss Charlotte E. Bloecher, the Columbia Recording Corporation, Mrs. Felix O. Derrick, Mme Lily Dŷmont-Mindus, Miss Nina Fletcher, Mrs. Ann Slade Frey, Miss Lillian Holland, Miss Lila Honig, Mr. Norman Hoyte, Mr. Willard Jaeger, Mr. Rue Knapp, Miss Ruth Krug, Miss Isabel Marting, Mrs. Alice H. McCullen, Miss Dorothy E. Means, Mrs. Josephine Murphy, Mr. Richard Nicklnus, the Radio Corporation of America (RCA Victor Division), Mr. Bertram Rowe, Mr. Israel Ben Scheiber, Mr. C. Dewar Simons, Mrs. Eric H. Smith, Mr. and Mrs. Samuel Sorin, Mr. Vernon Spitaleri, Mr. Salvatore Sullo, Miss Masuko Tanbota, and Mrs. Alberta Trotter.

Any biography that requires as many years of research as this book has called for needs subsidization for the same reason that a symphony orchestra needs it. I wish to acknowledge the generosity of Mr. and Mrs. C. Dewar Simons, who subsidized twelve months of research, and of the Schubert Fund Committee: Mrs. Ira Nelson Morris (chairman), Mrs. Josephine Braider (vice-chairman), Mrs. Edgar Stillman Kelley, and the late Madame Olga Samaroff Stokowski. The two chairmen raised a working fund, substantial contributions to which were generously made by Mrs. Robert Woods Bliss, Mr. and Mrs. Morris Llewellyn Cooke, Mrs. Colgate W. Darden, Mr. Henry S. Drinker, Mr. Henry Harkness Flagler, Mrs. John Henry Hammond, Mrs. Thomas W. Lamont, Mr. Otto T. Mallery, Mrs. Annie Nathan Meyer, Mrs. Dave Hennen Morris, Mrs. Ira Nelson Morris, Mrs. Frederick G. Platt, Miss Caroline Schauffler, Dr. Goodrich Schauffler, Mr. Henry Schauffler, and an anonymous contributor.

A large number of music lovers, including a number of the world's leading musicians, have assisted the Fund by subscribing early for the book at a considerable advance over the publication price.

Special thanks are due to Miss Marion Bauer for reading proof of the music cuts, arranging several musical examples, and helping to prepare the glossary; to Mr. Felix O. Derrick for lending me the ms. of the Peter Altenberg poem, and giving invaluable help with the chapter on Schubert's Vienna; to the psychoanalyst Dr. Edward Hitschmann for allowing me to quote from his psychogram of Schubert; to the Juilliard School of Music and Mr. Ernest Hucheson, its former president, who kindly allowed me to borrow Schubert scores for years, and authorized a private performance for me of Schubert's Mass in E Flat; to that school's chorus and soloists and Mr. Igor Buketoff, who not only rehearsed and conducted that splendid performance, but also helped me to study many of Schubert's rarely heard choral and dramatic works, and arranged a theme of the four-hand Sonata in B Flat for this book; to Mrs. Else Kurzbauer for her painstaking accuracy in copying many of the musical examples; to Mr. Donald W. MacArdle for his sure scholarship in preparing the index and the lists of compositions and of records; to the *Musical Courier* for permission to reproduce a dozen illustrations; to the Boston Public Library; to the New York Public Library, Mr. Franklin Lane Hopper, its former director, its Music Room staff, and Miss Gladys E. Chamberlain, librarian of the Fifty-eighth Street Music Branch; to Mrs. Augusta Scheiber for refreshing my memory of Schubert's piano works and, with Miss Dorothy Minty, of his music for violin and piano; to Mrs. C. Dewar Simons for much brilliant research; and to Mr. and Mrs. Dolf Swing who organized for me excellent readings of many Schubert part-songs, choral works, and operas.

R. H. S.

BIBLIOGRAPHY

The Most Important Books on Schubert

BIOGRAPHIES

Bates, Ralph, *Franz Schubert*. New York: Appleton-Century-Crofts, 1935.

Bie, Oscar, *Franz Schubert. Sein Leben und sein Werk*. Berlin: Ullstein, 1925. Eng. transl., *Schubert the Man*. New York: Dodd, Mead, 1928.

Bourgault-Ducoudray, L.-A., *Schubert*. Paris: Librairie Renouard, 1926.

Dahms, Walter, *Schubert*. Berlin: Deutsche Verlags-Anstalt, 1908.

Duncan, Edmondstoune, *Schubert*. London: J. M. Dent & Sons, Ltd., 1905.

Flower, Newman, *Franz Schubert, the Man and His Circle*. London: Cassell and Co., Ltd., 1928. Philadelphia: Frederick A. Stokes Company, 1928.

Frost, H. F., *Schubert*. London: Sampson Low, Marston & Co., Ltd., 1881.

Gérold, Théodore, *Schubert*. Paris: Alcan, 1923.

Goss, Madeleine, *Unfinished Symphony* (for young people). New York: Henry Holt & Company, Inc., 1941.

Heuberger, Richard, *Franz Schubert*. Berlin: Schlesische, 1920.

Hutchings, A. J. B., *Schubert*. London: J. M. Dent & Sons, Ltd., 1945.

Kobald, Karl, *Franz Schubert*. Zürich, Leipzig, Vienna: Amalthea, 1928.

Kolb, Annette, *Franz Schubert*. Stockholm: Berman-Fischer, 1941.

Kreissle von Helborn, Heinrich, *Franz Schubert*. Vienna: Gerold, 1865. Eng. transl. London: Longmans, Green & Company, Inc., 1869.

Kruse, Georg Richard, *Franz Schubert*. Leipzig: Velhagen, 1924.

La Mara, *Franz Schubert*. Leipzig: Breitkopf, 1921.

Landormy, Paul, *La vie de Schubert*. Paris: Gallimard, 1928.

Niggli, A., *Franz Schubert*. Leipzig: Reclam, 1925.

Pitrou, Robert, *Franz Schubert*. Paris: Émile-Paul, 1928.

Reissmann, August, *Franz Schubert*. Berlin: Guttentag, 1873.

Roggeri, Edoardo, *Schubert: La vita—Le Opere*. Turin: Bocca, 1928.

Silvestrelli, Anita, *Franz Schubert*. Salzburg-Leipzig: Pustet, 1939.

Stefan, Paul, *Franz Schubert*. Berlin: Wegweiser, 1928.

Vetter, Walther, *Franz Schubert*. Potsdam: Athenaion, 1934.

MISCELLANEOUS

Abraham, Gerald (ed.), *The Music of Schubert*. New York: W. W. Norton & Company, Inc., 1947.

Altmann, Wilhelm, *Handbuch für Streichquartettspieler*. Berlin: Hesse, 1928-1929.

Bauer, Moritz, *Die Lieder Franz Schuberts*. Leipzig: Breitkopf, 1915. Vol. I. Vol. II unpublished.

Brent-Smith, Alexander, "Schubert," in *The Musical Pilgrim* series. London: Milford, 1926.

Capell, Richard, *Schubert's Songs*. London: Benn, 1928.

Cobbett's Cyclopaedic Survey of Chamber Music. New York: Oxford University Press, 1929-30.

Deutsch, Otto Erich, *Franz Schubert: Die Dokumente seines Lebens und Schaffens*. Vol. II, Part I, *Die Dokumente seines Lebens*. Munich: Müller, 1914. Eng. transl. by Eric Blom, revised and augmented, *Schubert; A Documentary Biography*. London: J. M. Dent & Sons, Ltd., 1946. Amer. ed., *The Schubert Reader*. New York: W. W. Norton & Company, Inc., 1947. Vol. III, *Sein Leben in Bildern*. Munich: Müller, 1913. (Thematic catalogue and Recollections of Schubert unpublished.)

Feigl, Rudolf, *Klar um Schubert*. Linz: pub'd. by author, 1938.

Grove's Dictionary of Music and Musicians. New York: The Macmillan Company, 1904, 1906, 1927.

Hitschmann, Dr. Eduard, "Franz Schuberts Schmerz und Liebe," in *Internationalen Zeitschrift für ärtzliche Psychoanalyse*. Vol. III, 1915.

Kahl, Willi, *Verzeichnis des Schrifttums über Franz Schubert*. Regensburg: Bosse, 1938.

Klatte, Wilhelm, "Franz Schubert," in *Die Musik* series. Leipzig: Siegel's, 1907.

Költzsch, Hans, *Franz Schubert in seinen Klaviersonaten*. Leipzig: Breitkopf, 1927.

Mason, Daniel Gregory, *The Romantic Composers*. New York: The Macmillan Company, 1906.

Nottebohm, G., *Thematisches Verzeichniss der im Druck erschienenen Werke von Franz Schubert*. Vienna: Schreiber, 1874.

Oxford History of Music, Vol. V, *The Viennese Period*. New York: Oxford University Press, 1904.

Schubertforschung. Augsburg: Filser, 1929.

Spaun, Josef von, *Erinnerungen an Schubert*. (Georg Schünemann, ed.) Berlin: Atlantis, 1936.

Tovey, Donald Francis, *Essays in Musical Analysis*. London: Oxford University Press, 1935, 1936. Vols. I and IV.

Wells-Harrison, W., *Schubert's Compositions for Piano and Strings*. "The Strad" Handbooks. No. 2. London: Lang. New York: Charles Scribner's Sons, 1915.

GLOSSARY

Some Technical Terms Every Music Lover Should Know

ACCIACCATURA: A short, untimed grace note before the principal note, as in the final measure of the C Major Quintet.

APPOGGIATURA: A short note of embellishment suspending or delaying a note of melody.

ABSOLUTE MUSIC: That type of music to which no program or literary interpretation is attached by the composer. Sometimes called pure music.

ACOUSTICS: That branch of the science of physics dealing with the phenomena of sound.

ANSWER: The response to the fugue (q. v.)[1] subject. It resembles that subject but is in another key.

ARIA: One of the more ambitious instrumental forms originally used vocally in the older operas.

AUGMENTATION: Repeating a subject in notes of greater value: halves for quarters, etc. The opposite of diminution.

AUTHENTIC CADENCE: A closing formula consisting of the dominant triad (on the fifth degree) followed by the tonic triad (on the first degree).

BAGATELLE: A short simple composition, usually in song form.

BASSO OSTINATO: A bass part in which the same melodic figure obstinately recurs.

BINARY FORM: Two-part form. A movement with two themes.

CADENCE: (From Latin: *cadere,* to fall.) The close (fall) or ending of a phrase, period, part, movement, or work. The harmonic formula by which a phrase or period is ended, giving a sense of temporary or complete finality. Cadences are authentic, plagal, perfect, deceptive, etc.

CADENZA: An improvised florid passage usually brought in at or near

---

[1] Literally "which see."

the end of an instrumental movement or vocal aria. In the eighteenth century the cadenza was the part of the concerto best designed to exhibit the soloist's technical ability, introducing his own development of the subject matter of the movement. Later, not trusting to the powers of the artist, the composer himself wrote the cadenza. It is still the custom for composers or performers to compose new cadenzas for standard works, such as the cadenza Kreisler wrote for the Beethoven violin concerto.

CANON: A composition in which a subject sung or played in one voice is imitated note for note in the others, either at the same or at a different pitch. The old-fashioned round is in canon form (e.g., *Three Blind Mice*).

CAVATINA: A short aria (q. v.). The term is occasionally used for a songlike instrumental piece or movement.

CHAMBER MUSIC: Music meant to be played in a small hall or room by a limited number of soloists, or a group of instrumentalists, such as wood-wind combinations, string quartet, trio, etc., with or without piano.

CHORAL: Psalm or hymn tune. A broad simple song for many voices (chorale).

CHORD: The simultaneous sounding of tones built up in thirds from a given root or fundamental. A three-voiced chord is a triad; four-voiced, a chord of the seventh, etc. Today chords are sometimes arbitrarily built up in intervals other than the time-honored thirds.

CHROMATIC SCALE: One that proceeds in half steps.

CODA: A concluding phrase or section added to a vocal or instrumental work, not strictly necessary for completeness, but making a more positive and effective close. It may also occur at the end of a principal section or even of a period.

CONCERTO: In Beethoven's time, an elaborate work for solo instrument and orchestra. In form it is virtually a sonata (q. v.), usually of three movements.

CONTRAPUNTAL: Pertaining to counterpoint. Contrapuntal forms are canons (q. v.) and fugues (q. v.).

COUNTERPOINT: (Point against point. Point is an old term for note.) Two or more melodies written to sound simultaneously. Polyphonic or many-voiced style. Horizontal music as opposed to vertical or harmonic music.

CYCLICAL FORM: A composition laid out in a series of movements (as a suite or a sonata). Today we apply the term to inter-movement thematic relation.

DEVELOPMENT: The working out of a theme, subject, or group of subjects by every device for variation, expansion, etc., at the composer's command. The second section in fugue (q. v.) and in sonata-form (q. v.). Also called free fantasia, development section, or working-out portion.

DIATONIC: A scale proceeding by consecutive tone degrees, or a melody containing no tones foreign to the key.

DIMINUTION: Repeating a subject in notes of shorter duration: e.g., quarters for halves, eighths for quarters, etc. The opposite of augmentation.

DIVERTIMENTO (DIVERTISSEMENT): An early instrumental composition usually consisting of more than four movements, and of a cheerful, entertaining character.

DOMINANT: The fifth step of the scale; dominant harmony, the triad on the fifth degree (e.g., the dominant chord of the key of G major is D—F sharp—A).

DYNAMICS: Contrasts between loud and soft, and progressions from one to the other: one of the means of producing expression in music.

ECOSSAISE: A dance of Scottish origin.

ENSEMBLE: A particular combination of instruments or voices, as chorus, string quartet, orchestra, etc. Teamwork of instruments or voices. Chamber music is sometimes called ensemble music.

EXPOSITION: The thematic or subject matter set forth in the first part of a fugue or sonata.

FIGURE: A small melodic tone-group or motive.

FIGURED-BASS: A system of numeral-notation of a bass part to indicate the intended harmony. A stenographic method of writing keyboard music. Also called thoroughbass.

FINALE: The final movement of a composition in several movements.

FORM: The plan of a piece of music. The arrangement of material into symmetrical and effective order, as in the rondo, minuet, scherzo, sonata-form movement, etc. (q. v.).

FUGATO: A part of a composition built in the manner of a fugue (q. v.) but not carried out with its complication or completeness. The theme begins in one part and is successively imitated by the other parts.

FUGUE (From Latin: *fuga*, flight): An enlarged and elaborately developed canon (q. v.). The highest form of contrapuntal art. A fugue has a subject (q. v.), an answer (the subject repeated more or less exactly a fifth above or a fourth below), a counter-subject (a theme planned to dovetail contrapuntally into the answer), and episodes developed from the subject matter. Sometimes the first part, or exposition, is brought back with the subject inverted (*see* Inversion), augmented (*see* Augmentation), or diminished (*see* Diminution). The stretto (q. v.), in which the subject is shortened by telescoping in order to build up the climax of the composition, is followed by a coda (q. v.) in which there is often a long organ-point (q. v.) before the final cadence (q. v.). As it may be divided into exposition, developing portion, and recapitulation, it may be regarded as the precursor of sonata-form. Fugues are both instrumental and vocal.

GERM MOTIVE: A musical phrase which recurs, more or less disguised, in different movements of the same composition; used as an interlocking device to lend the whole work thematic unity. (E.g., the three notes of an ascending scale which run through the "*Unfinished*" and Ninth symphonies. See pp. 352, 355, and 356.)

GRACE NOTES: Ornaments written in very small notation.

HARMONY: The science that treats of chords—their construction, interrelation, and logical progression.

IMITATION: An echoing of the theme in other voice-parts but usually higher or lower than the original statement.

INTERVAL: The distance from one tone to another; the difference in pitch between two tones.

INTRODUCTION: A passage or movement at the beginning of a work, leading up to the principal subject (q. v.) or exposition (q. v.).

INVERSION:

    (a) Turning the two tones of an interval upside down.

    (b) Changing the position of the tones of a chord so that some other than its root serves as bass.

    (c) Reversing the intervals of a melodic line so that they go in contrary motion to their original order.

    (d) In counterpoint, exchanging the position of two lines of melody so that, e.g., soprano becomes alto, and vice versa.

KEY: Any particular scale or tone series binding the triads of that scale into a unity through relation to a tonal center that gives the key its name. "Key" and "scale" are used interchangeably (e.g., key of D). (*See* Tonality.)

LEITMOTIF: A term first used by Von Wolzogen in connection with the Wagnerian music-drama. A motive intimately identified with some character, situation, or idea in opera. The lineal descendant of the germ- and source motive (q. v.).

MASS: A choral setting, with or without accompaniment, of certain portions of the Eucharistic service in the Roman Church. Sung in Latin.

MINUET: A dance of French origin originally consisting of two eight-bar phrases in ¾ time and of moderate pace. A second minuet was added, contrasted in feeling and usually written in three-part harmony, from which it derived the name Trio. Beethoven speeded this form up and altered it emotionally into the scherzo (q. v.).

MODE: A type or species of scale. Today we have the major and minor modes in all keys, corresponding to the major and minor scales. The term was used in Hindu, Greek, and church music (Gregorian and Ambrosian modes).

MODULATION: The process of changing, in the course of a movement, from one key or tonality (q. v.) to another.

MOTIVE, MOTIF: A short melodic figure or note-group used as a structural basis for developing a composition.

MOVEMENT:

(a) Rhythmic motion.

(b) A principal division of a compound or cyclical work, such as a suite or sonata.

ORATORIO: An extended composition for solo voices, chorus, and orchestra, without stage setting or acting, usually illustrating some sacred subject.

ORGAN-POINT, sometimes called PEDAL-POINT: A stationary bass held for a considerable time, over which other voices move freely.

OVERTONES, also called UPPER PARTIALS: Tones of higher pitch which are present in a regular, mathematical series in every perfect musical sound. The higher overtones are more dissonant and—fortunately—fainter.

PLAGAL CADENCE: A closing formula which consists of the triad upon the fourth degree of the scale followed by the tonic triad (q. v.).

PROGRAM MUSIC: A composition, usually instrumental, to which a detailed program is affixed by the composer. Such a program, however, no more represents the exclusive meaning of the music than any other that may be attached to the piece by its millions of hearers. Music is too infinite to allow even its composer to pin it down to any one program. Calverley's line applies here:

And as to the meaning, it's what you please.

RECAPITULATION (or REPRISE): The restatement of a sonata or fugue exposition (q. v.). Succeeds the development (q. v.) with certain traditional changes in key relations.

RETURN: The change back to the recapitulation.

RONDO: A piece derived from the old round dance in which the main theme or subject is frequently repeated, separated by secondary themes, e.g., on the model ABACA, ABACADA, or ABACABA.

SCALE: A definite succession of tones within an octave, written on successive staff degrees. There are many varieties, ranging from the pentatonic, or five-tone scale of the Chinese, Scots, and many primitive races, and the modal scales of the Greeks and of the Medieval Church, to the diatonic major and minor, and chromatic scales in use today, as well as the whole-tone scale of Debussy, etc.

SCHERZO: Literally the joke movement. Usually the third movement in a larger instrumental work. Consists of two short sections built on three-part song-form (q. v.). The second section is known as the Trio. The typical scherzo usually begins fast, light, staccato, and in three-quarter time. Its Trio often brings in contrasting slower, smoother, and mellower music. This is followed by the more or less literal repetition of the first part.

SEQUENCE: The frequent repetition of the same melodic figure, starting on a different degree of the scale.

SONATA: (From Latin *sonare:* to sound; hence a "sound-piece.") An instrumental composition of three or four contrasting and more or less related movements. Most sonatas are for piano, or for piano and another instrument. Trios, quartets, quintets, etc., are really sonatas for groups of instruments. A symphony is a sonata for orchestra. The first movement is customarily in so-called sonata-form. The second, often a slow movement, is generally in extended three-part song-form. The third is usually in minuet or scherzo form. The fourth is frequently in rondo form, occasionally in sonata-form. Variation form may be used in any movement of a sonata.

SONATA-FORM: The form in which the first movement of the standard sonata is constructed. It is a development of the three-part song-form. The basic material of the typical sonata-form is found in two contrasting subjects, the first and the second, sometimes called "the masculine" and "the feminine," or vice versa, each of which may consist of one or more themes closely related by mood and key. The three main divisions of the form consist of:

(1) Exposition:
    (a) First subject in key of tonic, and modulation to
    (b) second subject in complementary key which is usually dominant, or relative major if (a) is in the minor.

(2) Development: in which these subjects are worked out with much modulation (q. v.), according to the imaginative fertility and technical resources of the composer.

(3) Recapitulation: a virtual repetition of the Exposition with prescribed changes of key (second subject in tonic, etc.).

The following diagram graphically represents the typical structure of sonata-form:

SONG-FORM:
    (a) The small, or simple, in two or three parts;
    (b) the large, or extended, in two or three parts.

(a) is the smallest independent form in use and is so named because it is in the form of a song. Much folk music and many songs are in the small two- and three-part song-forms. The third part is often a repetition, more or less exact, of the first part, and often a coda (q. v.) is added.

The large two-part song-forms embrace the old dance-forms such as Allemandes, Sarabandes, also Themes for Variations, and occasionally an entire movement. Many minuets, scherzos, and slow movements are in large three-part song-form.

SOURCE MOTIVE: A musical phrase that recurs, more or less identically, in a number of distinct compositions and produces in the group an effect of thematic unity.

STRETTO: A term used to denote quickening of time, especially in the fugue (q. v.), when the subject and answer are introduced in close succession, so as to overlap and crowd upon each other, producing an effect of climax.

SUBDOMINANT: The fourth degree of the scale. Subdominant harmony, the triad on the fourth degree (e.g., in the key of G major, the subdominant chord is C—E—G).

SUBJECT: A melodic figure or phrase taken as a theme for treatment throughout a movement. Used specifically in a fugue and as a general term in all forms of composition. Opposed to Answer (q. v.).

SUITE: A collection of idealized dance tunes put together in contrasting tempos, rhythms, and moods. Also called partita. A precursor of the form of composition in several movements which finds its highest perfection in the Beethoven sonata. Bach, Handel, Couperin, etc., wrote suites.

SYMPHONY: A sonata for large orchestra.

SYNCOPATION: Shifting the accent to the normally weak or unaccented part of the beat or measure and holding it over the strong or accented part, thus robbing the naturally strong rhythmic position of its normal accent. This rhythmic disturbance is often carried over from one measure to another by means of tied notes. See D Minor Quartet, start of Scherzo, p. 242, ex. 56, and *"Unfinished"* Symphony, First Movement, accompaniment of the famous second subject, p. 350, ex. 154.

THEMATIC WORK: The development of themes (*see* Development). The use in longer compositions of more or less disguised germmotives (q. v.).

THEME: A subject of a composition, or part of a subject.

THOROUGHBASS: Loosely, harmonic composition. Also Figured-Bass (q. v.).

TONALITY: All relations between degrees of a scale connected with a tonal center. A key or mode.

TONIC: The first tone of the scale (for instance, G in the scale of G).

TONIC CHORD: The chord based on the first tone of the scale, e.g., G—B—D in the scale of G.

TRIAD: A three-voiced chord, consisting of a root, third, and fifth. Triads are major, minor, augmented, and diminished.

TUTTI: Denotes the entrance of the full orchestra after passages for individual instruments.

VARIATION: The amplification or modification of a given theme. A form of composition called Theme and Variations.

INDEX OF COMPOSITIONS

Note: References in italics refer to examples in music type.

I. INSTRUMENTAL MUSIC

A. For Orchestra

B. For Violin and Orchestra

C. For String Instruments

1. For string quintet

Overture in C minor (1811)
Rondo in A for Violin and string quartet (1816)
String Quintet in C, Op. 163 (1828) — 5, 41, 51, 179, 186, 187, 193,
   197, 210, 218, 231, 232, 246, 252 ff., 269, 281, 331, 335, 362

2. For string quartet

3 string quartets "in changing keys" (1811–12) — 18
String Quartet in C (1812)
Overture in B Flat (1812)
String Quartet in B Flat (1813)
String Quartet in E Flat (1813)
String Quartet in C (1813)
String Quartet in B Flat (1813)
String Quartet in D (1813)
String Quartet in E Flat, Op. 125, No. 1 (1813) — 126, 227 ff., 231,
   234
5 German Dances and 7 Trios (1813)
5 Minuets and 6 Trios (1813)
Grave in C Minor (1814)
String Quartet in D (about 1814)
String Quartet in B Flat, Op. 168 (1814) — 27, 228, 250, 360
String Quartet in G Minor (1815) — 229 ff.
String Quartet in E, Op. 125, No. 2 (1816) — 126, 230, 231
String Quartet in F (1816)
Allegro assai in C Minor ("*Quartettsatz*") (1820) — 90, 230 ff., 232
String Quartet in A Minor, Op. 29 (1824) — 68, 90, 119, 125, 126, 204,
   206, 215, 225, 232 ff., 236, 239, 246, 248, 272, 289, 313, 329, 352,
   362
String quartet in D Minor (*Death and the Maiden*) (1826) — 36, 58, 90,
   153, 154, 183, 186, 204, 215, 232, 237 ff., 246, 248, 250, 290, 320,
   337, 362
String Quartet in G, Op. 161 (1826) — 158, 183, 186, 203, 210, 229,
   232, 236, 246 ff., 360

3. For string trio

Movement in B Flat (1816) — 44
Trio in B Flat (1817)

D. For Wind Instruments

"*Eine kleine Trauermusik*" in E Flat Minor (for wind nonet) (1813)
Minuet and Finale in F (for wind octet) (1813) — 23

E. For String and Wind Instruments

Additional 'cello part for Matiegka's *"Notturno for flute, viola and guitar"* (1814)
Octet in F for strings, clarinet, bassoon, and horn, Op. 166 (1824) — 125, 126, 168, 197, 203, 216, *220 ff.*, 248, 362

F. For Piano and Other Instruments

1. For piano quintet

Quintet in A (*Trout*) for piano, violin, viola, 'cello, and double-bass, Op. 114 (1819) — 58, 86, 204, 205, *213 ff.*, 220, 224, 263, 272, 294, 304, 307, 341

2. For piano, violin, viola, and violoncello

Adagio and Rondo Concertante in F (1816)

3. For piano, violin, and violoncello

Sonata movement in B Flat (1812) — 23
Trio in B Flat, Op. 99 (1827) — 183, *204 ff.*, 212, 214, 234, 294
Trio in E Flat, Op. 100 (1827) — 153, 180, 186, 188, *207 ff.*, 234, *277*
Notturno in E Flat, Op. 148 (about 1827)

4. For piano and flute

Introduction and Variations in E Minor on the song *Trock'ne Blumen*, Op. 160 (1824) — 218, 316

5. For piano and violin

3 Sonatinas in D, A Minor, and G Minor, Op. 137 (1816) — *216 ff.*
Sonata in A, Op. 162 (1817) — 216
Rondo brillant in B Minor, Op. 70 (1826) — *217*
Fantasy in C (with variations on *Sei mir gegrüsst*), Op. 159 (about 1827) — 182, 183, 218

6. For piano and arpeggione or violoncello

Sonata in A Minor (1824) — 134, *218 ff.*

G. For Piano Four Hands

1. Sonatas

Sonata in B Flat, Op. 30 (1818) — *295 ff.*
Sonata in C (*"Grand Duo"*), Op. 140 (1824) — 132, 150, 216, 269, *293 ff.*

Sonata, the 3 movements of which were published separately as Divertissement (Opus 63), Andantino varié (Opus 84, No. 1) and Rondo brillant (Opus 84, No. 2) (about 1825)
Sonata in E Flat Minor (1828)

2. Variations

Introduction and Variations in B Flat on an original theme (about 1818), Op. 82, No. 2 (authenticity doubtful)
Variations in E Minor on *Réposez-vous, bon chevalier,* Op. 10 (1818) — 100, 166, 300
Variations in A Flat on an original theme, Op. 35 (1824) — 132
Andantino varié, Op. 84, No. 1 (about 1825) — 299
Variations on a Theme from *Marie* by Hérold, Op. 82, No. 1 (1827)

3. Fantasies

Fantasy in G (1810) — 16, 299
Fantasy in G Minor (1811) — 299
Fantasy in C Minor (1813) — 299
Fantasy in F Minor, Op. 103 (1828) — 68, 183, 187, 263, 292 *ff.*, 300

4. Rondos

Rondeau (*Notre amitié est invariable*), Op. 138 (1818)
Rondo brillant, Op. 84, No. 2 (about 1825)
Grand Rondeau, Op. 107 (1828) — 187, 299

5. Dances

German Dances with 2 Trios (1818)
2 *Ländler* (1818)
2 German Dances, Op. 33, Nos. 8 and 9 (1824)
4 *Ländler* (1824) — 300
6 Polonaises, Op. 61 (about 1825) — 299, 300
4 Polonaises, Op. 75 (about 1825)

6. Marches

3 marches héroïques, Op. 27 (about 1818)
3 marches militaires, Op. 51 (1823 or earlier) — 298
6 grandes marches, héroïques, Op. 40 (about 1824) — *298*
Grande marche funèbre d'Alexandre I, Op. 55 (1825)
2 marches caractéristiques, Op. 121 (1825 or earlier) — 298
Grand marche héroïque au sacre de Nicholas I, Op. 66 (1826)
Kindermarsch (for Faust Pachler) (1827) — 177

7. Overtures

Overture in C (arranged by Schubert from orchestral version), Op. 170 (1817)

Overture in D (arranged by Schubert from orchestral version) (1817)
Overture in G Minor (1819)
Overture in F Minor, Op. 34 (1819)
Overture in F Minor (lost) (1819) — 87
Overture to *Alfonso and Estrella* (arranged by Schubert from orchestral version), Op. 69 (about 1825)
Overture to *Rosamunde* (arranged by Schubert from orchestral version), Op. 26 (1828 or earlier)

8. Miscellaneous pieces

Divertissement à la hongroise, Op. 54 (about 1824) — 68, 154, 272, 277, 298
Divertissement en forme d'une Marche brillante et raisonnée, Op. 63 (about 1825)
Fugue in E Minor, Op. 152 (1828) — 299
Allegro (*"Lebensstürme"*), Op. 144 (1828) — 160, *296 ff.*
Allegro moderato and Andante (date unknown)

H. For Piano Solo

1. Sonatas *

Sonata No. 1 in E (1815)
Sonata No. 2 in C (1815)
Sonata No. 3 in E (1816)
Sonata No. 4 in A Minor, Op. 164 (1817) — *264 ff.*, 279, 281
Sonata No. 5 in E Minor (1817)
Sonata No. 6 in E Flat (earlier version in D Flat), Op. 122 (1817) — *266*
Sonata No. 7 in F Sharp Minor (uncompleted) (1817)
Sonata No. 8 in B, Op. 147 (1817) — 266, 267
Sonata No. 9 in A Flat (1817)
Sonata No. 10 in C (uncompleted) (1818)
Sonata No. 11 in F Minor (uncompleted) (1818)
Sonata No. 12 in C Sharp Minor (uncompleted) (1819)
Sonata No. 13 in A, Op. 120 (1819) — *267 ff.*, 279
Sonata No. 14 in A Minor, Op. 143 (1823) — 115, *268 ff.*, 278, 281, 349
Sonata No. 15 (*"Relic"*) in C (uncompleted) (1825) — *269 ff.*
Sonata No. 16 in A Minor, Op. 42 (1825) — 143, 154, 175, 272, 281
Sonata No. 17 in D, Op. 53 (1825) — 154, 175, *273 ff.*, 281
Sonata No. 18 in G (*"Fantasy"*), Op. 78 (1826) — 208, 211, 214, *275 ff.*, 281

* This list does not include the three Sonatas in F (1815, 1816, 1818) listed on p. 257 of Nottebohm's *Thematisches Verzeichniss.*

2 German Dances (1824)
6 German Dances (1824)
16 *Ländler* (1824)
2 German Dances (1825)
Kotillon (1825 or earlier)
Grazer Galopp (1827) — 174
Grazer Walzer, Op. 91 (1827) — 174
6 German Dances (date unknown)
Valses nobles, Op. 77 (date unknown) — 277, 291
Last Waltzes, Op. 127 (date unknown) — 291
3 sets of 3 German Dances (date unknown)
2 German Dances (date unknown)
German Dance (date unknown)
4 Minuets (date unknown)
8 *Écossaises* (date unknown)

5. *Miscellaneous pieces*

Andante in C (1812)
Adagio in G (1815)
Adagio in G (second version, incomplete) (1815 or later)
2 Scherzos (B Flat, D Flat) (1817)
Adagio and Rondo in E, Op. 145 (1817)
March in E (1818)
Adagio in E (1818)
Andante in A (about 1818)
6 *Moments musicaux,* Op. 94 (No. 3, 1823 or earlier; No. 6, 1824 or earlier; Nos. 1, 2, 4, and 5, 1825–27) — 285 *ff.*
Hungarian Melody (arranged by Schubert from the *Divertissement à la hongroise* for piano four-hands) (about 1824)
Albumblatt in G (1825)
4 Impromptus, Op. 90 (1827) — 182, 285, 287 *ff.*
4 Impromptus, Op. 142 (1827) — 76, 119, 182, 234, 285, 288 *ff.*, 329
Allegretto in C Minor (1827)
3 *Klavierstücke* (1828)
5 *Klavierstücke* (date unknown)
Scherzo in D and Trio in B Flat (date unknown)
Pianofortestück in C (incomplete) (date unknown)
Allegretto in C Minor (incomplete) (date unknown)
Allegretto in C (incomplete) (date unknown)
Allegro moderato in C (incomplete) (date unknown)
Andantino in C (incomplete) (date unknown)
Adagio in C (incomplete) (date unknown)
Allegro in F Sharp Minor (incomplete) (date unknown)

II. VOCAL MUSIC

I. LITURGICAL MUSIC

1. Four or more voices, with orchestra and organ

Kyrie in D Minor (1812) — 23
Kyrie in F (1813)
Mass in G (No. 2) (1815) — 333 *ff.*
Stabat mater in G Minor (1815)
Offertorium in A Minor (*Tres sunt*) (1815)
Graduale, Op. 150 (1815)
Mass in B Flat (No. 3), Op. 141 (1815) — 39, 133, 334
Mass in C (No. 4), Op. 48 (1818) — 66, 334
Tantum ergo in C (1816)
Tantum ergo in C (1816)
Magnificat in C (1816)
Requiem (unfinished) (1816)
Tantum ergo in C, Op. 45 (1822)
Tantum ergo in D (1822)
Mass in A Flat (No. 5) (1822) — 106, 332, 334
Kyrie (unfinished) (1822)

2. Four or more voices, with orchestra

Kyrie in D Minor (1813)
Mass in F (No. 1) (1814) — 29, 332
Magnificat in C (1816)
Stabat mater in F Minor (1816)
Deutsche Messe (with supplement: The Lord's Prayer)* (1826) — 165, 332
Mass in E Flat (No. 6) (1828) — 187, 197, 314, 334 *ff.*
Tantum ergo in E Flat (1828)
Offertorium in B Flat (*Intende voci*) (1828) — 332
Hymne, Op. 154 (1828)

3. Four or more voices, with organ or piano

Mass in C (1810) — 16
Salve regina in F (1816)
Deutsche Trauermesse (1818) — 71
23rd Psalm, Op. 132 (1820) — 91, 332

4. Four or more voices, unaccompanied

Kyrie in B Flat (1813)

* Accompaniment also arranged for organ.

Salve regina in B Flat (*Hymne an die heilige Mutter Gottes*) (1816)
Antiphons for Palm Sunday, Op. 113 (1820)
Salve regina in C, Op. 149 (1824) — 331
Deutsche Messe* (1827)
92nd Psalm (1828) — 332

5. Two voices, with orchestra

Auguste jam coelestium (1816)

6. Solo voice, with orchestra and organ

Salve regina in F (1812) — 23
Salve regina in B Flat (1814)
Salve regina in F, Op. 47 (1815)
Offertorium in C (*Totus in corde langueo*), Op. 46 (1816)
Salve regina in A, Op. 153 (1819)

J. DRAMATIC WORKS

Des Teufels Lustschloss (opera) (1814) — 31, 106
Der vierjährige Posten (*Singspiel*) (1815)
Fernando (*Singspiel*) (1815)
Claudine von Villa Bella (*Singspiel*) (fragment) (1815)
Die Freunde von Salamanka (*Singspiel*) (1815) — 223
Der Spiegelritter (operetta) (fragment) (1815)
Die Bürgschaft (opera) (unfinished) (1816) — 41
Adrast (opera) (unfinished) (about 1819)
Die Zwillingsbrüder (*Singspiel*) (1819) — 80, 88, 90
Die Zauberharfe (overture and incidental music to play by Georg von
   Hofmann) (1820) — 89, 90, 328
Sakuntala (opera) (unfinished) (1820) — 90
2 additional numbers for *Das Zauberglöckchen* by Hérold (1821) — 99
Alfonso und Estrella (opera), Op. 69 (1822) — 89, 90, 103, 104, 135,
   175, 327, 328
Der häusliche Krieg† (operetta) (1823) — 119
Fierrabras (opera), Op. 76 (1823) — 90, 119, 327
Rosamunde von Cypern (incidental music to play by Wilhelmine von
   Chézy), Op. 26 (1823) — 89, 119 *ff.*, 234 289, 298, 327, 328 *ff.*
Der Graf von Gleichen (sketches only) (about 1827) — 90, 158, 192
Der Minnesänger (lost) (date unknown) — 42

* Arrangement of the Deutsche Messe for four voices and wind instruments.
† Original title (abandoned) *Die Verschworenen.*

K. OTHER WORKS FOR TWO OR MORE VOICES
(MIXED OR NOT STATED)

1. Four or more voices, with orchestra

Cantata for the name day of the composer's father (1815)
Cantata in honor of Joseph Spendou, Op. 128 (1816)
Cantata for the name day of Professor Watteroth ("Prometheus" Cantata)
   (1816) — 43, 90
Lazarus or Die Feier der Auferstehung (extant only in piano transcription) (1820) — 331
Constitutionslied, Op. 157 (1822)

2. Four or more voices, with piano

3 choruses: Gott im Ungewitter, Gott der Weltschöpfer, Hymne an den
   Unendlichen, Op. 112 (1815) — 326
Schwertlied (1815)
Round: Freundschaft und Wein (1815)
An die Sonne (1816) — 326
Lebenslust (1818)
Des Tages Weihe, Op. 146 (1822)
Gebet, Op. 139a (1824) — 132
Der Tanz (1825)
Cantata to celebrate Irene Kiesewetter's recovery (1827)
Miriams Siegesgesang, Op. 136 (1828) — 187, 331
Glaube, Hoffnung und Liebe (1828)
Begräbnislied (date unknown) — 326
Osterlied (date unknown)
Viel tausend Sterne prangen (date unknown)

3. Four or more voices, unaccompanied

Das Grab (1815)
Angels' Chorus (1816) — 326
Im traulichen Kreise (1819)

4. Three voices (with or without accompaniment)

8 Canons for three voices (1813)
2 Terzets: Erinnerungen; Andenken (1816)
Der Frühlingsmorgen, Op. 158 (1819) — 87
Der Hochzeitsbraten, Op. 104 (1827) — 326
3 Canons for three voices (date unknown)
Frühlingslied ("Die Luft ist blau") (date unknown)
Frühlingslied ("Grüner wird die Au") (date unknown)

5. *Two voices (with or without accompaniment)*

Five duets: *Frühlingslied, Mailied, Der Morgenstern, Jägerlied, Lützows wilde Jagd* (1815)*
Licht und Liebe (1816)
Vocal exercises for two voices and figured bass (1818)
Linde Lüfte wehen (1821)
Mignon und der Harfner, Op. 62, No. 1 (1826)
2 Canons for two voices (date unknown)

6. *Number of voices not stated*

Gretchen im Dom (unfinished) (1813)
Trinklied vor der Schlacht (1815)
Die Schlacht (unfinished) (1816)
Jagdlied (1817)
Gratulations-Cantate for the composer's brother Ferdinand (date unknown)

L. OTHER WORKS FOR TWO OR MORE MALE VOICES

1. *Five or more voices, accompanied*

Trinklied (1813)
Wer ist gross (1814)
Trinklied (1815)
Gesang der Geister über den Wassern, Op. 167 (1817) — 326
Rüdigers Heimkehr (1823)
Nachthelle, Op. 134 (1826) — 163
Zur guten Nacht, Op. 81, No. 3 (about 1826)
Schlachtlied, Op. 151 (1827) — 186

2. *Five or more voices, unaccompanied*

Sehnsucht (1819)
Mondenschein, Op. 102 (1826)†
Schlachtlied (1827)

3. *Four voices, accompanied*

Trinklied, Op. 131, No. 2 (1815)
Bergknappenlied (1815)
Trinklied (1815)
Naturgenuss, Op. 16, No. 2 (1816)
Das Grab (1817)

* For two voices or two waldhorns.
† With piano *ad lib.*

Das Dörfchen, Op. 11, No. 1 (about 1821) — 99, 325
Die Nachtigall, Op. 11, No. 2 (1821)
Geist der Liebe, Op. 11, No. 3 (1822) — 180, 325
Frühlingsgesang, Op. 16, No. 1 (1823)
Der Gondelfahrer, Op. 28 (1824)
Bootgesang, Op. 52, No. 3 (1825)
Widerspruch, Op. 105, No. 1 (1826)
Nachtgesang im Walde, Op. 139b (1827) — 325
Im Gegenwärtigen Vergangenes (date unknown)
Der Wintertag, Op. 169 (date unknown)
La Pastorella (date unknown) — 325
Morgengesang im Walde (date unknown)

4. Four voices, unaccompanied

Der Geistertanz (1816)
Cantata for Salieri's 50-year jubilee (1816) — 38, 39
Lied im Freien (1817)
Ruhe, schönstes Glück der Erde (1819)
Nachtmusik, Op. 156 (1822)
4 songs: *Jünglingswonne, Liebe, Zum Rundtanz, Die Nacht,* Op. 17
    (1823)
Trinklied aus dem 14ten. Jahrhundert, Op. 155 (1825)
Grab und Mond (1826)
3 songs: *Wehmuth, Ewige Liebe, Flucht,* Op. 64 (1826)
Frühlingslied (1827)
An der Frühling (date unknown)
Lob der Einsamkeit (date unknown)
Der Entfernten (date unknown)
Wein und Liebe (date unknown)
Fischerlied (date unknown)

5. Three voices (with or without accompaniment)

Die zwei Tugendwege (1813)
Cantata for the name day of the composer's father (1813)
Sprüche des Confucius (probably 1813)
Das Abendroth (1815)
Punschlied (1815)
Schlachtlied (1816)
Die Advokaten, Op. 74 (1822) — 326

6. Three voices, unaccompanied

13 *Terzetti* (1813)
Unendliche Freude (1813)

Bardengesang (1815)
Mailied (1815)
Trinklied im Mai (1816)
Trinklied im Winter (1816)
Frühlingslied (about 1816)
Totengräberlied (about 1816)

7. Solo voice, unison chorus, and piano

Lied eines Kriegers (1824)

M. OTHER WORKS FOR TWO OR MORE FEMALE VOICES

1. Five voices with piano

Ständchen, Op. 135 (1827) — 159, 164, 165, 170, 171, 186, 325

2. Four voices with piano

Gott in der Natur, Op. 133 (1822) — 325

3. Three voices with piano

Das Leben (1815)
Klage um Ali Bey (1815)
Das grosse Halleluja (1816)
Coronach, Totengesang der Frauen und Mädchen, Op. 52, No. 4 (1825)

N. SONGS FOR SOLO VOICE AND PIANO

Four groups of songs (Opp. 25, 52, 62, and 89) are sufficiently homogeneous in poetic and musical content to be properly known as song cycles. In January, 1829, a collection of fourteen songs was issued under the title of "*Schwanengesang.*" While this collection is not properly called a song cycle, the songs that are included date from Schubert's last months, and the collection is popularly known by the title that the publisher gave it.

Die schöne Müllerin, Op. 25 — 68, 123, 127, 160, 166, 303, 315 *ff.,* 349

No.		No.	
1.	*Das Wandern*	8.	*Morgengruss*
2.	*Wohin?*	9.	*Des Müllers Blumen*
3.	*Halt!*	10.	*Thränenregen*
4.	*Danksagung an den Bach*	11.	*Mein!*
5.	*Am Feierabend*	12.	*Pause*
6.	*Der Neugierige*	13.	*Mit dem grünen Lautenbande*
7.	*Ungeduld*	14.	*Der Jäger*

No.   No.
15. *Eifersucht und Stolz*   18. *Trock'ne Blumen*
16. *Die liebe Farbe*   19. *Der Müller und der Bach*
17. *Die böse Farbe*   20. *Des Baches Wiegenlied*

Seven songs from Walter Scott's "Lady of the Lake," Op. 52 — 144, 322

No.   No.
1. *Ellens I. Gesang*   5. *Normans Gesang*
2. *Ellens II. Gesang*   6. *Ellens III. Gesang (Ave Maria)*
3. *Bootgesang*°   7. *Lied des gefangenen Jägers*
4. *Coronach*†

Songs from "Wilhelm Meister," Op. 62

No.   No.
1. *Mignon und der Harfner*§   3. *Lied der Mignon*
2. *Lied der Mignon*   4. *Lied der Mignon*

Der Winterreise, Op. 89 — 116, 118, 165, 178, 179, 181, 191, 207, 246, 304, 316 ff., 323

No.   No.
1. *Gute Nacht*   13. *Die Post*
2. *Die Wetterfahne*   14. *Der greise Kopf*
3. *Gefrorne Thränen*   15. *Die Krähe*
4. *Erstarrung*   16. *Letzte Hoffnung*
5. *Der Lindenbaum*   17. *Im Dorfe*
6. *Wasserfluth*   18. *Der stürmische Morgen*
7. *Auf dem Flusse*   19. *Täuschung*
8. *Rückblick*   20. *Der Wegweiser*
9. *Irrlicht*   21. *Das Wirthshaus*
10. *Rast*   22. *Muth*
11. *Frühlingstraum*   23. *Die Nebensonnen*
12. *Einsamkeit*   24. *Der Leiermann*

Schwanengesang — 187, 305

No.   No.
1. *Liebesbotschaft*   5. *Aufenthalt*
2. *Kriegers Ahnung*   6. *In der Ferne*
3. *Frühlingssehnsucht*   7. *Abschied*
4. *Ständchen*   8. *Der Atlas*

° For male quartet and piano.
† For female trio and piano.
§ Duet.

Note: Words in parentheses following a song title are the first words of the song. They are given only in cases where the same title is used with different words and music.

An Chloen (1816)
An den Frühling Op. 172, No. 5 (two settings, 1815)
Andenken (1814)
An den Mond (Füllest wieder Busch und Thal) (two settings, 1815)
An den Mond (Geuss, lieber Mond) Op. 57, No. 3 (1815)
An den Mond (Was schauest du) (1816)
An den Mond in einer Herbstnacht (1818)
An den Schlaf (1816)
An den Tod (1817)
An die Apfelbäume, wo ich Julien erblickte (1815)
An die Entfernte (1822)
An die Freude, Op. 111, No. 1 (1815)
An die Freunde (1819)
An die Geliebte (1815)
An die Laute, Op. 81, No. 2 (1816)
An die Leyer, Op. 56, No. 2 (1822) — 305
An die Musik, Op. 88, No. 4 (1817) — 33, 58, 306, 323
An die Nachtigall (Er liegt und schläft), Op. 98, No. 1 (1816)
An die Nachtigall (Geuss nicht so laut), Op. 172, No. 3 (1815)
An die Natur (1816)
An die Sonne (Königliche Morgensonne) (1815)
An die Sonne (Sinke, liebe Sonne), Op. 118, No. 5 (1815)
An die untergehende Sonne, Op. 44 (1817)
An eine Quelle, Op. 109, No. 3 (1816)
An Laura (1814)
An mein Clavier (1816)
An mein Herz (1825)
An Mignon, Op. 19, No. 2 (1815)
An Rosa (Rosa, denkst du an mich?) (1815)
An Rosa (Warum bist du nicht hier?) (1815)
An Schwager Kronos, Op. 19, No. 1 (1816) — 320
An Sie (1815)
An Sylvia, Op. 106, No. 4 (1826) — 159, 213, 307 *ff.*
Antigone und Oedip, Op. 6, No. 2 (1817)
Arie aus "Didone" (1816)
Atys (1817)
Auf dem Flusse, Op. 89, No. 7 (1827) — 317
Auf dem See, Op. 92, No. 2 (1817)
Auf dem Strom, Op. 119 (1828)* — 186
Auf dem Wasser zu singen, Op. 72 (1823) — 305
Auf den Sieg der Deutschen (1813)†
Auf den Tod einer Nachtigall (1816)
Auf der Brücke, Op. 93, No. 2 (1825)

* With obbligato horn or violoncello.
† Accompaniment two violins and violoncello (no piano).

Das Rosenband (1815)
Das Sehnen, Op. 172, No. 4 (1815)
Das Wandern, Op. 25, No. 1 (1823) — 123, 191, 303, 315
Das war ich (1815)
Das Weinen, Op. 106, No. 2 (1827)
Das Wirthshaus, Op. 89, No. 21 (1827) — 320
Das Zügenglöcklein, Op. 80, No. 2 (1826)
Dass sie hier gewesen, Op. 59, No. 2 (1823)
Death and the Maiden: see *Der Tod und das Mädchen*
Delphine, Op. 124, No. 1 (1825)
Dem Unendlichen (1815)
Der Abend, Op. 118, No. 2 (Der Abend blüht) (1815)
Der Abend (Purpur malt die Tannenhügel) (1814)
Der Alpenjäger (Auf hohem Bergesrücken), Op. 13, No. 3 (1817)
Der Alpenjäger (Willst du nicht das Lämmlein hüten), Op. 37, No. 2
    (1817)
Der Atlas (1828)
Der blinde Knabe, Op. 101 (1825) — 165
Der Blumenbrief (1818)
Der Blumen Schmerz, Op. 173, No. 4 (1821)
Der Doppelgänger (1828) — 313, 336
Der Einsame, Op. 41 (1825) — 160
Der Entfernten (1816)
Der entsühnte Orest (1820)
Der Fischer, Op. 5, No. 3 (1815)
Der Flüchtling (1816)
Der Flug der Zeit, Op. 7, No. 2 (1817)
Der Fluss (1820)
Der Geistertanz (1814)
Der Goldschmiedgesell (1815)
Der Gott und die Bajadere (1815)
Der greise Kopf, Op. 89, No. 14 (1827) — 318, 319
Der gute Hirt (1816)
Der Herbstabend (1816)
Der Hirt (1816)
Der Hirt auf dem Felsen, Op. 129 (1828) — 135
Der Jäger, Op. 25, No. 14 (1823)
Der Jüngling am Bache, Op. 87, No. 3 (1815) (another setting, 1819)
Der Jüngling an der Quelle (1821)
Der Jüngling auf dem Hügel, Op. 8, No. 1 (1820)
Der Jüngling und der Tod (1817)
Der Kampf, Op. 110 (1817)
Der Knabe (1820)

Der Weiberfreund (1815)
Der Winterabend (1828)
Der Zufriedene (1815)
Der zürnende Barde (1823)
Der zürnenden Diana, Op. 36, No. 1 (1820)
Der Zwerg, Op. 22, No. 1 (1823)
Des Baches Wiegenlied, Op. 25, No. 20 (1823)
Des Fischers Liebesglück (1827)
Des Mädchens Klage, Op. 58, No. 3 (1815) (another setting, 1816) — 313
Des Müllers Blumen, Op. 25, No. 9 (1823) — 307
Des Sängers Habe (1825)
Die abgeblühte Linde, Op. 7, No. 1 (1817)
Die Allmacht, Op. 79, No. 2 (1825) — 150, 166, 186, 321
Die befreier Europas in Paris (1814)
Die Berge, Op. 57, No. 2 (1815)
Die Betende (1814)
Die Blumensprache, Op. 173, No. 5 (1817)
Die böse Farbe, Op. 25, No. 17 (1823) — 315
Die Bürgschaft (1815)
Die drei Sänger (1815)
Die Einsiedelei (1816) (another setting, 1817)
Die Entzückung (two settings: 1816, 1817)
Die Erde (date unknown)
Die erste Liebe (1815)
Die Erwartung, Op. 116 (1815)
Die Forelle, Op. 32 (1817) — 58, 64, 86, 215, 304
Die Fröhlichkeit (1815)
Die frühe Liebe (1816)
Die frühen Gräber (1815)
Die Gebüsche (1819)
Die gefangenen Sänger (1821)
Die Gestirne (1816)
Die Götter Griechenlands: see *Fragment aus "Die Götter Griechenlands"*
Die Hoffnung, Op. 87, No. 2 (1815)
Die junge Nonne, Op. 43, No. 1 (1825) — 166, 321
Die Knabenzeit (1816)
Die Krähe, Op. 89, No. 15 (1827) — 318
Die Laube, Op. 172, No. 2 (1815)
Die Liebe (1817)
Die liebe Farbe, Op. 25, No. 16 (1823) — 315
Die Liebe hat gelogen, Op. 23, No. 1 (1822)

Ein Fräulein schaut vom hohem Thurm, Op. 126 (1825)
Eine Leichenphantasie (1810) — 16, 109
Einsamkeit (Gieb mir die Fülle der Einsamkeit) (1818) — 67
Einsamkeit (Wie eine trübe Wolke), Op. 89, No. 12 (1827) — 318
Ellens I. Gesang (Raste, Krieger), Op. 52, No. 1 (1825)
Ellens II. Gesang (Jäger, ruhe von der Jagd), Op. 52, No. 2 (1825)
Ellens III. Gesang (Ave Maria), Op. 52, No. 6 (1825) — 144, 216, 222,
    314, 315, 322, 350
Elysium (1817)
Emma, Op. 58, No. 2 (1814) — 30
Entzückung (1816)
Entzückung an Laura (1816)
Epistel (von Matth. von Collin) (1822)
Erinnerung, Op. 108, No. 3 (1815)
Erinnerungen (1814)
Erlafsee Op. 8, No. 3 (1817)
Erl King, The: see *Erlkönig*
Erlkönig, Op. 1 (1815) — 9, 32, 35, 40, 59, 62, 64, 75, 82, 84, 92, 99,
    115, 123, 154, 166, 176, 180, 229, 244, 289, 304, 319, 321, 348
Erntelied (1816)
Erstarrung, Op. 89, No. 4 (1827) — 316
Erster Verlust, Op. 5, No. 4 (1815)
Fahrt zum Hades (1817)
Fischerlied (1816)
Fischerweise, Op. 96, No. 4 (1826)
Florio, Op. 124, No. 2 (1825)
Fragment aus "Die Götter Griechenlands" — 225, 235
Fragment aus dem Aeschylus (1816)
Freiwilliges Versinken (1820)
Freude der Kinderjahre (1816)
Frohsinn (1817)
Frühlingsglaube, Op. 20, No. 2 (1820) — 90, 304
Frühlingslied (Die Luft ist blau) (1816)
Frühlingslied (Geöffnet sind des Winters Riegel) (1827)
Frühlingssehnsucht (1828)
Frühlingstraum, Op. 89, No. 11 (1827) — 317
Fülle der Liebe (1825)
Furcht der Geliebten (1815)
Ganymed, Op. 19, No. 3 (1817) — 60
Gebet während der Schlacht (1815)
Gefror'ne Thränen, Op. 89, No. 3 (1827) — 316
Geheimes, Op. 14, No. 2 (1821)
Geheimniss (1816)

Mahomets Gesang (1817)
Margaret at the Spinning Wheel: see *Gretchen am Spinnrade*
Marie (1819)
Meeres-Stille, Op. 3, No. 2 (1815)
Mein, Op. 25, No. 11 (1823) — 307
Mein Gruss an den Mai (1815)
Memnon, Op. 6, No. 1 (1817)
Mignon (Heiss mich nicht reden) (1821)
Mignon (So lasst mich scheinen) (1821)
Mignons Gesang (1815)
Minnelied (1816)
Minona (1815)
Mio ben, ricordati (1820)
Misero pargoletto (1813)
Mit dem grünen Lautenbande, Op. 25, No. 13 (1823) — 307
Morgengruss, Op. 25, No. 8 (1823) — 145, 305
Morgenlied (Die frohe neubelebte Flur) (1816)
Morgenlied (Eh' die Sonne), Op. 4, No. 2 (1820)
Morgenlied (Willkommen, rothes Morgenlicht) (1815)
Muth, Op. 89, No. 22 (1827) — 323
Nach einem Gewitter (1817)
Nachtgesang (O gieb, vom weichen Pfühle) (1814)
Nachtgesang (Tiefe Feier) (1815)
Nachthymne (1820)
Nachtstück, Op. 36, No. 2 (1819)
Nachtviolenlied (1822)
Nacht und Träume, Op. 43, No. 2 (1825)
Nähe des Geliebten, Op. 5, No. 2 (1815)
Namenstaglied (1820)
Naturgenuss (1815)
Non t'accostar all' urna (1820)
Normans Gesang, Op. 52, No. 5 (1825)
Orest auf Tauris (1820)
Organ Grinder, The: see *Der Leiermann*
Orpheus (1816)
Ossians Lied nach dem Falle Nathos' (1815)
Parricide, The: see *Der Vatermörder*
Pause, Op. 25, No. 12 (1823) — 307
Pax vobiscum (1817)
Pensa, che questo istante (1813)
Pflichte und Liebe (date unknown)
Pflügerlied (1816)
Phidile (1816)

Skolie (Mädchen entsiegelten) (1816)
Son fra l'onde (1813)
Sonett I (Apollo lebet noch) (1818)
Sonett II (Allein, nachdenklich) (1818)
Sonett III (Nunmehr, da Himmel) (1818)
Sprache der Liebe, Op. 115, No. 3 (1816)
Ständchen (Horch, horch, die Lerch) (1826) — 96, 159, *306*, 331
Ständchen (Leise flehen meine Lieder) (1828) — 214, 307, 350
Stimme der Liebe (Abendgewölke schweben) (two settings: 1815, 1816)
Stimme der Liebe (Meine Selinde) (1816)
Suleika, Op. 14, No. 1 (1821)
Suleikas II. Gesang, Op. 31 (1821)
Täglich zu singen (1817)
Täuschung, Op. 89, No. 19 (1827) — 318
Thekla (Eine Geisterstimme), Op. 88, No. 2 (1817) (another setting, 1813)
Thränenregen, Op. 25, No. 10 (1823)
Tiefes Leid (1826)
Tischerlied (1815)
Tischlied, Op. 118, No. 3 (1815)
To Music: see *An die Musik*
Todesmusik, Op. 108, No. 2 (1822)
Totengräberlied (1813)
Totengräbers Heimweh (1825)
Totengräber-Weise (1826)
Totenkranz für ein Kind (1815)
Totenopfer (1814)
Trauer der Liebe (1816)
Trinklied (Bacchus, feister Fürst) (1826)
Trinklied (Ihr Freunde) (1815)
Trinklied vor der Schlacht (1815)
Trock'ne Blumen, Op. 25, No. 18 (1823) — 160, 218, 316
Trost (Hörnerklänge rufen klagend) (1819)
Trost (Nimmer lange) (1817)
Trost an Elisa (1814)
Trost im Liede (1817)
Trost in Thränen (1814)
Trout, The: see *Die Forelle*
Über allen Zauber Liebe (date unknown)
Über Wildemann, Op. 108, No. 1 (1826)
Um Mitternacht, Op. 88, No. 3 (1826)
Ungeduld, Op. 25, No. 7 (1823) — 305
Uraniens Flucht (1817)

RECORDED WORKS OF SCHUBERT

This tabulation is a representative list of recorded Schubert works currently available from American companies. Not all such records are included. No good end would be served by listing, e.g., all seventeen recordings of the *Ave Maria* found in the catalogues of the two largest American companies. Moreover, too many records are inadequately identified: if no more is catalogued than "Waltz by Schubert," no attempt has been made to determine *which* waltz it was so that the listing could be included here.

The following abbreviations are used:

AR	Allegro	EDA	Decca album
C	Columbia single record	K	Decca single record
CH	Concert Hall	Parl	Parlophone single record or
CJ ⎫			album
CM ⎬ Columbia album		V	Victor single record
CMX ⎭		VC ⎫	
DM	Mercury album	VM ⎬ Victor album	
		VP ⎭	

COMPOSITION	RECORD NO.
Symphony No. 2 in B Flat	
Columbia Broadcasting Orchestra (Barlow)	CM-420
Symphony No. 4 in C Minor (*"Tragic"*)	
New York Philharmonic Orchestra (Barbirolli)	VM-562
Symphony No. 5 in B Flat	
London Philharmonic Orchestra (Beecham)	CM-366
Boston Symphony Orchestra (Koussevitzky)	VM-1215
Symphony No. 6 in C	
London Philharmonic Orchestra (Beecham)	VM-1014
Symphony No. 8 in B Minor (*"Unfinished"*)	
London Philharmonic Orchestra (Beecham)	CM-330
National Symphony Orchestra (Fistoulari)	EDA-14
Boston Symphony Orchestra (Koussevitzky)	VM-1039
All-American Orchestra (Stokowski)	CM-485
and others	

COMPOSITION	RECORD NO.
Symphony No. 9 in C	
NBC Symphony Orchestra (Toscanini)	VM-1167
New York Philharmonic Orchestra (Walter)	CM-679
and others	
Overture in D, Op. 170	
National Symphony Orchestra (Unger)	K-1327
String Quintet in C, Op. 163	
Pro Arte String Quartet	VM-299
Budapest String Quartet	CM-497
String Quartet in E Flat, Op. 125, No. 1	
Guilet Quartet	CH-AE
String Quartet in A Minor, Op. 29	
Budapest String Quartet	VM-225
String Quartet in D Minor ("Death and the Maiden")	
Busch String Quartet	VM-468
Fine Arts Quartet	DM-14
Notturno for Flute, Guitar, Viola, and Violoncello	
Jaunet, Leeb, Kertesz, Mottier	CH-C9
Octet in F, Op. 166	
Hobday, Draper, Hinchcliff, Brain, and Lener Quartet	CM-97
Vienna Octet	EDA-104
Quintet in A ("Trout"), Op. 114	
Schnabel, Onnou, Prevost, Maas, Hobday	VM-312
Trio in B Flat, Op. 99	
Rubinstein, Heifetz, Feuermann	VM-923
Trio in E Flat, Op. 100	
Totenberg, Retjo, Baller	AR-1
Sonatina in D, Op. 137, No. 1	
Szigeti and Foldes	CMX-238
Rondo brillant in B Minor, Op. 70	
Menuhin and Menuhin	VM-901
Sonata in A Minor for Piano and Arpeggione	
Feuermann and Moore	CM-346
Sonata in E Flat for Piano (No. 6), Op. 122	
Long	EDA-26
Sonata in A Major for Piano (No. 13), Op. 120	
Casadesus	CMX-236
Sonata in A Minor for Piano (No. 14), Op. 143	
Kraus	Parl R-20388/90
Schnabel	VM-580

COMPOSITION	RECORD NO.
Sonata in C Major (*"Relic"*) for Piano (uncompleted)	
Lev	CH-B3
Sonata in D for Piano (No. 17), Op. 53	
Schnabel	VM-888
Szigeti and Foldes	in CMX-238
Sonata in G Major for Piano (*"Fantasy"*) (No. 18), Op. 78	
Minuet and Trio: Rubinstein	V-14276
Fantasy (*"Wanderer"*) (arr. Liszt)	
Kilenyi	CM-426
Ländler for Piano, Op. 171	
Nos. 1, 3, 4, 5, 6, 7, 8, 11: Casadesus	C-71466D
Valses nobles for Piano, Op. 77	
Kraus	Parl PXO-1039
March in E for Piano	
Schnabel	in VM-888
Moments musicaux for Piano, Op. 94	
All: Schnabel	VM-684
No. 2: Paderewski	V-17699
Paderewski	in VM-748
No. 3: Gieseking	C-17079D
Impromptus for Piano, Op. 90	
No. 2: Joyce	Parl E-11440
No. 3: Jonas	C-72047D
and others	
Impromptus for Piano, Op. 142	
No. 2: Paderewski	V-6628
Allegretto in C Minor for Piano	
Lev	in CH-B3
Rosamunde	
Overture, Entr'actes, Ballet Music, Shepherd's Melody: Halle Orchestra (Harty)	CM-343
Overture: London Symphony Orchestra (Krips)	K-2071
Ballet Music: Philadelphia Orchestra (Stokowski)	V-1312
London Symphony Orchestra (Walter)	V-12534
Boston Symphony Orchestra (Koussevitzky)	in VM-319
and others	
Song Cycle: *Die schöne Müllerin*, Op. 25	
Complete: Lehmann (S)	CM-615

COMPOSITION	RECORD NO.
12 songs: Crooks (T)	VM-1067
Separate songs:	
Wohin? (Opus 25, No. 2): Anderson (C)	V10-1327
Ungeduld (Opus 25, No. 7): McCormack (T)	in VC-3
Lehmann (S)	in VM-292
Kipnis (B)	C-9128M

Song Cycle: *Winterreise,* Op. 89

23 songs: Lehmann (S)	⎧ VM-692 ⎨ CM-466 ⎩ CM-587
12 songs: Tauber (T)	Parl P-9
Separate songs:	
Der Lindenbaum (Opus 89, No. 5): Kipnis (B)	in CM-89
Petri (pf.)	C-69620D
Der Wegweiser (Opus 89, No. 20): Kipnis (B)	in CM-89
Der Leiermann (Opus 89, No. 24):	
McCormack (T)	in VC-3
Am Meer	
Kipnis (B)	in CM-89
An die Musik, Op. 88, No. 4	
Lehmann (S)	V-10-1448
An Sylvia, Op. 106, No. 4	
Bjoerling (T)	V-12725
Hackett (T)	in CM-89
McCormack (T)	V-1306
Aufenthalt	
Anderson (C)	V-11-9836
Kipnis (B)	in CM-89
Auflösung	
Steber (S)	V-10-1099
Ave Maria: see *Ellens III. Gesang*	
Der Doppelgänger	
Anderson (C)	V-12-0580
Kipnis (B)	in CM-89
Lehmann (S)	C-71509D
Der Hirt auf dem Felsen	
Maynor (S)	V-12-0186
Der Jüngling und der Tod	
Anderson (C)	V-12-0580
Der Tod und das Mädchen, Op. 7, No. 3	
Anderson (C)	V-10-1327
Braslau	in CM-89

COMPOSITION	RECORD NO.
Der Wanderer, Op. 4, No. 1	
Tibbett (B)	V-1589
Kipnis (B)	in CM-89
Die Allmacht, Op. 79, No. 2	
Homer (C)	V-15-1011
Thorberg (C)	V-2148
Tibbett (B)	V-15891
Die Forelle, Op. 32	
Anderson (C)	V-1862
Braslau (C)	in CM-89
Stanton (S)	in CM-233
Die junge Nonne, Op. 43, No. 1	
Braslau (C)	in CM-89
Ferrier (C)	K-1632
Lehmann (S)	C-71509D
Du bist die Ruh, Op. 59, No. 3	
Alsen	in CM-89
Ellens III. Gesang ("Ave Maria"), Op. 52, No. 6	
Stevens (M)	C-7425M
Zimbalist (vln)	C-7275M
Crooks (T)	V-11-8570
Schumann (S)	V-8423
Boston "Pops" Orchestra	V-13589
Anderson (C)	V-11-9836
and others	
Erlkönig, Op. 1	
Braslau (C)	in CM-89
Kipnis (B)	C-9128M
Lehmann (S)	V-10-1448
Gretchen am Spinnrade, Op. 2	
Lehmann (S)	in VM-419
Alsen (S)	in CM-89
Baillie (S)	in CM-233
Ferrier (C)	K.1632
Petri (pf.)	in CM-362
Heidenröslein, Op. 3, No. 3	
Braslau (C)	in CM-89
Kipnis (B)	C-9128M
Tauber (T)	Parl RO-20442
Im Abendroth	
Lehmann (S)	in VM-292

COMPOSITION   RECORD NO.

Liebesbotschaft
  Maynor (S)   V-10-1372
Litanei auf das Fest aller Seelen
  Alsen (S)   in CM-89
  Primrose (viola)   in VM-757
Memnon, Op. 6, No. 1
  Williams (B)   in CM-233
Ständchen (*Horch, horch, die Lerch*)
  Houston (S)   in VP-39
  Tauber (T)   Parl PO-166
Ständchen (*Leise flehen meiner Lieder*)
  Maynor (S)   V-10-1372
  McCormack (T)   in VC-3
  Melchior (T)   in VM-990
  Crooks (T)   in VM-846
  Bjoerling (T)   V-12725
  Kullman (T)   C-9130M
  Elman (vln)   V-7461
  Rachmaninoff (pf.)   V-11-8728
  RCA-Victor Salon Orchestra   V-21253
    and others
Wiegenlied, Op. 98, No. 2
  Lehmann (S)   in VM-419
  Martin (S)   in CJ-17

INDEX